THE FURIOUS FLOWERING OF AFRICAN AMERICAN POETRY

Edited by Joanne V. Gabbin

UNIVERSITY PRESS OF VIRGINIA
Charlottesville

The University Press of Virginia
© 1999 by the Rector and Visitors of the University of Virginia
All rights reserved
Printed in the United States of America

First published 1999

∞ The paper used in this publication meets the minimum requirements of the American
National Standard for Information Sciences—Permanence of Paper for Printed Library Materials,
ANSI Z39.48-1984.

Library of Congress Cataloging-in-Publication Data
The furious flowering of African American poetry / edited by Joanne V. Gabbin.
p.   cm.
Includes bibliographical references and index.
ISBN 0-8139-1840-5 (cloth : alk. paper).—ISBN 0-8139-1841-3 (paper : alk. paper)
1. American poetry—Afro-American authors—History and criticism.
2. Afro-Americans in literature.   I. Gabbin, Joanne V.
PS310.N4F87   1999
811.009'896073—dc21   98-51964
                                                                              CIP

CONTENTS

Part 3. Writing a Literary History of African American Poetry

ACKNOWLEDGMENTS

The Furious Flower conference in 1994 was a great success because of the combined efforts of so many people who believe in the efficacy and beauty of poetry. The members of the Furious Flower Planning Committee, James Madison University, the Virginia Foundation for the Humanities and Public Policy, the major sponsors, and the poets and scholars who participated created an environment in which valuable insights about the critical theories, literary interpretations, and cultural roots of African American poetry were discussed and appreciated. Special thanks go to Alvin Aubert, Eugene Redmond, and Jerry Ward Jr., who chaired the major critics' roundtables that provided the theoretical framework for the conference. This book is a product of all of their combined efforts.

A collection of this kind requires patience and long-suffering. I am grateful to the contributors who shared their scholarship and commentary and saw the significance of this project. I also want to thank the entire staff at the University Press of Virginia who showed outstanding commitment and support in publishing this book with special thanks to Nancy Essig, director; Deborah Oliver, managing editor; and Julie Falconer, assistant project editor. I especially want to thank acquisitions editor Boyd Zenner, who has had faith in this project from the first time I proposed it in 1995. Her encouragement and gentle nudgings kept me going. Hers was truly the role of "literary gardener" to the Furious Flower.

I deeply appreciate the contribution of C. B. Claiborne, who was the official photographer for Furious Flower. His photographs provide lasting images and memories. I also appreciate the use of Erica Bleeg's photographs. My students and colleagues at James Madison University have been enthusiastic about this project. I am also grateful for the editorial assistance of my colleagues David Jeffrey, who proofread the manuscript, and Jason Corner, who provided valuable input with manuscript preparation and organization. I also want to thank my staff at the Honors Program, especially Bonnie Walker and Donna Shafer-Riha, who provided much-needed clerical support.

During the whole process, I have been fortunate to have inspiration radiating from many different sources. I am grateful to Gwendolyn Brooks, who has generously encouraged my scholarship and who wrote the magnificent lines in her poem "The Second Sermon on the Warpland" that provides the "furious flower" metaphor for black poetry. I am grateful to the late Margaret Walker, who added her sage voice to my life and this collection, and to Sonia Sanchez, Val Gray Ward, Judith Thomas, Daryl Dance, Opal Moore, Linda Jackson Jouridine, and Elizabeth Garbrah-Aidoo, who have sprinkled my days with their humor and understanding. I especially want to thank my sister-friends in the Wintergreen Women Writers' Collective, who have been a tremendous source of inspiration, support, love, ideas, and well wishes.

Finally, my family continues to be the gift for which I am eternally grateful. I give special thanks to my sister, Doris E. Hunt, who sings her love to me; to my daughter, Jessea Nayo Gabbin, who is my song; and to my husband, Alexander L. Gabbin, who for most of my lifetime has made me sing.

The authors and publisher wish to thank the following for granting permission to quote from copyrighted works:

Collected Poems by Langston Hughes. Copyright © 1994 by the Estate of Langston Hughes. Reprinted by permission of Alfred A. Knopf, Inc.

The Collected Poems of Sterling A. Brown, selected by Michael S. Harper. Copyright © 1980. Reprinted by permission of HarperCollins Publishers.

The Weary Blues by Langston Hughes. Copyright © 1926 by Alfred A. Knopf, Inc. and renewed 1954 by Langston Hughes. Reprinted by permission of the publisher.

Harlem Gallery by Melvin B. Tolson. Copyright © 1965. Reprinted by permission of Twayne Publishers.

Paul Vesey's Ledger by Samuel W. Allen. Copyright © 1975. Reprinted by permission of the author.

"Persephone in Hell," "Lost Brilliance," "The Bystro Styx," "Her Island," "Heroes," "Grief: The Council," "Mother Love," "*Wiederkehr,*" "Wiring Home," "Hades' Pitch," "Sonnet in Primary Colors," and "Demeter Mourning" from *Mother Love,* ©1995 by Rita Dove. Reprinted by permission of the author and W. W. Norton, New York.

"In the Tradition Too" by Ras Baraka, reprinted by permission of the author. From *In the Tradition: An Anthology of Young Black Writers,* ed. Kevin Powell and Ras Baraka. Copyright © 1992.

"The Ballad, the Hero, and the Ride: A Reading of Sterling A. Brown's *The Last Ride of Wild Bill*" by Mark A. Sanders was previously published in *CLA Journal* 38, no. 2 (Dec. 1993): 162–82, and is reprinted with permission from The College Language Association.

The Last Ride of Wild Bill by Sterling A. Brown. Copyright © 1975. Reprinted by permission of Broadside Press.

"Parapoetics" by Eugene B. Redmond. Copyright © 1991 by the author. Reprinted from

The Eye in the Ceiling: Selected Poems (New York: Harlem River Press, 1991) by permission of the author.

"A poem to complement other poems" from *Don't Cry, Scream* by Haki R. Madhubuti. Copyright © 1991 by Haki R. Madhubuti. Reprinted by permission of the author and Third World Press.

"It is Deep" from *How I Got Ovah* by Carolyn M. Rodgers. Copyright © 1968, 1969, 1970, 1971, 1972, 1973, 1975 by Carolyn M. Rodgers. Used by permission of Doubleday, a division of Bantam Doubleday Dell Publishing Group, Inc.

"Did This Happen to Your Mother? Did Your Sister Throw Up a Lot?" and "On Stripping Bark from Myself" from *Goodnight Willie Lee, I'll See You in the Morning* by Alice Walker. Copyright © 1978 by Alice Walker. Used by permission of Doubleday, a division of Bantam Doubleday Dell Publishing Group, Inc.

Excerpts from "Ballad of the Brown Girl" and "African Images, Glimpses from a Tiger's Back" from *Once: Poems* by Alice Walker, copyright © 1968 and renewed 1996 by Alice Walker. Reprinted by permission of Harcourt Brace & Company.

Excerpts from "Remember" and "Torture" from *Horses Make a Landscape Look More Beautiful: Poems by Alice Walker,* copyright © 1984 by Alice Walker. Reprinted by permission of Harcourt Brace & Company.

"When That Which Is Perfect Is Come" by Julia Fields. From *Slow Coins and New Poems (& Some Old Ones).* Copyright © 1981. Reprinted with permission of Julia Fields and Passeggiata Press (formerly Three Continents Press).

"'The Calligraphy of Black Chant': Resiting African American Poetries" by Aldon Lynn Nielsen was adapted from *Black Chant: Languages of African-American Postmodernism,* Cambridge University Press, 1997.

Black Writers of America by Barksdale & Kinnamon, © 1972. Reprinted by permission of Prentice-Hall, Inc., Upper Saddle River, NJ.

"The Self-Hatred of Don L. Lee," "The Primitive," and "a poem to complement other poems" by Haki R. Madhubuti. Reprinted by permission from Haki R. Madhubuti, *The Black Poets,* New York: Bantam, 1971.

"My Poem," "For Saundra," "Always There Are the Children," "The Women Gather," "Ego Tripping," and "Africa" by Nikki Giovanni. Reprinted by permission of the author. Copyright © 1968, 1996 by Nikki Giovanni.

"Ballad of Pearl May Lee," "The Anniad," "The Second Sermon on the Warpland," "A Sunset of the City," "the mother," *IN THE MECCA,* "Young Afrikans," "Malcolm X," "The Mother," "The Children of the Poor," and "A Song in the Front Yard" from *Blacks* by Gwendolyn Brooks. Publisher, Third World Press, Chicago. Reprinted by permission of the author. Copyright © 1987.

Good Woman: Poems and a Memoir 1969–1980, Next: New Poems, and *Quilting: Poems 1987–1990* by Lucille Clifton. Copyright © 1987, 1991 by Lucille Clifton. Reprinted with permission of Boa Editions, Ltd.

"Two-Headed Woman" by Lucille Clifton. From *Good Woman: Poems and a Memoir 1969–1980* (Boa Editions, Ltd.). Copyright © 1987. Reprinted with permission of the author.

Yusef Komunyakaa, "Facing It" from *Dien Cai Dau,* © 1988 by Yusef Komunyakaa, Wesleyan University Press, by permission of University Press of New England.

Yusef Komunyakaa, "Unnatural State of the Unicorn," "Touch-Up Man," and "How I See Things" from *I Apologize for the Eyes in My Head* © 1986 by Yusef Komunyakaa, Wesleyan University Press, by permission of University Press of New England.

Yusef Komunyakaa, "Anondyne" and "The Wall" from *Thieves of Paradise*, © 1998 by Yusef Komunyakaa, Wesleyan University Press, by permission of University Press of New England.

"I Wanna Be Black" by Michelle T. Clinton, reprinted by permission of the author. From *High Blood/Pressure*. Copyright © 1986 by West End Press.

"Gription" by Paul Beatty, from *In the Tradition: An Anthology of Young Black Writers*. Reprinted by permission of the author.

THE
FURIOUS
FLOWERING
OF AFRICAN
AMERICAN
POETRY

Introduction:
Essays and Conversations in African American Poetry

J O A N N E   V .   G A B B I N

The time
cracks into furious flower. Lifts its face
all unashamed. And sways in wicked grace.
— Gwendolyn Brooks

Y EPIGRAPH, TAKEN FROM GWENDOLYN BROOKS'S "Second Sermon on the Warpland," resonates strongly with the very act and agency of African American poetry. Whether Gwendolyn Brooks intended it or not, the term *furious flower* is a stunning metaphor for African American poetry because it implies a literature that is both rageful and resolute in its beauty. From the earliest attempts of African American poets in the eighteenth century to express their existence in a society that debated, and debased, their humanity to their intense exploration of their voice in the waning years of a racially charged twentieth century, African American poetry has been the aesthetic chronicle of a race struggling to lift "its face all unashamed."

In 1993 when I conceived of the idea for a poetry conference as a tribute to Gwendolyn Brooks, I wanted to bring her to James Madison University and invite a few of her friends and fellow poets to come in her honor. As I planned this gathering, the lines from her poem attached themselves tenaciously to my consciousness. Not only was Gwendolyn Brooks the embodiment of the "furious flower" but she was also part of a rich poetic tradition that expressed beautifully and ferociously our struggle for liberation. If I was to honor her meaningfully, the conference would have to be

1

expansive, like her poetic genius, and embrace three generations of poets who had nurtured a poetry that "swayed in wicked grace," a poetry that in the final years of the twentieth century was again experiencing renewal.

That genius and expansive renewal were dramatically evident at Furious Flower: A Revolution in African American Poetry Conference in 1994, when the largest gathering of poets, critics, and scholars in more than two decades met at James Madison University in Virginia to read, discuss, and celebrate. As if in stunning clairvoyance, Eleanor Traylor on the morning of the first day called Furious Flower the "coup of the century." For the first time, according to Jerry W. Ward Jr., African American poetry was getting the serious attention it deserves, and a remarkable number of poets and critics punctuated the importance of the confluence of ideas and creative energies that marked the event. They came from every region of the country, poised to deliver up the wisdom that we needed: Elizabeth Alexander, Samuel Allen, Jabari Asim, Alvin Aubert, Amiri Baraka, Gerald Barrax, Joanne Braxton, Gwendolyn Brooks, Rita Dove, Mari Evans, Nikki Giovanni, Michael S. Harper, Joyce Ann Joyce, Dolores Kendrick, Pinkie Gordon Lane, Naomi Long Madgett, Haki Madhubuti, E. Ethelbert Miller, Aldon Nielsen, Raymond Patterson, Arnold Rampersad, Bernice Johnson Reagon, Eugene Redmond, Sonia Sanchez, Clyde Taylor, Lorenzo Thomas, Askia M. Touré, Eleanor Traylor, Jerry W. Ward Jr., Val Gray Ward, and Sherley Anne Williams all converged on the campus of James Madison University on a weekend in late September when nature dressed itself in the brilliance and beauty of the Shenandoah Valley. Hundreds of students, faculty, and visiting scholars and writers traveled to the university and experienced what has since become the celebrated warmth and hospitality of the students and staff. In audiences that reached thirteen hundred people for major readings, we were vaguely aware that something was happening that would not likely happen again.

Contrary to an assumption among some literary scholars that African American poetry has all but ceased to exist since the 1960s, Brenda Marie Osbey said that the poets and scholars at the conference represented "the full range of creative output from the 1960s, '70s, '80s, and '90s." Gwendolyn Brooks first began publishing her poems immortalizing residents of Chicago's South Side in the 1940s and has since garnered a magnificent array of achievements, including being named the 1994 Jefferson Lecturer by the National Endowment for the Humanities. Samuel W. Allen, a scholar and translator of texts produced by the African-French Négritude movement, who had published, under the pen name Paul Vesey, the bilingual collection of poems *Elfenbein Zahne (Ivory Tusks)* in 1956, was in 1994 still writing poetry rooted in the surviving African oral traditions and the traditions of the southern black church.

Margaret Walker, who was honored in absentia at the Furious Flower conference, published in 1942 one of the singularly outstanding poems in American literature. In "For My People," the title poem of a volume that was introduced by Stephen Vincent Benét and won for Walker her first recognition as the winner of the Yale Young Poets Award, she accomplished a stunning psychological portrait of her people during the unsettling years of the Great Depression. Forty-seven years later Walker published "This Is My Century: Black Synthesis of Time," which shows her ability to create a persona expansive as the century.

Amiri Baraka, Sonia Sanchez, Nikki Giovanni, Haki Madhubuti, Askia M. Touré, Mari Evans, Eugene Redmond, and Lorenzo Thomas are counted among the number of significant literary figures who shaped the Black Arts Movement of the late 1960s. In these years of urgency and militancy, their strident call to reshape a society by speaking to the psyche of a people had resulted in change. Touré, in revisiting the 1960s and the Black Arts Movement, said that it "was the largest cultural upsurge that our people have had in this century, and we were organically linked—writers, activists, musicians, playwrights, and such." Now together, some for the first time in many years, some having survived fierce battles, ideological and otherwise, they took strength from the fact that they were still writing. Some who had fallen out with others over how best to get free were still talking about freedom. Their poetry called for increased political activism and drew on a strong black oral tradition mined by poetic precursors like James Weldon Johnson, Langston Hughes, Sterling Brown, and Robert Hayden. Their activism and empowering messages had an impact on the establishment of black studies programs on college campuses, the flowering of literary workshops and theatrical companies, the founding of black presses and journals, and the creation of an unprecedented demand for black writing. Significantly, the demand, as Lorenzo Thomas pointed out, was created within the community. Magazines and journals such as *Freedomways, Black Collegian, Black Scholar, Journal of Black Poetry, The Liberator,* and *Black World* (formerly *Negro Digest*) brought poetry out of the halls of academe to a black readership hungry for the word.

Several poets of the Black Arts Movement also demanded new and freer outlets for their poetry. Dudley Randall, the founder and editor of Broadside Press, pioneered in the black publishing industry and provided these outlets. Since 1956, Broadside Press produced 101 books, 94 broadsides, and 27 tapes of poetry, according to Julius E. Thompson, who spoke at the conference. Some of the most influential voices in African American literature since 1945 published their poems with Broadside Press, thereby making them accessible to a burgeoning black reading audience. Like Randall, Alvin Aubert and Naomi Long Madgett, accomplished poets in their own right, also did groundbreaking work in black publishing. In 1975 Alvin Aubert became the founder and editor of *Obsidian,* a literary journal that helped to launch the critical and creative work of emerging writers. Around the same time, Naomi Long Madgett became the moving force behind Lotus Press, the leading publisher of poetry by African Americans, listing more than seventy-five titles since 1975. Madgett proudly noted during the conference, "I think I've counted fifteen poets at this conference who had at least one book published by Lotus Press, and I'm very, very pleased with that."

And some of the voices from the sixties and seventies had been quieted. Like the leaves that Bernice Johnson Reagon sang about in her song "All the Leaves Are Falling," writers and poets like Hoyt Fuller, Henry Dumas, Larry Neal, Etheridge Knight, Sarah Fabio, David Llorens, and Addison Gayle had left a palpable void. So some, finally, had come to give homage to the elders as they themselves were, as Eugene Redmond put it, "slipping into elderhood."

Rita Dove, 1986 Pulitzer Prize winner and Poet Laureate of the United States from 1993 to 1995, acknowledged her own debt to the Black Arts Movement. She said that if it had not been for the Black Arts Movement, America would not be ready to accept a poet who explored a text other than blackness. In her tribute to Gwendolyn Brooks, Dove said, "Standing in front of this literary congregation as a grown woman, a woman who had entered her forties, I feel very strange thinking that when Gwendolyn Brooks was awarded the 1950 Pulitzer Prize for *Annie Allen,* her second collection of poems, I was not even, as people used to say then, 'a twinkle in my daddy's eye.'" Dove is one of a large group of poets who published their first poems during the 1970s and 1980s. Rita Dove, Michael S. Harper, Pinkie Gordon Lane, Sherley Anne Williams, Toi Derricotte, Gerald Barrax, and E. Ethelbert Miller were among those poets who made freedom both the medium and the message of their poetry.

The younger poets also added their sound, generating the kind of energy found now in the coffee houses, at open mikes, poetry slams, and spoken-word performances all over the country. The members of the Dark

Room Collective, Natasha Trethewey, Thomas Sayers Ellis, John R. Keene Jr., Sharan Strange, Kevin Young, and Carl Phillips were among the variegated voices that sprang forth during the first half of the 1990s. By creating a literary space for themselves, they have moved African American poetry to a new place, "diasporiz[ing] the country," in Elizabeth Alexander's words, as they shape metaphors and images in a fisted reading of contemporary life. At the Furious Flower Conference these three generations of poets carried with them the anlage for an explosive cross-pollination and harvest.

What happened that weekend is difficult to explain completely within the context of historicism and literary-critical significance. For there was a poetic energy, a spirit, that was palpable in the defining moments that have become our communal memory. Joanne Braxton, caught up by the spiritual contagiousness of the conference, said, "The air was thick with energy and excitement. That is to say, 'the joint was jumping' as brother and sister poets cross-pollinated, riffed, and vibed, not only on the stand, out in the hallways, over coffee, bourbon, checking out the fabulous book exhibit, the original art work. . . . Furious Flower was a coming together of such mammoth proportions as can hardly be imagined or held in the mind's eye."

Though we generally measure our lives in years, it is the moments that often mark time in ways only our hearts and minds can make connections. These moments, points on a continuum, are like poems that provide the concentrated, distilled images that, when recalled, burst forth full, fresh, and vivid. It was these moments that created out of this conference a poem. We were reminded of the uniqueness of this event, and its deep connection to the history that had come before it, in the midst of Val Gray Ward's dramatic roll call of our literary ancestors when she paused as she remembered Hoyt Fuller, friend and literary midwife of the Black Arts Movement. Her chanting voice, stopped in momentary memorial, gave evidence of the visitation of the spirits. Eleanor Traylor became another spiritual medium while invoking the anima of Larry Neal, Langston Hughes, and Henry Dumas. Inviting us to discover the spiritual legacy of African American poetry, she drew us as willing travelers into a discursive zone that Margaret Walker describes as "suffused with emotive content." In a virtuoso performance of the vernacular traditions that informed the poetry of Paul Laurence Dunbar, James Weldon Johnson, Langston Hughes, Robert Hayden, Margaret Walker, and others, she brought us into the realm of the oracular "where voices transmitting the spoken and measured word have dominion."

Ain't you nevah hyeahd Malindy?
    Blessed soul, tek up de cross!
Look hyeah, ain't you jokin', honey?
    Well, you don't know whut you los' . . .
Y' ought to hyeah dat gal a-wa'blin',
    Robins, la'ks, an all dem things
Heish dey moufs an' hides dey faces
When Malindy sings.

For a few moments we have an ear turned to the kitchen window out of which floats Malindy's melodious notes. Traylor suggested that when listening at the oracular place, the distinction between vernacular and tutored sound often blurs.

Clyde Taylor spoke of the transformative power of poetry as he recalled having his twelve-year-old libido stimulated when he heard Hughes read "Harlem Sweeties," his scintillating catalogue of the various skin tones of urban beauties, or being lovestruck by Gwendolyn Brooks when he was a student at Howard University as he heard her penetrating poetry that chiseled the details of urban life in dramatic, realistic relief. Taylor also recalled being stirred and agitated by a fiery speech given by Adam Clayton Powell that called for revolution and ended with Walker's "For My People." Taylor said that the poem represented the way poetry belongs to us as it captures the essence of our lives and added with considerable emphasis, "The poem is our way of belonging in poetry that was bequeathed by Margaret Walker." Taylor was one of the academics who were also poets who brought art together with scholarship: Raymond Patterson's gentle wisdom, Eugene Redmond's hip dexterity with concept and language, Joanne Braxton's incisive humor and verve, Jerry Ward's carefully weighed thoughts cupped in his deep sonorous voice, and Toi Derricotte's compassionate humanism.

Many of the most memorable moments happened as we witnessed the power of poets reading their own work. Few of us can forget the first night the stars came out when Amiri Baraka, Mari Evans, Michael S. Harper, and Sonia Sanchez touched us with original fire. Baraka burned red hot as he scatted and bebopped his own improvised accompaniment to "Heathens," a relentless attack on those people who choose death over life and a lie over the truth. One participant wrote, "To have read Baraka's *The System of Dante's Hell,* a sprawling masterpiece of modern disaster, is to know that he is a man of stormy passion. But to have read his essays and his poetry is to know that these storms are always kept in their territory of service to his art. When he read these lines from 'Lord Haw Haw (a Pygmy) # 37':

> 'We were here
>> *before*
> God
> We
>> *invented*
> Him.
>> Why?
> That's a good/god damn
> question'

some people laughed, others applauded, but many others just looked around, nervously. It's good to know that Baraka still has the ability to make people uncomfortable."

Mari Evans, radiant in gold and white, intoned "I Am a Black Woman." She was fully aware, as her song wafted through the auditorium, that we mouthed the words in emotional unison. Michael S. Harper burned cool blue. With his beret set saucily on his head, Harper recounted the tortured death of Bessie Smith in "Last Affair: Bessie's Blues Song":

> Can't you see
> what love and heartache's done to me
> I'm not the same as I used to be
> this is my last affair.

We were moved by his ability to sing our history and his own. And as Lenard Moore writes in a poem composed under the influence of the Furious Muse, Sonia Sanchez sizzled, "fire leapen, leapen / out of yo mouth." As another participant wrote, "Hearing Sonia Sanchez read is like having an hallucinatory vision of heaven and hell." As she read "Improvisation," her voice darting in small, tightly wound bursts of energy, we were both taken through the terrible depths of the slave ships and given that special, somewhat frightening joy that all great art gives us.

> It was
> the coming that was badddddddddddddd
> It was the coming that was baddddddddddddd
> across oceans across seas across eyes staring

Then there was the afternoon of the poet laureates. The packed auditorium bristled with kinetic excitement and expectancy. Students, not finding room to stand, sat precariously on the ledges of the balcony, getting as close as they could to living history. In the span of one sunny afternoon Gwendolyn Brooks and Rita Dove read and showed why their laurels rested so securely on their heads. Rita Dove, her eyes closed, her gaily painted fingernails adorning hands serenely pointed upwards as in prayer, delivered a reading that gathered its magic and flung it on the waiting crowd like confetti. I especially remember her brilliant poem "Parsley," which brought to life El General, the malevolent dictator who ordered 20,000 blacks killed because they could not pronounce the letter "r" in *perejil,* the Spanish word for parsley. We were all aware of the tittering in the audience when she read "After Reading *Mickey in the Night Kitchen* for the Third Time before Bed" and the magic she wove around innocence and a mother's love as a daughter discovers the wonders of womanhood.

When Gwendolyn Brooks walked in her determined way across the stage of the auditorium, her vigorous gait belying her seventy-seven years, the Furious Flower conference itself became the poem. As Gwendolyn Brooks read, occasionally interrupting herself to proclaim, present, or mildly persuade, she drew us to the locus of her kindness and made us feel as though we were the sole/soul object of her attention. It was her readings from *Children Coming Home,* a collection of portraits that fixed forever in our memory the vulnerability of the five-year-old boy in "Uncle Seagram," or the spirited pride of Kojo who asserts

> I am other than Hyphenation.
> . . . . .
> I am Kojo. I am A Black.
> And I Capitalize my name.
> Do not call me out of my name.

Gwendolyn Brooks read, moving from poem to poem, punctuated only by the applause from an admiring audience intent on returning her love. Joining her on stage, Haki Madhubuti, in a moving tribute, found the language to express our gratitude to this woman, "distinctive and proud at seventy-seven," whose kindness had left us inarticulate. "She wears her love in her language. If you do not listen, you will miss her secrets. We do not occupy the margins of her heart, we are the blood, soul, Black richness, spirit, and water-source pumping the music she speaks."

There was, in all we experienced at Furious Flower, the spirit of cele-
bration, for celebration is the affirmation of life. Lives that had been dedi-
cated to seeing with a clear eye, lives lived deeply and searchingly, lives
grown out of the need to question, describe, explore, reinvent, heal, re-
create, liberate, remember, consecrate, love. One evening we honored the
elders: Sam Allen, Gwendolyn Brooks, Mari Evans, Pinkie Gordon Lane,
Naomi Long Madgett, Raymond Patterson, and Margaret Walker. The
combined force of their power charged the air with excitement and rever-
ence and an awe-inspiring sense of significance that was at once historic and
primordial. We celebrated the melded voices of our singers and poets as we
listened to Val Gray Ward's big husky voice sweetened by a Mound Bayou
accent recite works by legendary poets. We celebrated as Bernice Johnson
Reagon took us to the source of poetry's original beauty. In her songs,
punctuated by the magical sounds of the shakaree, she sounded the notes
that connected us—spiritual, gospel, blues, freedom song were our links
to our cultural selves. We also celebrated, as Opal Moore said in her tribute
to Pinkie Gordon Lane, "the authors of the too-often uncelebrated, un-
memorialized acts of courage that have made context, have made all other
gains knowable."

But finally, it was Alvin Aubert who vivified such an act of courage.
On the last morning of the conference, Aubert stepped to the front of the
auditorium, book in one hand and cane in the other. (He was a recent
amputee learning to use a prosthesis.) His gait was steadied by them both.
He started to read his poem "Dream of the Heroes":

> Think of Miss Mandy on her front porch
> Wondering when her grandson Norris will get home
> The mosquitoes aren't much of a bother
> Nor the intolerable heat
> She's sipping lemonade
> Wouldn't it taste better
> with somebody to share it with?
> But it's not herself she's concerned with now
> It's Norris and all the Norrises in the City of
>   Detroit . . .

His voice broke. The words caught in his throat. "It is actually for all the
Norrises of Detroit that I'm shedding tears," he said. His words bore wit-
ness to why we were there. We were there because we love poetry and

know its power to charge our intellect with new ideas, excite our senses, change our hearts, and move us to action. For we all were dreamers and, in our way, heroes too. We had come together to assess the health of poetry, the beauty, truth, and spirit of it. We, like Alvin Aubert, had the health of a nation of Norrises on our minds.

The essays and conversations featured in this volume have been chosen on the basis of their contributions toward the task of assessing the health of African American poetry and building a larger critical framework in which to read and discuss it. Although the number of, and variety and quality of work by, black poets is currently on the wax and may well point toward one of the major moments in the history of American poetry, we are still in the process of developing a critical language to deal with this (r)evolution. When speaking at the conference, Eugene Redmond articulated the vast range of issues that such a language would have to address: territory, signs, semantics, geography, demography, performance and performative poetics, cross-fertilization and influences literary and extraliterary or nonliterary, indigenous and foreign ideologies, mother-myths and other-myths, multiculturalism, gender. The foregoing list, by no means an exhaustive one, should make it clear that African American poetry should *not* be conceived apart from the culture out of which it emerges; on the contrary, scholars and critics should seek the widest possible context.

The first grouping of articles deals with the question of "African American Poetry and the Vernacular Matrix," an area of concern for students of black poetry at least since Langston Hughes wrote these lines:

> Thump, thump, thump, went his foot on the floor.
> He played a few chords then he sang some more—
>   "I got the Weary Blues
>   And I can't be satisfied.
>   Got the Weary Blues
>   And can't be satisfied—
>   I ain't happy no mo'
>   And I wish that I had died.

Hughes's use of the blues idiom here is a keystone in the history of African American poetry's intermingling of folk and popular culture, an intermingling that raises such questions as those Alvin Aubert posed at the conference's roundtable on the subject: "At what point in the evolution of African American culture did the popular emerge from the folk? Assuming that such an emergence did occur. Or, we may ask, is the popular a discrete entity, or an evolutionary variant of the folk? Or is there a traceable evolutionary progression from the folk to the popular? And finally, to what extent, and at what point in the evolution of African American culture, did the folk and the popular become conflated to subsumibility under vernacular?" The very term *vernacular* has a complex and haunted resonance in African American culture; as Elizabeth Alexander has pointed out, the term derives from the Latin word for "slave." Thus, the cultural forms deriving from slavery, most obviously musical styles such as spirituals, are some of the earliest historical examples of the vernacular. Linguistic patterns original to African Americans—the dozens, capping, boasting—fall here as well, whether we are speaking of lyrics in hip-hop music or Michael S. Harper's reminiscences of his mother, in the kitchen, "telescoping complexity." Other areas of the vernacular addressed here and requiring further exploration include the dichotomies of rural/urban and northern/southern, musical and dance forms, and oratory including religious sermons and myths.

African American music being the major vernacular idiom, several essays in this section deal with poetry's relation to jazz and blues. Mariann Russell looks at the poets Langston Hughes and Melvin Tolson, uncovering a deep consonance between their use of the blues idiom and persona. Kalamu ya Salaam likewise examines the presence of the jazz idiom in Hughes's poetry, demonstrating Hughes's long poem *Montage* to be the first major piece of jazz poetry. Turning to the exploration of myth, Therese Steffen shows how Rita Dove launches out from the traditional ground of the Demeter-Persephone myth of betrayal and regeneration and, hovering within the aesthetic boundaries of the sonnet, reinitiates and configures a brown mother's encounter with fear, pain, grief, loss, joy, and renewal as she helplessly watches her daughter's loss of innocence. Eugenia Collier takes as her areas of concern black folk myth and legend as she explores heroic figures in the narratives of Sterling Brown. Edward A. Scott looks at Samuel Allen's poetry in the context of black religious tradition, particularly the sermon and the idea of witness, showing Allen's summoning of mythic time into the historical time with which his poetry deals. Also, in a conversation between Michael S. Harper and Aldon Nielsen, Harper discusses how he bridges his musical heritage and his literary one in his poetry.

The second group of essays deals with "Critical Theories and Approaches in African American Poetry." Jerry Ward suggests that theory is a bridge that helps to make understandable the relationships between those who create, their creations, and those who make use of their creations in the context of history and culture: "In that sense theory is necessary for rigorous examination of African American poetry. How might theory advance the study and appreciation of this body of poetry? How do such theories influence interpretive methods and approaches, and how must theorists themselves grapple with their own historicity in light of the evolution of African American poetry from orature to literature?" The questions raised by this section include questions about the adequacy of theoretical models like Marxism or deconstruction for assessing the works of African American poets. Joyce A. Joyce, for example, argues for a new language of critical theory drawn entirely from the culture of Africa and the African diaspora and suggests that the critical discourse will reflect the interconnection of language, politics, music, and religion, and its centrality to an exposition of African American poetry. Jerry W. Ward Jr., on the other hand, draws on speech act theory to explore the poetry of Don Lee (Haki Madhubuti); Ward challenges many of the assumptions of speech-act theorists, however, and shows in his study how the particular cultural situation of the African American poet helps fuel these challenges.

While this book does not attempt to resolve this debate, or even give a full picture of its dimensions, it is important that this debate be framed in terms that make it clear just what is at stake. The fight for inclusion of black authors in college literature courses and anthologies is a vital part of the fight for social justice on all levels in America, and the argument over literary theory—often charged, sometimes justly, with obscurantism and irrelevance—is an argument about how to talk about literature and culture. Jerry Ward, while speaking at the conference, challenged theorists to make their work available to a wider audience: "Perhaps the crucial question I raised has to do with linking, and I make the assertion . . . that theory is obligated to explain relations between people and artifacts in the context of history and culture. Now the matter of obligation and theory is very important to me, because through my training in theory, and what I teach, I very often feel that theorists believe that they are not obligated to anyone other than themselves, or to anything other than the signs in which they inscribe their ideas. And I find that very remiss in terms of human responsibility." Our responsibility to our readers, students, ancestors, and descendants is to develop a theoretical language that adequately links works of literature to the culture in which they exist and shows us how these works can serve to critique and change that culture.

The most fundamental assumptions about African American poetry are challenged by Aldon Lynn Nielsen's provocative essay "'The Callig-raphy of Black Chant': Resiting African American Poetries," which dem-onstrates that the presence of the written word has always been coupled with the better-understood oral tradition in black literature. Nielsen's argu-ment, though it covers massive historical ground, focuses on postmodern poets like N. H. Pritchard and Arthur Pfister and the reasons for their ob-scurity in the academy. Contributions to the theoretical language of African American poetics are made by Mark A. Sanders, who anatomizes the struc-tures of folk myths and details their contribution to Sterling Brown's depic-tion of heroism, and Ikenna Dieke, who works with the poetry of Alice Walker to reveal the presence of an earth-centered, ecofeminist sensibility in Walker. Jon Woodson, in his examination of three long poems on the Middle Passage, discusses theories of history found in African American poetry and those theories' relation to myth and their bearing on the future. Sherley Anne Williams and Deborah McDowell, in a conversation that ends the section, raise the issue of how to accommodate the new strains of rap and hip-hop expressions in a critical context that would allow for their ex-amination and assessment. Williams makes an acute criticism of misogyny in rap music and discusses the shifting constructions of memory and knowl-edge within the African American community.

The third grouping of essays, "Writing a Literary History of African American Poetry," deals with the construction of the literary framework in which we are to place poets and poetry. Writing this history is of the utmost importance for showing that American literature has always been an on-going conversation rather than a grand narrative; Henry Louis Gates Jr. uses the term *comparative American culture* as an example of a new model from which the humanities might profit.

A good literary history of African America would not, of course, be written in isolation from the literary history of white America—the spark-ing connections between, for example, Hughes and Whitman are too pow-erful. But it would also place black writers against the extraliterary back-drop of black history, from the Middle Passage through slavery and the civil rights movement to the present. The writing of such a history would have to take into account the history of vernacular culture that we have discussed elsewhere, as well as developments in the allied arts. And to be truly re-sponsible to the past, the writing of such a history would have to acknowl-edge the complications of characterizing a literary period: compare, for example, the aesthetics of Hughes and Cullen to see that the Harlem Re-naissance had multiple stylistic and formal faces.

The history of African American poetry is encapsulated by Raymond Patterson, from the nineteenth century to the post–Black Arts period, in an essay that explores the long development of the African American epic poem. Patterson delves both into the academy's given conventions about the epic, represented by his use of critics like Northrop Frye, and the specifics of the African American cultural condition that have made that epic tradition unique. Eric A. Weil dissects the dichotomy of I/we narrative voices in African American poetry, showing the continuing pattern among black poets to speak as a unified racial presence. Joanne V. Gabbin explores the early poetry of Gwendolyn Brooks with a special focus on her portraits of women in the context of the racial and social traumas of the mid-twentieth century. Hilary Holladay takes a similar approach to Lucille Clifton's poetry in her chapter "Song of Herself: Lucille Clifton's Poems about Womanhood" where she shows the poet speaking confessionals from the racial and social margins of American society. Conversations with Gwendolyn Brooks and Margaret Walker also add priceless insights into the lives and literary milieu of the foremothers of contemporary black poetry, of whom Nikki Giovanni said, "This Furious Flower was really planted and pruned by the two." Angela M. Salas creates a critical portrait of Yusef Komunyakaa, whose "beaten songs" thread through the raging history of the Vietnam War and civil rights era and whose poetic innovation, freedom, and density represent the present generation of poets. Finally, Jabari Asim looks to the new generation of poets who grow their words, informed by a long literary tradition, in a minefield of explosive new developments.

▲

(*Left to right*) Eleanor Traylor,
Elizabeth Alexander, and Alvin
Aubert (Photo courtesy of
C. B. Claiborne)

▲

Mari Evans
(Photo courtesy
of Erica Bleeg)

▲

Amiri Baraka (Photo courtesy of
C. B. Claiborne)

▲

Rita Dove (Photo courtesy of
C. B. Claiborne)

Sonia Sanchez
(Photo courtesy of
C. B. Claiborne)

(*Left to right*)
E. Ethelbert Miller,
Toi Derricotte, and
Gerald Barrax
(Photo courtesy of
C. B. Claiborne)

▶

Haki Madhubuti
(Photo courtesy of
C. B. Claiborne)

▼

Eugene Redmond
(*center, in cap*) talking
with other conference
participants (Photo
courtesy of C. B.
Claiborne)

Sharan Strange
(Photo courtesy of
C. B. Claiborne)

▶

Thomas Sayers
Ellis (Photo
courtesy of C. B.
Claiborne)

▶

Clyde Taylor
talking with
audience
members (Photo
courtesy of C. B.
Claiborne)

▲

D. J. Renegade (Photo courtesy
of Erica Bleeg)

▲

(*Left to right*) Adam David Miller, Askia Touré,
Brenda Marie Osbey, and Jerry W. Ward Jr. (Photo
courtesy of C. B. Claiborne)

▶

Samuel Allen
(Photo courtesy of
C. B. Claiborne)

▼

Val Gray Ward
(Photo courtesy of
C. B. Claiborne)

Bernice Johnson
Reagon
(Photo courtesy of
C. B. Claiborne)

Conference
participants in the
courtyard at James
Madison University
(Photo courtesy of
C. B. Claiborne)

▲
Gwendolyn Brooks
(Photo courtesy of
C. B. Claiborne)

PART 1

*African American Poetry and
the Vernacular Matrix*

Langston Hughes: A Poet Supreme

K A L A M U   Y A   S A L A A M

For the purposes of this essay, black poetry is poetry that (1) is grounded in the black experience; (2) utilizes black music as a structural or emulative model; and (3) "consciously" transforms the prevailing standards of poetry through an iconoclastic and innovative use of language.

No poet better carries the mantle of model and innovator than Langston Hughes, the prolific Duke Ellington of black poetry. Hughes's output alone is staggering. During his lifetime, he published over eight hundred poems. Moreover, he single-handedly defined "blues poetry" and is arguably the first major "jazz" poet. Early in his career he realized the importance of "reading" his poetry to receptive audiences. "When Alain Locke arranged a poetry reading by Hughes before the Playwriter's Circle in 1927 in Washington, a blues pianist accompanied him, bringing Hughes the artist and blues music one step closer together, even though Hughes felt that the piano player was 'too polished.' He suggested to his Knopf editor that they ought to get 'a regular Lenox Avenue blues boy' to accompany him at his reading in New York."[1] In the fifties Hughes was a major voice in the movement of recording with jazz accompaniment.

Although I have neither the space, inclination, nor ability to give a close textual reading of Hughes's poetry and although a large body of critical work already exists, I would like to focus on *one* piece by Hughes to evidence my case for his stature. That piece is the multipart, book-length poem *Montage of a Dream Deferred* (1951).

In *Montage,* which Hughes described in a letter to Arna Bontemps as "what you might call a precedent shattering opus—also could be known as a tour de force,"[2] Hughes addresses a number of critical problems facing black poetry: (1) how to affect a modern sensibility and at the same time maintain a grounding in the folk culture; (2) how to achieve the textual representation of the music, especially in terms of improvisation and variation of tone and timbre; and (3) how to use the vernacular without resorting to dialect.

Hughes realized that it was impossible to do what he wanted to do in one piece, so he composed a series of short poems that play off each other. Western literary thought values the long form, the novel in particular, as a statement of intellectual achievement and implicitly devalues short forms. For this reason a collection of short stories rarely receives equal critical attention as does a novel by the same author. In order to make the long form stand out, the author is expected to demonstrate complexity of plot and character development. But these and related concerns are simply a culturally biased valuation of a specific set of literary devices, often at the expense of other devices (many of which center on the sounding of poetry on the page). In a very important sense, modern American poetry was moving toward painting, that is, a composition of words placed on a page, and away from music, that is, an articulation of words that have both sense (meaning) and sound (emotion). Hughes clearly chose to emphasize black music, which increasingly meant dealing with improvisation.

The improvisation is implied in that certain themes, rhyme and rhythmic patterns, and recurring images ebb and flow throughout *Montage*—here spelled out in detail, there hinted at, and in another instance turned on their head. The above-quoted letter indicates that Hughes was conscious of what he was doing, and it is this self-consciousness that marks this as a modern poem. Indeed, *Montage* is almost postmodern in its mosaic of voices and attitudes contained in one piece.

Just as jazz simultaneously stresses the collective and the individual, Hughes's component poems are each individual statements, but they are also part of a larger unit(y). Significantly, Hughes as an individual is de-emphasized in the work, even as various individual members of the community speak and are spoken about. In other words, Hughes becomes a medium, a sensitive and subtle medium, but a medium nonetheless. In a seemingly simple form, Hughes serves as a sounding board for the articulation of people who are usually voiceless.

The work's modernity is the self-reflective nature of all of the voices speaking, and in speaking, coming to consciousness of themselves and their environment. Time and time again we hear voices self-consciously grappling with their Harlem realities, which include an international awareness of African American, West Indian, and African bonding. In the African American context "modernity" specifically refers to the post-Reconstruction, north-ern-oriented urbanization of African American life. No presixties black poet was more complete in expressing the black urban viewpoint than Hughes.

The ease with which Hughes voices the various personalities and points of view belies both the complexity and progressiveness of his achievement. Because of the brevity of the poems, Hughes's points are often made in passing and require reflection in order to appreciate just how far-reaching is *Montage*'s social commentary. "Cafe: 3 A.M." is one of the many short poems that make up the *Montage* series. This poem perfectly illustrates Hughes's musical use of bebop rhythms and phrasing mated to subtle social commentary.

Most critics consider Hughes reticent on the subject of homosexuality, yet *Montage* includes this double critique — one of homophobia and hetero-sexism and one of the criminalization of sexual activities.

Cafe: 3 A.M.

Detectives from the vice squad
with weary sadistic eyes
spotting fairies.
    Degenerates,
    some folks say.
    But God, Nature,
    or somebody
    made them that way.

Police lady or Lesbian
over there?
    Where?

Compare this to the work of any other poet publishing with a major house in the early 1950s.

In the headnote to *Montage,* Hughes declares, "In terms of current Afro-American popular music and sources from which it has progressed — jazz, ragtime, swing, blues, boogie-woogie, and be-bop — this poem on contemporary Harlem, like be-bop, is marked by conflicting changes, sudden nuances, sharp and impudent interjections, broken rhythms, and passages sometimes in the manner of the jam session, sometimes like the popular song, punctuated by the riffs, runs, breaks, and distortions of the music of a community in transition." [3]

Langston Hughes, a poet who had cut his teeth and made his mark as a *blues* poet, took up the challenge of writing a book-length *bebop jazz* poem! Although, just like the music, there is a bedrock of blues undergirding the structure, Hughes's objective and success was in creating a modern jazz structure that allowed for a broader range of themes, voices, and even styles. Some of the poems are epigrams, some are written as actual letters, some are conversations, and others are monologues; more than once we have poems that amount to sayings, folk definitions, and observations. Indeed, *Montage* is aptly named. In the whole history of American literature, no one has written a comparable poem that bases itself on a music form, and certainly no one has even come close in the context of jazz. All other efforts at jazz poetry pale in comparison.

Consider that Hughes does not take the easy way out. He chose not to emphasize the names of musicians or the names of musical compositions. There is no attempt to imitate the sound of the horns (as was common in much of the Black Arts music-based poetry). The mosaic quality of the music, the intensity of expression, the fluid, quicksilver rhythms, and the complex melodic counterpoint and harmonic daring of bebop are all achieved by a deft use of simple words, precise punctuation, and italics. The complexity of the overall composition notwithstanding, the individual parts seem too simple to be true, but *Montage* works so sublimely because Hughes figured out precisely how to get to the heart of the expression without bothering with or getting caught up in external floridness.

The third major achievement of this poem is Hughes's mastery of nuance and control of language. He suggests the dialect without resorting to the contractions and so-called broken English that mar(k)s most dialect poetry and some modern poetry by blacks. *Langston Hughes and the Blues,* Steven Tracy's detailed reading and explication of Hughes's blues poetry, more than adequately defines Hughes's consummate poetic artistry. Tracy pays particular attention to Hughes's subtle use of punctuation, a subtlety that completely escapes most critics of Hughes's work. Although Tracy does not focus on the bebop aspects of *Montage* and does not address *Ask Your Mama,* this is nevertheless the best starting point for a literary appreciation of Hughes's use of music in his poetry. Introducing an analysis of the textual revisions that Hughes made as he combined the techniques of the blues artist, the blues composer, and the poet, Tracy writes: "The pervasive influence of the oral tradition in Hughes's poetry might make an examination of Hughes's revisions of his blues poems seem like a futile, pedantic exercise, particularly given the variable nature of an individual blues lyric as the singer performs it. However, because Hughes was a literary artist, because he was tied to the written as well as the oral tradition, and because he made sometimes drastic revisions of his blues poems, such an examination helps to reveal his attitudes toward his material as they modulated over the years and to illuminate the nature of his use of the oral blues tradition in his written work."[4]

There is an African proverb used to express futility: "like singing to a white man." If one is unfamiliar with blues culture, how can one hope to appreciate fully or expertly critique Langston Hughes? The establishment's critical diminishing and dismissing of Hughes is based, to an astoundingly large degree, on the cultural illiteracy and unresponsiveness of establishment critics to the blues. In their ignorance they denigrated what they were both intellectually and emotionally unequipped to understand.

Montage gave us defining metaphors of the black experience—"the dream deferred" and "raisins in the sun." Only Dunbar's "caged bird" metaphor comes close, in terms of popular acceptance, as a cultural image of African American life. As important and innovative as *Montage* is, most of us are not fully aware of this book-length accomplishment because we have bought into the establishment assessment that Hughes had a limited poetic technique. In a similar way, the establishment assessed Thelonious Monk as having a limited piano technique. But just as few pianists are able to play like Monk and no musicians have been able to match his compositional authority; similarly, emphasis on Eurocentric poetic devices notwithstanding, few poets have been able to write from inside the black experience like Hughes, and no one has achieved as impressive a body of compositions, that is, "textual poems."

Langston Hughes was absolutely clear about the focus of his work and the danger inherent in articulating the history and vision, the realities and aspirations, of the sufferers.

Unfortunately, having been born poor—and also colored—in Missouri, I was stuck in the mud from the beginning. Try as I might to float off into the clouds, poverty and Jim Crow would grab me by the heels, and right back on earth I would land. A third-floor furnished room is the nearest thing I have ever had to an ivory tower.

Some of my earliest poems were social poems in that they were about people's problems—whole groups of people's problems—rather than my own personal difficulties. Sometimes, though, certain aspects of my personal problems happened to be also common to many other people. And certainly, racially speaking, my own problems of adjustment to American life were the same as those of millions of other segregated Negroes. The moon belongs to everybody, but not this American earth of ours. That is perhaps why poems about the moon perturb no one, but poems about color and poverty do perturb many citizens. Social forces pull backwards or forwards, right or left, and social poems get caught in the pulling and hauling. Sometimes the poet himself gets pulled and hauled—even hauled off to jail.[5] Contemporary white writers can perhaps afford to be utterly irresponsible in their moral and social viewpoints. Negro writers cannot. Ours is a social as well as a literary responsibility.[6]

An emphasis on dual responsibilities, social and literary, is in itself a particular feature of a black aesthetic. This is not new, or novel, but it does continue to be controversial precisely because it contextualizes art within the world as the world actually is, beset by dominant and dominating forces who enforce (sometimes under the rubric of "free enterprise") all manners of economic exploitation.

There is necessarily an opposition to "commercialism" inherent in the black aesthetic precisely because, from an African American perspective, the birth of the black experience, as archetypically illustrated by the Congo Square experience, was simultaneously the site of both black art as ritual and black art as entertainment, with the entertainment undermining the ritual. Moreover, the birth of the African American was as a chattel slave, as a commercial product. If anyone is by birthright opposed to commercialism, it is certainly the African American.

The advocacy of freedom and fighting against oppression and exploitation is not simply a question of content but also a question of the use of art. Langston Hughes was keenly aware of the dichotomy of content and aesthetic and also of the moral disaster of ignoring the reality and repercussions of such a dichotomy. Too many people in their literary criticism completely overlook social context and hence overlook as well the fact that the social thrust of poetry is integral to its aesthetics.

Langston Hughes, as subtle as he was, and as innocuous as he may seem by today's standards, is exemplary of a poet grounded in the culture, consistent in his use of music as both inspiration and model, and innovative and iconoclastic in his use of English. Yes, it was and continues to be revolutionary to insist on transforming English into a tool of ritual within the black community and not just a lingua franca of commerce or individual self-expression.

Finally, another aspect of Hughes's abilities that is also overlooked or ignored is that he was multilingual and masterfully translated poetry, including seminal work of Nicholas Gullien and Federico García Lorca. The importance of this observation is that this is another piece of irrefutable evidence that Hughes's writing style was not reflective of the limitations of an "undisciplined," unsophisticated, and provincial poet.

Much of the criticism of Hughes's poetry by textually influenced academicians would lead the reader to believe that Hughes was simply a hack writer who had some facility with musical imagery and styles. Such views allow the critic to pass over the difficult challenge of explaining how a man who comfortably spoke three languages, translated literature from Africa, the Caribbean, Europe, and elsewhere, and traveled incessantly, could be thought of as a relatively "unsophisticated," even "simple" poet.

In much the same way the Pulitzer judges refused to award their prize to Duke Ellington in 1965 because they did not think his work was serious enough, Hughes has been denied both appropriate formal awards and informal kudos, as well as significant posthumous awards from the American literary establishment. Perhaps there is no surprise here because the elevation of self-determined blackness, especially outside of sports and entertainment, is usually greeted by deafening silence from both the critical as well as the popular authorities of the status quo. How else could it be? To achieve blackness is inherently a liberating act, and liberation is necessarily disruptive of the status quo.

Notes

1. Tracy, 112.
2. Nichols, 236.
3. Rampersad and Roessel, 387.
4. Tracy, 236–37.
5. Berry, 149–50.
6. Ibid., 171.

Works Cited

Berry, Faith, ed. *Good Morning Revolution: Uncollected Writings of Langston Hughes*. New York: Citadel, 1992.

Nichols, Charles H., ed. *Arna Bontemps-Langston Hughes Letters, 1925–1967*. New York: Dodd, 1980.

Rampersad, Arnold. *The Life of Langston Hughes,* vol. 2, *1925–1967*. New York: Dodd, 1988.

Rampersad, Arnold, and David Roessel, eds. *The Collected Poems of Langston Hughes*. New York: Knopf, 1994.

Tracy, Steven C. *Langston Hughes and the Blues*. Urbana: University of Illinois Press, 1988.

Message to the Generations: The Mythic Hero in Sterling Brown's Poetry

E U G E N I A   C O L L I E R

Great poetry draws its strength from the life of mankind. . . . Whenever the
collective unconscious becomes a living experience and is brought to bear
upon the conscious outlook of an age, this event is a creative act which
is of importance for a whole epoch. A work of art is produced that
may truthfully be called a message to the generations.
—Carl Jung

A MEASURE OF THE GREATNESS OF ANY ARTISTIC FORM is the extent to which the artist is able to reach beyond the context of the age and to address the wider concerns of mankind. In assessing the poetry of Sterling Brown, we need to include in our examination the extent to which he delves into the area of these concerns—the realm of myth.

Myth encompasses our deepest truths, tested by the ages, as fresh to us now as to our earliest ancestors. It is "the embodiment of human aspiration and its appropriate imaginative form."[1] Thus myth makes tangible our human potential. Philosopher Joseph Campbell defines mythologies as "poetic expressions of transcendental seeing." Myth transcends time itself, linking us with our forebears and with future generations. Campbell points out that "if we may take as evidence the antiquity of certain basic mythic forms . . . the beginnings of what we may take today to be mystical revelation must have been known to at least a few, even of the primitive teachers of our race, from the very start."[2] Jane Campbell, in her study *Mythic Black Fiction,* defines African American myth as "a dramatic embodiment of cultural values, of ideal states of being found in Afro-American history and experience."[3]

I speak, of course, of two levels of myth: the local and the universal. Each culture has its own ethos wrought from historical experience. The myths of the Arabian Bedouins, for example, would differ in detail from those of the Eskimos. Yet undergirding the parochial level is the level of universal response. Joseph Campbell's *The Hero with a Thousand Faces* explains that despite the numberless conceptions of the hero arising from the different cultures of mankind, there are nevertheless discernible patterns that apply to the concept of the hero in all known cultures. Local myths, then, despite certain differences, draw from a pool of universal truths. "Mythology is the study of mankind's one great story . . . our search to find our place in the drama of the universe."[4]

Who, then, are the mythmakers? Who are the people charged with making tangible these sacred truths and setting them into place in this great, eternal drama? The artists are the mythmakers, for only they can plumb the depths of human experience and elicit from it the words, the sounds, the images to clothe in a particular culture's experiences the truths that are eternal. In the past, before the recent advances in technology, the artists remained unknown, and the songs of brilliant poets and musicians were honed and perpetuated by the people to whom they were meaningful. This, perhaps, was the ultimate test, for had the songs and narratives not contained the values of the people, they would never have lasted.

Individual experience is a vehicle by which the artist moves into the area of myth. "The poet," Carl Jung has written, "has plunged into the healing and redeeming depths of the collective psyche, where man is not lost in the isolation of consciousness and its errors and sufferings, but where all men are caught in a common rhythm which allows the individual to communicate his feelings and strivings to mankind as a whole." Jung further explains that "this re-immersion in the state of participation mystique" is what causes our profound response to great art, for "at that level of experience it is no longer the weal or woe of the individual that counts but the life of the collective."[5] "It is only from the insight of its own creative seers and artists that any people has ever derived its appropriate life-supporting and maturing myths."[6]

The poet is the ultimate seer; the art of poetry is the tangible form of the forces that support the life of a people. In the case of Sterling Brown, we don't just *read* his poetry; we *experience* it. We respond on a far more profound level than enjoyment or even—for us jaded old critics—

appreciation of its "literary" value. Brown's poetry "jes' gits hold of us dataway." In his brilliant essay "The Forms of Things Unseen," Stephen Henderson attributes our response to the presence of "mascon" words and images in Sterling Brown's poems. By "mascon" Henderson means "a massive concentration of Black experiential energy which powerfully affects the meaning of Black speech, Black song, and Black poetry—if one, indeed, has to make such distinctions."[7] Our response, then, arises from an area of the self that is beyond the individual self, that dips into what we call, for convenience, the black experience. Beyond even that area is the realm of universal myth.

I do not assume any deliberate attempt on Brown's part to utilize myth in his poems. Certainly his criticism does not call for mythic proportions in anyone's poetry. He does devote important scholarship to folk forms, revealing his reverence for and indebtedness to the black folk, contributing mightily to our understanding of this vital layer of our collective self. I do assume that we—writers included—are shaped by forces beyond our consciousness and that a writer, then, may call upon these hidden depths without conscious volition. One dips into myth instinctively, because only the most profound level of humanity can meet the most profound human need and thus create great art.

Much of Brown's poetry is obviously not mythic. Among these poems are the sonnets and many of the poems written in standard English. These are the personal poems, valued for other reasons. But it is in the public voice, the voice of the spokesman, that Brown's work becomes myth.

In examining Brown's *Collected Poems* to ascertain which could be said to be mythic, I used four guidelines: the presence of archetype, the use of ritual, the seriousness of effect, and the depth of my own subjective response. By *archetype* I mean an image that appears repeatedly in the historical experience and thus in the art of a particular culture and can be identified, although in different guises, in the art of other cultures. By *ritual* I mean the tangible, physical acting-out of myth. Joseph Campbell defines ritual as "the enactment of a myth." In another work he states, "Myths are the mental supports of rites; rites, the physical enactments of myths."[8] By *seriousness of effect* I mean that the effect of the work moves beyond entertainment or titillation or even accepted concepts of beauty. It addresses the reader on a deeper level; through symbols and mascon words and images it evokes deeply embedded memories of significant shared experience; it fosters a desire to read it or hear it again; it imparts wisdom or strength. The criterion is the depth of subjective response—which is, of course, unmeasurable but real. I am a black person. How does this poem move *me*? "Wherever [the tyrant monster] sets his hand there is . . . a cry for the redeeming hero, the carrier of the shining blade, whose blow, whose torch, whose existence, will liberate the land."[9]

A culture is defined—in part, at least—by its concept of the heroic, as embodied in the archetypal hero, by myths of all systems that have emerged from each culture's historical experience. Stephen Henderson has pointed out that certain folk forms "take us outside the dimension of history into the universal realm of the mythical. In the oral tradition," he continues, "the dogged determination of the work songs, the tough-minded power of the blues, the inventive energy of jazz, and the transcendent vision of God in the spirituals and the sermons, all energize the idea of Liberation, which is itself liberated from the temporal, the societal, and the political—not with the narcotic obsession to remain above the world of struggle and change and death, but with full realization of a return to that world both strengthened and renewed."[10]

I have discerned at least three faces of mythic heroism in Sterling Brown's poetry. The first is the quiet, law-abiding person who has tried for a lifetime to live within the boundaries set by an essentially violent and racist society. Something happens, some unendurable thing, or perhaps some final insult is added to a lifetime of insults, and the quiet person snaps. The perilous journey begins, out of the safety of passivity into the hell of direct resistance. It is the way of destruction, as the hero makes his choice, but he emerges transformed—though physically dead—into a hero, whose story, as the existence of the poem attests, is a beacon to his people. The second heroic archetype is the one who meets life with defiance and—yes—with style. Despite the dehumanizing force of racism, this hero has such a sense of himself, such a wholeness of spirit, that he remains unbroken. The third heroic archetype is the person whose heroism lies not in one magnificent gesture but in the lifelong struggle to Be, the struggle to maintain life and dignity and wholeness of self through the most arduous day-to-day effort, despite terrible losses. Life itself is the perilous journey, and the one who survives intact is the boon to other travelers along the "road so rocky." Here the wise elder is the archetype, known to every culture, carrying the seed of wisdom to succeeding generations. In African American culture, the wise-elder archetype merges with the hero archetype, because to survive to old age with wisdom and dignity is itself, in a system of total oppression, an act of heroism. "Invariably Brown's poetry reveals an exploration of self-hood, a celebration of the strength and stoicism of Black people, and an abiding faith in the possibilities of their lives. Brown becomes myth-maker, keeper of the images, preserver of values and definitions." [11]

The most obvious hero in Brown's poetry is a quiet, law-abiding (sometimes downright meek) person who has endured racial cruelties until finally he has simply *had* it. One final bitter drop causes the dam to burst, and the heroic journey begins. The hero ventures forth from the tenuous security of passivity and strikes out at the monster racism. He makes the choice deliberately, knowing the dreadful consequences but finding courageous death preferable to unendurable life. He becomes more than his individual self; he becomes the personification of resistance to overwhelming forces; he is the standard-bearer for black people from the first enslaved Africans to our last enslaved descendants and thus for all the heroic wretched of the earth.

A quintessential example of this hero is Crispus Attucks McKoy. With tight-lipped irony Brown recreates a modern version of the historical Crispus Attucks, the escaped slave who confronted the British on the Boston Common. Armed with only his conviction, Attucks became the first American to die in the Revolution and thus sacrificed his life for a freedom denied to him and to his progeny. "Crispus Attucks McKoy" is written in the form of a ballad. The irony is intensified by the mock-heroic language in which the ballad is rendered.

> I sing of a hero,
> Unsung, unrecorded,
> Known by the name
> Of Crispus Attucks McKoy. [12]

The balladeer evokes the names of others who have resisted oppression: Garvey, Trotter, Du Bois. These three men are among the giants of our culture: each had a lifelong commitment to resistance; each made immeasurable sacrifices; each took us a step closer to ultimate victory over oppression. By evoking their names the balladeer links McKoy to a heroic line.

McKoy works as a servant, hating every minute.

> No monastic hairshirt
> Stung flesh more bitterly
> Than the white coat
> In which he was arrayed. (141)

Again the irony is effective—the ancient monks wore hairshirts as a sign of willingness to suffer for religious ideals. McKoy's white coat symbolizes imposed subservience and inferiority—which he accepted unwillingly as a result of limited choices.

We encounter McKoy at the moment of extreme tension, when he has endured as much as is humanly possible. The balladeer need not enumerate the incidents that have brought him to this point: a black audience knows. The bitter humor of the next incident is based upon double entendres, as McKoy's mindset requires him to react with strong emotion to words uttered in an entirely different context. These are mascon words, uttered generations before Steve Henderson coined the term. Here Brown gives flesh to a dynamic as old as oppression and as complex as language: certain words evoke responses in the oppressed that are far different from those of the oppressor. Words can cut. And words can empower.

McKoy quits his job when a white woman at a bridge party bids one spade. For a moment he is free, but then a bootblack calls out, "Shine?" and McKoy lets loose a "blue streak" of curses. So it goes as McKoy, like an exposed nerve, is excruciatingly sensitive to the words that carry generations of insults. McKoy smashes a window of a bakery that advertises "brown Betties" (141). On the subway McKoy "could have committed murder / Mayhem and cannibalism" when a maid admonishes her little charge, "Come over here, darling / Here's a little shade" (142). Finally he goes to the boxing arena, "his refuge, / Recompense for insults, / Solace for grief" (142), where a black boxer, Slugging Joe Johnson, is fighting an Irishman, Battling Dan O'Keefe. At first McKoy expects to find solace as Joe is slugging it out with the white man, pounding him to a pulp, making recompense to all black people. Here, too, is the mythic battle of the leaders of contending armies. This arena is crowded with white people of various European backgrounds as "Crispus strode in / Regally, boldly" (142)—the only black person there.

Herein lies the tragic choice: McKoy invests great feeling into the battle—his pride, his raison d'être, assuagement for his pain are all riding on Slugging Joe. When Joe is momentarily getting the worst of the fight, someone right behind McKoy yells, "Kill the Nigger!" (143) and all the agony of all the years falls upon McKoy. The ballad endows him with the spiritual power and tragic dignity of classical heroes:

> Crispus got up
> In all his fury;
> Lightning bolts zigzagged

Out of his eyes.
With a voice like thunder
He blurted his challenge,
"Will the bastard who said that
Please arise." (143)

All rise—3,500 strong, Irish, Polish, Bohemian, Jew, gentile, and what-
ever, their differences unimportant, against this black man—"our hero /
Armed with his noble cause / Armed with righteousness / To battle goes."
McKoy perishes. The next three stanzas grimly catalog the various locales
in the Boston area—the very seat of democracy—where parts of McKoy's
body are found. But the ballad ends with the assertion that all over this
nation "the soul of our hero / *Goes marching on.*"

The effectiveness of the poem is due partly to Brown's masterful use of
the ballad form.[13] Here Brown recreates the traditional language of old
English balladeers, serious-faced but tongue in cheek. The contrast of the
orderly (or apparently orderly) world of jolly old England with the chaotic,
irrational, oppressive world forced upon black people, points out poignantly
the horror of McKoy's life. Gabbin says, "As a poet, Brown's most significant
achievement is his subtle adaptation of song forms, especially the blues, to
the literature. Experimenting with the blues, spirituals, work songs, and
ballads, he invents combinations that, at their best, retain the ethos of folk
forms and intensify the literary quality of poetry. Like his fellow traveler
Langston Hughes, Brown discovers how to enable one form to release the
power of another."[14]

"Crispus Attucks McKoy" is presented in a folkloric form, the ballad,
to portray an archetype in African American culture and indeed in virtually
all cultures—the tragic hero who chooses death over continued degrada-
tion. Each step along the way, as McKoy moves inevitably toward the mo-
ment of the final terrible choice, like Hector, and John Henry, McKoy's
steps lead to the ultimate ritual of physical destruction, a ritual enacted
repeatedly in our history—recall Denmark Vesey, Nat Turner, Medgar
Evers, and myriad nameless folk whose sacrifice will ever remain unnoted
and unrecorded. The ritual of gratuitous suffering and death for a principle
is, in fact, a cornerstone on which Christianity itself is founded.

Other Brown heroes also choose death over continued oppression.
Most fully drawn is Joe Meek, "soft as pie," who reaches the limit of for-
bearance when two policemen "throw a po' girl down" and then when Joe
politely inquires "ef they thought / They had done *just right,*" they beat
him into unconsciousness—a symbolic rebirth—a changed man, his asser-

tiveness released by raw injustice. He buys a gun and precipitates a shootout with the cops, the reserves, and the national guard—all the representatives of law and order arrayed against meek Joe Meek. Only through the treachery of the sheriff is Joe brought down, his last words reaffirming his rage.

Joe's story, too, is a ballad, this one sung by a black balladeer utilizing the black vernacular, who leaves us with this bit of folk wisdom:

> So you cain't never tell
> How fas' a dog can run
> When you see him a-sleepin'
> In the sun. (152)

Crispus Attucks McKoy and Joe Meek are both little people who tried to adjust to the system and to fit white America's historic definition of good, law-abiding black people. Our culture and our literature are replete with them. In their tragic choices, however, they become larger than ordinary life; they become heroes for the world's downtrodden little people to admire and perhaps even to emulate.

Old Lem tells of another hero who makes a choice. The poem uses spare, bare-boned language that is more effective than volumes of words. The narrator says simply, "I talked to Old Lem / And Old Lem said . . ." (170). We do not know why the apparently uneducated narrator sought out Old Lem. But we can infer that he went to this unlettered man who has lived and survived for so many years because in him there is life-sustaining wisdom. Old Lem's terse, bitter words capture the awful rituals of racism, the refrain reiterating the message:

> They don't come by ones
> They don't come by twos
> But they come by tens. (170)

Old Lem tells about his buddy, "Six foot of man / Muscled up perfect / Game to the heart" who "spoke out of turn / At the commissary." Unlike the ballads of Crispus Attucks McKoy and Joe Meek, this poem does not provide a full-blown scenario. Old Lem tells us only the essentials:

> They gave him a day
> To git out of the county.
> He didn't take it. (171)

Here the hero makes a deliberate choice. He has left the relative security of anonymity not by leaving home but by *staying* home and shedding the role white society has forced upon him. He "spoke out of turn." That is all we need to know. That is the start of the heroic journey—a swift, brief journey:

> He said, "Come and get me!"
> And they came and got him.
>
> . . . . .
>
> He stayed in the county—
> He lays there dead. (171)

The simplicity of Old Lem's words intensifies the horror of the ritual—a ritual so often repeated that it is indelibly stamped on our racial memory.

> Look at old Scrappy puttin' on dog,
> Puttin' on dog, puttin' on dog,
> Look at old Scrappy puttin' on dog,
> Steppin' like nobody's business. (227–28)

Heroism is easy to identify in tragic protagonists like Crispus Attucks McKoy, Joe Meek, and Old Lem's buddy. However, there is another type of heroism that is less obvious but just as real: here the hero repudiates the definition of the oppressed self and dares to live not meanly but flamboyantly. Unlike Joe Meek and Crispus Attucks McKoy, this hero has never played the role assigned to him by white racism. From the start he has refused to accept the role that white America imposes upon him and has dared to maintain his vision of himself.

Sterling Brown's poetry is peopled with vivid, vertical characters who maintain their selfhood in the face of ego-destroying forces. Joanne Gabbin's conversations with Brown reveal that these heroes are not paper dolls cut from the poet's imagination: they are real-life people whom Brown knew during his travels into America's black heartland—the South with its bloody, ineradicable history, its terrible testing of America's promise, its role as nucleus of African American culture in this sad land. In form as well as in content, these portrayals emanate from the blood-soaked soil from which our ancestors sprang.

It is, I think, very important that the first poem in Brown's classic

Southern Road is "The Odyssey of Big Boy." This poem sets the tone for the rest of the volume and establishes the strength and dignity of the folk. The poem is based upon an itinerate guitar-playing roustabout, Calvin "Big Boy" Davis, whom Brown knew in that significant period when Brown taught at Virginia Seminary. Big Boy inspired two other poems, "Long Gone" and "When de Saints Go Ma'ching Home," with the latter dedicated to Big Boy Davis "in memory of the times before he was chased out of town for vagrancy." The three poems are a trilogy that reveals a hero of mythic proportions.

"The Odyssey of Big Boy" begins and ends, as Gabbin has pointed out, with Big Boy's claim of immortality along with folk heroes Casey Jones, Stagolee, John Henry, Jazzbo, and "such like men." By evoking this lexicon of heroes, Brown has lifted Big Boy from the category of the colorful individual and made him the voice of the African American worker, whose labor has built this land. The poem, a ballad sung by Big Boy himself, is a catalog of the work Big Boy has done and the places he has traveled, as well as the listing of his sexual exploits along the way. Gabbin has written: "Big Boy represents the strong, resourceful Black worker who, denied the adventure of vertical movement in American businesses and industry, has wandered from job to job, from state to state, earning his wages with sweat and grit. . . . As Big Boy tells of his exploits in love and life, he assures his place in legend. Here, Brown is myth-maker. As the title helps to suggest a relationship between Big Boy and other heroes who had made their odysseys (Homer's Odysseus, Virgil's Aeneas, Dante's Pilgrim), Big Boy is raised to the level of mythic hero who embodies the values, attitude, *Weltshaung* of his people." [15]

Big Boy's heroic journey, then, as reiterated in "Long Gone" and "When de Saints Go Ma'ching Home," is the long and dangerous journey not only from place to place but also through life, a battle in which he is undefeated, from which he has clearly emerged as victor.

Slim Greer is another such hero: Slim Greer, the trickster figure cut from the same cloth as Bre'r Rabbit and Anansi the Spider. The real Slim Greer was a waiter in Jefferson City—

> Talkinges' guy
> An' biggest liar, [16]
> With always a new lie
> On the fire (77)

In a series of poems Slim Greer travels to "Arkansaw," Atlanta, and even Hell itself, where he slays the dragon of racism, escapes destruction, and returns to tell the tale. Slim not only survives but prevails to tell the story of his adventures and thus to teach and inspire.

> O you rascal, puttin' on dog,
> Puttin' on dog, puttin' on dog,
> O you rascal, puttin' on dog,
> Great Gawd, but you was a man! (228)

Big Boy, Long Gone, Slim Greer, Sporting Beasley, and Scrappy are flamboyant heroes who have confronted the system and triumphed. There is a third type of mythic hero in Brown's poetry—the wise elder, whose life has been a journey into chaos and back. It is a chaos well-known to African Americans, not needful of description because, in various ways, we have all been there. Brown's wise elder, in the manner of the Greek seer Tiresias, teaches us survival and more than survival, not only by overt statement but more by the force of *Being*. The wise elder shows us through his or her life the strength and wisdom we are all capable of.

Perhaps the strongest "wise elder" may be immortalized in "Sister Lou" and "Virginia Portrait," both portraits of Mrs. Bibby, the mother of one of Brown's students at Virginia Seminary. She was, as Brown told Joanne Gabbin, a "small, spry Indian-looking woman" who embodied the strength and wisdom that can emerge only from suffering. Gabbin writes, "On the many occasions that Brown was in her home, he became aware of her 'quiet nonchalance,' her 'courtly dignity of speech and carriage,' her 'strength and steadfast hardihood,' and her grief-tempered faith. Her disappointment when the crops were ruined by drought or by unexpected frost, her grief over her children who predeceased her, her simple joys are all captured in a pair of remarkably drawn portraits of a woman who was 'illiterate and somehow very wise.'" [17]

Ma Rainey, the great blues singer, was not really old enough to be an elder, but her designation as "Ma" reveals the nature of her image in the eyes of her listeners. She had seen so much, suffered so much, and emerged strong as steel tempered by fire. In her songs she told her heroic story and showed her listeners the way. In his poem "Ma Rainey," Sterling Brown the poet-mythmaker tells how Ma Rainey, the carrier of the culture, is needed, how folks from miles around "flocks to hear / Ma do her stuff."

Her art heals. She sings "Backwater Blues," which arose from the deepest sorrows of folks ravished not only by the cruelties of racism but also by the cruelty of nature. But the people rose from destruction, their humanity intact.

Ma's songs have had a profound impact on the audience, whose lives she has sung:

> An' den de folks, dey naturally bowed dey heads an' cried,
> Bowed dey heavy heads, shet dey moufs up tight an' cried,
> An' Ma lef' de stage, an' followed some de folks outside. (63)

Thus the artist merges with the people, and they become one.

Sterling Brown, too, like Ma Rainey and Mrs. Bibby, like Crispus Attucks McKoy and Joe Meek and Old Lem's buddy, like Old Lem himself and Big Boy Davis and Scrappy, like all the other heroes he has given us, all have melted into one another and added their strength and wisdom to a pool from which all of humanity can draw—now and into the unfathomable future. Thus Brown emerges as poet-hero, one who seized the sacred fire and offers its light to generations yet unborn.

Notes

1. Righter, 3.
2. Joseph Campbell, *Myths to Live By,* 30.
3. Jane Campbell, *Mythic Black Fiction,* x.
4. Joseph Campbell and Bill Moyers, *Power of Myth,* 54–55.
5. Jung, 104–5.
6. Joseph Campbell, *Myths to Live By,* 50.
7. Henderson, 44.
8. Joseph Campbell, *Myths to Live By,* 82.
9. Joseph Campbell, *Hero with a Thousand Faces,* 15–16.
10. Henderson, 20–21.
11. Gabbin, 4–5.
12. Brown, 141. Hereafter only page numbers will be cited for those poems appearing in this collection.
13. See Gabbin's analysis of the ballad in Brown's poetry, 161–69.
14. Ibid., 4.
15. Ibid., 162–63.
16. "Liar" here means teller of tall tales. Sterling Brown claimed to be "the best liar at Howard University."
17. Gabbin, 34–35.

Works Cited

Brown, Sterling A. *The Collected Poems of Sterling Brown*. Sel. Michael S. Harper. New York: Harper, 1980.

Campbell, Jane. *Mythic Black Fiction: The Transformation of History*. Knoxville: University of Tennessee Press, 1986.

Campbell, Joseph. *The Hero with a Thousand Faces*. Princeton: Princeton University Press, 1949.

———. *Myths to Live By*. New York: Bantam, 1972.

Campbell, Joseph, and Bill Moyers. *The Power of Myth*. New York: Doubleday, 1987.

Gabbin, Joanne V. *Sterling A. Brown: Building the Black Aesthetic Tradition*. Westport: Greenwood, 1985.

Gould, Eric. *Mythical Intentions in Modern Literature*. Princeton: Princeton University Press, 1981.

Henderson, Stephen. *Understanding the New Black Poetry: Black Speech and Black Music as Poetic References*. New York: Morrow, 1975.

Jung, Carl G. *Collected Works*. Princeton: Princeton University Press, 1953–79. Vol. 15.

Righter, William. *Myth and Literature*. Boston: Routledge, 1975.

Langston Hughes and Melvin Tolson: Blues People

M A R I A N N   R U S S E L L

Metaphors and symbols in Spirituals and Blues have been the Negro's
manna in the Great-White World.
—Melvin B. Tolson

Black authors [in 1965] rejected white literary standards, proclaiming
their own Black Aesthetic, which extolled literature written for the
common people, a literature that was distinctly oral, using the
language patterns and vocabulary of the street to arouse feelings
of solidarity and pride among Afro-Americans.
—Rita Dove

THE POETRY OF LANGSTON HUGHES AND MELVIN Tolson is sometimes thought to be antipodal. Hughes—man of the people and of the vernacular—and Tolson—elitist of the modern, poet of the abstruse—constitute clichéd images of the two poets. Hughes and Tolson, however, shared much—from the trivial to the significant, including a southwestern background with its musical/oral component, a thirties' commitment to the underdog in general and to the racial underdog, in particular, and a lifelong observation of and participation in the far-flung African American experience from Harlem to the Yazoo Bottom. All three of these interests converge in Hughes's and Tolson's "sampling" of blues in their work. My consideration of the blues/jazz component and its folkloric context will focus on Tolson's evaluations of Hughes's evolving use of blues/jazz.[1]

These two Lincoln University graduates both began their writing careers by producing poetry based on the vernacular, the language, form, and spirit of blues/jazz. Both poets later turned in their last full-length books to poetry cross-fertilizing the modernist with the oral and musical heritage derived from the blues, Hughes in *Ask Your Mama* (1961) and Tolson in *Harlem Gallery* (1965). Hughes's poetry in *Ask* approximates his own performances with jazz background. Tolson, a more oratorical/rhetorical poet, establishes a jazz/blues trope throughout *Harlem Gallery*.

Tolson, more the academic than the professional literary critic, was first attracted to Hughes's early books of poetry—*The Weary Blues* (1926) and *Fine Clothes to the Jew* (1927). Tolson also realized the complex nature of Hughes's later poetry, *Montage of a Dream Deferred* (1951) and *Ask Your Mama*. Tolson finally transcended the academic-to-text relation to embody poetically in *Harlem Gallery* (1965) the deeper import of Hughes's blues-inspired creations. Besides specific blues and blues-ballads, Tolson creates the figure of Hideho Heights, poet of the people and modernist, loosely based on Langston Hughes. In this way, Tolson evaluates and valorizes the poet Hughes through his relation to the blues subtext.

Tolson early evaluated the poet Hughes (whom he had met).[2] In a *Caviar and Cabbage* column in 1939, Tolson praised Hughes as a "radical" and as one of the "geniuses of the race." Tolson had defended Hughes—chiefly on ideological grounds—when he defended Hughes's controversial poem "Goodbye Christ."[3]

Further, in his master's essay, "The Harlem Group of Negro Writers" (1940), Tolson links Hughes's radical perspective to his poetic style when he calls Hughes an experimentalist as well as a radical. Tolson, in appraising the work of Hughes that had appeared at the time of his writing, saw Hughes's blues poetry as an ethnic poetry derived from his observation and love of the black masses. In his quest for beauty, unlike his friend Countee Cullen, Hughes found it among "the flotsam and jetsam" of life.[4] Tolson recognized that *The Weary Blues* "catches an undercurrent of philosophy that pulses through the soul of the Blues singer and brings the Blues rhythm into American versification. In the ethnic pattern, he portrays in a few bold impressionistic strokes, the setting, the theme, the atmosphere, the pathos, the climactic suspense, the Negro character and the odd denouement of the Blues" (37).

Thus Tolson valorizes the blues and Hughes's derivation from it with its "improvisational strokes, its incremental repetition, its spontaneity, rhythm and philosophy" (37). Tolson approves the blues strain both for its form and for its folk context; Tolson applauds Hughes's manipulation of the blues as a racially authentic artwork. The blues—sung by a single voice, expressive of many—evokes the racial heritage for both Hughes the artist and Tolson the critic.

Looking at Hughes's early work, one can see the impressionistic strokes noted as being relevant to Hughes's poetry. He himself used a rainbow as a metaphor for poetry. His poetry began with evanescent but meaningful experience or emotion. He sought to reduce such experience to its essence and then to recreate it in short flights. For him the poem is a life experience frozen in relatively short song.

However, Hughes's lyric poetry has overtones not usually associated with such verse. Hughes stated that 90 percent of his work involved "the Negro condition in America." Although he had written lyrics about "love, roses and moonlight, sunsets and snow," he felt that such poetry contradicted much of his and his people's day-to-day experience. Hughes makes a distinction between personal and public poetry, between "lyric" and "social" poetry when he says, "Some of my earliest poems were social poems in that they were about people's problems—whole groups of people's problems—rather than my own personal difficulties." [5] Influenced by Whitman and Sandburg, Hughes distilled his own kind of populist poetry, which Tolson the critic and "Christo-Marxist" esteemed.

At this time, Melvin Tolson clearly responded more to the social than the private poem, since he conceived a social role for the poet. He called on his readers to "use the Word. It is a two-edged sword for democracy and justice" (*Caviar*, 233). For Tolson as for Hughes the blues was a folk storehouse: its subject "personal catastrophe," its rhythm distinctly African American, its tone "tragic-comic" with emotion controlled by the blues singer's stoic affirmation—"Sun's gonna shine / Somewhere / Again." [6]

A look at the title poem of *The Weary Blues* volume will illustrate the kind of poetry Tolson found so praiseworthy. Here the blues, traditional in form and content, which the pianist plays and sings, crystallizes the tenor of the entire poem: "I got the Weary Blues / And I can't be satisfied / Got the Weary Blues / And can't be satisfied" (23). Embedded in the larger descriptive poem is the blues verse. Besides "classic" blues worked into the text here and in such poems as "Blues Fantasy" (37–38), there are other Hughesian blues-oriented poems such as "To Midnight Nan at Leroy's" (30), with blues commentary woven into the poem. In "Harlem Night Club" the blues pervades the night club glee from the first stanza's "Play PLay, PLAY," with its crescendo effect, to the last stanza with its onomatopoeia (32). A final example of a poem adapting the technique of blues/jazz music is "Jazzonia" (25) (another recreation of a Harlem nightclub), which both freezes and highlights the appropriate emotion. The poem's repetition, with variation and chiasmas, corresponds to jazz improvisation, here used to capture a racial aura. The rhythm of these imagistic poems is intended to evoke the rhythms of "natural" Africa, not the harsh rhythm of the white city.[7]

But beside the blues voice there is another—that of the persona, who is in some instances ambivalent in his perspective. In "The Weary Blues" the poet-persona hears beyond the joy the "sob" of jazz band and piano-playing bluesman. In "Lament for Dark People" (100), the ambivalent persona, having been removed from jungle, trees, and silver moon, finds himself "caged" in the "circus of civilization"; the circus image acts reflexively on the cabaret joys (100). The persona of "Disillusion" wishes to forget the "great dark city" and to escape Harlem: "Let me forget / I will not come / To you again" (104). An element of urgency in "Harlem Night Club" is derived from the carpe diem of "Tomorrow . . . is darkness / Joy Today!" (32). The persona, even more than the dancing boys and girls, is haunted by the pursuit of joy, triggered by the release of Harlem pain.

The dominant voice heard in *The Weary Blues,* then, is not the dialect voice but that of a modern poet who may occasionally use traditional imagery of night, sun, and dark. The persona's voice is that of the poet who sees his experience as of the same cloth as that of ghetto-dwellers and thereby discovers his individual voice. Such a process makes Hughes's voice a bardic one: "Bring me all of your dreams, / You dreamers . . . / That I may wrap them / In a blue cloud-cloth / Away from the too rough fingers / Of the world" (94). This poetry projects emotion too fragile to endure harsh reality. The poet keeps the dream alive.

In prose, Tolson responded to Hughes's invention of an ethnic vehicle—the rhythm, diction, and import of the blues—to portray the spirit of the folk. "Imitation must be in technique only. We have a rich heritage of folklore and history. . . . Our native symbols must be lifted into the universal."[8] In newspaper columns and in his master's essay, Tolson approves of Hughes, the laureate of the lowdown, the poet who values the experience from which the blues spring, the poet denied by many of the black middle class. But Tolson does not comment directly on Hughes's poetry exhibiting tensions caused by the difference between the poet-persona voice and that of the blues itself. Nor does Tolson's prose analysis of Hughes extend to the poet's later work in the blues/jazz idiom.[9]

Hughes further developed the blues/jazz idiom in *Montage of a Dream Deferred,* when he treated the unrealized dream in a book-length poem,

composed of approximately ninety short poems, poems united thematically
and stylistically. Aspects of bebop in diction, scatting, rhythm, and structure
are woven into poetry. The book is in many ways a reworking of the black
musical tradition Hughes first used in the twenties. His habit of public read-
ing with musical background is here evolved to working the jazz effects
into the text itself: "To me jazz is a montage of a dream deferred. A great
big dream—yet to come—and always yet—to become ultimately and fi-
nally true." [10] Thus the yoking of black musical evocation to social theme
that Tolson remarked on earlier is still being worked out by Hughes at a
later date. In this fifties book, Hughes experiments still further with musical
form used as trope for his theme. [11]

In a still later book, *Ask Your Mama,* Hughes used sight as well as sound
in pursuit of his blues/jazz approach. The album-shaped volume, printed
in blue and beige alternatively on salmon-colored paper, has musical direc-
tions in the margins and endnotes called liner notes "for the poetically un-
hep." Subtitling the book "12 Moods for Jazz" strengthens the musical con-
nection. The concept of the deferred dream is shaped again in specific
musical forms. The most important controlling figure is the "Hesitation
Blues": "Tell me how long—must I wait? / Can I get it now— / Or must
I hesitate?" (7). This leitmotif is a sixties version of the dream deferred.
Further, the musical directions complementing the text interact with it—
sometimes condensing, sometimes echoing, sometimes ironically under-
cutting it.

Beside the "Hesitation Blues" with its "figurines," there are incre-
mental repetitions of "Ask Your Mama" and the "quarter of the Negro" as
Hughes's blues/jazz ethnic mode moves from images to symbols. Associa-
tional organization, a trait of the blues, lends to expanding images not un-
like "mascons," symbols dense in themselves and acquiring nuances as the
text unfolds. Music, direct statement, and symbol embody the far-flung
dreamers of "freedom" as music and text act symbiotically.

Tolson was to capture in poetic expression these later innovations of
Hughes's blues trope as Tolson also changed poetic style while developing
his basic social theory; he still believed (as did Hughes) in the folk and en-
visaged for them an achievable American Dream. His major change is that
he no longer believed that the dream's fulfillment would come primarily
from the actions of the folk—black or white. Rather, he expanded his idea
of the social importance of the poet, of the artist as herald of a coming new
order. His ode, *Libretto for the Republic of Liberia* (1953), he says, "attempts to
bridge the dichotomy between poetry and politics . . . the private and the
public world, art and society." [12]

The development of Tolson's thought is concretized in *Harlem Gallery*. In the book can be found Harlemite protagonists—artists and art-lovers—who share the ghetto inhabitants' tragicomic blues. Such figures constitute the modern hero: "a flower of the gods, whose growth / is dwarfed at an early stage—" (153). Among the book's artist-protagonists is a figure who can be seen as Tolson's final word on Hughes.

Throughout *Harlem Gallery*, but especially in cantos "Lambda," "Mu," "Nu," and "Xi," the figure of Hideho Heights dominates the scene. The character draws on the flamboyant elements of the public personalities of Cab Calloway and of Tolson's former pupil, Henry Heights. A "charcoal Piute Messiah," Hideho, poet laureate of Lenox Avenue parallels the newspaper description of Hughes, as "poet low rate." Seen as antithetical to the black middle class, Hideho regards himself as the people's poet: as he says to the prostitute, "Sister, you and I belong to the people" (78). Described as the "vagabond bard of Lenox Avenue, / whose satyric legends adhered like beggar's-lice" (68), Hideho is fittingly the one who intones the blues poetry here. Further, Hideho sees the Curator's defense of art as bringing "highbrow stuff for the middlebrows who / don't give a damn and the lowbrows who ain't hip!" (68). This statement evokes, if it does not exactly reproduce, Hughes's views on folk culture, high culture, and modernist practice.

Hideho, who believes "Jazz is the marijuana of the Blacks" (74), appears in the Zulu Club cabaret scene where he recites for the ghetto-dwellers the blues-ballad of the legendary John Henry. "The poet and the audience one, / each gears itself to please" (81) recalls Hughes's popularity.[13] Hideho recites the "Birth of John Henry," rooting it in the African American community and constructs appropriate tall tales: "As he stoops to drink, Old Man River gets scared / and runs upstream to hide!" (82). The poet laureate sets the tone for a "poet's feast in a people's dusk of dawn" (83). Hideho's blues poems "counterpoint / protest and pride / in honky-tonk rhythms" (83). Hideho's later story of the turtle gnawing its way through a shark's entrails conveys racial pride in an unforgettable image.

Hideho is then truly a bard, intoning in the Harlem Gallery a blues-ballad about the African American hero Louis Armstrong. Hideho's blues poems with their insistent rhythm and rhyme and hyperbole cause his auditor, The Curator, to recall the old blues greats, female and male. Hideho recites the Satchmo blues: "Satchmo's / gravelly voice and tapping foot and crazy notes" (70). The poem ends in hyperbole: even Gabriel finds himself second to the premier trumpeter of the universe, Satchmo (70).[14]

But there is another side to the people's poet, a side that recalls Hughes, the dreamkeeper. Hideho's private poem in the modern vein questions the worth of his vocation while expressing his irrevocable dedication to that endeavor. Also reflecting the other side of the people's poet is The Curator's hearing "a gurgle, a gurgle—a death rattle" (69) just before Hideho's recital of the Satchmo poem. Later, after the presentation of the John Henry poem, the flow of the jazz community's happenings subsides. His audience "absent" or "ugly" or "tight," Hideho "slumped in the shoal of a stupor, / slobbers and sobs / My *people, my* people— / they know not what they do" (92).

Michael Berube addresses this division in his discussion of *Harlem Gallery*. In a modernist poetic critique, he sees the poem as divided between The Curator and Hideho. Hideho *seems* to be the legitimate vox populi. His blues-ballads and parable of the turtle illustrate his power. Hideho's popularity seems to overwhelm The Curator's "autobiofragment," but the discovery of a "private poem" compromises Hideho's populist position. Modernistic in technique and tone, the private poem indicates a failure of nerve if not an outright betrayal of the people. According to Berube, it allows the voice and avant-garde position of The Curator to wrest control of the poem from Hideho.[15] The defeat of Heights as champion of oral, narrative poetry is sealed by his own written words, "words to the effect that, well, poetry makes nothing happen" (121).

To sum up, in *Harlem Gallery*, major African American characters are split—displaying assurance in their public creations and hesitance in their private endeavors. The public poems can link Hideho to Langston Hughes; the private doubts in another, less accessible style may reflect Hughes's poet-persona's hearing the jazz band "sob" and his alluding to death in the final words of "The Weary Blues." The opposition between Hughes's creation of blues poems and the tone of his poet-persona, in some instances, is relevant here. The "stridency" and frustration underlying the jazz high in some of Hughes's poetry may appear here in Hideho's distress. Tolson, noting the popular and private poet in Hideho/Hughes, is saluting in a final form the complex nature of literary blues, the racially authentic poetry of Langston Hughes, keeper of the dream—bluesman.

Notes

1. Of course, Langston Hughes knew well the differences among jazz and blues and spirituals. He also knew the different types of jazz; however, he sees all these as different elements in a single tradition with thematic and technical commonalities more important

than differences: "Jazz is a big sea. . . . there're all kinds of water" (*Reader, 492–94*). Melvin Tolson shares the same perspective in *Harlem Gallery*, 83: "O spiritual, work-song, ragtime, blues, jazz." Further references included in text.

2. The two met not only in Harlem but in their travels throughout the country: "Tolson addressed audiences with Langston Hughes everywhere from college auditoriums to county jails" (Flasch, 44). One of the many nonliterary coincidences is that Tolson moved to Langston University and was four-time mayor of Langston, Oklahoma. Both school and town were named for Hughes's great-uncle James Mercer Langston: "It was the same town where his [Hughes's] parents had met some thirty-four years before" (Berry, 147).

3. Tolson, *Caviar and Cabbage*, 40. For more on Tolson's involvement with Hughes's "Goodbye Christ" and its context, see 4–5. Further references included in text.

4. Tolson, "Harlem Group," 31. Further references included in text.

5. Hughes, "My Adventures as a Social Poet," 205.

6. Hughes, *Weary Blues*, 37. Further references included in text.

7. For further discussion of musical elements and structure of Hughes's literary blues, especially *The Weary Blues*, see Crossland, 9–21. See also Tracy for a full discussion.

8. Flasch, 70.

9. For a full discussion of the later relationship between Hughes and Tolson, see Rampersad 2: 234–36 and elsewhere.

10. Hughes, *Reader*, 494.

11. Berube comments on "the production of *Libretto* [by Tolson] and [Hughes's] *Montage of a Dream Deferred* in the midst of the decade of bebop . . ." (156). Further references included in text.

12. Tolson, "Notebooks."

13. Berube suggests that the reference to the *"howl-howl-with-the-Combo* quacks" (*HG*, 144) may be Tolson's reference to Hughes and his practice of reading poetry to the accompaniment of live music (186).

14. Hughes dedicated *Ask Your Mama* to Louis Armstrong, "the Greatest Horn Blower of Them All."

15. Berube, 124.

Works Cited

Berry, Faith. *Langston Hughes: Before and Beyond Harlem*. Westport: Lawrence Hill, 1983.

Berube, Michael. *Marginal Forces—Cultural Centers—Tolson, Pynchon, and the Politics of the Canon*. Ithaca: Cornell University Press, 1992.

Crossland, Dawn, et al. "Langston Hughes: Griot and Troubadour." *Langston Hughes Review* (spring 1988): 9–21.

Flasch, Joy. *Melvin B. Tolson*. New York: Twayne, 1972.

Hughes, Langston. *Ask Your Mama: Twelve Moods for Jazz*. New York: Knopf, 1961.

———. *The Langston Hughes Reader*. New York: George Braziller, 1971.

———. "My Adventures as a Social Poet." *Phylon* 8 (1947): 205–12.

———. *The Weary Blues*. New York: Knopf, 1926.

Rampersad, Arnold. *The Life of Langston Hughes*, vol. 2, *1941–1967*. New York: Oxford University Press, 1988.

Tolson, Melvin B. *Caviar and Cabbage: Selected Columns by Melvin B. Tolson from the Washington Tribune, 1937–1944*. Ed. Robert Farnsworth. Columbia: University of Missouri Press, 1982.

———. *Harlem Gallery: Book 1, The Curator*. New York: Twayne, 1965.

———. "The Harlem Group of Negro Writers." Master's essay. Columbia University, 1940.

———. "Notebooks." Melvin B. Tolson Papers. Manuscript Division. Library of Congress.

Tracy, Steven C. *Langston Hughes and the Blues*. Urbana: University of Illinois Press, 1988.

Bardic Memory and Witness in the Poetry of Samuel Allen

E D W A R D   A .   S C O T T

> *Each time that he returned to England*
> *where he had never been*
> *with his saxon name*
> *and mists of english memories*
> *and his dark blood*
> *and his dubious blood*
> *black and Lewis Carroll white,*
> *he never ceased to be amazed*
> *at the enormity*
> *Of these four hundred years.*
> —*Samuel W. Allen,* Paul Vesey's Ledger

> *I have only the life you give me. Remember me!*
> —*Juan Ramón Jiménez,* The Complete Perfectionist

WITNESS IS COMMON THESE DAYS TO OUR reflections concerning African American culture in most, if not all, manifestations: historical, religious, political, literary, musical, and social. Samuel Allen's poetry is a rich attestation of the power of witness to recover *and* transform the sense of self and alterity necessary to the creation of community within a space that is as spiritual as it is geographical. One finds in his poetry this ambient facility for dualities, often harsh, but ever responsive to the hope of final judgment and higher orders of conciliation. The poem quoted as epigraph speaks to this form of witness that I wish to address in this paper. The weight of slave history is charged with this sense of tension carried by the polarity of dark (black) and "dubious" (white) blood. That history, in turn, makes a very particular and complicated form of identity and life possible. Is it any wonder that the subject of the poem is "amazed"? Whatever the ambiguities attendant upon this "affective disposition,"[1] it should be clear that we have to deal with oppositions that demand a dialectical rapprochement: reason and feeling, understanding and imagination, the abstract and the concrete. Allen's poetic practice is both traditional and prophetic in ways I intend to make clear in the following. Accordingly, I propose a reading here that gathers its hermeneutic power from the poems themselves. I do not claim that the poems are self-interpreting, but I do think they resist any exercise of exegesis that would be imposed from some transcendental point of view.

I am primarily interested here in that collection of poems comprising *Paul Vesey's Ledger* and others that have been frequently anthologized. If Allen's poetry emphasizes witness, as I claim, it is because of the strong temporal pull that gathers and disseminates the numerous tensions and oppositions about which I have already remarked. By temporal pull I mean the concentrated manifestation of concern for the past as a necessary condition for acts of remembering, the present as mystery and discovery, and the future as call and promise. It is this temporalizing spontaneity that accounts, in part, for this poetry's witness in the registers of historical time and mythic time. Indeed, the transformation of historical time into mythic time and the anchoring of mythic time by historical time are fundamental features of this poetry as witness. Consider the form of recollection in the well-known panegyric for Satchel Paige.

> Sometimes I feel like I will never stop
> Just go forever
> Till one fine morning
> I'll reach up and grab me a handful of stars
> And swing out my long lean leg
> And whip three hot strikes burning down the heavens
> And look over at God and say
> How about that! (Adoff, 167)

This is a time so full and complete that it gathers past, present, and future at once in one blazing act of dynamic, godlike joy. But we know because we remember, because we are made to recall the harrowing plague of racism that might have destroyed Paige's singular gift. We also know the gift was greater, in the end, than the plague haunting it and that, whatever future may come, the hope of overcoming calamity is not empty but ordained.

This form of mythic temporal distillation is evident again in *Paul Vesey's Ledger.* One of the poems collected (none are specifically named) is charged with the pathos and urgency of escape from slavery. It is one of several Allen devotes to this subject. It too lifts its subject to the level of mythic figure by imbuing historical event with poetic elaboration. Harriet Tubman *is* Moses. The poetic utterance that discloses this tableau fixes the time of runaway slaves, predatory patterollers, and the heroic resolve of one lone black woman. It does so with a quickening clarity. The repeated use of the word *move* accents a future of risk and promise, in this instance, of liberty. I cite but a portion of the poem here, though one should keep in mind the *sound* of poetic performance in a public setting. Even physical gesture invokes a mythic presence of Tubman that memory seals in a time beyond time. Allen renders Tubman immortal by speech and by act. I have noted in his performance of this piece the modulation of his tone and the rhythm of his enunciation. The Homeric effect is deliberate and measured in a way that makes witness a moral and communal obligation. The act of rescue is a performance of deed and a performance of word.

> Moses pulled out her revolver and she quietly said:
>   Move or die.
>
> You ain't stoppin' now
> You can't stop now
> you gonna move
> move or die.
>
> If you won't go on
> gonna risk us all
> I'll send your soul to glory, move
> move or die.
>
> Long time now, I got it figgered out
> every child of God got a double right, death
> or liberty. I said move
> move or die. (*Paul Vesey's Ledger,* 7)

Here poetry is a mirroring of the courage and tenacity required to *be* free. Word is bound to deed in the echoing resonance of then and now. Poetry becomes an exercise of heroism and mythic creation.

Similarly, in a poetic retrieval of one of the bloodiest slave rebellions in our history, Allen brings us to a nearly sacramental recollection of Nat Turner. Poetry transmogrifies the historical Turner into a mythic Turner. That it may do so is a power belonging to word but only as memory may enact this process in imagination. *There must be something to remember.* In this poem memory links the contemporary African American religious conversion experience to past rebellion experience. Each is an exercise of the power of religion generally and the persuasive oratorical gift of the black preacher particularly. In his recitation of the poem (Allen reads a later incarnation of this poem than the one I cite here) Allen takes pains to make clear that Turner was a slave preacher and that religious assembly of slaves was closely monitored. The observation underscores the continuity of religion as a moving force in African American experience and makes evident the dangers visited upon such practice:

> And his face hardened
> and we heard, again, the voice, calling
>   whosoever will
>   let him come
>   let him come, now
>   let him come
>   let him come
>   let him come (6)

The incantatory iteration of "let him come" is an enactment of an oratorical constant in African American culture. In this poem it fairly tolls the hour of redemption but with an ambiguity that makes the heart race and tremble. We know this moment will conclude tragically, that it must conclude that way "whate'er betide." Repetition evinces "eternal return" and discloses human will in raw negotiation with necessity.[2]

Prophetic agency is here, as well, because what has been is possible again, because freedom must overcome bondage, laughter must overcome crying. Joy must come in the morning. And if it comes it often comes at great expense and consequence. The poet's song is joined once more to that more primordial song the preacher sang—of freedom out of the letting of blood. Preaching poet begets remembering poet who begets a ceaseless return of transposition—recollection and regeneration. Looking forward is looking backward. And yet we are required to recognize the force of dialectical understanding. What laughter can be deep without the mediation of crying, or freedom precious without the threat of enslavement? When read by Allen, the following refrain sends a bolt of terror that resolves the will to resistance:

> I did not climb the apple trees in Sussex
> Or wait upon the queen in London town
> They courted me in sweltering Mississippi
> With birch and thong to bring the cotton down (5)

Allen ingeniously exploits a near blueslike riffing on the use of the word *down* to intensify the palpable destruction of flesh and the deformation of time and space. The songlike clarity of these later lines in the same poem suspends us between agony lived and agony witnessed.

> they descended by the Delta, down
>   into the pit
> forsaken by Shango and Damballah, down
>   to the fist and the terror, down
> to the whiplash and the whim
> to the blazing heat of the field by day and the raging lust
> of the big house by night and all pale and ravenous things.

Variation in repetition brings us round again to the unrelated relatedness of Sussex, London, and the broiling suffocation of the state of Mississippi.

> I did not climb the apple trees in Sussex
> I'll never hail the queen in London town
> I spent eternity in Mississippi
> whose grace was death, to bring the cotton down. (5)

On the two separate occasions when I heard these lines recited by Allen, audible gasps were summoned from the audience as if called. Down we did go Ulysses-like into that hell of no return. What abandonment can be more damning than that of gods so awful and sublime as Shango and Damballah?[3] How might one survive the irregulation of time when day and night dissolve to common horror?

Perhaps nowhere in Allen's corpus is the despair of time more exhausted than in the lines that lament the assassination of King. Because past and future have unraveled into chaos, the present is existentially paralyzed. The only relief would appear to be the weak "perhaps" preceding an ellipsis that trails off into an indeterminate time that itself discloses a vague and anxious future.

> It was a splendid dream, cracked
>   by a rude technology,
> it was a glorious dream
>   bushwhacked by reality.
> "We shall overcome"
>   our voices bravely sang.
> We have yet to overcome
> an air cooled engine with a country blues
> an anti anti missile with a fat back pot of soul.
> Perhaps the time will come
> when the dream will merge with matter
> in the gleam
> of some apocalyptic fusion
> perhaps . . .
> in time . . . (10)

What is the substance of witness now? I have attempted to show the operation of configuring in Allen's poetry as a function of temporal harmonizing. The ecstasies of time are ranged voices made to sing a deep song of human being. What the poetry reveals is the strum of time just as one might produce overtones on the piano or a guitar by a sympathetic vibration of different notes in other octaves. But these lines just cited suggest that the remarkable élan of black culture may not be enough to "overcome" the sheer energy and force of hatred. Allen's lines posit troubling questions concerning the effective verve of the "country blues" and the magnetic draw of down-home soul. The sense of weariness and ennui is raised to a nearly unbearable pitch by the expression of this lament in poetic art. How can it do what the blues (itself a high form of poetic art) and the personality of black spirit seemingly fail to do? We will know that reconciliation is not cheap. Imagination is not free of dread and anguish. The *Ledger* is a record, after all, of atrocity. But that is why it is so powerful an instrument for demystifying history and enabling the present. The witness born of those who have died, those who were lost, those who were killed, is an acme of apotheosis. These are ancestors who in our remembrance are gods. The poet's narrative is a story of triumph because it is a story first of assault and destruction. It is, therefore, a poetic *j'accuse* in search of justice, a justice that reintegrates time and experience beyond fault and chaos. In the following passage Allen uses a device of double voicing to demonstrate simultaneously the moral corruption of slavery and the authenticity of the moral claims against it.[4] In doing so, he presupposes in his reader a capacity for moral outrage and an appetite for justice.

> In the dungeons of Goree
> > *This sale will be carried out*
> were the children safe,
> > *in a lawful manner—*
> in the ship's hold
> > *Order*
> on the auction block
> > *we must have order*
> were the women safe?
> > *cried the auctioneer.*
>
> From the sheeted Klan
> > *What do I hear*
> from the smiling sheriff
> > *going*
> were our fathers safe
> > *The gentleman in the black tie*
> are they
> > *Gone.*
>
> safe?
> Are they safe? (12)

The form of destruction is specified here in concrete and ideal terms. Families are generative and regenerative of men, women, and children. But where none of these are safe, families are annihilated. What is engendered instead is a clamorous and undisciplined disorder of wailing and license: *"we must have order."* The long political association of law with order makes us ponder, in the present context, how any genuine law or order might be had in the absence of justice. Corruption and perversion at the concrete level of black bodies and the abolition of black communities have an ideal correlate: the savage and barbaric miscarriage of justice, moderation, and wisdom. Can we hear the poet's query over the din of the auction? Are they safe, even now, the children, the women, the fathers? Can human community be salvaged from the wreckage of slavery's past? How do we proceed in building a sense of self mediated by interaction with others? The questions fall upon us from the fallout of the poem. How do we proceed indeed?

Poetry provides a clue in its very practice. Have we not been discussing it all along? Can we ever be a people without a founding of culture in story, without the poet to sing our misery and our joy, our bondage and our freedom? Are the resources of a literate imagination deep enough to construe who we have been, who we are and what, yet, we may become? We may not be rid of poets, whatever Plato may have argued.[5] Poetic word is *poiêsis* in the strong sense of "bringing forth" the Greeks championed. The mythic force of poetic witness comes now into sharper focus. It beatifies "the martyrs" (Allen, 20) and thereby creates a bond to the present that negates the negation of slavery. This Hegelian double negation to which Allen referred in his essay on the African poet applies to Allen's own search for the higher truths into which we may be gathered.[6] Poetic mimesis is the condition for the very possibility that such a gathering may ever be performed.

But if poetry is to be a formative power for life, what word may it pronounce on death, the great, undoing death, the leveling death, the death that dissolves our relation to the world, each other, and even ourselves? I turn to this question now because witness must contend with the mute mystery of death's eruption if it would establish concord between those gone and those who survive them. How, in fact, we may be able to conceive our posterity and be moved existentially by our meditations and reflections on posterity may depend upon the confrontation of death and witness. In "Dylan, Who Is Dead," an elegiac performance that signifies on Dylan Thomas's "Do Not Go Gentle into That Good Night," Allen makes exceedingly clear the seriousness of what is finally lost to us in death:

> The fevered brow, the trembling hand that bore,
>   that lifted, now are still.
> He is forever gone out from us
>
>   . . . . .

Stuck to his measure there is none
Nor seed in womb to bring forth the glory that
is fallen (4–6, 12–13)

And yet the poet expresses a faith in the word that death would silence. It is as if the sacred mystery of the abyss separating the quick and the dead had been bridged by poetic speech:

Bitter is the wind that whirls up out of the shorn isle
And voiceless the void of his farewell
Hail oracle, shine
in that dark night! (15–18)

Here poet calls unto poet and in a way that transcends questions concerning reference and reality. We see that remembering is as much hearkening to a call as making one. It is a form of prayer in this respect. "Hail oracle" is, at once, recognition and a request to be addressed from the shine of word *"in that dark night!"* Mystery is not erased but secreted in a language that requires attentive deciphering. We must hear before ever we may speak. Paul Ricoeur's meditations on metaphor, time, and narrative assist us here. Narrative constitutes a singular endowment we deploy for describing and refiguring the world.[7] We have seen how this occurs in Allen's narrative poetry. Story and imitation are infrangibly bound into a whole that binds the opposites with which we began. "The conjunction of *mythos* and *mimêsis* is the work of all poetry."[8] Owing to this "conjunction" poetry is able to gather in that way Aristotle regarded as its primary effect. The poetry performs something in us: a gathering of wisdom in the gathering of the order of things.[9] In Allen's poetry this gathering is wide and redoubtable. In the threnody for Dylan Thomas, Allen would gather life and death, light and dark, word and silence, saying and hearing, sacred and profane. Indeed, it would appear that nowhere is this conjoining of heavens and earth more complete than in "If the Stars Should Fall," the poem that would threaten to undo our thesis, a poem of despairing weariness over the grind of time:

Again the day
The low bleak day of the stricken years
And now the years. (1–3)

Earthly, profane indifference ("And I grow cold / And care less / And less and less I care") is a cosmological infection:

> If the stars should fall
> I grant them privilege;
> Or if the stars should rise to a brighter flame
> The mighty dog, the buckled Orion
> To excellent purposes appear to gain—
> I should renew their privilege
> To fall down. (9–15)

The "If" here is the signaling of a hypothesis, an analogy of inner and outer. The collapse of the self is a crash of sky and its divine retinue:

> It is all to me the same
> The same to me
> I say the great Gods, all of them,
> All—cold, pitiless—
> Let them fall down
> Let them buckle and drop. (16–21)

The same tone is struck in "Ivory Tusks":

> Inconsolable inconsolable
> all that matters lost
> ice ages of days and I will not be comforted. (14–17)

What then of witness when universal calamity is proclaimed? Can poetry sustain when poetry begs silence? Or perhaps poetry protests the fall of the sky by speaking the unspeakable. Here is the final victory of this voice: to stare unblinkingly into the abyss, to pronounce its horror. Had abyss not won where no word could be spoken, ranged in order of rhythm and meter? Witness calls to us to hear, to remember, to think, to wonder, to cry, to laugh, to see and feel. It calls us to life and larger union, to sympathies hard won, and a wisdom darkly brightened. One senses this call to recall in "Africa to Me." It is call and calling, the counterstroke to forgetfulness and oblivion:

They say we have forgotten;
That we parted, and forever, at the shore
In the shadow of the ships attending,
Flickering still the flame and death, the branding,
Amid the cries of terror which long ago they bore (17–21)

So long as a poet may lift his voice, remembering shall sustain and renew the life we share. The horror of war and betrayal, of loss and death, of capture and flight cannot still his song but grounds his song instead. We would see Agamemnon and Achilles, Odysseus and Calypso, our Tubmans and our Turners. Odysseus cries in knowing the costly glory he has won in hearing the song of the bard in the courts of Alcinous. We too know the glory won "of many thousands gone," glory to ponder in Allen's songs of awful and sublime witness. The gathering force of the bard has come down to Allen and to us over the vast and trackless ages. What was true then is true still. "It is right that bards should receive honour and reverence from every man alive, / inasmuch as the Muse cherishes the whole guild of singers / and teaches to each one his rules of song." [10]

Notes

1. See Allen, "The Black Poet's Search For Identity," 197. Allen makes reference to Heidegger's notion of *befindlichkeit* to underscore the black poet's condition of "being-in-the-world" as a clarification of the concept of *négritude*. The context of this reference is ironic, for the thesis of Allen's text is that African poets acquire an authenticity of voice by virtue of their ability to attenuate the conceptual schemata of Western thought and literary practice. That Heidegger's ontological characterization of "our being" as mood is appropriated in this way is not, in my view, without merit, however ironic. Heidegger's redetermination of thinking is radically conceived here in a way that contests traditional Western norms. It, nonetheless, indicates an opening on forms of life and thought that amplify the features limned by Allen as intrinsic to *négritude*: "an act, an active becoming, a vital force dynamically, but patiently and stubbornly, active in the earth and sky and the elements" (ibid., 198). Still, Heidegger's analyses of *Da-sein's* attunement to the world is not as positive as Allen's *négritude*. The former will underscore the tendency of *Da-sein* to evade its being. "Attunement discloses Da-sein in its thrownness, initially and for the most part in the mode of an evasive turning away [*Die Befindlichkeit erschließt das Dasein in seiner Geworfenheit und zunächst und zumeist in der Weise der ausweichenden Abkehr*]" (Heidegger, 136). For an analysis of mood in connection with poetry, see Frye, 80–81. See also Ricoeur, 216–56. Ricoeur's work, it must be allowed, is the primary influence upon my own approach in this present essay.

2. For a brilliant and original analysis of this concept in connection with African American culture see Snead, 59–79. Snead profoundly underscores the temporal circling intrinsic to repetition and unfolds the insuperable connection between past and future such repetition founds and betokens (71). He points out, as well, the centrality of the black church tradition in the maintenance of this figure: "The black church must be placed at the center of the manifestations of repetition in black culture, at the junction of music and language" (70).

3. For an instructive account of the death of the African gods among slaves in North America, see Raboteau, 44–92. We know that Shango is a thunder god (19) and that Damballah, whose corporeal emblems are the rainbow and the snake, is the "governor of men's destinies" (75). We understand, therefore, with lucid foreboding what Allen's poem signifies: what life might be, had to be, without an opening of sky and bereft of the ordering of time. And yet mytho-poetic declaration of lost gods is, at once, a calling to those gods.

4. See also Allen, "A Moment Please," 585–86. In this poem Allen uses the same device throughout. Its stunning play on space and time in its penultimate line reconfirms any suspicion we may have concerning the fragility of identity and consciousness in our being with others who cannot see *us*.

5. Platonic dialogue is ambivalent on the issue of poetry. Its condemnation of the poets is well known (*Republic*). However, the inspiration of the poets is surely displayed in Socrates' most transporting moments (*Phaedrus* and *Symposium*). Most noticeable, even curious, is Socrates' claim on the day of his execution that he had been admonished, *by means of a dream,* to "get to work and compose music" (*Phaedo*, 60e). For a careful exposition of the "exile of the poets" in Plato's *Republic*, see Gadamer, *Dialogue and Dialectic,* 39–72. For an engaging and provocative discussion of poetry in constructive relation to philosophy, see his *Relevance of the Beautiful.*

6. "Negritude in African poetry is an antiracist racism; it is the moment of negativity as reaction to the thesis of white supremacy. It is the antithesis in a dialectical progression which leads to an ultimate synthesis of a common humanity without racism" (Allen, "Black Poet's Search," 199). There is a strong "elective affinity" here between the practice ascribed to the African poet and the practice Allen undertakes in his own poetry.

7. Ricoeur, 239.

8. Ibid., 245.

9. See Aristotle, *Rhetoric and Poetics,* 227. Aristotle underscores our delight in the *witnessing* of tragic action poetically figured.

10. Homer, *Odyssey,* 8.538–40.

Works Cited

Adoff, Arnold, ed. *The Poetry of Black America: Anthology of the 20th Century.* New York: Harper, 1973.

Allen, Samuel. "Africa to Me." In *Black American Literature: 1760–Present,* ed. Ruth Miller. New York: Macmillan, 1971.

———. "The Black Poet's Search for Identity." In *African Heritage: An Anthology of Black African Personality and Culture*, ed. Jacob Drachler. London: Collier, 1963.

———. "Dylan, Who Is Dead." In Adoff, 167.

———. "If the Stars Should Fall." In Adoff, 168.

———. "Ivory Tusks." In *Understanding the New Black Poetry: Black Speech and Black Music as Poetic References*, ed. Stephen Henderson. New York: Morrow, 1973. 227–28.

———. "A Moment Please." In Miller, 585–86.

———. *Paul Vesey's Ledger*. Heritage Series 27. London: Breman, 1975.

———. "To Satch." In Adoff, 167.

Aristotle. *Rhetoric and Poetics*. Trans. W. Rhys Roberts and Ingram Bywater. New York: Modern Library, 1954.

Frye, Northrop. *Anatomy of Criticism: Four Essays*. Princeton: Princeton University Press, 1957.

Gadamer, Hans-Georg. *Dialogue and Dialectic: Eight Hermeneutical Studies on Plato*. Trans. P. Christopher Smith. New Haven: Yale University Press, 1980.

———. *The Relevance of the Beautiful and Other Essays*. Trans. Nicholas Walker. Cambridge: Cambridge University Press, 1986. Trans. of *Die Actualität des Schönen*. Stuttgart: Reclam, 1977, and *Kleine Schriften, Band II, IV*. Tübingen: J. C. B. Mohr, 1967.

Heidegger, Martin. *Being and Time*. Trans. Joan Stambaugh. Albany: SUNY, 1996. Trans. of *Sein und Zeit*. Tübingen: Max Niemayer Verlag, 1953.

Homer. *Odyssey*. Trans. T. E. Lawrence. Oxford: Oxford University Press, 1991.

Jiménez, Juan Ramón. *The Complete Perfectionist: A Poetics of Work*. Ed. and trans. Christopher Maurer. New York: Doubleday, 1997.

Plato. *Phaedo. Great Dialogues of Plato*. Trans. W. H. D. Rouse. New York: The New American Library, 1956.

———. *Phaedrus. The Collected Dialogues of Plato*. Ed. Edith Hamilton and Huntington Cairns. Princeton: Princeton University Press, 1961.

———. *Republic*. Trans. Allan Bloom. New York: Basic Books, 1968.

———. *Symposium*. Trans. Alexander Nehamas and Paul Woodruff. Indianapolis: Hackett, 1989.

Raboteau, Albert. *Slave Religion: The "Invisible Institution" in the Antebellum South*. Oxford: Oxford University Press, 1978.

Ricoeur, Paul. *The Rule of Metaphor: Multidisciplinary Studies of the Creation of Meaning in Language*. Trans. Robert Czerny with Kathleen McLaughlin and John Costello, SJ. Toronto: University of Toronto Press, 1977.

Snead, James. "Repetition as a Figure of Black Culture." In *Black Literature and Literary Theory*, ed. Henry Louis Gates Jr. New York: Routledge, 1990.

Rooted Displacement in Form: Rita Dove's Sonnet Cycle *Mother Love*

THERESE STEFFEN

The freedom of fine cages!
—Rita Dove

This will sound masochistic: I like cages,
I like working under that kind of pressure.
—Rita Dove

The Sonnet as Talisman

LOSS AND PAIN CONTAINED IN THE FINE CAGE OF A sonnet has a long tradition in writing as a survival strategy. With his 1840 sonnet "Thirty Years," the Cuban slave Juan Francisco Manzano initiated the movement of abolition in his country.[1] And from Phillis Wheatley's exquisite handling of the form, in 1772, which convinced eighteen of Boston's most notable citizens of the poetic abilities of a slave girl,[2] to Gwendolyn Brooks's breakthrough in 1950 (Pulitzer Prize), the sonnet has marked momentous personal and public turning points in African American careers. Countee Cullen uses the Shakespearean sonnet after the breakdown of his marriage, and Langston Hughes fights isolation and despair with a blues version of the form.[3] Yet it was Claude McKay's "If We Must Die," first published in *The Liberator* (1919), that enshrined a new idea of resistance, racial consciousness, and aesthetic rendering. This sonnet, motivated by the black blood that flowed in the race riots of the "Red Summer" of 1919, came to express the dignity of the New Negro at the outset of the Harlem Renaissance. As a Petrarchan sonnet, "If We Must Die" fuses a romantically inspired poetic structure with a theme that appears to cover revolutionary ground.

60

The highly emotional dichotomy of love and war, ideally housed in the sonnet, overshadows the fact that the structure is also an important form of aesthetic transfer. Introduced by Petrarch in the fourteenth century, the sonnet lent itself to a new consciousness, a wider horizon of thought reaching its apogee in the Renaissance. At this crucial moment in history, sonnets and sonnet writers came to embody the lifestyle of lyrical subjects who asserted themselves as self-contained and autonomous. Rita Dove is aware of the inherent power of the sonnet and the criticism waged against it. When she was told that "some modern poets, women particularly, have rejected the sonnet form, calling it outdated, false, patriarchal, even fascist," her reply was clear: "I think that it is bogus to talk about patriarchal form in art. . . . I became . . . interested in the early stages with how I could make the sonnet fresh again." [4] In her foreword to *Mother Love,* she calls the sonnet "an intact world where everything is in sync, . . . any variation from the Petrarchan or Shakespearean forms represents a world gone awry." Its charmed structure nonetheless acts like a talisman against the vicissitudes of fortune and serves as a sanctuary while chaos reigns outside.

"The Changing Same" of Myth

"The Demeter-Persephone mythic cycle of betrayal and regeneration is ideally suited to this form since all three—mother-goddess, daughter-consort, and poet—are struggling to sing in their chains," Rita Dove writes in her foreword to *Mother Love.* [5] Wrestling with fate, life through death, is indeed inseparable from wrestling with composure and form. Myth, the oldest and most widespread form of "speaking about gods" in the ancient world of oral tradition, is above all determined, even overdetermined material whose narrative inscribes itself into history with "blood and fire." [6] It is a holy scripture that allows for an unlimited number of reinterpretations but whose essence remains inviolable.

The gist of the myth is Kore (the girl)/Persephone's abduction by Hades, the god of the underworld, while she is gathering narcissi in Sicily. This date rape within the Olympian family is sanctioned by the bride's father, Hades' brother Zeus,[7] but occurs against her mother's will. Demeter's grief over the loss of her daughter and subsequent neglect of her duties as goddess of agriculture is finally appeased by Persephone's semiannual return to earth. The plot is handed down in variations through the *Homeric Hymn to Demeter,* to Ovid's *Metamorphoses* (5), and more recently by Margaret Atwood and Jorie Graham.[8] The secret of this particular cycle lies hidden in the seeds of a pomegranate. Pomegranates as apples of love are well known. Less familiar is what Artemidor von Daldis notes in his *Book of Dreams:* "The pomegranate's color suggests wounds, its spine torture, and due to the Eleusinian mystery, bondage and submission."[9] One line in the second poem of part 3 of *Mother Love* subsumes the myth's essence and inscribes the poet-mother-daughter in her own name: "my dove my snail" (*ML,* 25).[10] While the pomegranate links the realms of life and death, "snail" and "dove" acquire meaning beyond the animalistic male and female principle. "Like a bird soaring over land and sea, / looking and looking" the Lady Mother "sped off," *The Homeric Hymn to Demeter* reports (1.43). Beyond Demeter's search from a bird's-eye view, Persephone's abduction is linked to birds in several ways: In the fifth book of the *Metamorphoses,* Ovid recounts the muses' pledge of secrecy when they sing of her erotic initiation. They compete to perform the song but disunite over the task: while the "good" muses, the peace-loving doves, render death as an orgasmic "little death," the "bad" muses, the talkative magpies, foreground a violent act of rape by Death personified.[11] Is Rita, the muse, a dove or a magpie? She is all in one, withholding the secret yet telling the story.

Let us return to the main plot. Having tasted the mortal seven seeds of the pomegranate upon her good-bye to Hades—part 3, "Persephone in Hell," and *Mother Love* comprise seven parts each—Persephone remains caught in the signifying chain of deferred desire, a *Wiedergängerin* between the realms of life-in-death with Hades and death-in-life with Demeter. The only German title in the sequence, "Wiederkehr" ("Return," *ML,* 38), foregrounds this liminal state between a mother and a lover who ultimately rejects her: "He only wanted me for happiness / to walk in air / and not think so much . . . Which is why, / when the choice appeared, / I reached for it." Persephone is ready for "Wiring Home" (*ML,* 39).

The site of Persephone's abduction, I argue, is also a decisive mythopoetic spot at the intersection of life and death. The omphalos, the cult object in the temple of Apollo in Delphi, the navel of the world, or the navel of life is indeed "a symbol for the connection between child and mother, between human and earth, and as such for ideas about being centered, about a site of origin and termination of being," as Elisabeth Bronfen maintains.[12] Life, we are forced to perceive, is always tainted with death. Myth and regeneration, we might recall at this point, inevitably begin with death through sacrifice.[13] It is the poet-narrator's task to reinitiate and configure extreme feelings of pain, loss, and joy that surround the blind spot of initiation and to render them not only durable in words but endurable through artistic enspacement.[14]

Beyond Rita Dove's passion for and expertise at experimenting with form and theme stands her experience as daughter and mother. "I hadn't anticipated the vulnerability of being a mother; the vulnerability of accepting that there are things you can't do anything about in life; that you can't protect another person completely; that in fact when you were the daughter, you didn't want to be protected. The feeling of exposure and helplessness is something I was trying to explore in this book. But I learned that the mother can still be strong through all this conflict as well, that she can still turn around and stare Hades down, so to speak, and say, You didn't think about the consequences." [15]

A Sign of Her Own: Rita Dove's *Mother Love*

Rita Dove's poetical concerns—the magic of words, the polyphony of voices, and an artistic third space growing out of a revised tradition—are as finely tuned in *Mother Love* as in her Pulitzer Prize–winning *Thomas and Beulah*. No longer writing directly about her family, she bases her lyric sequence on myth and at the same time transforms overdetermined source material into something deeply personal. The result is a Demeter-Kore/Persephone plot in a contemporary setting and idiom in which Rita Dove as a daughter-mother-poet remembers and deploys all the voices and stages of sacrifice and metamorphoses she can imagine: protagonists, a chorus of witnesses and bystanders, wiggling tongues, the Olympians. Whereas the mythic abduction is played out on a vertical axis of upper- and underworld, this worldly modern version develops horizontally between the stereotypes of an innocent America and a Paris of erotic experience. While the Greek model features a white girl in a dark world, *Mother Love* highlights a dark girl in a white world.

Rita Dove drives us along a maze of thirty-five poems in seven parts, mirroring the seven seeds of the pomegranate. Seven times two equals the sonnet's magic number of fourteen lines. Yet in giving her audience but half of the whole, she keeps the cycles of both sonnets and myth open to recreation. Except for part 3, counted as one poem, and "Lost Brilliance" closing part 4, most of the poems can loosely be termed sonnets. They gesture at rhyme, then pull back off meter and constantly regroup the fourteen lines to dovetail form with theme. Thus comforted and held in place are ambiguities already palpable in the title. Mother Love, the German *Mutterliebe*—or should we rather read Mother and/or Love?—oscillates between gain and loss, fertility and barrenness, innocence and erotic initiation. The cycli-

cal reiteration between Eros and Thanatos, death and rebirth, opens with a
short introductory fable, "Heroes," followed by part 2, a series of mother-
daughter pieces that drift between myth and autobiography. Part 3 is the
seven-section piece "Persephone in Hell," a memory of the poet's, her
daughter's, or any teenager's descent into Paris's erotic "underworld."
There are no sonnets in hell, as a dramatic monologue with a latter-day
Hades from the city's artistic *bohème* reveals. Yet the form still lingers on
the margins of the underworld, for two times seven equals fourteen. Dove
loves number puzzles, as John Greening notes.[16] Part 4 prepares the ground
for an anxious mother meeting her dizzily damned daughter in "The Bystro
Styx." Parts 5 and 6 concentrate on Demeter's sense of loss, the inescapable
hell of watching a daughter sacrifice her innocence and finally coming to
terms with her own narcissistic fixation. Part 7 consists of an exquisite cycle
of eleven sonnets entitled "Her Island." The tourist-visit of Rita Dove's
family to Sicily, one of the classical sites of Persephone's abduction, devel-
ops into a true ars poetica.[17] Dove equates life and poetry in the symbol
of a racetrack surrounding the lake that marks Persephone's abduction by
Hades' chariot: "To make a sport of death / it must be endless: round and
round / till you feel everything you've trained for— / precision, speed,
endurance—reduced to this / godawful roar, this vale of sound" (*ML*, 76).[18]
Of course, the structure of this closing section is circular with sonnets
whose first and last lines overlap into one big ring around the abyss.

Crucial to our discussion of the dialectic between artistic freedom and
formal constraints, is the redefinition of myth within the sonnet form and
the interaction of theme and form. In a few signature poems we shall dis-
cuss to what extent and to what result form interacts with theme.

Rita Dove introduces and summarizes *Mother Love* on nonpersonal
absolute grounds. Her prologue, "Heroes," could be the conclusion, her
final poem (*ML*, 77) as well the opening piece, with one distinction: while
the first poem focuses on heroes and plot, the last and following one pre-
sents site and poetic enspacement.

> Through sunlight into flowers
> she walked, and was pulled down.
> A simple story, a mother's deepest
> dread—that her child could drown
> in sweetness.
>   Where the chariot went under
> no one can fathom. Water keeps its horrors

while Sky proclaims his, hangs them
in stars. Only Earth—wild
mother we can never leave (even now
we've leaned against her, heads bowed
against the heat)—knows
no story's ever finished; it just goes
on, unnoticed in the dark that's all
around us: blazed stones, the ground closed. (*ML, 77*)

Two parts rotate around an axis of two half-lines that connect and sever
the sonnet into a factual upper world and an underworld of elemental pow-
ers. "Water," "Sky," "Earth," and "blazed stones" (fire) join the poet to
recreate a story never finished. Though Earth, "wild / mother" to whose
ground we are bound is the only stable, tied down element, she "knows"
with a poetic vision what is going "on, unnoticed in the dark that's all /
around us."

Back to the book's beginning. The first poem thwarts the reader's ex-
pectations: not a sonnet, "Heroes" features nine tercets (and one extra line)
as if to represent the three protagonists involved: a hero/thief/killer/poet
figure, a plucked poppy, a woman losing flower and life. In twenty-eight
lines—two times fourteen—innocent details keep snowballing into an
inevitably tragic flow: the flower is plucked, the woman's only joy de-
stroyed.[19] Because she refuses to accept "a juicy spot in the written history"
as consolation prize for the loss of her flower, the angry stranger kills her
and turns into fate's victim, mirrored in a fugitive, explanatory single line
in the end: "O why / did you pick / that idiot flower? / Because it was the
last one / and you knew it / it was going to die" (*ML, 3*). Only, the poppy
would have died had it not been plucked, as Lotta Lofgren points out: "The
flower's near-miraculous task is to form new roots; this is its only chance at
sustained life. Disintegration, separation, alienation, all are essential ingre-
dients for growth."[20] Yet why would *Mother Love,* whose central image is
plucked narcissi, open with a picked poppy? According to Ovid, Kore was
gathering "violets or white lilies," symbols of death and resurrection.[21] Pop-
pies, however, together with the ears of grain, are constant attributes of
Demeter,[22] and the Eleusinian mysteries use drugs in her honor.[23] The pop-
pies' soporific and soothing qualities are also associated with the narcotic
essence of narcissi.[24] Poppy further foreshadows decisive features of the
pomegranate whose addictive seeds keep Persephone under Hades' spell.
The flower recalls Hades' antihero Orpheus as well. Rainer Maria Rilke's

sonnet 9 to Orpheus reads: "Only he who has eaten / poppies with the dead / will not lose ever again / the gentlest chord."[25] This is how Rita Dove accentuates various sources and begins to unfold a constant dialogue between "the given and the made."[26]

The Demeter-Kore/Persephone myth, the absolute myth of womanhood, discloses the dramaturgy of an abduction that pairs rape with enrapture. Sanctioned by Zeus, who fathered Persephone, the deed bereaved Demeter in favor of Zeus' brother Hades, whose queen his daughter was destined to be. As a goddess, daughter of Rhea, Mother Earth, Demeter should know how to conform to the dynastic Olympian law whose stability rests on two imperatives: never abdicate, always procreate. Demeter's narcissistic grief and neglect of duty that interrupt the regenerative-procreative cycle, affect the welfare of the community and illustrate the conflict between personal and official obligations. In questioning the hierarchy of these duties, Demeter may win the sympathy of mortals but doubtless the contempt of immortals: "Grief: The Council" (ML, 15–16) frames a double demand for compliance and composure by the Olympians and a chorus of well-meaning neighbors and friends. No single voice in a sonnet but various strands of speech in stanzas of changing size and typography furnish advice.

> I told her: enough is enough.
> Get a hold on yourself, take a lover,
> help some other unfortunate child.
>
>> *to abdicate*
>> *to let the garden go to seed*
>
> Yes it's a tragedy, a low-down shame,
> but you still got your own life to live. Meanwhile,
> ain't nothing we can do but be discreet
> and wait
>
>> . . . . .
>
> I say we gotta see her through
>
>> . . . . .
>
>> *at last the earth cleared to the sea*
>> *at last composure* (ML, 15–16)

Form, poise, and self-control result in a downpour of re-creative rain, an oxymoron of abundance in containment. This effective Olympian council is strikingly African American in its speech (double negations, colloquialisms) and references to self-help, maybe a subtle hint that form and composure as sources for creation and re-creation might well be of nonwhite ancestry. In this praisesong for the spirit of black sisterhood, Sister Jeffries could drop in with one of her Mason jars of soul food, "something / sweetish, tomatoes or bell peppers" or "Miz Earl can fetch her later to the movies— / a complicated plot should distract her." Inner-city poise and neighborhood help equal Olympian strategies. What the well-meaning sisters cannot perceive at this point is: there is no escape route from fate. Every detour like the one they suggest, a "car chase through Manhattan, / loud horns melting to a strings-and-sax ending" (*ML*, 16), points but back to the very center of the despair they want Demeter to forget: Hades' pursuit of Persephone.

In the title poem, "Mother Love," form and theme interact to expound the ambivalence of love and duty from the archetypal mother Demeter's perspective. The first part depicts a moral mother's call to duty in casual language.

> Who can forget the attitude of mothering?
>   Toss me a baby and without bothering
> to blink I'll catch her, sling him on a hip.
>   Any woman knows the remedy for grief
> is being needed: duty bugles and we'll
>   climb out of exhaustion every time,
> bare the nipple or tuck in the sheet,
>   heat milk and hum at bedside until
> they can dress themselves and rise, primed
>   for Love or Glory—those one-way mirrors
> girls peer into as their fledgling heroes slip
>   through, storming the smoky battlefield. (*ML*, 17)

"Mothering" rhyming with "bothering" is indeed duty's bugle call until "those one-way mirrors / girls peer into as their fledgling heroes slip / through" appear. Then the primary narcissistic identification of a child with the mother is replaced by a teenager's narcissistic identification with a "fledgling hero." The image of the mirror and its function as idealizing exaltation bring the poem back to Persephone's abduction and mirror a mortal mother's sense of duty against Demeter's mythic or, rather grotesque, dimension of coping. Hers is a more elaborate speech, garnished with heavenly mockery:

So when this kind woman approached at the urging
    of her bouquet of daughters,
(one for each of the world's corners,
    one for each of the winds to scatter!)
and offered up her only male child for nursing
    (a smattering of flesh, noisy and ordinary),
I put aside the trousseau of the mourner
    for the daintier comfort of pity:
I decided to save him. Each night
    I laid him on the smoldering embers,
sealing his juices in slowly so he might
    be cured to perfection. Oh, I know it
looked damning: at the hearth a muttering crone
    bent over a baby sizzling on a spit
as neat as a Virginia ham. Poor human—
    to scream like that, to make me remember. (*ML*, 17)

The goddess presents herself by three anaphoric decisions: "I put aside the trousseau of the mourner . . . / I decided to save him . . . / I laid him on the smoldering embers." Mother love leads Demeter to try to preserve her ersatz child by searing him in immortalizing fire. Thus she wanted to thank Metaneira, who had offered her late-born son for her to nurse, as the Greek sources reveal. Despite the best intentions, mother love may develop grotesque, even cruel and deadly traits of overprotection. Form reflects theme: We could read the poem as two single sonnets slightly gone awry. The first part, marking Persephone's absence, lacks two lines; the second one, featuring the ersatz child, exceeds in two. We could as well read the two parts as one epic sonnet of long split lines. The sestet, dedicated to the mortal mother, is lighter and colloquial in tone. The goddess's octave is statelier, more formal. Yet in tune with the content, division and fragmentation persist in form, either vertically (sestet before octave) or horizontally (split lines).

    Part 3 is the archetypal Persephone's seven-part descent into the hell of Paris, "the stone chasms of the City of Lights" (*ML*, 23). Rita Dove renders this journey into life-in-death from the perspective of the girl, who is less a naive victim than one curious about life. Except for the final poem, where two parallel columns of fourteen lines each signal a return to poetic shape, hope, and light, this is no sonnet world but rather the most realistic part of the sequence, a prosaic realm, if not a hell of prose. "Lost Brilliance" (*ML*,

51) at the end of part 5, which depicts Persephone's return to Hades, is no sonnet either. Part 3 features various voices: the lyrical self's, the party small talk of American expatriates, a mother's "super-ego": "are you having a good time / are you having a time at all" (*ML*, 27).

Visiting "a former schoolmate who'd married / onto the Ile"—the Seine is the river Styx—the girl reaches the bottom pit of the underworld. In one of Dove's witty anticlimactic reversals, this is "a two-room attic walk-up / crammed with mahogany heirlooms," an "offensive tin sink," and "gargoyles," props of a stale past world full of artifice and "bad sculpture" like "upright coffins"—containers for dead material—and worse, neither form nor theme for language but small talk centering on "dog shit." "Crudités, peanuts" all over. The poet's message is clear as light in darkness: Death resides wherever artifice and make-believe have replaced art and life, good sculpture, and "meaningful conversation" (*ML*, 27).

Poem 5 presents a self-revealing interior monologue in which Hades, a French gallery owner and a stage villain by Dove's standards, exposes his inner racist, rightist, undiscerning self.[27] Absence of artistic enspacement— this is but "an incomprehensible no-act play"—signals an atmosphere of death and decay. Hades' voice, longing for change, is typographically distinguished.

> I need a *divertissement:*
> The next one through that gate,
> woman or boy, will get
> the full-court press of my ennui.
>
> *Merde,*
> too many at once! Africans,
> spilling up the escalator
> like oil from lucky soil (*ML*, 30)

Distilled in a tercet ushered in by Hades' comment "Merde," Rita Dove commemorates the collective abduction of African victims into American slavery, "spilling up the escalator" like human leftovers from the "Middle Passage," "like oil from lucky soil," drifting on the waters of a growing diaspora.

Section 4 still plays in Paris. Yet the four poems in sonnet form signal the daughter's increasing composure and willingness to meet with her mother. "Wiederkehr," "Wiring Home" (*ML*, 38–39), and the meal of

Demeter and Persephone in "The Bystro Styx" (*ML*, 40 – 42) counteract the opening of "Hades' Pitch." At this decisive moment in the sequence axes turn, and the poet-daughter becomes the poet-mother or, rather, the true blood artist who notices the mannerisms of her daughter's dark uniform. Her "gray," "graphite," and "brushed steel" are Hades' noncolor imprints grafted onto her personality, besides the "blues and carmine," half American, half French, he drapes her in private. "Are you content to conduct your life / as a cliché and what's worse, / an anachronism, the brooding artist's demimonde?" the artist-mother asks. How sad for her to see her daughter regress into the state of passive muse, the object of a male gaze, instead of a subject with a voice and style her own. The third sonnet, however, offers consolation in the form of real soul food shared, a "Chateaubriand," "smug and absolute / in its fragrant crust, a black plug steaming / like the heart plucked from the chest of a worthy enemy." This is real meat set against the daughter's "posing nude for his appalling canvases, / faintly futuristic landscapes strewn / with carwrecks and bodies being chewed / by rabid cocker spaniels." Hades remains a flat and banal figure. "And he never thinks of food. I wish / I didn't have to plead with him to eat," the daughter complains in the fourth sonnet. In "The Bystro Styx," though the primordial fusion with Persephone has been broken, and union with Hades has engendered consciousness and separation, Demeter is at least able to provide nourishment for her starving daughter. By the time they reach dessert, however, she realizes how far she is removed. This is the last of the five strung sonnets:

> I stuck with café crème. "This Camembert's
> so ripe," she joked, "it's practically grown hair,"
> mucking a golden glob complete with parsley sprig
> onto a heel of bread. Nothing seemed to fill
>
> her up: She swallowed, sliced into a pear,
> speared each tear-shaped lavaliere
> and popped the dripping mess into her pretty mouth.
> Nowhere the bright tufted fields, weighted
>
> vines and sun poured down out of the south.
> "But are you happy?" Fearing, I whispered it
> quickly. "What? You know, Mother"—

she bit into the starry rose of a fig—
"one really should try the fruit here."
I've lost her, I thought, and called for the bill. (*ML,* 42)

Instead of having her "cream child" back (*Grace Notes,* 41), the mother is "stuck with [ersatz] café crème." After the girl "bit into the starry rose of a fig" full of seeds,[28] Demeter knew her to be gone for good and graciously asks "for the bill" for this last meal, not the check, this is Paris.

Section 5 still shows "Demeter Mourning" (*ML,* 48) but poised: "I'll not ask for the impossible; / one learns to walk by walking . . . but it will not be happiness, / for I have known that." Freed from her task of mothering and bothering, as "Nature's Itinerary" (*ML,* 46) suggests—"Irene says it's the altitude / that makes my period late; / this time, though, it's eluded / me entirely. I shouldn't worry (I'm medically regulated)" (*ML,* 46)—Rita Dove's lyric self explodes and rises above the dichotomy between the inexperienced American and the experienced European, which has enjoyed currency from the time of Henry James to that of James Baldwin. A third world, Mexico with its open skies, becomes the artistic new ground where the poet is "prepared / for more than metaphorical bloodletting among the glad rags / of the Festival Internacional de Poesia." The cycle of art and nature, however, is still threatened by temptation, "a beer— / a man's invention to numb us so we / can't tell which way the next wind's blowing" (*ML,* 46).

Blood plays an important role in rites of passage, be it in the menstrual apparent death of a young girl, in Mark 5:23–42, in Apuleius's *Amor and Psyche,* or in Dove's short story "Fifth Sunday." [29] In all cases "dying" refers to a sexual initiation that sees no end in death but a transformation: the girl dies and becomes a woman. These metamorphoses and ritual cleansings or stoppings of blood—in Dove's *Mother Love* a halt in "Nature's Itinerary" (*ML,* 46)—finally make room for a moment of true art. The only sonnet in the cycle that bears the name of the form in its title is "Sonnet in Primary Colors" (*ML,* 47). No longer in sultry Paris but in the high altitude of Mexico,[30] poetry is again possible and dedicated to the painter Frida Kahlo.

This is for the woman with one black wing
perched over her eyes: lovely Frida, erect
among parrots, in the stern petticoats of the peasant,
who painted herself a present—

wildflowers entwining the plaster corset
her spine resides in, that flaming pillar—
this priestess in the romance of mirrors.

Each night she lay down in pain and rose
to the celluloid butterflies of her Beloved Dead,
Lenin and Marx and Stalin arrayed at the footstead.
And rose to her easel, the hundred dogs panting
like children along the graveled walks of the garden, Diego's
love a skull in the circular window
of the thumbprint searing her immutable brow. (*ML,* 47)

"One black wing" and "parrots" immediately link Frida Kahlo with the birds of Demeter. Yet as a mater dolorosa who suffers in her supporting corset but continues to paint, she conquers her excruciating physical and mental pain by shaping it into art. Thus her creative though maimed body symbolizes another common ground, or third space, where suffering woman and artist meet and at the same time overcome their barren grief. Frida Kahlo, married twice to the philandering Diego Rivera, who comes and goes like Persephone, masters anger and loss through her brush. The thin air, the stark primary colors, her signature blue, yellow, and red, and the mental strength of Frida Kahlo maintain a high, clear counterpoint to the decadent underworld of Hades' Paris. Cultural space, not the fixation of a beloved person, is the ultimate home for the displaced and deprived.

Part 6 finds Demeter in her second, more sedate cycle of mourning and coping with a fate ancient and modern. With Persephone pregnant in "History," and "Rusks" (*ML,* 58, 59, 61), Demeter is able to perceive her fate as one she shares with others. From Hades ("Demeter's Prayer to Hades," *ML,* 63) she seeks but knowledge and understanding. "There are no curses— only mirrors," and mirrors reveal without judging.

Mother Love ends with section 7, a cycle of eleven sonnets entitled "Her Island," depicting a tourist visit to Sicily (Persephone's island) by Dove, her German husband, and their daughter. Two concentric circles ark the final sequence. As if to unwind the past, the family drives "counterclockwise" (*ML,* 73) around Sicily, and then watches a race around the site of Persephone's abduction, the lake of Pergusa in the center of Sicily.[31] The increasingly circular movement is enhanced by eleven strung sonnets in which the last line of each poem becomes the first in the next. The section also opens and closes with a slight but significant variation of the same line: "Around us: blazed stones, closed ground" and "around us: blazed stones, the ground closed" (*ML*, 67, 77). Whereas myth, symbolized in the archeological remnants of a "closed ground"—"These monstrous broken sticks, . . . Sicily's most exalted litter" (*ML*, 74)—first invites to be unearthed, the "ground" may be "closed" after myth's revision and revaluation. The final sonnet, however, is the poignant realization that "no story's ever finished," including this one.

Rooted Displacement in Form: Conclusion

In *Mother Love* Rita Dove uses and recharges the sovereignty of two significant structures: the theme of myth and the form of the sonnet. Both are particularly suitable carriers for variety within repetition, an interplay of freedom and form. Dove, who otherwise resists and rejects limiting demarcations, explicitly welcomes these artistic borders whose inclusions and exclusions she renegotiates at her will. What renders the rewriting of myth so attractive is the absence of a single canonized original. Given the variants, what should be enhanced? In *Mother Love* a mother mourns her daughter, not her sons, and Demeter has sons, according to various sources one to three: Jachos, Plutos, and the holy horse Arios. Though including a range of voices and perspectives, Rita Dove chose to enhance the mother's perspective: how to let loose, how to come to terms with loss, grief, humiliation, and prostration in the face of Olympian power. Yet she does so without subordinating Hades' love to the love of mother and daughter. Remember that in *The Homeric Hymn to Demeter,* Hades has Persephone only for a third of the year. A compromise with never-healing wounds is reached. Mother and Lover share the young woman equally—"half a happiness is better / than none at goddam all" (*ML*, 61)—death and life continue to take each others' toll. Two metamorphoses, however, are crucial to the myth's solution: Demeter's reconciliation with loss and pain and Hades' transformation from uncle/rapist to power-sharing and loving consort. The fruit of this resolution is not only the happy family life present in the poet's visit to Sicily (*ML*, 67–77), but also the mystery revealed at Eleusis: the recognition of identity in difference, the fulfillment of the individual through communion.

Notes

1. Manzano, *Obras*, vii; Manzano, *Poems,* 101.

2. When asked whether she was Wheatley's spiritual heir, Rita Dove stressed socio-logical rather than literary parallels (Interview, 30–31).

3. See Cullen, 301; Hughes, "Seven Moments of Love," subtitled "An un-sonnet se-quence in Blues," 217–20.

4. Kirkpatrick, 36.

5. "The Changing Same (R & B and New Black Music)" is Amiri Baraka's designa-tion for the interplay between tradition and the individual talent in African American music. *Black Music* (New York: William Morrow, 1967).

6. Treusch-Dieter, "Analyse des Demeter-Kore-Mythos," 176–77.

7. In her foreword to *Mother Love* Rita Dove states that "the Olympians disapprove of the abduction," but in the *Homeric Hymn,* Helios, who greatly respects Demeter and feels sorry for her, also informs her of Zeus' explicit sanction of the deed (see Pindar, ll. 75–80; see also Hesiod, 289–325). An excellent survey of plot variants is still Foerster's 1874 study.

8. See Pindar, ll. 1–495, especially l. 445 f (Here, Persephone divides the year differ-ently: Zeus "assented that her daughter, every time the season came round, would spend a third portion of the year in the realms of dark mist underneath, and the other two thirds in the company of her mother and the other immortals"); Atwood; Graham, 59–63. See also Treusch-Dieter, "Analyse des Demeter-Kore-Mythos," 176–212.

9. Artemidor von Daldis, *Book of Dreams,* lib. 1, c. 73; Treusch-Dieter, "Analyse des Demeter-Kore-Mythos," 199.

10. On Dove's punning on her own name, see "The Event" and "Courtship," *Thomas and Beulah,* 141, 146, and Cushman, 131.

11. Treusch-Dieter, "Analyse des Demeter-Kore-Mythos," 192 f.

12. See Bronfen, 151.

13. Before a young headhunter can be permitted to marry and father children, he must go forth and have his sacred kill. "Unless there is death, there cannot be birth." See Campbell and Moyers, 111.

14. "Because the person in [physical] pain is ordinarily so bereft of the resources of speech, it is not surprising that the language for pain should sometimes be brought into being by those who are not themselves in pain but who speak *on behalf* of those who are" (Scarry, 6).

15. Kirkpatrick, 37.

16. See Greening's review, 41–42.

17. Graves maintains that "it may have been at Sicilian Enna; or at Attic Colonus; or at Hermione; or somewhere in Crete, or near Pisa, or near Lerna; or beside Arcadian Pheneus, or at Boeotian Nysa, or anywhere else in the widely separated regions which Demeter visited in her wandering search for Core" (1:90).

18. Arcadia, the Greek vale of undisturbed bliss, also features various entrances for Hades. It is Death who says "et in arcadia ego." Death and bliss are always intertwined.

19. Cushman observes "that the key to Dove's sonnets lies not in accentual-syllabic meter or regular rhyming but in their various arrangements based on the number fourteen . . . for Dove counts lines and stanzas and strophic groupings" (132).

20. Lofgren, 140.

21. Ovid, 5:392.

22. Upon Zeus' suggestion, Demeter must have taken poppy seeds to forget her pain. Compare Foerster, 62. See also Ovid, 4:531, where Demeter is said to have broken her lent because she has eaten poppy.

23. Burkert, 108.

24. Graves, 1:96, 1:288.

25. In order to complete an orphic circle, the poet must experience the worlds both of joy and of sorrow. See Rilke, 19.

26. A quote from Graham, 61.

27. Introduced and developed to perfection by Robert Browning.

28. The Italian "fica," "fig," is a slang term for female genitals.

29. See Treusch-Dieter, "Das Märchen von Amor und Psyche"; Dove, *Fifth Sunday*, 8–9.

30. Notice that "Mexico" in Robert Lowell's sonnet cycles—he too writes about father, mother, and daughters—is no place of art but one of erotic initiation and rejuvenation (201–6).

31. In *Der Raub und die Rückkehr der Persephone,* Foerster traces the myth from its attic Greek origin to Sicily (65).

Works Cited

Atwood, Margaret E. *Double Persephone.* Toronto: Hawkshead Press, 1961.

Booth, Alison. "Abduction and Other Severe Pleasures. Rita Dove's *Mother Love.*" *Callaloo* 19 (1996): 125-30.

Brelich, Angelo. *Paides e Parthenoi.* Rome: Edizioni dell'Ateneo, 1969.

Bronfen, Elisabeth. "From Omphalos to Phallus: Cultural Representations of Femininity and Death." *Women: A Cultural Review* 3 (1992): 145–58.

Burkert, Walter. *Ancient Mystery Cults.* Cambridge: Harvard Univ. Press, 1987.

Campbell, Joseph, and Bill Moyers. *The Power of Myth.* New York: Doubleday, 1988.

Cullen, Countee. In *Black Poets of the United States,* ed. Jean Wagner. Urbana, Chicago: Univ. of Illinois Press, 1973.

Cushman, Stephen. "And Dove Returned." *Callaloo* 19 (1996): 131–34.

Dove, Rita. *Fifth Sunday.* Charlottesville: Univ. Press of Virginia, 1990.

———. Interview by Mike Hammer and Christina Daub. *Plum Review* 9 (1996): 30–31.

———. *Mother Love.* New York: W. W. Norton, 1995.

———. *Grace Notes.* New York: W. W. Norton, 1989.

———. *Thomas and Beulah.* Pittsburgh: Carnegie Mellon Press, 1986.

Foerster, R. *Der Raub und die Rückkehr der Persephone* [The Abduction and the Return of Persephone]. Stuttgart: Albert Heitz, 1874.

Frischmuth, Barbara. *Traum der Literatur, Literatur des Traums.* Münchner Poetik-Vorlesungen. Salzburg, Wien: Residenz Verlag, 1991.

Graham, Jorie. "Self-Portrait as Demeter and Persephone." In *The End of Beauty.* New York: Ecco Press, 1987.

Graves, Robert. *The Greek Myths*. 2 vols. Harmondsworth: Penguin, 1960.

Greening, John. "Vendler's List." *Poetry Review* (summer 1995): 41–42.

Hesiod. "To Demeter." In *The Homeric Hymns and Homerica*. Trans. H. G. Evelyn-White. Cambridge: Harvard Univ. Press, 1982.

Hughes, Langston. "Seven Moments of Love." In *The Collected Poems of Langston Hughes*, ed. Arnold Rampersad and David Roessel. New York: Alfred A. Knopf, 1995.

Kirkpatrick, Patricia. "The Throne of Blues: An Interview with Rita Dove." *The Hungry Mind Review* 35 (1995): 36–37, 56–57.

Leisi, Ernst. *Rilkes Sonette an Orpheus*. Tübingen: Gunter Narr Verlag, 1987.

Lofgren, Lotta. "Partial Horror: Fragmentation and Healing in Rita Dove's *Mother Love*." *Callaloo* 19 (1996): 135–42.

Lowell, Robert. *Selected Poems*. New York: Noonday Press; Farrar, Straus and Giroux, 1995.

Manzano, Juan Francisco. *Obras*. Habana: Instituto Cubano del Libro, n.d.

———. *Poems by a Slave in the Island of Cuba*. Ed. and trans. R. R. Madden. London: 1840.

Ovid. *Metamorphoses*. Books 1–15. 2 vols. Cambridge: Harvard Univ. Press, 1994.

Pindar. *Homeric Hymn to Demeter*. Trans. Gregory Nagy. Lecture script. Harvard University (fall 1992): 1.75–80.

Rilke, Rainer Maria. *The Sonnets to Orpheus*. Trans. Stephen Mitchell. Boston: Shambhala, 1991.

Scarry, Elaine. *The Body in Pain: the Making and Unmaking of the World*. New York: Oxford Univ. Press, 1985.

Sourvinou-Inwood, Christiane. *"Reading" Greek Culture. Texts and Images, Rituals and Myths*. Oxford: Clarendon Press, 1991.

———. *Studies in Girls' Transitions. Aspects of the Arkteia and Age Representation in Attic Iconography*. Athens: Kardanitsa, 1988.

Treusch-Dieter, Gerburg. "Analyse des Demeter-Kore-Mythos." In *Mythos Frau. Projektionen und Inszenierungen im Patriarchat*, 176–212. Ed. B. Schaeffer-Hegel and B. Wartmann. Berlin: Publica, 1983.

———. "Das Märchen von Amor und Psyche." *Manuskripte. Zeitschrift für Literatur*, 1983/84.

———. "Der Mythos von Demeter und Kore" (The Myth of Demeter and Kore). In *Mythos Frau. Projektionen und Inszenierungen im Patriarchat* (Mythos Woman. Projections and Dramaturgies in Patriarchal Society). Berlin: Publica, 1984.

Ziegler, Konrad, and Walther Sontheimer, eds. *Lexikon der Antike, Der kleine Pauly*. München: dtv., 1979.

Conversation:

MICHAEL S. HARPER
and
ALDON LYNN NIELSEN

NIELSEN: Gwendolyn Brooks is being honored here at the Furious
Flower conference, and I was remembering that the very
first time I ever saw you read was at the Library of Congress with Robert
Hayden and Gwendolyn Brooks, at which point you read your poem for
Gwendolyn Brooks as she was beaming behind you. Now, of course you
couldn't see the beam; I don't know, maybe you felt it. Was that the first
time you ever read that to her?

HARPER: Yes, yes it was. You know Gwendolyn is responsible for
my first book being published, and she chose my book
before she met me, *Dear John, Dear Coltrane*. I owe her plenty and you
can't repay this. Gwendolyn has been very friendly, supportive, and a kind
of sage, setting the pace for everybody, and I have done my homework
retrospectively. That is to say, I've been to see the house she was born in,
in Topeka, and I know some of her relatives, and they tell me, "Gwendolyn
is not the only substantial person in this family, you ought to come to
church on Sunday." They're just correcting people. They're very solid
folks. So she comes from solid people.

I owe her much more than I can pay her and I wrote her a citation
for an honorary degree in 1974 at Brown. We were going to a luncheon
and I escorted Gwendolyn and her husband and son and daughter, and
I was about to leave, and she said, "Where are you going?" I said, "I'm
not invited to this luncheon." She said, "You know, I don't have to go to
this luncheon; in fact, I don't even have to stay here." She said, "I've had
other honorary degrees." So I said, "How many honorary degrees do you
have?" She said, "Oh, about fifty." That was in 1974.

NIELSEN: I was about to say, it must be about a hundred and fifty by now.

HARPER: But then I explained to her that Judge Sirica had been honored because of the Watergate business and everybody wanted to sit at lunch with him, and that what you ought to do is read a poem. I'm going to read one because I love this poem and people are always misreading it. They don't know how Gwendolyn reads this poem and so I'm going to read it in her honor. Furious Flower is dedicated to her, and this is partial payment. It's a great poem. I was corresponding with her over the summer, and you know Gwendolyn does all kinds of surprising things. Just when you think generosity has reached its level, she just takes it to another level.

NIELSEN: That's true.

HARPER: She had been on campus to give a convocation a few years ago and a lot of students came out. I was teaching her poems. She had published a collection called *Blacks*. The bookstore couldn't get distribution.

NIELSEN: It had some very good poems.

HARPER: Yes. And we couldn't get copies in the bookstore, so I wrote to her: "Listen, we've got this seminar and we need books. Would you just arrange or call somebody, or tell me who to call?" And in the next couple of days, I got a package in the mail. Twenty books of *Blacks*. In her scrawl, which is distinctive, she writes: "I do not want any money for these," which meant give them to the students, which I did. So we were reading on Sterling Brown's birthday at the Guggenheim Library, and I had gone to the bookbinder at the John Hay Library who binds books from the fourteenth, fifteenth, sixteenth century, given him a copy of *Blacks,* and said, "I want you to bind this in the best leather you can find." He said, "Well, it's a paperback." I said, "Well, do whatever you have to do." And when I walked up to her on Sterling's birthday—Sterling was dead, he had died in 1989—I just handed this to her and said, "This is in appreciation for all the things you've done for me." And for the first time, that I have seen, she had nothing to say.

Then when it came time to read, she said the highest compliment a poet can pay to another poet is to do what that poet would not do for him or herself. How many of us are binding our own books in leather?

NIELSEN: Well, the only person I knew was Wallace Stevens, who did it all the time.

HARPER: Well, he was working in insurance; he had an expense account, we all know that. But Gwendolyn is wonderful and I owe her plenty. She's been a marvelous example and, not only that, her generosity is widely known among many people. But more than anything else, what I love is what she does for children and young folks.

NIELSEN: When she was Poetry Consultant at the Library of Congress, she was insistent about visiting the schools in particular; much more so than any later poet laureates had done until probably Rita Dove. That reading was also the occasion where they announced that Robert Hayden was going to be the Poetry Consultant. Now, what a lot of us don't know is that he had been offered that position once before, and because of things having to do with his position at Michigan, had to turn it down at that point. But you were sitting between him and Gwendolyn Brooks, who was the next African American poet laureate and the first African American woman. I'm not predicting necessarily that you'll be the next one in line or something, but it was a curious situation because along with Sterling Brown those are two of the most important people in terms of their appearance in your own work.

HARPER: Absolutely.

NIELSEN: I remember hearing you read that poem. It wasn't too much longer after that you did *Chant of Saints,* which had a considerable amount of Robert Hayden's work in it as well, along with Sterling Brown's. Let me ask you something about that first book. You mentioned several times during the Furious Flower Conference Gwendolyn Brooks's participation in selecting that for the prize. When I go back to that book, it's striking in retrospect that, far more than most poets I read, it seems that most of the characteristic Michael Harper elements are already there. That is, your primary thematic sources—history, music, family, art—are the primary sources already, and structurally the poems seem to have already found the major formal methods that you'll use the rest of your life. It makes me feel a little bit like when Emerson got Whitman's first book and said, "There must have been a long apprenticeship." I was wondering if you could speak a little bit about the development of that first book.

HARPER: Well, I was already in my early thirties when that book was published and I think that's one of the things. I came along at a time when most poets did not even think about publishing a book until they were in their late thirties. Two of my mentors at undergraduate college were both alumni of the Iowa Writers Workshop. I was aware, for example, that the workshop had a kind of undercurrent of encouragement to black artists and musicians because Iowa was graduating Ph.D.s in dentistry and music composition as early as the 1920s. You could attend the school, but you couldn't get an apartment unless you lived in student housing or married housing. That's a whole other story because they've got no convention of black folks living in that town, with the exception of athletes.

But I was lucky enough to come along at a time when one spent all one's time kind of doing one's own background. You never expected to get paid. All the time I went to undergraduate school, I was working in the post office on graveyard and that meant that I was in the company of people who had Ph.D.s in all kinds of disciplines, but the best job they could get was working in the post office. So they were constantly keeping me on my toes. They would say, "Young blood, what are you reading now?" And I'd say, "I'm reading Dostoevsky." They would say, "Oh, yes, Dostoevsky . . ." and then they would give me a quiz. I mean, going to school was a picnic in comparison to just working in airmail. I would be walking around going through airmail, and there was Charles Mingus's sister sitting there and she said, "Don't walk around and act like you're a musician," because I always had a book in my pocket. Dexter Gordon and Mingus and Wardel Gray, these were all household names.

At that time the Watts local was still going; that is to say, a trolley car going to Watts. What they really need now in L. A., as you know: the mass transit problem has just gotten astronomical.

NIELSEN: Well, they took the trolley cars out of all the American cities.

HARPER: Of course they did. When I first got to L. A., they had
                 the Watts uprising. My parents left Brooklyn, where I
was born in 1938, in order to save us from gang fighting. So, of course, we
went to L. A. The first thing they were doing was bombing black people's
homes as you crossed the great divide. At that time the great divide was
Crenshaw, then it became LaBrea. My dad was working in the post office
and he had transferred out there and we were asked to finish school; at the
time, I was finishing the eighth grade. When we came out there, talking
about trauma, oh Lord, being in L. A. It was tremendous. In fact, I never
recovered.

    A lot of people think my development is mostly concerned with being
in Los Angeles. But actually, I got all my real good training in New York. I
was living in Brooklyn at a time when Brooklyn was a suburb of New
York. That is to say, people lived in New York because you could get a
commodious house that had tree-lined streets. The street that I was born
on, which was called Lafayette Avenue, was chestnut-lined, and the hurri-
cane in 1948 blew all those trees down.

NIELSEN: When you think of Brooklyn, you don't think of
                 hurricanes.

HARPER: No, you don't. And you don't think of snow either, but
                 we had twenty-six inches of snow in 1947, and my old
man was shoveling snow and that's when he decided to go to California.
He said, "I'm not gonna die on this stoop." So I am an urban type, but I
was influenced by music long before. My parents had good record collec-
tions and I already knew about Parker. I got to Los Angeles and nobody
had ever heard of Charles Parker, especially in the school.

NIELSEN: When was this?

HARPER: This was in 1951. Nobody knew this for many years; for
                 example, when the Supreme Court decision came down
in 1954, this was not discussed in civics class. We had no precedent for the
kind of historic dialogue which you would think would go on in a "pro-
gressive state." The school that I went to was an antiearthquake building,
which meant it was one floor and a geometric pattern. It was built on land
that had been appropriated from Japanese Americans. It had been a rice
field.

NIELSEN: During the internment period.

HARPER: Yes. You have all of that unwritten, undiagnosed history.
                That was part of it. So I was not all that young during
the Black Arts Movement when people were publishing magazines. I was
living in San Francisco; I was listening to Coltrane and Art Blakey and the
Jazz Messengers and Horace Silver and listening to Sarah Vaughan sing
and all of that sort of stuff. So I had a whole repertoire and a whole frame
which was entirely different.
    My literary exposure and literary background was pretty much an in-
dependent thing. In fact, I taught the first black literature and black history
courses, because I was in places where there was no precedent for it, and
the administrators said, "Well, all you have to do to do black literature is
to teach the books," as though there were a lot of them. I'm talking about
anthologies. There weren't. So I read the original material; I mean Gwen-
dolyn Brooks and Hayden and Sterling and Margaret Walker.

NIELSEN: At that time it was hard to get Sterling Brown.

HARPER: Very much so. There was a record that Folkways Re-
                cords had made, so one could hear that. I was actually
riding on the freeway in San Francisco and I heard a tape of a voice and
I said, "This is not a West Coast voice." I waited until the end, because
at that time I had never heard Sterling except by record and he was giving
a lecture on the Negro character in American literature from the nine-
teenth and twentieth centuries and his diagnosis.

NIELSEN: His book was one of the first on that subject.

HARPER: It was unreal. Oh, and to hear him teach. This was a
                lecture he gave at Berkeley. So I was lucky in that way.
I was just riding along and you'd have FM on the educational radio and the
next thing you know you hear this. Also, I did so much of my work in iso-
lation. When I went to Iowa, for example, in the writer's workshop my
friends were foreign students. There was a guy from Ghana who taught me
the Anansi stories. Miriam Makeeba came to campus, and I was the one
they used to come and get. I used to wear hats all the time, these great big
hats. They used to say "Padre"—they called me Padre—they would say,
"Padre, you have to go and represent us in there." I said, "What do we

have to do now?" They would say, "We'll tell you about it." They didn't
have any money and Miriam Makeeba would give a concert. It would cost
$7.50 to get in, and we couldn't afford that, so I would be sent as emissary.
And I went with a bouquet of flowers and knocked on the door and I wel-
comed her to campus. This was in the mid-afternoon. I explained that
there were all these football players and basketball players and random
motley people collected around the jukebox. She said, "Well, where are
they?" I said, "Right down here." She said, "Just a minute." She came
down and she sang for us for 45 minutes a capella. So they thought I had
some magical power. All I had said was there were some people that are
not going to be at your concert that would love to hear you sing.

NIELSEN: And gave her some flowers.

HARPER: Yeah, and gave her some flowers. These are some pa-
                trician people. I don't care if they're tribal blacks from
South Africa, they got their own traditions. She was magnificent. So these
little highlights. That was the same year that W. H. Auden read. I was a
student in Chris Isherwood's class. Auden would come to Isherwood's
class. Isherwood would bring his friends. Charles Laughton came to class.
I said, "Man, that looks like the hunchback of Notre Dame, boy," and then
he'd come. Isherwood would never say anything; he would just bring him.
   So I read Richard Wright and Langston and people like that who were
household names to me. We subscribed to the *Crisis* magazine and I used
to clip Langston's poems out of the magazines and put them on the wall.
So when a person asked me, did I want to be the new Langston Hughes,
that was sacrilegious talk. I thought, what is wrong with these people?
He's still walking around! But that was the only black name they knew,
so they would run that.

NIELSEN: Still is for a lot of people.

HARPER: Oh, yeah. Oooh, I get tired of that. You try not to be
                insulting because they're making efforts. So I would, in
witty fashion, say, "I'm trying to be a W. B. Yeats," and they used to take
that seriously. People would write me letters and say, "Where did you get
the idea for this poem?" I would say, "I was reading Dante," and they'd
write that down. So now, some of my poems in the Norton Anthology,
for example, "Nightmare Begins Responsibility"—everybody assumes

that's Yeats or Delmore Schwartz. Well, I don't need those two to write a poem of that sort. Anybody can just look at the subject matter. Where'd the technique come from? I don't sound like Iowa poets.

NIELSEN: I was going to ask you about that. I haven't seen too
                 much discussion about this. The structure of your poems
isn't like any of the sources you've been talking about. You seem to have a sort of phrasal structure that's unique.

HARPER: This is the man that's got real critical acuity. I love it.

NIELSEN: Well, it's not hard to notice.

HARPER: No, it isn't. All you have to do is read it. The answer to
                 the question is, I've tried to put together two different
forms. There is a kind of phrasing that the great musicians—see, I grew up with Lester Young who would go to the Savoy Ballroom and he would play to the dancers. He would get ideas from watching people dance and especially on kitchen mechanics' night, which was Thursday night, when it cost a dollar to get in. He'd watch these dancers and he'd come up with this phrasing. People were wondering where the phrasing came from. For every musician, every session is a new day. They don't sound like the soloists on the record because that was just one time. These people are improvising all the time. When you've got geniuses out there, I say to myself, "Now that's the source."

    Now, how to make the bridge from that musical linkage to a literary one was always the issue for me. You could live under the security blanket of the metronome, but that struck me as enormously boring, and since Hayden and Gwendolyn had already done that—they'd written beautiful sonnets and ballads and they'd kind of carved out that territory—there was no point in imitating them. I was trying to kind of build on what they had done. You notice how Gwendolyn and Hayden and Sterling were always working against the tradition at the same time. They were already conversing in it. But they were adding to it in a kind of theory of adaptation. They would take elements of it and they would run with them, just to give you a kind of semblance of what they were doing, and then they would bring other elements to it. Oftentimes it came from Afro-American folklore or Afro-American speech patterns. The critics would come along and say, "These people are not conforming to the pattern." They weren't trying to. They were already conversing in this. They were really pioneers; they were pioneers not only because they were well educated in terms of the nuances and creativity and all that. They understood the creative process. The creative process is always one-on-one, no matter what your preparation is when you enact your writing, or when you enact your singing. Everything depends on that moment. The whole weight of one's life in training comes to pass then. That's what I was trying to do.

NIELSEN: You seemed to have solved a problem that a lot of writers, post–early modernists, have faced, and that's the difficulty of a narrator using modernist techniques. Your phrasal structures aren't exactly the sort of collage juxtapositions that you find in a lot of writers. Somehow you manage to, particularly in your history poems, manage to have a narrative without having narrative-style sentences. Then again, it's not what the so-called new narrative poets are doing, which is really just going back to a very old form.

HARPER: If you listen to the solos of the great musicians, or you listen to the phrasing of the great singers like the Sarah Vaughans and the Billie Holidays, these are always people who are looking for the epiphanies in things, and they turn the whole melody, the whole chordal structure, on just a phrase or two, and the exposition as well as the highlights turn on these kinds of moments. That's what I'm trying to do in a certain kind of analogical way; I'm trying to build on that.

This is also part of my sensibility: the way I was raised. You know the way in which black Americans talk, particularly in the kitchen, is something which is extraordinary to me because they always telescope complexity. They'll give you just . . . Stephen Henderson calls it mascon. Henderson said to me—I'm using it as an illustration—he said to me a beautiful thing once. The Coltrane poem, "Dear John, Dear Coltrane," is a poem which has been looked at not only by me, but by others. He said to me one day, "Were you thinking about Du Bois and Sam Hose at the beginning of that poem?" He's the only person who understood the context of that poem and it pleased me so for him to say that. We were just walking across the campus at Howard when he came up with that. So there's a certain kind of intelligence and a certain kind of literacy which is not necessarily written down, which is always in dialogue because we're always participating in what I call a long dialogue. That's one of the reasons why the Ellisons, Haydens, and the Gwendolyns are most important.

[Following are three poems that Michael Harper wrote in tribute to Gwendolyn Brooks:]

Wizardry:
The Poetic Saga in Song of Gwendolyn Brooks

When you wrote YOU WERE MY CLEAR WINNER
a telegram followed, wanting to publish,
but I held out for the critical word
from your typewriter; only later,
after my citation as honorand,
when Judge Sirica reigned
over Watergate, but did not jail
the real culprits—only then
did I appreciate, internalize,
conjure the special meaning
of your bold HOLD ON!

What you had learned in Topeka,
the rhythmic ropesters
dancing the neighborhood beat,
and how the count went up
IN THE MECCA, at vespers
in the baptist rectory,
which could have been a library
but had to feed the children
rereading their stories
you wrote for them.

We are lying about the 60's—
promise of any age—
when liberation is not Tupelo,
Natchez, including the trace,
and Hattiesburg
where women of great song
and elbow grease
sat down through the floorboards
and gave their children up

into coldwater flats
and the ash and beeswax
of the 47th St. Y.

On the Brooklyn College campus
I spoke about the South African
connection with my ancestors
who bought the freehold land
before the Union became the Union,
and why the AME bishopry
had its gangster bishops
who sang their own religion,
with or without the spirit
which always rose to buzzard's
roost, to the rafters,
and on the choir's bench
satin dolls, and the rollaways
of our deep song,
louder than Bessie Smith's
"my house fell down and I can't live
there no mo"

And IN THE MECCA we could,
and in that narrative, sorrow songs
for the marathon of your committal.
The prizes in our hands were your words.

Sorbet (GB: 6 7 97)

Morsel or ton exquisite, the power
of taste in sonics, the power of theme
endurance, the well you go to for thirst.

I wore my basque beret
in duplicate
in your honor:

standing in Atlanta
in a squad
I was asked by a Guadalupan
just back from the Sorbonne
"how much basque blood
I had";
host of tuskeegeans
backed off the microphone
as if the wizard
were approaching
with a cane
(maybe the one used on him
in new york city);

no vestryman
from St. Phillips
could approach the dais;
uptown and downtown
leaps of song synapsed

and in Chicago
nothing is trivialized:

you get down
for a pedestal at cape
and up
into the choir
of allegiance:

this woman has carried mail
on every bad day for good;
she is our project;
for this junebug

open your screens
and bring your spoons:

elixir, essence,
all that you can take away

(bring some to get some)
homemade is the best

Double Sorbet 6 7 98/ for G.B.

This is sherbet but it is DuBoisian
with flavoring so sorrowful shenanigans

shake to meltdown and we are eating again
The palate of observation exquisite

everpresently in a prosody of lace
embroidery strengthened in homespun

patterns of speech the skipping rope
in alleyways compost on thoroughfares

commence symphonic tones of yesteryear
odors from the kitchen balm for hungers

only slightly felt in the name of bbq
sauce homemade the vinegar and salt

equations you can never solve without touch
do not eat "hold on" sorbet in GB's name

a perfect temperature woven in the corner
of the frigidaire too many morsels to eat

at one sitting the doubling overdraft
in the bank deposits one cannot save

but remembers in tintypes only she had made
an album still crisp with baccanalia

refrains of living on the edge of traintracks
north and south of the equator

she navigates in some nightrain discourse
with the other cautionary tales

only sage can know and being 81
a tune Miles Davis played on Calumet

she is the traveler as archetypal jaguar
convivial enough as embers reach dusk

comfortable in the treeline off the ground
eating a catch mysterious and polish off

by double sorbet essences of fruit fructose
too sweet to be eaten before the meal: and saved

for edification in the logos of the race
above the veil, inside it, dawn to dusk

composed at Yaddo 6 7 98
in honor of Gwendolyn Brooks's
birthday: $9 \times 9 = 81$
superlatives
and sacred names

Conversation:

E U G E N E   R E D M O N D
and
J A B A R I   A S I M

ASIM: We're here with Eugene Redmond on the campus of
              James Madison University at the Furious Flower Confer-
ence. Last night at the reading, one thing I was struck by was the number
of poets of major stature under one roof, and I saw you moving around,
taking pictures of them and things like that. I wonder what your thoughts
were while that was taking place.

REDMOND: I was reveling in the wonder of it all and in the historic
              presence; the cultural, multicultural, artistic, and, specifi-
cally poetic ambiance, or atmosphere. Yeah, I was very much struck by it,
especially since we've been losing some writers—these kinds of gatherings
serve a lot of ends. So I was very moved: moved in the way I was think-
ing, moved in the way I was feeling, and then I was moved in another way
that's hard to describe or put your finger on; I was inundated, energized,
maybe in the spirit, you know, in a "church" kind of way.

ASIM: One thing that struck me was the endurance of those
              particular writers that were featured; and not just them,
but some of the writers that were in the audience, giving them vocal en-
couragement. And when you go back and look, you see that a lot of these
people emerged during the Black Arts Movement, in *Black Fire, New Black
Voices,* things like that. So one of the achievements of these poets, as I see
it, is not just that they have consistently improved their talent, but that
they have endured and continued to write, because a lot of the people
in those anthologies—"Whatever happened to so-and-so?"—made that

appearance, and then they never appeared again. And these poets here to-
day have continued to be at the forefront as decades have passed.

REDMOND: Well, James Baldwin used to say, "Do the work; just keep
                doing the work"; and you do it because you have to, you
do it because you need to, you do it because you're being pushed in a kind
of healthy way by the people around you, your peers, and by the genera-
tions of writers aborning, and you're being pulled by the writers who are
moving toward the other end of the tunnel. Askia Touré and Val Gray
Ward and I were just talking about slipping into elderhood without know-
ing it. And part of it's age, part of it is just through a process of attrition,
where the older writers die or the not-so-older writers leave the scene, and
somebody's got to fill that vacuum. And you can never fill their steps, you
can never take their place, but you stand there because you want their
light, and you want to be transfused, you want that transfusion from the
elderhood, from the history, from the culture. But also, you're a guardian:
you're a vault, you're a bank, you're a repository. You're at the crossroads,
like so many of those deities from the various cultures found in the Pan-
African world. Somebody's always standing at the crossroads, watching
out—you see that a lot in the community anyway, somebody's always
looking around, checking out for folks.

      The perseverance, the wherewithal, the stamina, the stick-to-it-iveness,
is all part of it, and I continue to be amazed by the perseverance; pleased
and amazed in the sense that not as much attention, or not as much sup-
port, or not as much reinforcement or exposure comes to many of the
lights, even singular lights who are quite good, who've kept the watch,
who've been vigilant and wakeful and faithful and productive for so many
years. That's why this conference is so important, is so major.

ASIM: Right, and to get back to the reading last night, you're
                talking about the opportunities for even the major lights,
in terms of exposure. I've read Michael Harper for years, really know his
stuff, really admire his stuff, and one of the things I was thinking when I
got in was, "I've got to get to the reading, because I've never had the op-
portunity to see him in person. As big as he is within our world, it's not
like he's going on a world tour, it's not like he's going to stop in St. Louis
for a few days. You've got to catch him while you can."

      Now, the other thing that comes to mind is a lot of these poets
emerged during the sixties, with what I call street credentials. And in the

criticism of the time, there was a lot of discussion of a dichotomy between academic poets and poets of the street. And the implication was that the poets of the street had a more authentic voice. Thirty years later, most of those poets of the street are employed by the academy. That's a sea change. So does that result in our redefining what academic poetry is? Has the academy influenced them; or, have they influenced the academy? What is the effect, then, on the poetry that they've produced?

REDMOND: It's a two-way process, a two-way road of influence; and it's reciprocal, but it's also conflictual, contentious, combative, and rich in mutual reinforcement, détente, and, sometimes, mutual dislike. We're wrestling with that issue now; it's afloat and afoot: the issue of dissension and institutions. In fact, a book that I contributed an article to is just coming out of the University of Illinois, and it's called *English Studies/Culture Studies: Institutionalizing Dissent,* and one question it raises is: Does the change agent who comes into the institution with street heat get completely remade in that fire, or does the change agent change the institution? There are several approaches to this, but my feeling is that a parallel institution in the community must always be maintained. And you know the way I work, so I've just done that all my life. If I'm someplace for two weeks, you're going to find me in a church in that community; I'm going to be in a church or a basement before I leave there, a barbershop or something. Wherever I've been, within virtually no time I've tried to set up a parallel operation or apparatus.

And you do it for salvation! For the salvation of your heart and your soul, for one; but also you owe that, you owe it to people who can't get a hearing or who don't have someone to lobby for them. And also, they need some things that are in that institution: there are some technologies, some information, there are some systems that I think people in the so-called streets can use, and certainly the institutions need their knowledge: what we call the old wives' and old husbands' wisdom of the community—the residential community—so there's this seesaw of residential/campus energy.

ASIM: Now you've done a lot of that since your return to your home base of East St. Louis while teaching at Southern Illinois University. You've done a lot of community-based projects; quite a few have resulted in a lot of publications like the *Original Chicago Blues Annual, Literati Internazionali, Break Word with the World* series, *Drumvoices*

Revue, and when you go to these conferences and you set up your table, you've got all of these things that you've produced in this relatively small region. It's quite a bit of things. Now, contrast this to your book, *The Eye in the Ceiling;* that was your first book of poetry in how many years?

REDMOND: Eighteen years.

ASIM: And there was a parallel situation in Chicago when I was in college, and Haki Madhubuti published a book of poems; that was his first book of poetry in ten years. So there's a parallel there between people such as yourself and Haki Madhubuti who spend a lot of time doing grassroots organizing and institution-building. So obviously, you think, I guess, the rewards are equal, that we benefit as much from the institution-building you've done. I think it was Melvin Dixon who was writing a piece praising your shepherding of Henry Dumas's work through the years. And he said, the only downside of Redmond doing all this beautiful Dumas work is we've had less from Eugene himself. What is your response to that?

REDMOND: Yeah, this has been said by some other people, June Jordan and a number of people. In fact, just to speak personally about this, I do have friends, close friends, and some who are much better known than I could ever be—better known than all the poets here together—they have even suggested that I pull back from Dumas, that I could've been cutting myself off at the knees by doing the Dumas work.

But people look at you—and, of course, you love them—but we're all on different tracks, grooving on different systems, and we all have different perspectives and different takes on this thing. So I would say that I think: always try to define poetry or creativity in its widest setting; and for me, what I do is all part of being a poet. Being a father is part of being a poet, being a teacher, being an activist, railing against the twenty-two dump sites in East St. Louis—repeat, there are twenty-two toxic waste dumps in East St. Louis!—railing against that is part of being a poet. I think that's something we inherit, and I don't know anybody who doesn't have projects of sorts that they do. And then, of course, there's more to being a poet than publishing: I read a lot, and you teach and you do workshops for teachers and you do consciousness-raising forums, and the poet comes out of you.

It's like Alice Walker talks about how during the years when a lot
of black women writers weren't writing, they were doing quilts. She has
this wonderful essay on the ways that black women who were writers
at heart, perhaps, or creative artists at heart, did other things; they were
known for cooking the best this, or preparing the best that, and she said
that's almost like the waiting years. And you see it, I see it, all those men
of my generation, the generation of my *young* youth, who went to the
post office. Or went into the packinghouse. Who played great horns, and
played great guitars, but forfeited their artistic careers because the girl-
friend from high school said, "If you're going to go on the road, forget it.
I'm going to stay here and create a family." The John Coltranes and the
Charlie Parkers.

ASIM: Well, speaking of modes of expression, I was hoping
                 you'd share some of your work with us that's included in
the publication that accompanies the program.

REDMOND: Sure, I'll read two or three stanzas from this poem. And
                 speaking of poets and poetry and service to poets and
service to the community, "Barbequed Cong: or We Laid My Lai Low" is
dedicated to Larry Neal, who called me when he saw this poem in *Black
Scholar* and said, "Hey, I dig what you're doing." So I'll read three stanzas
from it. It was written in 1969.

i

at my Lai we left lint for lawns
feathered with frameless wingless birds,
barbequed and bodyless heads of hair
hanging from the charcoal gazes of burnt huts.
rice-thin hides harbored
flesh-flailing pellets,
unregenerative crops trigger-grown from the trunks of branchless
mechanical trees.
as barbeque grills grew hotter, with ghost-hot heat
mothers cooked children and causes
in the grease of blood-glazed breasts,
resigned in the weighty whisper that:
"one can only die once."

iv

my lands! My Lai!
puppet shows and portable pentagods soar or sneak from saigon.
Shine came on deck of the mind this morning and said:
"there's a sag in the nation's middle.
which way extends the natal cord—
north or south?"

I lay down my life for My Lai and Harlem.
I lay down my burden in Timbuctu, East Saint Loo, and Baltimore.
we waited long and low
like low-strung studs for My Lai
when we reared and rammed her
with spark-sperm spitting penises
then withdrew westward 6000 miles
(a pacific coffin of the mind between us)
to vex canned good consciences
and claim the 5th Amendment.

ASIM: When you talk about the close of the sixties, as the de-
                   cades change, do you think there's an easily determined,
classified change in the approach of the poetry, or does it not work that
neatly?

REDMOND: Doesn't work that neatly; in some ways, they spill over,
                  and there are certain triggers. It's like when people say
sixties, I ask, which one of the sixties; just like when I run into an English
professor and he or she says, "I teach English," I ask, "Which one?" Be-
cause I've got an *English* too! So, which sixties: is it the antiwar sixties? The
free speech sixties? Is it the environment-conscious sixties? Is it the civil
rights/early sixties? The Black Nationalist–Black Power–Black Arts late
sixties? The Black Studies sixties? The Chicago Eight, Memphis Nine, New
York Seventeen? Which tier of sixties? Are you looking at the West Coast
black sixties? US? Panthers? There was a difference. So, yeah, there are dif-
ferent triggers, different themes in the decades.

ASIM: Thank you very much.

PART 2

*Critical Theories and Approaches in
African American Poetry*

Bantu, Nkodi, Ndungu, and Nganga: Language, Politics, Music, and Religion in African American Poetry

J O Y C E   A .   J O Y C E

HISTORICAL OVERVIEW OF AFRICAN AMERICAN poetry reveals the presence of similar linguistic, political, musical, and religious features in Phillis Wheatley, Jupiter Hammon, George Moses Horton, James Monroe Whitfield, Frances Ellen Watkins Harper, James Edwin Campbell, Paul Laurence Dunbar, Fenton Johnson, James Weldon Johnson, Jean Toomer, Claude McKay, Countee Cullen, Melvin B. Tolson, Georgia Douglas Johnson, Helene Johnson, Alice Dunbar Nelson, Angelina Grimke, Langston Hughes, Frank Marshall Davis, Waring Cuney, Sterling Brown, Owen Dodson, Gwendolyn Brooks, Margaret Walker, Robert Hayden, Pinkie Gordon Lane, Naomi Long Madgett, Mari Evans, Gloria Oden, Henry Dumas, Askia Touré, Etheridge Knight, Amiri Baraka, Sonia Sanchez, Haki Madhubuti, Audre Lorde, Jay Wright, Lucille Clifton, Jayne Cortez, Sterling Plumpp, Eugene Redmond, Michael Harper, June Jordan, Pat Parker, Al Young, Calvin Forbes, Nikki Giovanni, Angela Jackson, Marilyn Nelson Wainek, Rita Dove, Alexis de Veaux, Ntozake Shange, Essex Hemphill, Hattie Gossett, E. Ethelbert Miller, Quincy Troupe, Daryl Holmes, Elizabeth Alexander, Wanda Coleman, Michael Warr, Ruth Forman, Kevin Powell, Ras Baraka, D-Knowledge, and Marvin Gladney.

This catalogue is made deliberately overwhelming with the intention of underscoring the diversity, productivity, and richness of our poetic tradition and of presenting a historical pool of writers, most of whose works (with amazingly few exceptions) to varying degrees and in varying ways reflect the interconnection of language, politics, music, and religion in African American poetry. This interconnection is clearly obvious in the works of the young writers whose poems appear in *In the Tradition: An Anthology of Young Black Writers*, edited by Kevin Powell and Ras Baraka, which was published in 1992. I would like to suggest that any theory of African American poetry must place these four features at the center of its exposition.

In the engaging study *A Profile of Twentieth-Century American Poetry*, editors Jack Myers and David Wojahn present a collection of essays that trace the development of American poetry from 1908 until the 1990s. What emerges clearly from this study is that white writers before the 1960s did not look to black poets when they sought craftsmen or women poets as role models and that the major influences on twentieth-century white American poetry are Walt Whitman, Emily Dickinson, Robert Frost, T. S. Eliot, and Wallace Stevens. If we are going to be successful at identifying a theory of African American poetry, we must look to the works of our own writers and develop the theory from within our tradition, from their works and not from the outside. We must not follow the established trend of black theoreticians who have theorized about fiction by imposing alien terminology from outside the culture or who have cleverly taken an African folktale and imbued it with Eurocentric intellectual thought that has nothing to do with the culture from which the tale is taken.

The nature of our poetic tradition demands that criticism and theory of black poetry be grounded in black folk or popular culture. Because of the elitist nature of Eurocentric critical theory, black writers who have suggested that our folk culture is the source of our literature have been perceived as either propagandistic or negligent in addressing aesthetic issues. The critical ideas of Langston Hughes, Richard Wright, Larry Neal, Hoyt Fuller, Addison Gayle, and Stephen Henderson, from varying perspectives, have demonstrated that folk speech (both rural and urban and folktales), music (spirituals, folk songs, blues, jazz), religion (sermons, Islam, Christianity), and liberation politics (freedom from oppression in the diaspora and in Africa) are the elements of an African American poetic aesthetics.

The most engaging and widely known study to address the aesthetics of African American poetry is Kimberly Benston's "Performing Blackness: Re/Placing Afro-American Poetry" (1989). Although this essay demonstrates the serious thought that African American poetry demands, it also reflects the dangers of a contemporary theoretical process and language that operate at a high level of abstraction and fail to move beyond the level of theorizing. Benston writes, "A division persists between our knowledge of the poetry as text and our awareness of it as performance." [1] Ironically, perhaps the most important characteristic of our poetry is its orality, the transformation of words into performance. However, my use of *perfor-mance* here is not synonymous with Benston's use of the term. In contemporary theoretical parlance, *performance,* the noun form of *performative,* refers to "a kind of utterance that performs with language the deed to which it refers . . . instead of describing some state of affairs." [2] Thus Benston calls for a metalinguistic analysis of black poetry that never moves beyond discussions of language about language.

Such discussions of the performative act of black poetry must move beyond exclusively intellectual exercises about the intricacies of language to analyses that merge aesthetics with political commitment and meaning. Benston's essay rejects the entire social, political, and cultural content that underlies the conception of most black poetry. He explains,

> I think we need to see Afro-American poetry not as a static alignment of proclamations (reflecting either some preconstituted "reality" *or* its own stagnant pool of tropes) but rather as a performative activity that sees itself in struggle with other practices. A corollary point: we must recognize our own relation to this process, understanding interpretation as an inescapably mediatory act that will itself be a transformative process. Thus, as we contemplate our movement past the juncture of Black Arts and formalist impulses that situates much of our work today, we must be careful not to retreat into a nostalgic humanism which ignores the differences *within* black discourse(s) as well as their conflicts with other discourses. Conventional oppositions of praxis/theory and history/discourse which occupy so much of our internecine exchanges will no longer serve. Our readings are performances which theorize their relations to other readings. They, too, continuously (re)construct their "subjects." [3]

Numerous questions beg for answers here. What is the purpose of theorizing about the relationship of our performances to other readings? What is the purpose of discourse? If interpretation is "an inescapably mediatory act that will itself be a transformative process," what is this process being transformed into? In other words, why are we critics engaged in the critical process? If our words are limited to the academy, why is it that we do not use them as a process or means by which we can change the academy so that it becomes more involved in what's happening in the outside world of which the academy is a part? Only those of us who are from a privileged group or who identify with such a group would call humanism "nostalgic." Real humanism has yet to be realized on this planet, in this country.

Why is it that instead of refining, retuning, or reshaping what is defined as those weaknesses of the Black Aesthetic, we immerse ourselves deeper in the very Eurocentric aesthetic the theoreticians of the Black Arts Movement fought against? Haki Madhubuti's comments succinctly capture the essence of the Black Aesthetic creed. He says, "Writers write. What they write about tells the reader to what extent they are involved with the real world. . . . Writers should be questioners of the world and doers within the world."[4] Most of our creative artists, and particularly our poets, have stressed in their works the need for black creative artists to maintain connections to their people, not to "metapeople." J. Saunders Redding's presentation of the essential qualities of good poetry analogously describes the qualities necessary for the critic or theorist of black poetry if the scholar intends to remain inside the tradition of African American poetry. Saunders says, "The essential quality of good poetry is utmost sincerity and earnestness of purpose. A poet untouched by his times, by his conditions, by his environment is only half poet, for earnestness and sincerity grow in direct proportion as one feels intelligently the pressure of immediate life."[5]

The most immediate cultural environment for the scholar of African American poetry is the poetry itself with its political and linguistic or verbal consistencies that have endured for well over a century. The terminology we use to theorize or critique African American literature, in this case poetry, should come from within Africa or black culture in the diaspora. A method I propose is one that uses terms taken from the Charleston, South Carolina, area where an incredibly large number of African slaves were taken, slaves whose homes were in Angola, Gambia, the Congo, Sierra Leone, Senegambia, and Guinea. At least 70 percent of all incoming Africans into South Carolina were Bantu from the Angola region near the Congo River. "For [these] Africans in South Carolina, the first stage in the acculturation process was the melting of numerous West and Central African elements in a culture such as Gullah. The creation of this Creole culture allowed these Africans to form a kind of lingua franca, enabling them to communicate with each other as well as with the planters."[6] Consequently, the largest and most homogeneous group in the area, the Bantu, had great influence over other African groups in the area. "Also, since the Bantus were predominantly field hands or were used in capacities that required little or no contact with European-Americans, they were not confronted with the problem of acculturation, as the West African domestic servants and artisans were. Coexisting in relative isolation from other groups, the Bantus were able to maintain a strong sense of unity and to retain a cultural vitality that laid the foundation for the development of African-American culture."[7]

Continuing the Bantus' tradition of unity and affirming their strong cultural identity, in the title of this essay and in the exploration to follow, I use the word *Bantu* to refer to those characteristics of black speech, such as plantation, rural, and urban dialect, folktales, sermons, the dozens, signifying, and all other historical characteristics of black speech, such as those listed by Stephen Henderson in his *Understanding the New Black Poetry*.

The Bantus were clearly a political people. This political consciousness and a deeply spiritual component have always been integral aspects of African American poetry. The most pervading aspect of late nineteenth- and early twentieth-century African American poetry to date is the theme of liberation or consciousness-raising against the evils of oppression. I refer to this characteristic as *Nkodi*, a BaKongo word for specialists who sent messages to the dead.[8] The *Nkodi* are closely related to the *Nganga*, in BaKongo a priest who employed life-affirming *nkisi* to heal and ward off *kindoki* (evil). Thus in the Bantu cultures in the diaspora as well as in Africa, the religious and the political are intertwined. In the tradition of African American poetry, politics and Christianity are sometimes wedded, as they are in the poetry of Frances Harper, James Whitfield, and Margaret Walker, or they are diametrically at odds, as they are in some of the poetry of Frank Marshall Davis, Amiri Baraka, and Haki Madhubuti. Henry Dumas's poetry combines an understanding of African spirituality with consciousness-raising.

Instead of following the tradition of isolation and despair that characterizes much contemporary Euro-American poetry, African American poetry celebrates life, is life affirming. African music on the continent and in the diaspora also reflects this affirmation of life. And although James Edwin Campbell and Paul Laurence Dunbar perfected the use of dialect before Langston Hughes, Hughes was the first to bring the blues and jazz rhythms to black poetry in America. Following Hughes and Sterling Brown, many of the poets of the 1960s who are still writing and reciting today—Nikki Giovanni, Haki Madhubuti, Eugene Redmond, Asia Touré, Amiri Baraka, and Sonia Sanchez—perform their poetry with musical groups. Music not only becomes part of the subject matter of their poetry, it also appears in the typography of the poem and in the poets' use of their voices or in what some would refer to as their utterances. This use of music as a group activity continues the African tradition. In discussing the function of music in African societies, Kwabena Nketia writes, "Music making is generally organized as a social event. Public performances, therefore, take place on social occasions—that is, on occasions when members of a group or a community come together for the enjoyment of leisure, for recreational activities, or for the performance of a rite, ceremony, festival, or any kind of collective activity."[9]

As in Africa, music is integral to all aspects of African American life, as demonstrated by the development of our musical tradition, which includes folk spirituals, folk gospels, gospel choirs, gospel quartets, contemporary gospel, work songs, field songs, protest songs, game songs, social songs, rural blues, ragtime, vaudeville blues, boogie-woogie, New Orleans jazz, big band, rhythm and blues, urban blues, bebop, rock'n'roll, soul, soul jazz, civil rights songs, jazz fusion, funk, disco, rap, techno funk, go-go, and house music. I use the word *Ndungu*, the name of the long drums used in Haitian dance with their origins in the Kongo or Zaire, to represent the role music plays in the history of African American poetry.

In this essay, I would like to explore the predominance and merger of *Bantu* (black speech), *Nganga* (religion), *Ndungu* (music), and *Nkodi* (politics) in African American poetry by providing a brief overview of the prevailing subjects and stylistic features of the poetry in four seminal and available anthologies of African American literature: *Black Writers of America, The New Cavalcade: African-American Writing from 1760 to the Present, Black Poets,* and *In the Tradition: An Anthology of Young Black Writers.* I offer here a practical interpretive piece, based on a specific theory of interpretation. Such an approach takes African American literary theory out of the realm of abstraction, where words and utterances only refer to a more involved level of words and utterances, and secures the interpretive act inside the tradition of African American literary history. When Stephen Henderson says in his response to Benston's essay that the challenge of the modern world requires sophisticated African American criticism of black poetry, he makes it clear that this criticism, in order to be a part of the continuing tradition, must maintain its cultural, folk, and popular roots. So the dilemma that emerges is how to keep our folk base, which demands a kind of humanism that has been under attack for years in the academy, and at the same time focus on aesthetics with the "sophistication" that moves us beyond the 1960s.[10]

Addressing the politics of academia and those of the world discussed in the writer's art is an essential aspect of the paradigm I propose here. It is the absence of this political component that enables contemporary theoreticians to ignore the environmental background of black fiction and poetry. This political component demands that we talk / write about how we treat each other (our humanism or our lack of it) and that we address the inherent hypocrisy of a literary endeavor that seeks to be solely metaphysical. As for formalism, any reader who peruses my book on Richard Wright's *Native Son* and sees nothing that goes beyond Aristotle's *Poetics* or grammatical, generic, and syntactical form also refuses to examine the merger of politics and aesthetics, a process that privileges neither form nor content.

Although poststructuralist theories are to be celebrated for disrupting assumptions and predictable reading patterns in fiction, they do not provide the direction we need to address: the merger of black speech, politics, religion, and music in our art, especially our poetry. For all of these characteristics of black poetry have at their roots black survival. They emerged and continued to thrive in a context that is always environmentally and socially grounded.

The four anthologies listed above all demonstrate the folk origins of African American poetry that emerge as a people's expressive responses to the social, political, and psychological forces that dominate their lives. The folk songs (both secular and sacred), of course, precede Phillis Wheatley and her learned poetry. Thus while much of contemporary African American poetry, especially the poetry by the young writers collected in Kevin Powell and Ras Baraka's *In The Tradition,* reflects the stylistic features of an African oral tradition, which manifests in folk songs and early folk poetry, African American poetry has also developed intermittently through the works of those poets who, like Wheatley, perfected the Eurocentric features of their poetry. James Monroe Whitfield, Frances Harper, Paul Laurence Dunbar, William Stanley Braithwaite, Fenton Johnson, Georgia Douglas Johnson, Countee Cullen, Claude McKay, Melvin Tolson, Owen Dodson, Samuel Allen, Robert Hayden, and Gwendolyn Brooks are examples of some of these poets who, before the influences of the Black Arts Movement of the 1960s, crafted their art primarily on the models of mainstream poetry. Contemporary black poetry reflects the merger of the tenets of the Black Aesthetic and Eurocentric features. This wedding is characterized by some combination of the presence of black speech, music, religion, and politics, the characteristics of folk poetry.

Dudley Randall begins his edition of *Black Poets* with folk poetry, which he divides into folk seculars and spirituals. Even a cursory glance at the titles and content of these secular folk songs reveals the slaves' outrage over the conditions that stifle their lives. Songs such as "He Paid Me Seven," "Run, Nigger, Run," "Promises of Freedom," "Song to the Runaway Slave," and "The Old Section Boss" combine folk speech, music, and political commitment while folk spirituals like "Go Down, Moses," "Josha Fit de Battle of Jericho," "Steal Away to Jesus," and many others illuminate how biblical stories and allusions serve as parables to the slaves' reaction to their bondage.

While *The New Cavalcade* does not include a separate section on folk poetry, Keneth Kinnaman and Richard Barksdale's well-known *Black Writers of America* has four sections of folk poetry that record folk poetry from the seventeenth century to the 1970s. Thus *Black Poets* and *Black Writers of America* demonstrate the folk origins and continuum of the folk tradition in African American poetry. More contemporary and comprehensive than Randall's and the Barksdale-Kinnaman anthologies, *The New Cavalcade* provides an overview of the historical development of African American literature, including sixty-two poets that span the centuries from Phillis Wheatley to E. Ethelbert Miller. Before Langston Hughes's poetry, no one poem reflects the merger of music, politics, religion, and black speech, although many poems reflect the presence of any one of these features.

The idea that Phillis Wheatley does not concern herself with the issue of slavery is now in literary circles an unlearned cliché that was dispelled by critics like John C. Shields. In fact, some of Phillis Wheatley's poetry is equally as political as that of James Monroe Whitfield and George Moses Horton. Her poem "To the University of Cambridge, in New England" confirms the subtlety that describes her political voice. Addressed to the students at the university, the poem warns them that morality, virtue, and religion must not be shunned for knowledge and education. The poem's last stanza captures Wheatley's subtle, almost camouflaged critique of white society.

> Ye blooming plants of human race divine,
> An *Ethiop* tells you 'tis your greatest foe;
> Its transient sweetness turns to endless pain,
> And in immense perdition sinks the soul. (12) [11]

It is highly ironic that one brought to America to be a slave, and thus perceived by the students as inferior, is the one to tell the students that the joys of sin, their greatest foe, are transient. The lines "Remember, Christians, Negroes, black as Cain / May be refin'd, and join th'angelic train" found at the end of "On Being Brought from Africa to America" confirms Wheatley's condemnation of racial oppression. Because of the presence of religious faith and her use of it to challenge mainstream notions of virtue and morality, Phillis Wheatley, then, is both at the beginning and the center of the African American poetic tradition.

Following Wheatley, James Whitfield and Frances Harper wrote more overtly political poetry. But a name less known than theirs is James Edwin Campbell, a master of the plantation dialect before Paul Laurence Dunbar. The few poems of Campbell collected in *The New Cavalcade* illustrate his sharp ear for plantation dialect and the connection between music and religion in the plantation's cultural life. Quite similar to Campbell's poetry, Paul Laurence Dunbar's frequently anthologized "An Ante-Bellum Sermon" illustrates, like the spirituals, how the slaves used religion to camouflage their condemnation of slavery. Using Moses' successful defeat of Pharaoh as the crux of his sermon, the preacher denies that his words have any meaning outside the biblical story:

> An' de lan' shall hyeah his thundah,
> Lak a blas' fom Gab'el's ho'n;
> Fu' de Lawd of hosts is mighty
> When he girds his ahmor on.
> But fu' feah some one mistakes me,
> I will pause right hyeah to say,
> Dat I'm still a-preachin' ancient,
> I ain't talkin' 'bout to-day. (303)

The preacher clearly knows that he must protect himself and that he cannot trust everyone indiscriminately in his audience. Although he is not educated in the fashion of Phillis Wheatley, he uses a rhetorical technique similar to paralipsis. Telling his audience something that he says he is not going to tell them, he ironically denies that his sermon relates at all to the slave masters.

In addition to "An Ante-Bellum Sermon," the most anthologized of Dunbar's poetry are the poems "When Malindy Sings," "Sympathy," and "We Wear the Mask." Like his "Ode to Ethiopia," collected in *The New Cavalcade,* both "Sympathy" and "We Wear the Mask" address the African Americans' reaction to their oppression. Recorded in African American literary history as some of the most well-honed poetry, Paul Laurence Dunbar's poetry manifests the features of religion, music, language, and political commitment. Just as Dunbar is the first African American poet to make a living from his writing, he is also the first to integrate these features throughout the canon. His ear for the plantation dialect in "An Ante-Bellum Sermon," "When Malindy Sings," and many other dialect poems brings a melody and rhythm to African American poetry that remained unchallenged until Langston Hughes's blues and jazz poetry.

In his masterful adaptation of urban black folk speech and his transformation of blues and jazz music into a literary form, Langston Hughes emerges as the artist whose works are a culmination of the folk songs and folk poetry and of Paul Laurence Dunbar's plantation dialect pieces. Consequently, in tracing the continuum in African American poetry, Langston Hughes had the same irrevocable influence in the twentieth century that Dunbar had on black poetry in the late nineteenth century. Although it is undeniable that numerous other poets of the Harlem Renaissance, such as Claude McKay, Countee Cullen, Georgia Douglas Johnson, Alice Dunbar-Nelson, Anne Spencer, Helene Johnson, Gwendolyn Bennett, Effie Lee Newson, and others were skillful poets, Langston Hughes emerged as a poet "of the people," and, for numerous reasons, we now distinguish him from the group.

In the 1920s, publishers were clearly interested in black male writers who highlighted racial issues in their art. Both McKay and Cullen wrote poems that have nothing to do with racial issues, such as McKay's "Spring in New Hampshire" and Cullen's "To John Keats, Poet, at Springtime," but they are best remembered for those poems that do. McKay's "Harlem Shadows" and "If We Must Die" and Cullen's "Heritage" and "Yet Do I Marvel" are their most anthologized pieces. Women writers of the Harlem Renaissance, like Georgia Douglas Johnson, Anne Spencer, and others are far less visible than McKay and Cullen in the annals of literary history because their most frequently anthologized poems address such subjects as love, death, pain, and the futility of war. Maureen Honey's edition of *Shadowed Dreams: Women's Poetry of the Harlem Renaissance* remains the only anthology that provides a broad coverage of the women poets of the renaissance. Part 2 of the anthology, subtitled "Heritage," presents twenty-five poems that have black life as their subject. These poems focus on the beauty of black life and thus lack the rebelliousness or anger that describes McKay's and Cullen's poems. Because most anthologies of Harlem Renaissance writers either ignore the women poets or publish those poems that do not emphasize blackness, most readers think that these women neglected to write on racial subjects.

The politics of the times, literary history, and his unsurpassed genius have made Langston Hughes one of the most widely known poets of his time and ours. Despite an understandably small black reading audience, Hughes's poems were addressed to blacks as well as whites. However, the voice he uses in most of his poems—those written in dialect and those written in standard English—is the voice of the common person. His "Theme for English B" and the companion pieces "Low to High" and "High to Low" demonstrate how Hughes could take standard English and transform it into a form that lies between black dialect proper and standard English. The first two lines of "Negro Dancers," "Me an' ma baby's / Got two mo' ways," compared to the lines "How can you low-rate me / this way?" from "Low to High" illustrate my point here.

As with much of Hughes's poetry, "Theme for English B," "Low to High," and "High to Low" address the ramifications of racism. While the two companion pieces highlight the intraracial class conflict within the black community, "Theme for English B" informs white society that the black man and woman are as much American as the white man or woman: "You are white— / yet a part of me, as I am a part of you." Hughes captures the African American's historical journey to America in what is perhaps his signature poem, "The Negro Speaks of Rivers." Dedicated to W. E. B. Du Bois and using water or the river as a metaphor for the source of life, the poem traces the movement of black life from the Euphrates and Nile rivers in Africa to the Mississippi. Hughes subtly couches his admonishment of slavery and racism in the refrain "My soul has grown deep like the rivers." The first time the line appears in the poem it follows the poet's assertion that he has known rivers "ancient as the world and older than the flow of / human blood in human veins." The poet here identifies himself and his blackness with the first human beings. The second and only other time the line appears in the poem occurs after the poet has made reference to Mississippi, New Orleans, and Abe Lincoln. He places the lines "My soul has grown deep like the rivers" at the end of the poem, this time suggesting that he is no longer the same man who "bathed in the Euphrates" and "built [his] hut near the Congo." He is now a black man who has experienced the pain of slavery and racism, and his soul now bears the imprint of these experiences.

So far the poems discussed reveal Langston Hughes's political commitment and make some suggestions about his use of black speech. But one of the poems that best captures the full range of the stylistic innovations Hughes brought to African American poetry and identifies him as the prototype for the Black Arts Movement of the late 1960s is "The Cat and the

Saxophone." Because the poem is short and all its elements inextricably interwoven, I cite it in full:

> EVERYBODY
> Half-pint,—
> Gin?
> No, make it
> LOVES MY BABY
> corn. You like
> liquor,
> don't you honey?
> BUT MY BABY
> Sure. Kiss me,
> DON'T LOVE NOBODY
> daddy.
> BUT ME.
> Say?
> EVERYBODY
> Yes?
> WANTS MY BABY
> I'm your
> BUT MY BABY
> sweetie, ain't I?
> DON'T WANT NOBODY
> Sure.
> BUT
> Then let's
> ME,
> do it!
> SWEET ME.
> Charleston,
> mamma!
> ! (556)

The scene of the poem is a jazz club at two o'clock in the morning, and, of course, the cat is the man talking to his woman or someone he wants to be his woman. As the man raps to the woman, a saxophone player performs. And either he or someone else sings the blues lyrics that

Hughes represents in capital letters. The poem is a tightly integrated network that vacillates between the dialogue between the man and the woman and the words of the singer. In addition to being the lyrics to the blues song, the words in all capitals also set the rhythm of the poem as they capture the saxophone's melody.

"The Cat and the Saxophone" exemplifies all those qualities of Hughes's poems that presage the black poetry of the 1960s. Although Sterling Brown, too, perfected transforming blues music into poetic form and captured with a sharp ear the urban and rural black speech, it was Langston Hughes who opened up its possibilities for black poetry with much the same effect Richard Wright achieved in fiction. The features of music (blues, jazz), language (black speech), religion, and political commitment summarize the predominant stylistic and thematic characteristics of Hughes's poetry. Despite that fact that *The New Cavalcade* does not include any of Hughes's religious poems, such as "Prayer Meeting," "Feet o' Jesus," "Angels Wings," "Judgment Day," and "Prayer," the reader familiar with African American culture knows that the mother in the frequently anthologized poem "Mother to Son" is steeped in a religious faith that is her ideological foundation and gives her the power to tell her son not to expect life to be a crystal stair.

The daughter of a Methodist minister and educated in church schools, Margaret Walker joins Sterling Brown, Robert Hayden, and Gwendolyn Brooks as four well-known black poets whose initial publications follow Langston Hughes and precede the Black Arts Movement. Like Phillis Wheatley, the stylistic features of Gwendolyn Brooks's and Robert Hayden's poems reveal their success at honing Eurocentric poetic forms. And also like Wheatley, their subject matter manifests a political commitment that comprises part of the continuum of the African American poetic tradition. Moreover, Brooks shares a passion for ballads with Sterling Brown and Margaret Walker. Such ballads as Brooks's "Ballad of Pearl May Lee," Brown's "Old Lem," and Walker's "Ballad for Phillis Wheatley" confirm their use of music and black speech as poetic references. The content of these poems positions them at the center of a poetic tradition that attacks racial oppression. Brooks's "Ballad of Pearl May Lee" in its focus on the white woman's betrayal of the black man and Brown's "Old Lem" in its concentration on the overwhelming force the white world wields over black society address contemporary racial issues.

Although they both began publishing their work in the 1940s, Gwendolyn Brooks and Margaret Walker continue to write and publish poetry that reflects the influences of the times and experiences through which they have lived. In her *Report from Part I,* Brooks documents her first encounter with Amiri Baraka and the ideology of the Black Arts Movement. Manifesting the influence of the new movement, Brooks, after 1967, no longer used the sonnet form, which is so pervasive in her early poetry.

Students of African American literature sometimes fail to realize that more mature poets, like Gwendolyn Brooks, Margaret Walker, Lance Jeffers, Dudley Randall, and Robert Hayden, also make up the black poetic tradition of the 1960s. In fact, a look at the single most important publication of the Black Arts Movement in the 1960s, Amiri Baraka's and Larry Neal's edition of *Black Fire: An Anthology of Afro-American Writing,* reveals that a number of the poets in this volume did not survive the test of time. Despite the fact that Gwendolyn Brooks, Margaret Walker, Lance Jeffers, Dudley Randall, and Robert Hayden were never identified with the Black Arts Movement as defined by Baraka and Neal, these older poets have all made their indelible mark on the African American poetic tradition.

While some younger, contemporary writers, such as Trey Ellis, attempt to replace the Black Aesthetic or Black Arts Movement with what Ellis refers to as the *New Black Aesthetic,* the Black Aesthetic Movement of the 1960s and early 1970s changed the course of African American poetry irrevocably. Following the lead of black jazz musicians Ornette Coleman, Sonny Rollins, Pharaoh Sanders, Sun Ra, and John Coltrane, black poets with Amiri Baraka, Larry Neal, Sarah Webster Fabio, Sonia Sanchez, Haki Madhubuti, and Nikki Giovanni in the vanguard began to redefine themselves and their poetry by grounding their art in black speech and black music. Taking up the legacy handed to them by Langston Hughes, these young poets were far more outspoken than he about their intent to merge the political and the aesthetic in shaping their art. They went further than Hughes in making it clear that they were addressing a black audience with the goal of spiritual awakening and sharpening political consciousness.

The four landmark publications that present the political and aesthetic ideology of the Black Aesthetic are the already mentioned *Black Fire,* published in 1968; Addison Gayle's edition of *The Black Aesthetic,* published in 1971; Stephen Henderson's *Understanding the New Black Poetry,* published in 1972; and a series of essays published in the *Negro Digest* from September 1968 to November 1969. Except for Henderson's collection, the anthologies include literary critics, dramatists, and fiction writers. Yet it was the poets who were at the vanguard of this movement. Haki Madhubuti,

Keorapetse Kgositsile, Carolyn Rodgers, and Sarah Webster Fabio all have essays in these late 1960s issues of *Negro Digest* where they discuss the technique and direction of black poetry. These essays discuss stylistic innovations and particularly black subjects that challenge Euro-American definitions and expectations of poetry.

Although these young poets redefined black poetry in the 1960s, the essential component of their art manifests the same integration of music, language, religion, and politics that constitutes the development of black poetry from Phillis Wheatley to the present day. Their contributions emerge as a sharpened political focus and an innovative honing of their use of black speech and black music.

This defiance of Euro-American aesthetic standards reflects the 1960s poets' political commitment to move away from the white mainstream's cultural expectations. Thus the traditional focus on religion that imbued Phillis Wheatley's, Dunbar's, Hughes's, and Margaret Walker's poetry was replaced by a rejection of Christianity and the adoption of Islam. Many of these writers, such as Sonia Sanchez, who in the early 1970s was associated with the Nation of Islam and later moved away from the group, manifested an interest in spirituality that went beyond institutionalized religion.

The focus on spirituality centered on African history with particular attention given to traditional African religions. An essential component of this return to African culture emerges in the manner in which poets like Sanchez, Baraka, Giovanni, and others read their poetry. Their dramatic performance finds its source, like the folk songs and folk poetry, in the oral tradition in African culture. Almost all of these poets identified with the 1960s Black Arts Movement, and those who joined their company in the 1970s, 1980s, and 1990s demonstrate the indigenous African oral tradition in black poetry through various combinations of references to African history and Egyptian gods and goddesses, the accompaniment of spirituals, jazz, blues, African percussion, and chanting.

Perhaps nothing better demonstrates how the 1960s and 1970s poets enriched the legacy they received from Langston Hughes and Sterling Brown than the contrast between Sanchez's reading/performance of her poetry and Langston Hughes's readings of his. Fortunately, literary archives provide us with a few recordings of Langston Hughes's readings of his poetry. They are rather dry and casual with very little attempt at dramatic effect. Influenced by Hughes's transformation of blues and jazz into literary art, the black poets of the 1960s enriched this poetic legacy by extending the transformation so that the performance of the poem itself becomes a jazz or blues song or an African chant. Although Amiri Baraka, Eugene Redmond, Jayne Cortez, Quincy Troupe, and Nikki Giovanni all deliver spellbinding readings of their poetry, Sonia Sanchez emerges as the priestess whose performances combine music, religion, politics, and black speech so indigenously that she brings to these historical characteristics a heightened aesthetics. In her performance of any number of her poems—"Kwa mama zetu waliotuza," "Letter to Dr. Martin Luther King"—she challenges the listeners'/readers' Eurocentric perception of reality by calling on the spirits of the ancestors to heal black people's physical and psychological wounds and to enlighten their political awareness. These incantations forbid indifference or political neutrality from whites as well as blacks, but their black speech, their psychological emphases, and their origins in African culture suggest that a black audience is Sanchez's primary focus.

Even the titles of the works of the poets in the vanguard of the Black Arts Movement illustrate the writers' goal of awakening the spiritual and political consciousness of a black audience. Amiri Baraka's *Black Art/Black Magic, It's Nation Time,* Mari Evans's *Where Is All the Music?,* Carolyn Rodgers's *Song of the Blackbird,* Sonia Sanchez's *Home Coming, We a BaddDDD People, Blues Book for Blue Black Magical Women,* and Haki Madhubuti's *Think Black, Black Pride,* and *Don't Cry, Scream* reflect the momentum to which these poets used their art to expose the social, political, and psychological impediments to black well-being. To affirm their connection with their African heritage, some of these writers and those that followed changed their Euro-American names to African or Arabic names: for example, Don L. Lee became Haki R. Madhubuti, Rolland Snellings became Askia Touré, Jewell Latimore became Johari Amini, Paulette Williams became Ntozake Shange, and LeRoi Jones became Amiri Baraka.

Perhaps no poet demonstrates the presence of black music, black speech, politics, and religion in contemporary African American poetry more effectively than Amiri Baraka's son Ras Baraka. Because most of the poets who came into the limelight in the 1960s continue to dominate the African American poetic arena, Ras Baraka, twenty-five years old and already an accomplished poet, and his generation both confirm the irrevocable influence and contributions of his father's generation to African American poetry and presage the direction of that poetry. The 1990s have so far produced five anthologies of African American poetry: Michael S. Harper and Anthony Walton's *Every Shut Eye Ain't Asleep: An Anthology of Poetry by African-Americans since 1945,* Keith Gilyard's *Spirit & Flame: An An-*

thology of Contemporary African American Poetry, E. Ethelbert Miller's *In Search of Color Everywhere: A Collection of African-American Poetry,* Clarence Major's *The Garden Thrives: Twentieth-Century African-American Poetry,* and Kevin Powell and Ras Baraka's *In the Tradition: An Anthology of Young Black Writers.*

The title of Powell and Ras Baraka's anthology clearly distinguishes it from the others, which present the works of older, better-known poets. At even a slight glance, the typography of the poems in *In the Tradition* substantiates the virtuosic (to use one of Stephen Henderson's terms) free verse that best describes the arrangement of black poetry in the 1990s. Ras Baraka's poem "In the Tradition Too," dedicated to Amiri and Amina Baraka, powerfully recalls a tradition in African American poetry in which politics and aesthetics are inextricably interwoven.

Using the title of one of his father's well-known poems, "In the Tradition," Ras Baraka's "In the Tradition Too" (which is much like Amiri Baraka's poem "Black Art") is a poetic manifesto that uses black political and literary history as sources for black strength and survival. This "African war song" includes references to various types of African American music, such as spirituals, blues, and jazz; references to rap artists, such as Flavor Flav and Public Enemy, Big Daddy Kane, and Melody; references to rap recordings, like "Rebel without a Pause" and "Stop the Violence"; and references to reggae musicians, such as Bob Marley and Steele Pulse. While the spirituals and blues are creative outcomes of the pain of racial oppression, jazz, reggae, and rap evolve as rhythmical and vocal attacks on racial oppression, imperialism, capitalism, and the like. Ras Baraka places these musicians in a "tradition of workers and fighters" whose resistance joins forces with literary fighters, such as his father, W. E. B. Du Bois, Toni Cade Bambara, Toni Morrison, Sonia Sanchez, Langston Hughes, James Baldwin, and his own mother, Amina.

Echoing Haki Madhubuti's latest collection of poetry, *Killing Memory, Seeking Ancestors,* and serving the same purpose as Sanchez's chants, Ras Baraka's poem announces that the poet pays the debt of memory to all those who were enslaved and lynched. Typical of black poetry of the sixties, "In the Tradition Too" catalogues those situations and black figures whose lives have made an impact in the struggle against racism both nationally and internationally. He includes Tawana Brawley and Howard Beach, Malcolm X, Medgar Evers, Martin Luther King Jr., Patrice Lumumba, Fred Hampton, George Jackson, and Kwame Nkrumah. This catalogue of national and international figures reflects the poet's communal, global, or

Pan-African aim of bringing the worldwide black family together under one umbrella of identification and resistance.

The poem ends on a note of resistance and the commitment to building heritage:

> I wanna be blackness, I wanna be peace.
> I wanna be Amiri and Amina too. I wanna
> be both of you! And I will carry the
> tradition on in good times and bad and build
> and create, create and build, build and create
> create and build . . . .
>   THE KLAN WILL DIE AND
>   BLACK PEOPLE WILL BE VICTORIOUS! (89)

Reminiscent of both the "Black Power" and "Black is Beautiful" slogans of the 1960s, these last lines demonstrate the message of the entire poem. The son of two of the most well known figures in African American poetic history, Ras Baraka pays tribute to his mother and father—his literary ancestors—who bequeathed him a tradition in which poet and political activist are one. Ras Baraka's use of anadiplosis (the repetition of the last word of one clause at the beginning of the following clause) and polysyndeton (use of many conjunctions) extends the length of lines so that form and meaning are parallel. He and the lines build heritage.

This Pan-African heritage focuses inward exclusively on black people. The Klan becomes a symbol of all those forces that conspire to ignore, distort, or destroy the multifaceted black tradition. If black people worldwide are to be victorious as the poet suggests at the end, then all areas of African American intellectual, political, social, and psychological lives must be directed toward black survival. A major source of strength and inspiration, the continuum in African American poetry, from Phillis Wheatley to Ras Baraka, reflects the interrelationship of black speech (*Bantu*), music (*Ndungu*), religion (*Nganga*), and politics (*Nkodi*) as poetic references.

Notes

1. Benston, 165.
2. Ibid., 164.
3. Ibid., 182–83.

4. Madhubuti, 21–34, 21.
5. Redding, 108–9.
6. Holloway, 1–19, 9.
7. Ibid., 9.
8. Ibid., 152.
9. Nketia, 21.
10. Henderson, 192.
11. All poems quoted from Davis, Redding, and Joyce with the exception of "In the Tradition." Only page numbers are cited.

Works Cited

Baraka, Amiri, and Larry Neal. *Black Fire: An Anthology of Afro-American Writing*. New York: William Morrow, 1968.

Baraka, Ras. "In the Tradition Too." In *In the Tradition: An Anthology of Young Black Writers*, ed. Kevin Powell and Ras Baraka. New York: Writers & Readers, 1992.

Benston, Kimberly. "Performing Blackness: Re/Placing Afro-American Poetry." In *Afro-American Literary Study in the 1990s*, ed. Houston A. Baker Jr. and Patricia Redmond. Chicago: University of Chicago Press, 1989.

Davis, Arthur P., Saunders Redding, and Joyce A. Joyce, eds. *The New Cavalcade: African-American Writing from 1760 to the Present*. Vol. 1. Washington, D.C.: Howard University Press, 1991.

Dunbar, Paul Laurence. "An Ante-Bellum Sermon." In Davis, Redding, and Joyce.

Henderson, Stephen. *Understanding the New Black Poetry: Black Speech and Black Music as Poetic References*. New York: Morrow, 1975.

Holloway, Joseph. "The Origins of African-American Culture." In *Africanisms in American Culture*, ed. Holloway. Bloomington: Indiana University Press, 1990.

Honey, Maureen. *Shadowed Dreams: Women's Poetry of the Harlem Renaissance*. New Brunswick, N.J.: Rutgers University Press, 1989.

Hughes, Langston. "The Cat and the Saxophone"; "High to Low"; "Low to High"; "The Negro Speaks of Rivers." In Davis, Redding, and Joyce.

Kinnaman, Keneth, and Richard Barksdale. *Black Writers of America*. New York: Macmillan, 1972.

Madhubuti, Haki. "Haki Madhubuti (Don L. Lee)." *A Capsule Course in Black Poetry Writing*. Detroit: Broadside, 1975.

Nketia, Kwabena. *The Music of Africa*. New York: W. W. Norton, 1974.

Randall, Dudley. *Black Poets: A New Anthology*. New York: Bantam, 1971.

Redding, Saunders. *To Make a Poet Black*. Chapel Hill: University of North Carolina Press, 1939. Rpt. Ithaca: Cornell University Press, 1988.

Wheatley, Phillis. "To the University of Cambridge, in New England." In Davis, Redding, and Joyce.

The Ballad, the Hero, and the Ride: A Reading of Sterling A. Brown's *The Last Ride of Wild Bill*

M A R K   A .   S A N D E R S

IN 1975 ONE OF THE MOST AGGRESSIVE PROPONENTS of the Black Arts Movement, Broadside Press, published *The Last Ride of Wild Bill and Eleven Narrative Poems*, Sterling A. Brown's final collection. As he points out in his preface, Dudley Randall had been requesting, for some time, permission from Brown to reissue much of his poetry; Randall was especially concerned that *Southern Road* was out of print and therefore largely unavailable to a new generation of highly politicized readers. But Brown's eye was on a new configuration of older works—most of them not found in *Southern Road*—and a new poem to introduce the collection.

Broadside, a press very much involved in the heated racial politics of the late sixties and early seventies, by definition sought out writers who directly engaged the various ideologies of Black Power and Black Arts. It serves as testament to Brown's longevity and insight that such a press would aggressively pursue a figure much less preoccupied with the immediate polemic than with the continuum of cultural aesthetics. But Brown's enduring applicability is not inconsistent with the times, for throughout the civil rights movement and the subsequent Black Power movement, Brown was lionized for his strident defense of grassroots folk and for his astute appraisal of African American culture. As an immensely popular teacher at Howard University, he served as mentor to a number of future political leaders— Stokely Carmichael (Kwame Ture) being one of the most prominent—and worked as advisor to NAG, the Nonviolent Action Group. In fact, the more radical students at Howard agitated to rename the institution "Sterling Brown University."[1] And as James G. Spady, a devoted Brown admirer, aptly illustrates, Brown's poetry and politics fostered a conceptual and cultural continuum from New Negro to Black Power activist. Recalling a "magnifying reading at Howard University," featuring luminaries such as Sonia Sanchez and LeRoi Jones (Amiri Baraka), Spady reflects:

> Despite the many light bombs dropped that night it was Sterling who completely detonated the audience, old and young alike. Remember this was doing [sic] the seething sixties when some considered anyone over thirty to be an uncle tom. As a matter of fact some of Howard University's finest professors had been burned in effigy. Why were Sterling Brown's poems so enthusiastically applauded? . . . They have simplicity, they are vivid, they are often humorous, sometimes sad, more often heroic but always capable of moving the listener. They have sense and sound. Most important they are timeless. That is the reason "Old Lem" could move both my grandparents and me. And everybody knows that Jim Fox ain't easily moved.[2]

In short, both the political activists of the Black Power movement and the aestheticians of the Black Arts Movement fully embraced Brown as mentor and progenitor; in him they found a viable antecedent for their political and cultural agendas; and as such, Brown was celebrated as a Black Arts activist far ahead of his time.

Yet given the accolades and attention produced in the late sixties and early seventies, Brown's poetics stood apart from, if not in direct opposition to, the dominant aesthetics of the day. Although *Last Ride* occupies the same historical moment as BAM poets such as Nikki Giovanni and Don L. Lee, Brown continues a much older tradition focused on rural and southern idioms. By presenting the dynamics of African American culture as its own liberating agent, the poem, for Brown, does not become the polemic but an aesthetic means of celebrating essential strengths and potential. In a sense *Last Ride* is largely anachronistic: Black Arts aesthetics notwithstanding, Brown rejects the encroaching dissonance of postmodern poetics and its emphasis upon language's chronic instability. Instead, Brown harkens back to the forms and traditions that shaped his first collection. Indeed, completing a continuum beginning with *Southern Road* and advanced in *No Hiding Place*, *Last Ride* reconceptualizes African American culture in modal process. Like his previous collections, *Last Ride* explores the means by which the culture itself actualizes its own progression and propels itself toward its own visions. In this particular collection Brown cites heroism and the omnipresent heroic spirit as the catalytic agents animating African American culture. Brown's cultural heroes—figures produced by the folk and embodying their essential strengths and aspirations—singularly confront the multiple forms of white authority and its stifling influences. Through defiance, and often martyrdom, these figures reveal a vital impulse toward autonomy and self-realization. Be they perpetually rebellious or only occasionally so, all reflect a cultural will that continues to inspire defiant acts commensurate with heroism.

With Brown's emphasis on heroism in mind, understanding *Last Ride* as a book of and about ballads becomes vitally important. Brown takes the ballad, an essential medium of folk culture (a "communal art form"), and reconstructs it in a search for essential cultural strengths.[3] In this collection of ballads the process of narrating itself holds center stage; the tradition of exaggeration and tall tales fuels the collection and points to its metaphoric focus. Both the folk ballad and Brown's literary ballads take up the figure of the folk hero, but where the folk ballad validates the hero's mythic stature, *Last Ride* seeks to examine the fundamental nature of heroism—how and why it exists, and what broader meaning it imports. Brown presents an extended address of the cultural hero, invoking the conventions of lies and toasts, but goes beyond the mere appropriation of folk idioms in order to examine the essential motivations behind the hero's perpetual rebelliousness.

If heroism is predicated upon the physical act of rebellion, so too are the various iconographic forms Brown's heroes take. The badman, the renegade, the humble worker trying to do right all combine to provide an array of personas destabilizing social conventions. By creating a diversified or multidimensional face for the heroic impulse, Brown eventually makes a strong case for its ubiquitousness. Moving beyond the stasis of a single cultural image, Brown attempts to portray the cultural dynamic, the specific catalyst that prompts the culture as a whole to confront imposed limitations. In short, *Last Ride,* moving through various avatars of the heroic spirit, asserts the ubiquitous yet often hidden heroic impulse—an impulse anterior to the heroic act yet gesturing toward numerous possibilities. Thus Brown's ballads seek to locate power and potential implicit yet dormant within the culture.

This gesture toward hidden potential fixes the hero in the broadest metaphoric spheres; here the hero is an ultimately transformational figure, one alluding to liberation through reformulation of self, community, and relations with white authority. *Last Ride* begins with an examination of the hero's power to transform confining surroundings, then embarks upon a linear progression in two modes—comic and tragic—toward ever-expansive implications in transformation. Each specific face of the cultural hero reveals new possibilities, both individual and collective, culminating in Joe Meek's encompassing gesture toward the transcendent nature of heroism itself. Brown enriches the metaphoric development of heroism and its transformational potential with an intricate dialogue between comic and tragic modes. Beginning with the comic, Brown establishes the resonant folk voice. Invoking the tradition of the toast, tall tales, and hyperbole, Wild Bill, Slim Greer, and John Bias offer various forms of the exaggerated and the burlesque, but gradually acquire undertones of tragic implications. Brown effectively blurs the distinctions between the two modes, achieving a final unity in Joe Meek—a product of the tall tale yet a tragic hero of epic proportions. Thus by reformulating the mode of their representation, Brown underscores the overt transformational qualities of his heroes. On yet a more fundamental level, Brown critiques traditional balladry through his experimentation with new narrative forms. As we will see in "The Last Ride of Wild Bill," the ballad form itself serves as yet another site for Brown's invocation of liberating and rejuvenating potential in heroic resistance.

Brown achieves both formal and thematic unity through his central metaphor, "the ride." In practical terms the trope refers to narrative itself, both the episodic progression toward resolution and the formal transformation that underscores such a progression. As a central metaphor, the trope invokes the liberating possibilities inherent in the heroic act. The superlative romantic gesture of freedom and autonomy, the ride signals the broadest symbolic movement from the palpability of the physical act itself to its expansive metaphoric implications.

Thus Brown introduces this collection of ballads and heroes with a signature poem, largely defining the tenor and import of the book. In "The Last Ride of Wild Bill" Brown concerns himself primarily with transformation itself; in terms of form, theme, action, and final metaphor, "Last Ride" points toward the power and agency of change, toward the potential in reordering and redefining oppressive circumstances, and ultimately toward the fundamental value systems that create them.

Furthermore, "Last Ride" establishes the expansive implications of the central trope—and by extension those of the entire collection—by laying claim to epic stature. As the embodiment of collective cultural aspirations and as one willing to battle forces threatening the community, Wild Bill serves as epic hero in folk form. From Wild Bill's extended and detailed journey to his descent into the underworld, the poem takes on the trappings of high epic and thus a depth and breadth in metaphoric resonance.

But even with its epic scope, "Last Ride" announces itself as a ballad in the traditional sense—"verse narratives that tell dramatic stories in conventionalized ways."[4] Yet immediately evident are the reordered conventions. Brown replaces the standard quatrain structure and its regular meter with a new form that self-consciously calls attention to its own unconventionality. In fact, Brown holds true to only the most basic tenets of balladry, often constructing for the reader a set of expectations, then systematically violating them, thereby instituting the concept of flux within the very matrix of the poem. Brown's lines range broadly in length. And though most lines consist of two or three stresses, the stresses themselves constantly move; so too, quasi-conventional lines seldom succeed each other for more than two or three lines, again breaking a regularity that is tenuous at best. For example, "Challenge" begins the poem with a six-line stanza proclaiming volatility and flux as major organizing principles for the poem:

> The new chief of police
> Banged his desk
> Called in the force, and swore
> That the number-running game was done
> And Wild Bill
> Would ride no more. (121)[5]

Here Brown demonstrates his range in length of line and his perpetually mobile stresses. That he consistently uses masculine endings and rhymes "swore" and "more" serves to create some sense of regularity. Throughout the poem these nearly sporadic reminders of regularity (hard stops, masculine endings, and occasional rhymes) strain to harness the potentially discursive energies of the poem, strain, in effect, to hold the poem back from free verse, and thus from a full departure from folk oral and musical traditions. Yet all the while Brown utilizes short lines, enjambment, and irregular stresses in order to sustain a sense of rapid movement, almost a sense of tumbling.

As a result of this perpetual tension between regularity and irregularity, between conformity and freedom, the larger metaphoric implications of poetic form come into focus. Here Brown's self-conscious denial of formal expectations stresses the palpable and symbolic importance of transformation. By consistently breaking convention, and thus refusing to meet standard expectations, Brown underscores Wild Bill's significance beyond the immediate poem. As motion and progression emerge from the very matrix of the poem, they contribute directly to the effect of the narrative and the symbolism of the ride. Perhaps this symbolism goes so far as to suggest Brown's own transformational powers in his revision of Western balladry in order to create new conceptual space for black agency.

As the narrative structure begins to give itself over to metaphor, it gives rise to the progression of the ride—the physical movement across the city and the symbolic agitation against confinement. In both senses the ride serves as transformative act with Wild Bill looming as the symbolic figure embodying potential in transformation. As a folk form of the epic hero, the badman, Wild Bill possesses special qualities in subverting and transforming the status quo. Stressing such abilities, Brown devotes a conspicuously large section of the poem to the reaction of the community rather than focusing strictly on the dramatic events of the chase. The wit and humor with which the various communities respond to the central conflict reveal the essential power behind Wild Bill and his ride:

> These were the people
> That the bug had bit,
> Betting now
> On a sure-fire hit:
> Kiwanians, and Rotarians
> Daughters, Sons, Cousins
> Of Confederate Veterans,
> The Kleagle of the Ku Klux Klan,
> The Knights of the Pantry
> And Dames of the Pan,
> The aristocrats, the landed gentry,
> The cracker, and the jigaboo
> Hoi-polloi
> All seemed to think well
> Of their boy,
> Were eager to lay
> Their bucks on Bill.
>
> On Druid Hill
> An old-stock cavalier tried to bet
> His yard-boy part of his back-pay due
> But Mose he believed in Wild Bill too. (123–24)

Here, with much ironic humor, Brown allies groups that ordinarily would be diametrically opposed by class and racial divisions. White/black, rich/ poor, powerful/powerless, Wild Bill effectively dismantles these oppositions fundamental to the very meaning of the community. In subverting the status quo, he creates new conceptual ground where the rudimentary potential for redefinition lies.

Much of this potential rests on Wild Bill's symbolic meaning, assigned by the newly united community. Even beyond the prospect of making money from his triumph, the community at large embraces Wild Bill as a repository of values far more significant than monetary gain. As "their boy," he implicates an expansive iconographic field incorporating the American badman, renegade, and hero. Defining himself on his own terms and thus occupying conceptual space outside of cultural conventions, Wild Bill invokes fundamental American myths celebrating the frontiersman, independence, and unbridled individuality; and it is precisely his ability to embody these mythic precepts that draws the admiration of the community.

Wild Bill states:

> "Ride my route
> Again today;
> Start at noon,
> End at three.
> Guess it will have
> To be you and me." (125)

He here sets conformity and self-reliance in practical and symbolic opposition. In doing so, he does not so much threaten the community as uphold its fundamental beliefs. Here Wild Bill as outlaw is not simply a metaphor for disruption, the trickster destabilizing the oppressive rhetoric of authority;[6] to the contrary, he looms as a sanctioned representative of agency. More than checking the forces of authority, he agitates for space within the community for both freedom and independence.

Brown completes this notion of liberating transformation through an apotheosis redefining a highly symbolic space. Although Wild Bill lands in hell, the final site and evidence of his transformational abilities, his hell is a reconstructed one that reverses the assumed value of temporal and permanent life:

The devils rushed at him
In a swarm,
And the cool
Wild Bill
Grew awful warm.
It looked like he'd
Broke up a meeting;
But this was the Convocation's
Greeting:
They climbed all over
His running board,
"Wild Bill, Wild Bill!"
Their shouting roared
And rang through all the streets of Hell:

"Give us the number,
Wild Bill,
Tell us
What fell!" (135)

Underestimating his own prowess, Wild Bill expects the Judeo-Christian notion of hell, one in which he will pay for a life of sin through eternal torment. But instead he finds a transformed hell that ultimately affirms the qualities for which he was killed. Here the final reversal relies on the juxtaposition of earth and hell. As the devils embrace Wild Bill as hero, earth and temporal reality become the site of perpetual persecution; conversely, Wild Bill's reconstructed hell then becomes the final site of resolution. In this apotheosis he expands as metaphor to represent a myriad of regenerative transformations. By subverting traditional and confining oppositions, by militating against oppressive authority, by living and dying according to self-defined principles, Wild Bill points toward a range of possibilities that lie beyond stasis and conventionality.

Thus by creating conceptual space for himself, he also points toward the possibilities suggested by the ensuing heroes and ballads. In response to this potential suggested through comedy, "He Was a Man" pursues potential in tragic representation. Returning to conventional balladry, Brown addresses the sobering brutality of folk life and the exorbitant costs of self-assertion. The poem, like "Last Ride," works through ironic inconsistencies that conspire to defeat heroism; yet Brown meticulously constructs Will as the embodiment of social stability, one firmly grounded within the community, and one defined by stabilizing notions of work and family. As such, Brown affirms the fundamental ties that supposedly hold cultures together. In order to add pathos to Wild Bill's stature, the speaker declares that these attributes disqualify Will as hero:

> He wasn't nobody's great man,
>   He wasn't nobody's good,
> Was a po'boy tried to get from life
>   What happiness he could,
> He was a man, and they laid him down. (136)

Brown pits Will's agency against that of the community; in these tragic circumstances Will's act of self-assertion in self-defense is met with a greater act of assertion. Killing a man in self-defense, he willfully accepts the truth of his actions—"Didn't catch him in no manhunt." But even more boldly the whites "Didn't hide themselves, didn't have no masks, / Didn't wear no Ku Klux hoods." And with a final ironic twist, at the site of social justice they destroy his claim to autonomy. Clearly, here Brown calls into question the concept of justice and ultimately deems the term void of meaning as the sheriff and coroner decline to pursue it. Thus irony becomes tragic as allegedly just officials turn murderous, killing one wholly in support of the community they vow to protect.

Brown's elliptical style also contributes to the cathartic force of the poem. As opposed to "Last Ride," which provides an abundance of detail and celebrates the process of telling the tale, "He Was a Man" gains much of its force through omission. Simply the facts of the lynching speak for themselves; and only the one-line incremental refrain allows for much editorial comment. As the refrain connotes a fatigued and tragic inevitability, it also identifies the essential vitality of the hero, a vitality that exists beyond physical life, a vitality that in fact emerges through martyrdom. That Will was a man, a black man no less, in the scheme of this poem, and within the broader politics of the South, demands his destruction; yet his destruction validates his agency. For both Will and Wild Bill, much of their heroism derives from the willingness to die for their convictions and from the culture's compulsion to curtail such rebellious assertions of self. Although the individual impulse toward self-assertion and the societal impulse to deny black selfhood collide to destroy the physical hero, they also conspire to create the symbol and thus the sustenance of the omnipresent spirit. Therefore the poem laments Will's loss but implicitly validates an immortality that will manifest itself in ensuing poems.

As this second poem inaugurates the theme of tragic representation, it looks forward to "Sam Yancey" and the further extension of the tragic mode. "Sam Yancey," "Crispus Attucks McKoy," and "Break of Day" all represent the hero as liberating potential tragically cut short. In each poem the hero embodies essential strengths common to the culture yet threatening to white authority. In each instance, in the classic mode of the hero, he asserts these strengths, strives to defend them, and ultimately dies as a result of his agency. Martyrdom serves as the supreme affirmation of heroism, where superlative sacrifice in defense of self and culture ostensibly points toward an irrepressible continuity in heroic spirit. Each time the physical avatar is struck down another manifestation of the spirit appears, insuring sustained agitation for freedom and independence.

Having established this strident sense of agency, in both comic and tragic modes, Brown presents the Slim Greer series, which examines both the strengths and limitations of the comic hero. Following "Sam Yancey," Brown moved away from the high price of heroism to complete the Slim Greer series and to explore humor's potential. In 1932 Brown first presented Slim Greer in *Southern Road,* with only the first three poems—"Slim Greer," "Slim Lands a Job?," and "Slim in Atlanta." With this configuration Greer clearly conforms to the standard definition of the trickster, consistently subverting white authority through wit and humor. His introductory poem, "Slim Greer," sketches his persona and demonstrates both his ability to circumvent social restrictions and his ability to use them for his own gain. Beyond the immediate action of the drama, though, Slim's ability as comic figure reveals his superlative gifts in absurdity and burlesque. His outlandishness and the circumstances in which he finds himself acquire dramatic force, as Greer uses his rhetorical skills to diffuse oppressive situations, transforming them into moments of celebration.

It is within this context that the first three Slim Greer poems add a humorous dimension to the master trope, "the road" in *Southern Road.* But by completing the series and placing all five poems in *Last Ride,* Brown implies critically different connotations. First, by moving away from high burlesque, the later two poems incorporate more ominous implications for both Greer's character and his ability to affect his surroundings.

Furthermore, in relation to the broader signifying field of *Last Ride,* the Slim Greer series exposes the limitations of comic representation and thereby alludes to its final subsumption in "The Ballad of Joe Meek."

Following "Slim in Atlanta," "Slim Hears 'The Call'" continues the mode of burlesque, but raises serious questions concerning Slim's use of his transformative powers. Simply the title stressing "the call" questions its ultimate meaning, anticipating an ironic call to make money rather than to serve God. Furthermore, "Slim Hears 'The Call'" deviates from Brown's standard presentation in that it is Greer's own narrative. Rather than a third-person narrative celebrating Greer's ability to outwit whites and to undermine potentially oppressive circumstances, Greer tells his own story of victimizing the powerless. The poem begins by invoking the tradition of exaggeration and hyperbole; and much of its amusing quality stems from Greer's mastery of style and form. In the first two stanzas Greer recreates his adversity in order to elicit laughter, not pity; rather than illustrating the severity of his condition, he better demonstrates his rhetorical skills and mastery of form, a mastery implicitly asserting control over much more than oratorical tropes:

> Down at the barbershop
> Slim had the floor,
> "Ain't never been so
> Far down before.
>
> "So ragged, I make a jaybird
> About to moult,
> Look like he got on gloves
> An'a overcoat.
>
> "Got to walk backwards
> All de time
> Jes' a-puttin' on front
> Wid a bare behime.

Indeed, Greer's display of rhetorical expertise serves as prelude to his mastery of a cultural form, "de bishopric"; thus his tale is one of apprenticeship in preparation for his next money-making scheme. Greer retells, with humorous irony, the mercenary practices of a fraudulent clergyman; that his friend misrepresents himself, steals from his congregation, and ultimately undermines the religious imperative of his position, for Greer constitutes the epitome of cunning and shrewdness. Greer's admiration ultimately is for the ability to control, manipulate, and make money with the least amount of effort:

> So here he was de head man
> Of de whole heap—
> Wid dis solemn charge dat
> He had to keep:
>
> "A passel of Niggers
> From near an' far
> Bringin' in de sacred bucks
> Regular."

And Greer ends his apprenticeship and his amusing tale with a resounding endorsement of this enterprise, and with an embracing call for everyone, so inclined, to do as he does. On the one hand, Greer successfully promotes the same persona celebrated in the previous three poems; he is witty, resourceful, and above all farcically entertaining. But as he shifts the focus of his talents away from the empowered to the dispossessed, he begins to work against the iconography previously assigned him. He no longer ridicules and dismantles figures and forces of oppression; he now reinforces them. Clearly, Brown pokes fun at the disreputable figures in the African American clergy; clear enough too is the attempt to add levity to the sobering reality of African American exploitation in one of its most important institutions. But in terms of Greer's development, and in terms of his broader implications within the collection, "Slim Hears 'The Call'" constitutes a serious departure from the established metaphoric development.

Greer's willful exultation of his own ability to exploit begins to indicate the limitations of burlesque. At this point the mode of the tale subsumes the overt politics of the content; humor begins to serve its own ends—pure entertainment—and thus divorces itself from a broader political context.

This implication, that the very form Greer represents necessarily embodies severe limitations in terms of historical vision, receives further treatment in the last poem of the series. More so than "Slim Hears 'The Call,'" "Slim in Hell" entertains a number of potentially sobering ironies, while sustaining the tradition of the burlesque. The premise of the poem—Greer in an odd situation—automatically advances the comic mode of the series. But given the comic conventions, that Greer finds hell to be in truth the South strikes a poignantly accurate note. As St. Peter corroborates Greer's encroaching suspicions, comedy quickly becomes satire:

> Then Pete say, "You must
> Be crazy, I vow,
> Where'n hell dja think Hell *was,*
> Anyhow?

This acerbic indictment of the South and its racial politics works in and of itself to darken the implications of the poem. But that the poem ends, not with the realization of such a harsh reality but with Greer's expulsion from heaven due to his limited vision, shifts the focus from the injustice of the South to Greer's misunderstanding of its ramifications:

> "Git on back to de yearth,
> Cause I got de fear
> You'se a leetle too dumb,
> Fo' to stay up here."

As a product of the South, and as one having resisted many of its stifling forces, Greer fails to perceive the literally cosmic implications of racial oppression. In the broadest of religious schemes, hell and Dixie hold the same literal meaning that its victims are expected to understand. That Greer fails calls into question his understanding of his own gifts and the implications of their application. Although he perceives and fights the oppression directed specifically at him, he does not or cannot read beyond his own circumstances, nor does he invoke an appreciation for a continuum of oppressive forces. Simply put, Greer exists in a historical vacuum, employing only ad hoc measures of resistance. That Brown ends the series with Greer's expulsion from heaven due to his misreading implicates the entirety of his progression and finally raises the issue of his limitations. As the trickster fails to see or act beyond his own self-interest—thus he perpetually assumes a defensive rather than offensive political position—Brown begins to circumscribe the comic mode of the hero within a limited metaphoric and political sphere, limited at least relative to the final expansion of the tragic hero and his import.

Brown responds to the subtle but serious encroachment upon Slim Greer's levity with an unequivocal canonization of a figure fully aware of the political imperatives of his circumstances. "Crispus Attucks McKoy" explores the transcendent heroic spirit, a spirit completely dedicated to both individual and collective liberation. As in "Last Ride," Brown creates a dramatically new ballad form in order to stress the monumental precedent McKoy represents. Yet in contrast to the continual changes in "Last Ride," the form of "Crispus Attucks McKoy" is uniform and immediately self-evident. Brown's regimented eight-line stanzas, complete with regular rhyme and meter, first create a strident sense of regularity and clarity. As the speaker asserts an uncompromising vision of heroism, so too does the form affirm a sense of strength and assurance. Equally as important, but somewhat less obvious, Brown borders on formal rigidity in order to emphasize a consistent historical progression linking past, present, and future. Just as each stanza succeeds the previous one in a predictable fashion—almost marching toward the inevitable apotheosis in martyrdom—that "The soul of our hero / Goes marching on" ultimately affirms the inevitable progression of the heroic spirit.

Following the profundity of martyrdom, Brown advances the exchange between comic and tragic, presenting John Bias in "A Bad, Bad Man." Setting "A Bad, Bad Man" against "Break of Day," John Bias serves as the farcical antithesis to the self-determined tragic hero, while Big Jess epitomizes the tragic martyr. Where Big Jess completes the tragic lineage begun with Sam Yancey, Joe Meek picks up both strands of representation in order to provide the broadest array of transformational possibilities for both kinds of heroes.

As the first and last stanzas indicate, Brown frames Joe Meek's ballad within two illustrations suggesting a wealth of meanings residing just below surface appearances. "The Ballad of Joe Meek," as Brown's final representation of the hero, affirms the ubiquitous nature of the heroic spirit and thus completes Wild Bill's transformational ride. Joe Meek becomes "Joe Hero"—a compelling combination of ordinariness and extraordinariness—championing the cause of the downtrodden and illustrating the heroic potential lurking in the most unlikely individuals.

Stressing the intrinsic meaning hidden behind deceptive surfaces, Brown constructs the poem around the tension between the external and internal, between superficial illusion and permanent meaning—"You cain't never tell / How far a frog will jump, / When you jes' see him planted / On his big broad rump." In a conversation with Clark White, Brown comments:

"The Joe Meek piece is an ideal peace and it's [*sic*] meaning is: don't believe the appearance of my people by the way they look . . . with Joe Meek the dramatic turn was the injustice. . . . we can take so much and then take no more." [7] Initially the form itself invokes and advances the absurdity developed in the Slim Greer series. The short lines and regular quatrains convey a light homespun folk voice that seems to indicate yet another tall tale in the burlesque. Yet the form and its comic implications belie the intrinsically political ramifications of Joe Meek's narrative. In sharp contrast to its form, the poem's content follows the basic pattern of hero construction initiated in "Last Ride." The solitary figure, stridently committed to his own principles, dares to combat the established order bent on compromising those principles. Of course, this battle ends in martyrdom; thus in terms of fundamental patterns, Joe Meek echoes Wild Bill's implications and completes a lineage including Will, Sam Yancey, Crispus McKoy, and Big Jess.

Thus we find that beneath the surface of the comic voice and form lie both the tragedy of potential destroyed and the promise of transformation. In this sense "The Ballad of Joe Meek" culminates the exploration of the heroic nature and finds its potential omnipresent. The title itself constructs Joe as the most unlikely candidate for martyrdom. Mild mannered and conciliatory to a fault, his fundamental disposition would usually allow the status quo to exist undisturbed and unchallenged. Yet given a catalyst for transformation, Meek becomes the epitome of the cultural hero. The catalyst here, heat, promotes aberrant behavior in beetles, pet bunnies, and babies, but exposes in Meek an essential and permanent nature. That "Joe didn't feel / So agreeable" is certainly a direct result of the heat, but after "The sun had gone down" and "The air it was cool," Joe continues his defiant behavior. In both cases, Joe's actions serve as manifestations of a latent heroic nature. In a typically mild manner he asks the officers if they had done "just right," and asks at his death for "one kindness / Fo' I die." These gestures and his willingness to battle an entire police department transform his "meekness" into strength and conviction, and finally reveal his heroic essence.

Finally affirming his heroism, Brown places Meek in direct reference to John Henry:

> "Won't be here much longer
>   To bother you so,
> Would you bring me a drink of water
>   Fo' I go?" (151)

Just as John Henry asks for a "Cool drink of water 'fore I die," Joe Meek asks for the same practical and symbolic solace. In a mode similar to Big Boy Davis, of "Odyssey of Big Boy" fame, Joe Meek invokes the tradition that holds the permanent meaning for both his life and death. Where Big Boy Davis invokes the rhetorical form of his idol John Henry, Joe Meek quotes him directly, attempting to achieve a similar affinity. Furthermore, Brown assigns Joe a greater degree of metaphoric weight by linking his martyrdom, and the vision of justice his martyrdom represents, to that of John Henry, perhaps the broadest symbol of black cultural agency.

In addition, Brown lends even greater resonance to his encompassing notion of transformation through the conversion of comic into tragic. "The Ballad of Joe Meek" serves as an apt conclusion to a collection of ballads and heroes in that it combines the two dominant modes of portrayal in order to utilize the most expressive traits of each. This ballad reinvokes the tradition of tall tales, but as we have already seen, Brown calls into question the broader scope of the comic hero's abilities. As Slim Greer makes explicit, neither he nor Wild Bill sees or acts beyond his own self-interest. Moving beyond the confines of self-concern is the tragic hero's task, particularly Joe Meek's, to exercise agency in a public sphere, to act on behalf of the surrounding community; in doing so, the tragic hero extends the nearly limitless potential of transformation to incorporate acts of liberation. Thus, both in mode and metaphor, Joe Meek successfully subsumes the comic hero and reconstructs him as a public agent for the greater community.

Returning to the framing notion of deceptive appearance, Joe Meek's tale ends alluding to the heroic possibilities lying dormant in unlikely places, thus ending a collection that celebrates the folk hero by ultimately democratizing the figure. Here, finally, Brown's notion of heroic transformation achieves its broadest scope. With Joe Meek as central metaphor for the collection, Brown creates conceptual space for the reader. Joe the commoner validates the patently unromantic, yet he stresses that we all are heir to the legacy John Henry and Wild Bill represent. As the collection ends, "The soul of our hero / Goes marching on"; unimpeded by the murders of specific figures, the idea and symbol of the hero remain immortal and continue to point toward future incarnations.

Indeed, by employing a number of cultural icons—the badman, the renegade, the humble worker trying to do right—and various ballad forms, the collection creates a diversified or multidimensional face for the heroic impulse, one perpetually agitating against social conventions and white authority. The ride, formally and metaphorically, invokes progression, movement from specific to general, from renegade (and therefore aberration) to commoner, symbolically embracing all. Through this movement beyond the stasis of a singular cultural image, Brown attempts to portray a dynamic that prompts the culture as a whole to confront imposed limitations. In short, Brown's ballads seek to locate power and potential latent within the culture. Having done so, the collection has discovered and affirmed an essential means by which African American culture attempts to realize its own liberation.

Notes

1. Gabbin, 59.
2. Spady, 35.
3. Smith, 396.
4. Laws, xi.
5. These poems, first published in Brown's *The Last Ride of Wild Bill and Eleven Narrative Poems,* are, with the exception of "Slim Hears 'The Call,'" available in *The Collected Poems of Sterling A. Brown.* When citing from this collection only the page numbers in text will be used hereafter.
6. Jackson suggests that the prototypical badman serves as a "challenge to hegemony," 31.
7. White, 114–15.

Works Cited

Brown, Sterling A. *The Collected Poems of Sterling A. Brown.* Sel. Michael S. Harper. New York: Harper, 1980.

———. *The Last Ride of Wild Bill and Eleven Narrative Poems.* Detroit: Broadside, 1975.

Gabbin, Joanne V. *Sterling A. Brown: Building the Black Aesthetic Tradition.* Westport: Greenwood, 1985.

Jackson, Bruce. *"Get Your Ass in the Water and Swim like Me": Poetry from Black Oral Tradition.* Cambridge: Harvard University Press, 1974.

Laws, Malcolm, Jr. *The British Literary Ballad: A Study in Poetic Imagination.* Carbondale: Southern Illinois University Press, 1972.

Smith, Gary. "The Literary Ballads of Sterling A. Brown." *CLA Journal* 32 (1989): 393–409.

Spady, James G. "Ah! To Have Lived in the Days of That 'Senegambian,' Sterling Brown." *Sterling A. Brown: A UMUM Tribute.* Ed. Black History Month Museum Committee. Philadelphia: Black History Museum UMUM Publishers, 1982.

White, Clark. "Sterling Brown, 'The ole sheep, they know the road . . . Young lambs gotta find the way': An Essay Dedicated to ole 'skeeta Brown." Sterling A. Brown UMUM Tribute. Ed. Black History Month Museum Committee. Philadelphia: Black History Museum UMUM Publishers, 1982. Black History Month Museum Committee.

Illocutionary Dimensions of Poetry: Lee's "A Poem to Complement Other Poems"

J E R R Y   W .   W A R D   J R .

POSTSCRIPT IN THE FOREGROUND:

"Furious Flower: A Revolution in African American Poetry" was a landmark moment in late twentieth-century discourse on the literature and literacy of black Americans. The exchanges among poets, scholars, critics, and students authenticated the primacy of speech, of talking with other people about how languages reshape thought and lives. When I introduced the critics' roundtable on theory, I was obligated to mention that poetry "may well demand that theory be cognizant of what its speculative strategies may be responsible for; it may demand of critical theory a critical honesty." Such honesty, for me, includes presenting again this paper, first published in the spring 1977 issue of *JuJu: Research Papers in Afro-American Studies*. Offering it as a historical document, I have reprinted it without changes in content or documentation, with minor changes in format to fit this volume. The essay is a segment of the past brought into the present for future inspection, a template for critical creation. Pied Pipers of the postmodern can and should expose the limits of how I oriented theory in an act of topical reading. They can critique the essential value of the performance and construct more sophisticated models for applying speech act theory in considerations of the poet, the text, the reader, and the contextualizing environments.

The study of literature might profit if more attention were given to speech acts embodied in prose and poetry. Literature is an act of speech, despite the accumulated criticism that argues otherwise. Like speech, literature requires minimal linguistic units, a lexicon and grammar, and at least one person as a producer. There is reason to believe that the procedures used in understanding literature are identical with those used in understanding everyday speech.[1] While it is valid to maintain distinctions between the language of literature and the language of ordinary speech, excessive discrimination promotes the kind of literary analysis that is ahistorical and divorced from what happens when we engage literature.[2] A more adequate kind of literary analysis can be derived from using aspects of speech act theory, dependent as that theory is on empirical observations about acts of language.

Although philosophers and grammarians have been aware for many years that grammar alone fails to explain the contractual relations implicit in discourse, the Oxford philosopher J. L. Austin was the first to make systematic explanations about the conditions required for successful spoken communication. Delivered as the William James Lectures at Harvard in 1955, Austin's examination of action in linguistic usage was published posthumously in 1962 as *How to Do Things with Words*.[3]

Starting with premises about the function of utterances in communication, Austin was able to construct a performance-based theory of language. A specific formulation of speech acts, based on his contrast of "constative" utterances and "performative" utterances, is the hub of his theory. According to Austin, three kinds of speech acts, interrelated by action, exist in communication.

1. Locutionary acts: speaking, the simple uttering of speech sounds
2. Illocutionary acts: what the speaker does *in* speaking, e.g., asking a question, making a promise, giving a command
3. Perlocutionary acts: what the speaker does *by* speaking, the consequences of speaking, e.g., persuading, inciting, appeasing[4]

Austin devoted careful attention to illocutionary acts and to the rules that govern a successful performance of asking a question or making a promise. Austin proposed six conditions. Richard Ohmann, who has done significant work in adapting speech act theory to literary analysis, reduced those conditions to four critical rules.

1. The circumstance must be appropriate.
2. The persons must be the right ones.

3. The speaker must have the feelings, thoughts, and intentions appropriate to his act.

4. Both parties must behave appropriately afterward.[5]

When we attempt to apply these rules in literary analysis, we encounter problems originally raised by certain qualifications in Austin's theory of speech acts.

In *How to Do Things with Words,* performative utterances that did not conform to the rules of smooth or "happy" functioning were summarily excluded from discussion. It was claimed that the language of literature occurs in special circumstances and that "language in such circumstances is in special ways—intelligibly—used not seriously, but in ways *parasitic* upon its normal use."[6] If one accepts such a distinction between literary and ordinary languages, one inadvertently assigns an abnormal character to literature. Moreover, dismissal of literary performatives on what I take to be socio-linguistic grounds is not sufficient to show the conventions governing a successful illocutionary act cannot be identical for literature and nonliterature. It may be possible that certain kinds of poetry do satisfy the conditions of explicit performative given in Austin's theory and still maintain poetic identity in the mind of the reader/hearer.

Until now, no theorist has been willing to risk the possibility that the language of literature is nonparasitic. Understanding that literature is rooted in speech acts, Richard Ohmann yet contends, "Writing (or speaking) a literary work is evidently an illocutionary performance of a special type, logically different from the seeming acts that make it up. The contract between poet and reader or hearer does not put the poet behind the various statements, rejoiners, laments, promises, or whatever, that he seemingly voices. His word is not his bond, in just this way. Perhaps the only *serious* condition of good faith that holds for literary works and their authors is that the author not give out as fact what is fiction."[7] It is clear that Ohmann believes that illocutionary acts of literature have a privileged mode of existence. African American literature and criticism, especially some of the poetry of the sixties and seventies, pose a real challenge to such a belief.

How do you analyze literature that theoretically disavows a privileged mode and seeks to locate its authenticity, in part, in social bonding and the writer's responsibility to his potential audience? In cases where poetry is governed by such a contract, how a poem functions ought to be described as transactions between utterance and receiver. The rules of smooth functioning should be derived from the transaction, for otherwise one is imposing philosophical and logical assumptions that militate against an accurate description. Understanding the illocutionary dimensions of the new black poetry depends very much on description of praxis.

Part of what made black poetry "new" was a sense that literary acts are not separate from other language acts and that poets had a special burden to speak truth to the people. Keorapetse Kgositsile's statement was typical of prevailing thought: "Poems are acts in motion. And acts, processes which involve action and reaction, lead inevitably to other acts." [8] In short, a poem might be different in style from everyday discourse; the "rules" governing its reception were thought to be those that govern the reception of all utterances made in a social context. A poem has the same illocutionary force as certain kinds of monologue, as orations, sermon, or lectures; [9] as was claimed in the 1968 trial of the *State of New Jersey v. LeRoi Jones*, a poem can have perlocutionary effects.

The context in which a poem operates is conceived as one of dynamics rather than one of stasis. Literature is no parasitic language game. It is discourse designed to inform, persuade, incite, reassure, and so forth. Many new black poets wrote with just such aims in mind and with the understanding that they and the acts (poems) they performed had consequences. They regarded their use of language as serious, and it was a serious condition of good faith that the author's "fiction" be commensurate with "fact." So in theory, and in fact, the new black poetry intensified the normal illocutionary forces.

One example of a black poem that meets all the conditions set by speech act theory for a felicitous performative is Don L. Lee's "a poem to complement other poems." [10] A brief analysis of its illocutionary dimensions reveals the applicability of speech act theory to the discussion of a poetic text. The analysis follows the order of rules given by Ohmann.

Are there any instances in which this poem in the imperative mode fails to meet the conventional procedure for the performance of a *command* or an *exhortation*? The answer seems to be *no*, for Lee's poem (utterance) is addressed to an audience for which the rhetorical stance and the message are commonplaces, i.e., the poem is directed to a black speech community by a black poet, and the determinants of felicity are those involved in black-to-black speech acts.

Just as coming to know the meaning of non-black poetic utterance depends on recognition that the utterance issues from a particular microepisteme, coming to know the meaning of black poetic utterance often depends on recognition of linguistic features having greater significance for black speakers. The definitive commentary on this point was made by Stephen E. Henderson in *Understanding the New Black Poetry*. Of course, the principle is not distributive. It cannot be applied to all poetry written by African Americans. But it is valid for poetry constructed on the premises of Lee's poem.

The first fifteen lines of Lee's poem can be understood without a special knowledge of black speech and lifestyle. However, some items in the locution evoke special meanings for a black audience.

> change.
> life if u were a match I wd light u into something beauti-
>   ful. change.
> change.
> for the better into a realreal together thing. change. from
>   a make believe
> nothing on corn meal and water. change.
> change. from the last drop to the first, maxwellhouse,
>   did. change.
> change was a programmer for IBM, thought him was a
>   brown computer. change.
> colored is something written on southern out-
>   houses. change.
> greyhound did, I mean they got rest rooms on buses.
>   change.

The illocutionary force of the poem to line fifteen is carried by the verb "change." The audience, specified in later lines, is *commanded* to change. In no sense would the lines be understood as *pleading*, for the conventional grammatical and lexical signals of pleading are not used. Lee *commands* on the grounds that change itself is desirable in a society where change is unavoidable. Thus, the references to "maxwellhouse" (a brand of coffee, a kind of advertising, an American industry) and IBM (the monopoly technology has on culture). The allusion to "southern outhouses" is regional and racial, evoking some bitter memories of public restrooms in the South. The mention of "greyhound" refers to transportation, though for some it evokes memories of Freedom Rides and humorous lines from the late comedienne Moms Mabley. The shift into nonstandard phrasing ("thought him was" instead of "he thought he was") lets the hearer know "where the speaker is coming from." I do not suppose the ungrammatical usage would be misunderstood by any audience familiar with contemporary American speech. The slang phrase in line 5 ("a realreal together thing") has currency in a variety of speech communities.

Lee's poem was written in 1969, and appropriate circumstances did exist for such an utterance. What gives the poem an illocutionary dimension appropriate only for a black speech act is the initial use of "nigger" in line 17 ("change nigger"). The word has a semantic range from endearment to damnation within the black speech community. Even within that community the meaning is determined by intonation and context. In Lee's poem, an exhortation, the black hearer would understand the word to be expressive of Lee's anger and as an attempt to remind the hearer of his commonality with other blacks in America. For a non-black to use "nigger" in expressing a *command* would be an insult that invited the performance of violence upon his or her person.

Having specified his audience, Lee *informs* the audience about political types.

> saw a nigger hippy, him wanted to be different. changed.
> saw a nigger liberal, him wanted to be different . . .
>   changed.
> saw a nigger conservative, him wanted to be different. (ll. 18–21)

He *suggests* what are some behavioral and linguistic contradictions in the black community.

> niggers don't u know that niggers are different. change.
> a doublechange. nigger wanted a double zero in front of
>   his name; a license to kill. (ll. 23–25)

And he *warns*

> niggers are licensed to be killed. change. a negro: some-
> thing pigs eat. (ll. 26–27)

He *asserts* credibility by admitting an inability ("like I / don't play / saxophone but that doesn't mean I don't dig 'trane.'") (ll. 28–30), *insisting* the inability does not preclude a shared interest in the complex jazz of John Coltrane.

Line 44 ("know the realenemy") marks a change in illocutionary function. The basis on which change is desirable is no longer natural or abstract social process; the real basis becomes racial self-interest, a matter of modifying the interactions of black and white communities. The "realenemy" is to be identified with a conditioning process in American society, a process that urges us to confuse symbol with substance. It is implicit that both blacks and whites share in this conditioning process, but Lee wishes to exploit black aspects.

> change nigger: standing on the corner, thought him was
>   cool. him still
>   standing there. it's winter time, him cool.
> change,
> know the realenemy,
> change: him wanted to be a TV star. him is. ten o'clock
>   news.
>   wanted, wanted. nigger stole some lemon & lime
>   popsicles,
>   thought them were diamonds. (ll. 46–55)

The hearer recognizes the irony intended from the juxtaposition of "cool" behavior and "cool" temperature; and from the implied distinction of "TV star" and "ten o'clock news."

The final section of the poem is a chant designed to *command* acquisition of knowledge and a specific kind of change not by rational statement but by incantation.

> know the realenemy. change. know the realenemy. change
>   yr/enemy change know the real
> change know the realenemy change, change, know the
>   realenemy, the realenemy, the real
> realenemy change your the enemies / change your change
>   your change your enemy change
> your enemy. know the realenemy, the world's enemy.
>   know them know them know them the
> realenemy change your enemy change your change
>   change change your enemy change change
> change change your change change change.
> your
> mind nigger. (ll. 64–76)

In repeating the words "know," "real," "enemy," and "change" in combinations that stress rhythmic values, Lee manipulates the hearer to concentrate on ideas of knowing, reality, opposition and danger, and transformation. The two final lines hit with maximum force. The hearer is forced to realize that Lee has all along been talking about thought patterns.

The illocutionary dimensions of "a poem to complement other poems" are dependent on the way certain lexical items register in the black speech community. They rely also on the special status habitually given to oral artistry. Lee's speech act is a variant of the rap, so his feelings, thoughts, and intentions are taken as appropriate for the public discourse in which he engages. If one insists on further evidence for intentions, it can be found in Lee's literary and political essays. Do both parties behave appropriately afterward? The behavior required is changing one's habitual assumptions. Lee kept his end of the bargain. His word was his bond. He changed his name to Haki R. Madhubuti. The audience has either changed its thinking about Lee / Madhubuti or about American society. "To participate in discourse," Ohmann suggests, "is to set in motion one's whole awareness of institutions, social ties, obligations, responsibilities, manners, rituals, ceremonies." [11] Lee / Madhubuti's poem qualifies as successful discourse because it meets, from a black perspective, the conditions of speech act theory. It is a speech act with consequences of the usual sort.

Few poems will meet *all* the requirements of speech act theory, even when the rules are based on transaction. But virtually all poems will embody speech acts. Let us take two other samples of new black poetry to indicate formal and contextual features which seem to operate in shaping statements about illocutionary dimensions. Eugene Redmond's "Parapoetics" begins

> Poetry is an *applied science:*
> Re-wrapped corner rap;
> Rootly-eloquented cellular, soulular sermons.
>
> Grit reincarnations of
> Lady Day
> Bird
> & Otis;
> and ends
>
> *Carry* your poems.
> Grit teeth. Bear labor-love pains.

Have twins and triplets.
Fertilize poem-farms with after-birth,
Before birth and dung (rearrange old words);
Study/strike tradition.

Caution to parapoets:
Carry the weight of your own poem.
. . . it's a *heavy lode.*[12]

What is performed in the illocution is *instruction* and *warning,* but the mode is more poetic than discursive. Unlike "a poem to complement other poems," "Parapoetics" invites us to do the impossible. Redmond is using this speech act to *define* the act of poetic creation and the audience. The defining is not bound by in-group reference but by what the references impute to "lode." The illocutionary dimensions here involve principles of contextual closure.

Or we might consider the second stanza of Carolyn Rodger's "IT IS DEEP."[13]

My mother, religiously girdled in
her god, slipped on some love, and
laid on my bell like a truck,
blew through my door warm wind from the south
concern making her gruff and tight-lipped
    and scared
that her "baby" was starving.
she, having learned, that disconnection results from
        non-payment of bill   (s).

The illocutionary act is that of *describing* past experience. The dictional choices and the metaphoric vision that inform this segment of a speech act involve what Stephen Henderson calls saturation: "(a) the communication of Blackness in a given situation, and (b) a sense of fidelity to the observed and intuited truth of the Black Experience."[14] Saturation necessitates the use of subliminal recognitions to build meaning, and the illocutionary dimensions of a speech act in which saturation occurs are controlled by the hearer's choosing to participate on the grounds of specialized interest or knowledge. Perhaps that is why we seek to make our nonpoetic descriptions of our own past experiences so colorful.

Henderson has demonstrated, incontrovertibly, that black speech and black music as poetic references are crucial in seeking to understand the new black poetry. But analysis should go beyond the recognition of those important features to the kind of interpretation and explanation that requires knowing what is being done *in* the acts that constitute the poetry. A poem is only one segment of the total range of discourse available to human beings. The more seriously literature is considered as an event, as an act, the more important becomes accounting for the illocutionary dimensions of that act. Recognition of the kind of illocution being performed in a specific black poem is dependent on common knowledge of the "rules" of discourse and on a special knowledge of how the "normal" rules may be modified or disregarded within the black speech community. To recognize the illocution is to recognize both that a departure from Standard American English discourse has been made and that the departure is or is not sanctioned by the historical "norms" of black speakers. The illocutionary dimensions of black poetry are relative not absolute, specific not general. And since they are grounded in similarities and differences that also occur in the illocutionary dimensions of non-black speech acts, they are to be accounted for by actual responses, not by logical, philosophical rules about how human beings should respond. Certainly, the more we know about how literature communicates, the stronger will be our defense of literary study as a practical contribution to human knowledge.

Notes

1. For an extensive discussion of this point see Hancher.

2. Brown, 56–66. Brown insists "the crucial meaning distinction, which allows us to separate poetry from everyday speech, is . . . our knowledge that an author is behind the fictive speaker and his fictive audience" (61). It is precisely this notion of "fiction" that a number of black writers eschew.

3. A fine bibliography of work in speech act theory is Marcia Eaton's "Speech Acts: A Bibliography," *Centrum* 2 (fall 1974): 57–72.

4. Austin, 94–107.

5. Ohmann, 50.

6. Austin, 22.

7. Ohmann, 53.

8. Kgositsile, 256.

9. An observation by Hirsch seems cogent: "A genre conception is constitutive of speaking as well as of interpreting, and it is by virtue of this that the genre concept sheds its arbitrary and variable character" (78).

10. I refer throughout to the text as printed in *Don't Cry, Scream*, 36–38.

11. Ohmann, 51.

12. Redmond's poem is quoted from Henderson, 371–72.

13. Rodgers, 11–12.

14. Henderson, 62.

Works Cited

Austin, J. L. *How to Do Things with Words.* Ed. J. O. Urmson. New York: Oxford University Press, 1973.

Brown, Robert. "Intentions and the Contexts of Poetry." *Centrum* 2 (spring 1974): 56–66.

Hancher, Michael. "Understanding Poetic Speech Acts." *CE* 36 (1975): 632–39.

Henderson, Stephen. *Understanding the New Black Poetry.* New York: William Morrow, 1973.

Hirsch, E. D., Jr. *Validity in Interpretation.* New Haven: Yale University Press, 1967.

Kgositsile, William Keorapetse. "Paths to the Future." In *The Black Aesthetic,* ed. Addison Gayle. Garden City, N.Y.: Doubleday, 1971.

Lee, Don L. "a poem to complement other poems." *Don't Cry, Scream.* Detroit: Broadside, 1969.

Ohmann, Richard. "Speech, Literature, and the Space Between." *NLH* 4 (1972): 50.

Redmond, Eugene. "Parapoetics." In Henderson, 371–72.

Rodgers, Carolyn. "IT IS DEEP." *How i got ovah.* Garden City, N.Y.: Anchor, 1975.

Conversation:

A M I R I   B A R A K A
and
A S K I A   T O U R É

TOURÉ: Hey, man. It's good for us to slow down so we could have some dialogue here at the Furious Flower Conference at James Madison University in Virginia, which is bringing together many of the serious minds in African American literature and culture. These are people who I feel are the motive force in this, and show so by their continuance of excellence through the decades. . . . I'm seriously concerned that you, being one of the great revolutionary thinkers, writers and creators for our people, and by implication for the world, that people like yourself, Larry Neal, and other Black Arts Movement visionaries and activists are not given credit. It is almost treason. We were together recently at the National Black Arts Festival and we had some struggles. It seemed to be an attempt to rewrite history!

BARAKA: Yeah.

TOURÉ: We have one of the seminal writers and thinkers here, and you have people bandying the name "Black Arts" around, and yet there's no mention of Amiri Baraka and his pioneering work and his continuance.

BARAKA: Well you know, I think like you said, "This is a period of deep reaction." Du Bois said the Sisyphus Syndrome. They thought we were supposed to die, and because we haven't died, they have to pretend that something has happened that hasn't happened.

TOURÉ: That's right.

BARAKA: But I also remember Ngugi's story "Petals of Blood";
that novel where the Mau Mau have to fight the British,
and the Negroes that will not fight the British are put in charge of the
country, you understand. And the Mau Mau are on the sidewalk selling
apples or selling oranges. So it's like that because it's a neocolonial situ-
ation, and all the Negroes who were fighting for the status quo are still
fighting for the status quo. It's just now they have used our efforts; almost
like martial arts, they used our strength against us in a sense. You can un-
derstand it. But I think fundamentally, and I say in the end, it has to come
back to you, though, because no one finally can do anything for you ex-
cept that which you permit to be done.

That's why I got pissed off last night when that all-white jazz band
was playing there and my son is locked up in jail. You understand what
I'm saying? It finally has to do with us. Where are the institutions that we
have created? Where are the magazines? Where are the theaters? Where
are the movie companies? And as cold as that might be, that's what I be-
lieve. Because I believe that we have two struggles: we have the struggle
for equal rights in America, because we're supposed to be Americans; we
know that's a sham, but we have the struggle for equal rights, but you
can't even fight for equal rights successfully unless you have something to
struggle with. And that's the question of self-determination. You must at
least create the stick if you're going to fight for equality in this country,
and that stick has got to be some institution or some organization.

TOURÉ: That's one of the things that I credit brothers like Eugene
Redmond and people like that with, because I think it's
critical, engaging in ongoing institution-building: the work you're doing in
Newark, things that we're trying to jump off in Atlanta, and building a
mass-populace base for the culture and developing young minds out of
neighborhood people and neighborhood youth and so forth. I would say
it's critical that we build regionally but also not lose track of developing
national organizations.

BARAKA: But you see, that's important. It just occurred to me, like
when we were talking about black art, when we talk
about Spirit House. The most important thing about that, and you, Askia
Touré, if there are five people in your neighborhood that want to hear the
history of Afro-American literature—you understand what I'm saying?—
if there are three little boys and little girls who want to know that, then

they know that. The whole idea of competing with, for example, Virginia Tech. We had five people, ten people at the Spirit House; we had audiences of thirty people, but see, they can say they saw that and say that changed their lives. So no, if we want to talk about the history of our thing, what do we want? How many people are up in those high-level seminars up in Yale, four? How many people in those high-level seminars at Oxford, three?

We mistake mass work, which is necessary, but there's also advanced work! There weren't thousands of people flocking to Du Bois. They were flocking somewhere else. It's got to be done; you can't confuse this. If you have an advanced class in theater, Val is teaching theater, it's thirty-three students. That's like they would be in Yale or Oxford. And that's the way you have to take it. You can give them all of it. It doesn't have to be the thousands that you have to deal with. I'm for the mass thing and I work for that, but at the same time, you cannot get so crazed in terms of the popular notion, because some of the stuff you are saying is not going to be popular at first. It's like Lenin talking about the First World War when people were talking about opposing the war, "don't join the war." People were running him off the stand. They were saying, "Get out of here." They don't want to hear that.

TOURÉ: It's like being a lonely voice.

BARAKA: Exactly, exactly.

TOURÉ: And not going along with the "popular trend."

BARAKA: But like Du Bois: they busted him for being an agent of a foreign power, which was a lie, and all the Negroes jumped ship, and he still said, "No, no, no. It ain't that way. It ain't that way."

TOURÉ: Would you then suggest, whether in theater or other aspects of literature, in terms of traditions, that we are actually the guardians of the culture. I think what you so aptly wrote in your beautiful long poem "In the Tradition" is correct: we are the guardians of the traditions and, therefore, the national spirit.

BARAKA: Absolutely.

TOURÉ: People are talking about spirituality, using that term,
            sometimes very extravagantly and it usually ends up be-
ing strictly some churchmen.

BARAKA: Exactly, that's what it is.

TOURÉ: My thing is, how can you compare some of the folks like
            the John Coltranes or the work we've done in literature
or theater. I think of the walls of respect from the sixties: we embody the
role of the national spirit, the spirit of our people. Our national spirit and,
of course, within that the ongoing will to self-determination.

BARAKA: The problem is this: the problem is that we have not
            prepared, in a formal way, a continuation of that. Obvi-
ously, people pick up stuff you say, but the idea of having the theater
school was correct. There should be an institute for advanced studies in
Afro-American aesthetics. It should be, if it ain't but ten professors and
fifty students. Why? Because *they will know*. And they will have a paper
that says, yes, we studied with these people, and no matter what Yale,
Oxford, Columbia, University of Virginia say, you ain't got this stuff.

TOURÉ: People like us. We teach the professors.

BARAKA: That's right! That's it! Nobody can do it but you.

TOURÉ: We are the primal center.

BARAKA: When I was in Berlin, I went to East Berlin before democ-
            racy came back; I was over there in the Berlin Ensemble
Theatre. There were Chinese, Indians, Africans, Europeans, Americans.
I asked this person, "Why are all these people here?" They said this is the
only place you can see Brecht. If they were doing a play of Askia's and you
said, "Well, they're not doing my plays over here and over there"; no,
they will not do them, but if you are doing them somewhere, then any-
body that wants to see them has got to go there. That's the same thing
we're doing in Newark: say you want to see a play of Baraka's, you're not
going to see it there, or there. The only place you'll see it is in a fifty-seat
theater in Newark. You can go there and you can see that.

TOURÉ: So, in that sense, the struggle, the vision, and so forth is embodied in that.

BARAKA: Exactly. You have to hold it up. Even though they're rushing in the wrong way, you still have to hold it up and say, "No, that ain't happening, and you'll find that out in a minute." But you still have to dig in. That's what I'm yearning to see. Not only these kinds of conferences where it's momentary, but where we have at least the vision to see each summer, for two months, an institute for the study of advanced Afro-American aesthetics or political science; for two months, where you get the minds together and if it ain't but fifty youth who come there.

TOURÉ: But out of that fifty youth will develop a leadership that will take a vanguard role.

BARAKA: Absolutely. Who would have advanced training and not just snippets of the mass.

TOURÉ: One of the things I wanted to raise with some of the writers, activists, and intellectuals in New York, and I know it's going to sound a little controversial, but unfortunately I didn't get a chance to talk with Sam Anderson and some of the other people: now, this whole thing with Spike Lee. My position on that, and a lot of the things that you all forwarded I definitely agreed upon; my difference was, the reason why those vacuums are there—and you can have opportunists that can come into them—is because not enough of us as a generation have done the advanced work that you are speaking of.

BARAKA: That's true.

TOURÉ: I feel you're going to have that, how can you not have that with the tricksters and the reactionaries and stuff. I.e. Lenin, "What Is to Be Done?" What is to be done? We then have to become the embodiment of that forward motion of history. And this is what disturbs me: we are going to have this confusion as long as the advanced voices and thinkers don't begin to come together and do precisely what you were pointing out. In other words, a vacuum is not going to be allowed to exist so the opportunists and the tricksters will come into it. The weight is still on us as a generation.

BARAKA: Yeah, the point is, you said, "we are," or who we config-
                 ure as "we." See, if after the struggle for self-determina-
tion or whatever people thought they were struggling for, or equal rights—
which none of it happened anyway—then people fall back and say, "My
job now is, based on what I have done, to get a good gig in America along
with the Americans." You understand that? The first thing you're doing is,
you've abandoned any alternative to what the Americans are doing. All
you are doing is waiting to let the Americans give you a gig doing what
they decide you're doing. You see what I'm saying? And I'm saying that
whatever the Americans are doing, it's cool, let the Americans do that, be-
cause they're going to do that if they want to anyway, with or without
you. The point is, what are the Afro-Americans doing?

TOURÉ: That's their role.

BARAKA: Right, exactly. They are always going to do what they
                 want to do, and it ain't shit you can say about it. You
may say, "Man, I don't like that, that's corny." The point is, you have to be
doing something. OK, a man got 30 million dollars to make a movie about
Malcolm X that I thought was backwards and attacks black people funda-
mentally. The point is, where are the $100 movies? Where are the $200
camcorder movies? Where's the $500 feature on Malcolm X that we are
passing around in the street piece by piece?

TOURÉ: Piece by piece.

BARAKA: Where is the history of Afro-American music made
                 for $5,000 that we pass around? The point is, we're so
hooked up on America as an ideology and as a method of looking at
things that we don't understand that number one, in terms of the actual
facts, we are Americans in name only, which is what we've been fighting
about! We've been fighting about that. Objectively, we are black—nobody
can doubt that. They'll always tell us we're black. The thing that is in con-
tention is whether we're Americans. So we can struggle about the Ameri-
canness of it; but the point is, the blackness ain't never been in contention.
Where is that? What have we done about that? And that's the only thing
I've been saying. I want to make sure that what you acknowledge I am is
registered. The thing we're fighting about, Americanism—that might go
on for a long time.

TOURÉ: Centuries! Because this country is still formularizing and
                  still trying to forge its identity and so forth. Looking at
work, mentioning films like Halie Gerima's *Sankofa,* Sister Julie Dash's
Daughters of the Dust, we see that we have a tradition in film that is being
forged. And in line with what you just pointed out, why couldn't Julie or
Halie or other progressive black filmmakers come together and make
something on brother Malcolm similar to what you said?

BARAKA: Well, that's what I'm saying. I'm saying that the point is
                  that we're so obsessed with being an American that we
don't move on the objective fact of *not* being in it.

TOURÉ: Very stimulating that you pointed out the idea of an in-
                  stitute of advanced studies. One of the recent things here:
Jabari Asim interviewed Eugene Redmond, and in the course of their dis-
cussion, the thing came out, and I became conscious of the fact, that many
of the young, progressive, evolving leadership don't know about us: what
our overall philosophy is, what our worldview is.

BARAKA: Where would they learn it?

TOURÉ: What was Larry [Neal]'s view of the music in conjunc-
                  tion with the poetry and the drama? How did you and
Larry formulate these things? What was the theory of the Black Arts
Movement? What were the roles of the revolutionary journals that we
forged? The liars are telling the youth that it was a bunch of mad anar-
chists, protest writers who had no theory. Now, we can say the theory
was not as refined in the sixties, but it was a basis, it was a theory, it was
a worldview forged through our journals and an organic relationship. I
think in terms of the work and the concerts you organized with Coltrane,
Sun Ra, musicians who were actually in and of and out of the Black Arts
Movement. My contention is that the Black Arts Movement was the larg-
est cultural upsurge that our people have had in this century and that we
were organically linked writers, activists, musicians, playwrights, et cetera.
I think that is the thing that they want to try to suppress.

BARAKA: See, they can suppress that because, you see, America
                  has no responsibility to tell the truth about us. That's
why we're fighting for equality so there will be. They have no responsi-

bility. So that when we are shocked to see the people who work for them lie about what we did, that's naïveté on our part, and that's finally what keeps me cool and not punching people in the mouth recently in the last few years.

TOURÉ: You've come very close.

BARAKA: Close. But knowing that you are actually the one. I can't put down Uncle Sam's Negro for doing what Uncle Sam pays him to do. You know what I'm saying? That's stupid. What do you say: "I want him to do my gig"? The point is, you need to do your gig and, to the extent you do your gig, you're going to neutralize Uncle Sam's Negro, and that, I think, is what I've come to the realization of in the last decade. Deep in politics as we were, what we forgot is that you are an artist, you are a writer, and the strongest political work you can do, *the strongest political work you can do is in the arts.* And I mean that in the sense of who is going to be reached, most broadly. That's what I'm saying.

TOURÉ: Coupled with that now, I agree: continuing the work, our creativity, our innovativeness must be manifested in journals or else the boule will write us out.

BARAKA: That's what I'm saying. You have to create the institutions. . . . You have to create your magazines. I came down here with all these books. I don't have them anymore, and why? I made them on my machine and I sold them; that's my work. I sold my little two hundred books. That's my work. Now I can't complain about so-and-so didn't publish me. He ain't supposed to publish me. Would you publish somebody telling you, "You need to die, Askia"? Would you say, "Send me that poem, I want to publish it right away"?

TOURÉ: Very good. So that pretty much sums up that we have to see that the responsibility lies within us, the buck stops with us, and that we have to engage not only in the theory, which is very important, but again the practice and that we become, by so doing, centers of the forward movement of our people for self-determination.

Consciousness, Myth, and Transcendence: Symbolic Action in Three Poems on the Slave Trade

J O N   W O O D S O N

THIS ESSAY DISCUSSES THREE POSTMODERN LONG poems by African American poets: Robert Hayden's "Middle Passage," Melvin B. Tolson's *Libretto for the Republic of Liberia,* and Clarence Major's "The Slave Trade: View from the Middle Passage." The motivations behind such an enterprise are several, not the least being that African American poetry is seldom approached with the idea of comparatively evaluating the supreme performances of African American poets. Another is the need to define more closely the connection of African American poetry to the majority literary tradition. The practice of poetry by black poets is inextricably linked to the practice of poetry by poets of the majority culture, and nowhere is the connection between black poets and white poets more problematic than in relation to the high modernist long poem.

Like other poets who wished to compose long poems in the mode of *The Waste Land,* Robert Hayden had not only to resolve the many problems inherent in such a project, but he also had to negotiate another complement of difficulties occasioned by the distance from which he was forced to contemplate American society. Hayden's account of his own appropriation of the long poem is revealing. The most striking feature of Hayden's career is that he did not begin as a modernist poet. Reading Stephen Vincent Benét's poem *John Brown's Body* (1928) moved Hayden to attempt the writing of an epic poem about the efforts by blacks to gain their freedom during the slavery era, the Civil War, and its aftermath.[1] Hayden began his epic in a style similar to Benét's and won the Hopwood Award in 1942 with sections of "The Black Spear," written in blank verse. In an interview with Paul

McCluskey in 1972, Hayden's description of the creation of "Middle Passage," the opening section of "The Black Spear," does not address Hayden's shift from classical to high modernist poetics: he observed that he was dissatisfied with "The Black Spear" because it was too much like Benét, and that after a year of revising "gradually a form began to suggest itself."[2] Hayden added, "The style, or method, might be thought of as, in a way, cinematic, for very often one scene ends and another begins without any obvious transitional elements." In the same interview, Hayden comments that his poem contains different voices—the voice of the poet that "at times . . . seems to merge with voices from the past, voices not intended to be clearly identified" as well as the voices of the traders, of the hymn-singers, and "perhaps even of the dead."[3]

Despite Pontheola Williams's assertion of Hayden's uniqueness and brilliance in the face of her acknowledgment of Hayden's debt to Eliot and Pound,[4] Hayden did not so much realize the form that his poem *could* take as much as he realized the form his poem *should* take.[5] Had Hayden refused to accommodate the demands of high modernist practice, African American poetry would have remained aesthetically archaic, removed from contemporary discourse, and a further demonstration that blacks were culturally retrograde. The most salient breakthrough that Hayden accomplished was the realization that whereas the "mythic histories,"[6] "the poems including history"[7] of Eliot, Pound, Crane, and Williams, fell outside of the concerns of most Americans, "mythical histories" written for African Americans would necessarily find a captivated audience.

In constructing "Middle Passage," Robert Hayden borrowed directly from Eliot, Pound, and Crane much more than has been acknowledged by his critics. Hayden's use of the "cinematic" technique of montage can ultimately be attributed to Eliot's stylistic innovation; however, Hayden's most numerous and consistent direct appropriations are from Pound and Crane as well. From Pound, Hayden derived the use of documents and the use of a "historic character who can be used as illustration of intelligent constructivity."[8] From Crane, Hayden derived the narrator who is a "floating singer,"[9] the catalogs of the names of ships, and some of the vocabulary (e.g. "corposant").

"Middle Passage" has a deceptively simple structure: the poem consists of three sections, each of which tells a brief story. The materials that are cinematically collaged serve to disguise and complicate this simple narrative structure, for they intersperse fragments of *history* in the form of names, diaries, and snatches of disembodied ruminations in the interest of deepening the temporal scope. Despite Hayden's adoption of Pound's documentary method of introducing history into poetry, his goal differs from Pound's, who never moves away from the contents of his own mind.[10] Like the symbolist poet Yeats, Hayden seeks to revive a mythic past, yet he must accomplish this by means that are essentially realistic and self-articulated.[11] Hayden's goal was, then, to erect a racial myth out of the materials of history.

After the speech of the outraged Spaniard, the poem concludes with a six-line coda: in these lines Cinquez is identified by the poet-narrator and thereby personifies the "deathless primaveral image" of "the deep immortal human wish, / the timeless will." The poem is brought to an end with the lines that have been used to establish a motif, appearing formerly in the first section and in a varied form at the beginning of the third section: "Voyage through death / to life upon these shores."

Hayden's method is to present historical detail as though historical events compose a body of evidence that incriminates the slave traders, and, by extension, Western Christian culture. Hayden's faithfulness to the Eliotic doctrine of impersonality has determined the narratological strategy of "Middle Passage": the slaves are never presented directly, and they do not speak for themselves. In its simplest form, the poem pairs examples of the worst horrors of the slave trade with examples of the religious hypocrisy of the Christians who profited from its merciless operation. Yet because the poem opens cinematically with a sweeping "objective" gesture—the recitation of the names of the slave ships that has the effect of a pan of the camera—the slave traders also are distanced and are not yet allowed to speak for themselves: these distancing devices are largely responsible for endowing the poem with an aura of self-articulated historical event. However, the poem's self-articulation is challenged by the discontinuous presentation of the scenes, for when this effect is examined, the narratological consciousness that orders and presents the scenes soon becomes evident. What the poem musters as history must now be recognized as *argument*.

Thus, the history in Hayden's epic is illusory, a matter of semantic interpolations. The names of the ships are mere names, and, as signs, are not containers of history. While their semiotic value is that, for the poet-narrator, they are icons of the discourses of Christianity, sailing, and commercial enterprise, they are not in themselves, as the poet-narrator *must* say, "ironical." The poet-narrator wishes to present the ships as objective correlatives of the failed moral code of Christianity and thereby to indicate that a naturally occurring semiotic (and symbolic) situational irony exists in the conjunction of the names and function of the slave ships. This type of irony, however, actually exists as a substitutive myth that is being fabricated by the associative and sign-making efforts of the poet-narrator. "Jesus, Estrella, Esperanza, Mercy": to the namers of the ships, the Christian myth that enfolded and motivated their activities was as solid a conceptual map of their culture as the poet-narrator's rejection of the interpretants of European myth and the conception of an African American antimyth is indicative of his own cultural mythmaking.

The "impersonal" rhetoric of Hayden's epic is designed to disguise the fact that an operation of mythic inversion is taking place: the poet-narrator has taken the approach that the documentary depictions of the depredations of the Christian enslavers of the Africans are all that need to be shown in order that the poem will establish the "mirage and myth and actual shore" that the poet-narrator sees blended in the history of the building up of the Americas. However, we have only to realize the implications of Hayden's argument in order to grasp the absolutist and ideologically conservative nature of his discourse. Hayden's rereading of history might at first seem inevitable and inescapable because the poet-narrator speaks from the point of view of the "good" in order to show the "evil" of the traders in slaves. However, we may deconstruct this view of the slave trade by reflecting upon the fact that the poem does not enact Cinquez's transfiguration so much as it justifies and then dramatizes Cinquez's slaughter of the crew of the Amistad. The poem avoids the direct engagement of moral problems by shifting the ground of its argument to the symbolic mode of agency: "Middle Passage" enacts a relativistic reversal of the controlling myth from the Christian and imperial law of the Europeans and substitutes for it the mythic agency of the revolutionary "will" of the Africans. What we see of this retributive "will," as it is expressed in the person of Cinquez as a transfigured agent, is that he is as ruthless as the self-righteous Spaniard who narrates the climactic events of the mutiny in the poem's final section. As in The Tempest, which serves as the paradigm of "Middle Passage," the action proceeds judicially, while those on trial remain unaware of the ongoing process. However, because the poet-narrator is at once Ariel, Prospero, and Caliban, there is no voice to take on Ariel's role as sympathetic intercessor for Sebastian and Antonio ("if you now beheld them, / your affections / would become tender," 5.1.18–19) and, likewise, to speak against the condemnation of the Spaniard who has been cast in the role of villain by the poet-narrator.

The dramatic structure of "Middle Passage" places Cinquez parallel to The Guinea Rose and King Anthracite as recipients of the actions of the Europeans, who are the poem's prime agents until the entrance of Cinquez; moreover, we also see Cinquez in a speech that attempts to reassert action upon him. However, the semiotic relationship between Cinquez and the other Africans who figure in the narratives that precede the Spaniard's diatribe is quite different, for we are not presented with the example of King Anthracite and The Guinea Rose in order to see in them examples of deathless "will" or transfiguration, as we are in the case of Cinquez. Perhaps we do not see the agency of "will" in its problematic relation to the poem until we try to ascertain Cinquez's role in the poem. The poem establishes a group/individual dialectic alongside the more obvious black/white dialectic: this group/individual dialectic is problematic, since the European speakers represent "history" and appear in an African American poem as concrete examples of their culture's moral failure. In opposition to these acts of history speaking for itself through documents that are supposedly objective and impersonal, we have only the example of Cinquez as interpreted by the poet-narrator after we are presented with the Spaniard's speech—the speech that we must interpret ironically, because the poet-narrator, who is also the judge, implies that its meaning is ironical. Cinquez, then, comes to signify the "transfiguration" of a group, the collective entity of the slaves, even though he is presented to us as an individual, a name, and a hero. Conversely, actions of individual evil committed by the Europeans signify only at the collective level, for otherwise their actions would not be ironic.

Hayden's "Middle Passage" is rather like a *Tempest* in which Caliban is not allowed to speak for himself. At first we seem to see the actions from the view of an impartial poet-narrator, and what we are shown seems to be history. However, when we ask who the poet-narrator is, we soon recognize that Caliban does indeed speak, for he has taken on the powers of Ariel: as Ariel, Caliban shows us his debased and silent state through the consciousness (and consciences) of his oppressors. Later we see Caliban finally rise against Prospero to assume the power of the former master, and we do not question what we see because the special effects are so deft. Hayden has, for example, employed allusions to remove the poet-narrator's need to present the slaves directly, allusions to two European literary works ("The Rime of the Ancient Mariner" and *The Tempest*), both of which (ironically) wrestle with issues of power and forgiveness and betrayal and reconciliation.

By alluding to Coleridge's "Rime of the Ancient Mariner," Hayden is able to suggest the problem of European guilt: in contrast to Coleridge's narrator, the Ancient Mariner, the three dominant voices who speak in each section of "Middle Passage," "the deponent," the slave-catcher, and the Spaniard, show no signs of remorse or awareness of their evil. These three speakers represent the destruction, respectively, of African social relations, African civil order, and (again, ironically) European religious/moral and legal/civil order. The writer of the "8 bells" section is problematic, however, for in this fragment of a ship's log we have the suggestion of a figure who is able to recognize and express the criminal nature of the actions that have been committed in the name of the salvation of the African pagans: thus Hayden invokes a European text to indicate the moral failings of European culture. Hayden had no choice but to include this assessment within the poem, since the recognition of the contradictions within European culture is an important component of that culture; however, to allow European texts to voice a realization of European immorality undercuts the absolutist thrust of the poem's dialectical articulation of history.

That Hayden's employment of myth is so reductively absolutist also has the effect of forcing him to shift historical factuality into mythmaking. Since the poem restricts itself to only the *middle passage,* it cannot evaluate the theme of "life upon these shores" even while evoking the themes of futurity and transcendence in the poem's concluding lines: "Voyage through death / to life upon these shores." We are allowed to witness the triumph of Cinquez's survival but not the historical *facts* of his escape: thus his slavery alone is life, while his life is reduced to the voyage. Moreover, we are being asked to ignore the fact that "deathless" Cinquez's survival is paid for in the same bloody coin as the lives of the Europeans, by the destruction of the Other: yet this remorseless violence is the agency of Cinquez's transfiguration.

To engage in moral absolutism with regard to history, as Hayden does in "Middle Passage," is to construct a myth and to revise history with an eye toward a distinctly moral interpretation. The revision is particularly evident when we learn that Cinquez was not a prince but a rice planter, was made a hero by the white Americans who freed him, and did not remain in America but returned to live out his life in Africa. In Hayden's scheme the two emblems of European purpose, religion and law, are shown to be bankrupt; "the timeless will" of the poem's concluding movement, on which the poem hangs its meaning, is the same will as that which is the driving force of European civilization, yet it has been rendered unrecognizable as will by the destruction of its mythic icons in the three sections of the poem. The will to which Hayden points is the same will to power that exists in all humans, African and European, the will that the Europeans express by conducting the slave trade: in speaking of Nietzsche's book *The Genealogy of Morals,* Hayden White has observed that "men looked at the world in ways that conformed to the purposes which motivated them; and they required different visions of history to justify the various projects which they had to undertake in order to realize their humanity fully." [12] This idea may be neither comforting nor savory, nor is it pleasant to realize that Hayden's attempt to transfigure Cinquez is a semiotic adjustment; what does Cinquez signify if not the dialectical conversion of Caliban into Prospero and, thereby, the ahistorical man into the historical man?

By rising against Prospero, Caliban merely becomes Prospero: the inadequacy of the symbolic means to accomplish Cinquez's transfiguration is made tangible in that Hayden himself felt that the conclusion of the poem did not ring true in his ears and that after four revisions it still required a strengthening that it never adequately received.

The conceptual fault in "Middle Passage" is that Hayden overlooked the fact that *The Waste Land* and *The Cantos* achieve their synthesis by assuming, in the final analysis, a superhistorical stance expressive of spiritual wholeness and a transcendence of the dualities and tautologies within which Hayden's poem remains marooned. History, in "Middle Passage," is present as *text:* it is the textual presentation of what happens to the historyless and unhistorical Africans. Finally, Cinquez's "transfiguration," which the poet-narrator speaks into existence in its closing lines, is Cinquez's entrance into history as an individual, a name, a consciousness, a monad of the historical will.

Written in 1953 to commemorate the founding of the Republic of Liberia in 1847 by African American settlers, Melvin B. Tolson's occasional poem *Libretto for the Republic of Liberia* is officially celebratory and in that sense more public than Hayden's "Middle Passage." Tolson's 770-line poem is 336 lines longer than *The Waste Land* and 591 lines longer than "Middle Passage." *Libretto for the Republic of Liberia* recalls *The Waste Land* in many ways: it is difficult, written in sections, and highly allusive; it uses a mixture of languages; it has extensive notes that are ironic, playful, and unhelpful; and it has an omniscient "protagonist" (see *Libretto,* note 367) comparable to Tiresias. Moreover, it alludes to *The Waste Land* throughout, and gives name to it in line 50.

The rhetoric of the more public aspects of *Libretto* is derived from "The

Bridge," which it also resembles in its versification and which in both texts is more conventional than Eliot's. Crane's influence is particularly evident where Tolson followed Crane in assuming a Pindaric stance toward his materials. Tolson's Pindarism is evident throughout *Libretto*, for he writes inspirationally out of faith in a Hegelian / Marxist dialectic of history that cannot but bring about a future golden age to the Africans. At least the surface of the poem, which is comic in outcome, unfragmented in rhetoric, and buoyant in tone, militantly expresses these eschatological convictions. However, beneath the enthusiastic public rhetoric, the requisite modernist form of the poem holds a quite different subtext coded in "deepi-talki"— a level of text that is inaccessible to the poem's uninitiated, horizontal, "public" audience.

The contrast between Tolson and Hayden is striking. Tolson's starting place is (in a sense) Hayden's "Middle Passage"; however, Tolson views history as a "force," and his poem is an attempt to depict the action of that force through one octave of rising or descending moment, the historical line of Liberia's coming into being. In contrast, the ground of Hayden's scene is myth: while he only suggests the outlines of his argument, it is clear that his work is an attack on the centrality of the Western worldview. Tolson's poem, in contrast to those by Eliot, Pound, and Hayden, may be understood not as a heap of fragments but as a unified dynamism, or as the interplay of discrete, measurable forces. Tolson's departure from the Eliotic approach appears primarily on the formal level, where this revised epistemology is enacted through Tolson's rejection of the discordant, cinematic, associative techniques of modernist poetics.

Libretto for the Republic of Liberia begins with a question, "Liberia?," that is an oblique allusion to the third stanza of "Heritage," Countee Cullen's pseudo-Keatsian meditation on Africa, which importunes: "Africa? A book one thumbs / listlessly, till slumber comes." It is not Cullen's poetic that Tolson finds objectionable, for he pursues his satire of Cullen in meter and rhyme, nor is it Cullen's attempt at a reductive textualization of Africa; it is, instead, the being out of which Cullen's attitudes project. In contrast to Cullen's decadent limpness, Tolson's poet-narrator speaks in the indomitable voice of the Nietzschean superman, and from that towering vantage he satirizes Cullen's under-manly romanticizing of African historical reality.

The Pindaric gist of Tolson's opening movement, "Do," is that Liberia is an example of the "will" that is necessary if the forces ranged against liberty are to be overcome: thus Tolson sets up a dialectic between freedom and "an alien goad." Liberia is "no waste land yet" since the Liberian moment in the "Heraclitean continuum" has not been exhausted, its "will" used up, though the "protagonist of the poem" is able to look forward to the moment in which Liberia falls like the empires of the past.[13]

It is tempting to read the second movement, "Re," as the description of the past glories of Africa and their destruction at the hands of European invaders; however, much more transpires here: Tolson is refuting Hegel's assertion that Africa "is no historical part of the World."[14] Yet none of this "argumentation" is on the surface of the poem, for Tolson's Pindaric project, his celebratory lyric, must be allowed to soar. Below the song resides the dross of an ideological substitution of universal history for ethnocentric history. To allow himself more room for the transaction of politico-historical argument, Tolson has relegated these matters to his extensive notes. Rather than being notes that explicate his poem, Tolson's notes are designed to mislead the reader without allowing the reader to realize that he or she has gone astray. Thus, the notes do not provide a gloss indicating that the "micro-footnote in a bunioned book" of the second line is a key allusion to Oswald Spengler's *Decline of the West,* in which Spengler asks the rhetorical question—"Do we not relegate the vast complexities of Indian and Chinese culture to footnotes, with a gesture of embarrassment."[15] Again, as with Hegel, the "protagonist of the poem" (here revealed as a universal historian who holds up "the Good Gray bard" as a mediating persona) casts before the reader the *historical* reality of Africa in the face of its obliteration by Hegel and Spengler. Thus, Tolson's poem is positioned as a countertext to the European philosophy of history in which Africa is theorized into historical nonexistence. In other words, the subject of Tolson's *Libretto* is not so much the founding of Liberia as a questioning of the nature of historical reality.

To keep before us the Pindaric strategy of digressive mythical narrative that Tolson employs in *Libretto,*[16] let us recall that Hayden presents Cinquez much in the way that Crane presents Pocahontas, as a real person "transfigured" into a mythic significance in a digression that presents her narrative. Similarly, Tolson builds his poem toward his world-historical hero, Jehudi Ashmun, the founder of Liberia, by digressing through five sections: "Do," the invocation; "Re," a consideration of historical change; "Mi," an expository movement that summarizes the conception of "the wren Republic"; and "Fa," an imagistic treatment of the Heraclitean alternation of peace and strife as the engine of history, only reaching the climax of the poem's narrative with "Sol," the account of the founding of Liberia led by Elijah Johnson.

Even though *Libretto* narrates the return of African slaves to their original continent, the poet-narrator finds it necessary to turn to the subject of Hayden's poem, in order to conjure up the etiological horrors accompanying the transformation of African to slave: "This is the Middle Passage: here / Gehenna hatchways vomit up / The debits of pounds of flesh. / This is the Middle Passage: here / The sharks wax fattest and the stench / Goads God to hold His nose!" (152–54). Tolson reverses Hayden's practice, giving Elijah Johnson only nine lines where the griots receive forty-two lines in which to speak the aphoristic wisdom of their "vertical" tradition.[17] In speaking of vertical culture, Tolson was alluding to his idea that in every age there existed few individuals who were aware on an esoteric, or "vertical," level, while the majority comprised a mass who were aware on a limited "horizontal" level.

The language of the description of "today" in the first eighty-five lines of "Do" perhaps owes much to the prose of Joyce's *Finnegans Wake*. The scope of Tolson's practice is illuminated by Altieri's comment that "the epic and the joke become necessarily fused elements in a process of losing and finding the letters that can return 'his tory' to the state of the anagogic book, which must, therefore, also be an antibook."[18] Lest the reader miss Tolson's aim to write an antipoem, he spells this out in the extraordinary fourth stanza of "Do," in which the protagonist offers a description of himself: among the labels is "a pataphysicist" (509): the relevant part of note 509 reads, "Cf. Jarry, Gestes et Opinions du Dr. Pataphysicien," thereby confronting the *attentive* reader with the text of an antinovel that, like Tolson's *Libretto,* is divided into eight sections, is metasemiotic in method, contains an occult subtext, explicates its own generation, and provides for the unmasking of its own subtext.

Dialectically, the opening movement of "Do" looks toward the text of the future, for the imagined/prophesied future is incommensurate with the "chaos" of Today. The protagonist looks for the glory of the past in the future because he sees no sign of its becoming in the destruction of "Today": "only the souls of hyenas whining *teneo te africa* / only the blind men gibbering *mbogan* in greek / against sodom's pillars of salt / below the mountain of rodinmashedstatues *aleppe*" (551–54). However, the text contains the resolution and reconciliation of even these universal oppositions. Like all anagogic texts, *Libretto* is an initiatory text that looks simultaneously to the fool in need of initiation and to the griot, superman, or alchemist that represents the end of initiation. Thus, Tolson's protagonist is, like *The Waste Land*'s Tiresias, simultaneously inside and outside of history. On the symbolic level, Tolson's poem enacts the transformation of Caliban, the Fool, into Prospero, the Magician; however, Tolson's concern is more for Prospero's book of knowledge than for the man himself. History must be textualized if it is ever to be conceptualized, for the shape of history can only be passed down through the text. Yet it is through the reading of the text that the Calibanic reader becomes metamorphosed into Prospero, the Magician. Thus, Tolson has tried to write an ultimate poem that, like Joyce's *Finnegans Wake,* we do not know how to read unless we become as well versed as Prospero.

That Clarence Major wrote his poem "The Slave Trade: View from the Middle Passage" assures a critique of both "Middle Passage" and *Libretto;* for Major to write his poem at all points to a recognition of the inadequacies of Hayden's poem, and suggests, perhaps, an underappreciation of Tolson's *Libretto.* In other words, the textualization of the slave trade was for Major an unwritten text. At 575 lines, Major's poem is more than three times longer than Hayden's poem and 200 lines shorter than Tolson's 770-line "encyclopedia." We should also note that it compares to *The Waste Land* in length, coming closest, of the poems under discussion, to the ur-epic of high modernism's 434 lines.

With the first word—"I"—of "The Slave Trade: View from the Middle Passage," Major makes plain his intention to employ a different method from those of Hayden and Tolson: where their poems are characterized by the modernist doctrine of impersonality, the postmodern "I" with which "The Slave Trade" opens announces that the subject of the trade in Africans is to be broached directly and personally. It is rather a capitulation, then, when in the third line the protagonist's narrative shifts to the third person. This shift from first to third person places Mfu at a distance from the reader that is necessary since he is, like Eliot's Tiresias, Crane's "floating singer," and Tolson's magus-protagonist, a supernatural narrator, here, a "water spirit, / a voice from deep in the Atlantic." We find in the third line, in which the distancing shift of person occurs, that "Mfu jumped ship, made his escape, to find relief / from his grief on the way." Thus Mfu, Major's speaker, may be identified as one of the figures Hayden's poet-narrator has reified in the diary entry in "Middle Passage": "three leaped this morning with crazy laughter / to the waiting sharks, sang as they went under." Another departure is that of casting his narrator as nonhuman, a water spirit. In jumping from the ship to the sea, Mfu has transposed from Caliban to Ariel. Thus, Major's "Slave Trade" is presented as an explicitly revised *Tempest* in which events are narrated from Ariel's point of view. Mfu seems to have been suggested by Hayden's reworking of Ariel's song: resurrected in Major's poem, Ariel/Mfu is free of Prospero and "free to speak his music." His existence as an interpreter has a reversed polarity, for Mfu's song indicates the polarity of sight, not the blindness that was the subject of Hayden's and Tolson's allusions to Ariel's song.

Though Mfu can admit at the beginning that he did not know the destination to which he was bound, while under the power of his white captors he has determined his own direction by leaping into the spiritual beyond: once transfigured into a spirit, Mfu, a "floating singer" like Crane's and Hayden's narrators, is free to summon up historical tableaux vivants at will. However, like Pound's poet-narrator, his purpose is to analyze the historical and cultural conditions that have so impacted upon him: he states that his intention is to "look generously in all directions / for understanding of the white / men / who came to the shores / of his nation." Thus, Mfu's goal is to pursue an inquiry that Hayden's narrator was not psychically equipped to pursue and ascertain the reasons behind the slave trade. Though Mfu enacts the role of Prospero, he behaves with the humanity of Ariel, or, he is the transfigured Prospero of the end of the play.

While Tolson and Major pursue similar assessments of historical meaning through the examination of discrete historical details, just as Hayden's "protagonist" does (although their conceptions of the form and meaning of history are radically different), and Tolson made both his quest and his answers esoteric, in comparison with Hayden and Tolson, Major makes plain the motives that propel the dialectical engine of history. Mfu makes his first categorical assignments by dividing Europe into "good" Europe and "bad" Europe: Mfu is "baffled" by the division of European culture into "bad" and "good," yet he resolves to work through the dialectical quandary by first picturing the "good" Europe, then the "bad" Europe. What Mfu actually summons are images of the *effects* of European missionary work. The argument is confused by the presentation of slave ships as "objective correlatives" that contrast to the actions of an abstracted "good white monk" whose activities in Africa occupy nearly one hundred lines. A further difficulty is introduced through the irony that results as the white monk prays to black saints and to a black Madonna "who certainly must know something he doesn't / know." Throughout the presentation of the "good" Europe, Mfu remains "puzzled." As he presents vignettes of specific and generalized historical events, even actions that "led to no good for anybody," Mfu is unable to resolve the enigma of the moral dualism that he has set up.

Prospero-like, Mfu continues his "trial" as he ironically wonders

whether the "jolly good sinless deeds" make it necessary to "give ex-
amples / of the deeds of *bad* white men." The third section is a 139-line
treatment of the bad deeds: this section includes a variety of allusions, from
European fairy tales and historical atrocities to cartoons from eighteenth-
century newspapers. The section ends with another "objective correlative,"
a coin given Mfu by an Ashanti Ju Ju girl: tellingly, the coin that commemo-
rates the abolition of slavery in the Danish West Indies was given to the girl
by a kind white man.

The concluding section resolves Mfu's historical and moral quandary
by placing "hope" opposite "insanity": the "objective correlative" of hope
is "the gentle face / of say, Carl Bernhard Wadstrom, / white man, bent
over Peter Panah, black man, / teaching him to read." Hope is, however,
insufficient because for Mfu the "configuration" means less than it says.
The final movement summons up the words of Equiano: "We are almost a
nation of dancers, musicians, and poets." The poem presents a long catalog
in which the living and the dead are invoked to "Come on, ya'll / . . . and
make . . . some sounds mean / what they're supposed to mean."

By substituting Equiano for Cinquez and moving the poem to a cele-
bration of the creative and renovative faculties, Major has banished the
problem of the historical moment by summoning up a timeless transcen-
dent "space" in which the dead and the living are at one. Less visible is the
shift of agency from the mutinous retaliation of Hayden's Cinquez and
the proletarian revolution of Tolson's "unparadised nobodies" (486) to
the image-changing capabilities of the artist: this ambiguity of agent is due
to Major's embrace of "cotton pickers, computer punchers, migrants / and
retreaters." Major settles on the agency of the magic of the word, for a
closer look at the catalog shows that he names far more writers and musi-
cians than revolutionaries and political leaders.

Finally, the role of agent is settled on Equiano. Mfu/Caliban-become-
Ariel now tells the story of Caliban-become-Prospero. Mfu's Prospero is
aptly named, for he is a prosperous merchant, a bourgeois, and also the
author of the story of his own life. Through Equiano, the man who sur-
vived the Middle Passage, entered into a full life in the Americas, bought
his freedom through his own efforts, and wrote his own story, Major directs
his evocation of myth away from the glories of the African past (as in the
early sections of *Libretto*) and into a transcendent, though as yet untrans-
acted, future. We see, in comparison, that the chief strength of Tolson's
conclusion is the exactitude of his imagined future. Major's entire concep-
tion of futurity belongs to lines that privilege improvisational solipsism:

"Do it your way. / It's nobody's business but your own" (520–21). This allusion to Billie Holiday's defense of her abusive paramour is not an impressive platform for the fashioning of a redemptive weltanshauung.

Major's future is not the distant future of Tolson's "Futurafrique," in which a radically new model of man evolves but an immanent future to which one can travel instantly through an act of will. Major's conception of the future invokes the myth of the eternal return, for his future is the golden past that he summons up through the magic words of Equiano—the man who accomplished the translation from African to American, the man who has made the voyage and textualized it, preserving that voyage for all time, while transcending it.

The final section of Major's poem appropriates the triumphant tone of a typical Pindaric conclusion. The dancer-musician-poet is invited to "gather in a sky chorus today, with all those gone and all those / coming, / with Josephine and Leopold the King, / and make, he says, sounds mean what they're supposed to mean." The conclusion of "The Slave Trade" takes its origin in the concluding section of *The Waste Land*, "What the Thunder Said": "at the end of the poem, the proliferation of tongues, the fragments shored against ruin, must be seen as emanating from the thunderous 'DA.' Fragments they are, but fragments with a common origin, fragments within a tradition that begins with a moment of revelation." [19]

Major does not shore fragments of culture against ruin, for his subject is not artworks but lives: it is the lives of the past that he wishes to commemorate, the living of the present that he wants to inspire, and the lives of the future that he wants to ensure. Major's poem is the culmination of the African American public poem on the slave trade, for it treats issues of morality, history, and cultural identity in a balanced way, while also managing to construct a myth that resonates authentically against the confused context of postmodern nihilism and iconoclasm.

Notes

1. Fetrow, 14.
2. Hayden, *Collected Prose*, 169.
3. Ibid., 171.
4. Williams, 79.
5. It should also be pointed out that such terms as *brilliance* and *uniqueness* are irrelevant and inapplicable after the assaults of high modernist experimentation.
6. Walker, 138.

7. Longenbach, 64.
8. Dickie, 116.
9. Walker, 140.
10. Longenbach, 149.
11. See Ross.
12. White, 332.
13. Tolson, 79, n. 79.
14. Hegel, 98.
15. Spengler, 17.
16. Walker, 122.
17. Tolson, 170.
18. Altieri, 122.
19. Longenbach, 233.

Works Cited

Altieri, Charles. *Canons and Consequences.* Evanston: Northwestern University Press, 1990.
Dickie, Margaret. *On the Modernist Long Poem.* Iowa City: University of Iowa Press, 1986.
Fetrow, Fred M. *Robert Hayden.* Boston: Twayne, 1984.
Hayden, Robert. *Collected Prose.* Ed. Frederick Glaysher. Ann Arbor: University of Michigan Press, 1984.
———. "Middle Passage." *Afro-American Writing,* ed. Richard A. Long and Eugenia W. Collier. University Park: Pennsylvania State University Press, 1992. 471–76.
Hegel, George Wilhelm Friedrich. *The Philosophy of History.* New York: Dover, 1956.
Longenbach, James. *Modernist Poetics of History.* Princeton: Princeton University Press, 1987.
Major, Clarence. "The Slave Trade: View from the Middle Passage." *African American Review* 28 (1994): 11–22.
Ross, Andrew. *The Failure of Modernism.* New York: Columbia University Press, 1986.
Spengler, Oswald. *The Decline of the West.* New York: Knopf, 1926, 1939.
Tolson, Melvin B. *Libretto for the Republic of Liberia.* London: Collier, 1970.
Walker, Jeffrey. *Bardic Ethos and the American Epic Poem: Whitman, Pound, Crane, Williams, Olson.* Baton Rouge: Louisiana State University Press, 1989.
White, Hayden. *Metahistory.* Baltimore: Johns Hopkins University Press, 1973.
Williams, Pontheola T. *Robert Hayden: A Critical Analysis of His Poetry.* Urbana: University of Illinois Press, 1987.

Alice Walker: Poesy and the Earthling Psyche

I K E N N A   D I E K E

IN WHAT HAS NOW BECOME ONE OF THE MOST SIGNIFI-
cant books of essays in the rich repertoire of African American criticism,
In Search of Our Mothers' Gardens, Alice Walker enunciates a preoccupa-
tion with the artistic imagination that might well be dubbed the earth-
ling subjectivity. Reacting angrily to a reader's disparaging remark that "a
farmer's daughter might not be the stuff of which poets are made,"[1] Walker
insists that the raw material out of which the poet constructs the world of
her art must necessarily originate from the common people for whom she
clearly writes. "A shack with only a dozen or so books is an unlikely place
to discover a young Keats. But it is narrow thinking, indeed, to believe that
a Keats is the only kind of poet one would want to grow up to be. One
wants to write poetry that is understood by one's people, not by the Queen
of England."[2]

If we put aside the narrow context of this apparent though unintended
slight against the English monarch, the expression "Queen of England"
should be construed in a much wider sense, as an intentional trope by ne-
gation designed, first, to express the idea of art as the inspired response to
the ordinary, the commonplace, the experiences of common people, and,
second, to highlight the marked difference between this kind of art and that
which has as its primary focus the high and mighty in society, the privi-
leged elite. It is a distinction between high mimetic art and that of the low
mimetic.[3] As Walker sees it, the enduring aspect of art is the artist's extraor-
dinary capacity to hallow the commonplace, to imagine the limitless pos-
sibility of the extraordinary in the common run of affairs—in the words
of Ralph Waldo Emerson, to see the miraculous in the ordinary everyday
reality.[4] This sensibility is displayed at every level of her writing, but most
energetically in her poetry. In fact, her poetry, from *Once* to *Revolutionary
Petunias,* and from *Good Night, Willie Lee, I'll See You in the Morning* to *Horses*

Make a Landscape Look More Beautiful, reads like one grand pastoral meta-phor of the earthling consciousness, which attempts to redeem through the poetic medium a world thought to be of little worth. It is very much like dining with Keats and being swept away by his doctrine of negative capa-bility—"the abandoning of one's self to a selfless sympathy with common everyday things."[5]

Walker's poetry, therefore, like the verse of John Greenleaf Whittier, Thomas Gray, Robert Burns, Oliver Goldsmith, Henry David Thoreau, Walt Whitman, and William Wordsworth, does significantly share in many of the essential motifs of the earthling subjectivity, motifs neatly jelled and goulashed in the unique cadences of the familiar and the commonplace in the experiences of a woman of color in America and beyond. The essential characteristic elements of this earthling subjectivity are expressed through a preoccupation with certain themes and concerns.

First, the imagination that informs the earthling psyche is an imagina-tion that originates from the artist-poet's concern with the affairs of com-mon people. According to J. Bard McNulty, the earthling, or low mimetic, psyche is informed by a certain verisimilitude since the experiences it seeks to construct, or in some cases reconstruct, strike us as being true to life.[6] This quasi-populist realism intersects with feminism, or better yet "womanism," in that the focus of its subject now shifts from a concern with dominating powers and wills to an interest in, a sympathy with, the lowly and the commonalty, their hopes and aspirations, their secret dreams and disappointments, their sorrows and moments of incandescent joy, even personal triumphs. Appealing to the common run of people and things is for Walker a measure of power, both in a personal as well as in a political sense.

In "Remember," the first poem in Walker's fourth poetry collection, *Horses Make a Landscape Look More Beautiful,* the poet assumes the persona of one who evokes and honors the memory of an unassuming, humble, almost self-effacing young girl "with dark skin / whose shoes are thin." With characteristic modesty, the girl declares: "I am the girl / with rotted teeth / I am the dark / rotten-toothed girl / with the wounded eye / and the melted ear." Her nobility and dignity come not from class or high birth but rather from her humanness; in other words, her capacity to respond to and satisfy human needs and desires. She is the one on whom we always call to hold our babies, to cook our meals, to sweep our yards, and to wash our clothes. But in spite of her meekness and lowly disposition, or perhaps because of them, she achieves, at least in the eyes of the poet, the highest honor and distinction as the repository of hope for humanity, hope for regenerative healing and wholeness.

In "Ballad of the Brown Girl," the twenty-third poem in her first volume of poetry, *Once: Poems,* Walker writes about the tragic suicide of an ordinary girl of color. The reason for her suicide is that she lives in a society that does not tolerate interracial love relationships. The poet's sympathy is unquestionably with the girl. In fact, the last lines, a question, are meant to dramatize in bold relief the poet's anger and dismay, dismay at the fact that "here love fails to cross the racial barrier."

> "Question—
>
> did ever brown
> daughter to black
> father a white
> baby
>   take—?"

In the first movement/canto of *Revolutionary Petunias,* Walker's second poetry volume, the poems "Burial" and "Women" continue this sympathetic interest in the affairs of common people. In "Burial," the occasion is a solemn one, the burial of the poet's father's grandmother, Sis Rachel Walker, alias "Oman." In a tone reminiscent of Thomas Gray's persona in "Elegy Written in a Country Church Yard," the speaker visits the gravesite of her departed immediate forebears and surveys the sense of neglect and desolation brought on by the passage of time. She grieves over the fact that she alone mourns amidst the crumbling tombstones that once "mark[ed] my family's graves." She is particularly distraught because what is supposed to be a final resting place of honor for the dead has now been turned into a place of near disuse and neglect. Where once stood the grieving mourners at the funeral ceremonies for her departed family members, the transhumant cattle now graze with ardent abandon in what has become a weft of weedy pasture. But the poet, despite all that, is still interested in renewing her contact with the dead, mindful of "the old, unalterable roots" that supply a large chunk of the emotional and social matrix that binds her to them.

In "Women," the poet turns historicist and pays homage to a generation of black women, contemporaries of her mother, ordinary women with tireless industry who have achieved extraordinarily. Their raw physical strength, their fortitude and endurance expressed metaphorically as "Headragged

Generals / Across mined / Fields / [and] Booby-trapped / Ditches," and their pioneering work in minority education, all are for the poet, decisive terms of personal endearment. The politics of ancestral memory and the passionate intensity of remembering these otherwise ordinary womenfolk are consistent with Walker's avowal to keep the tradition and memory of African American women alive and to let that be a constant source of inner strength and personal wholeness. In *In Search of Our Mothers' Gardens*, Walker writes: "There are countless vanished and forgotten women who are nonetheless eager to speak to her—from Frances Harper and Anne Spencer to Dorothy West—but she must work to find them, to free them from their neglect and the oppression of silence forced upon them because they were black and (also because) they were women." [7]

In "Did This Happen to Your Mother? Did Your Sister Throw Up a Lot?," the first poem in Walker's third volume of poetry, *Good Night, Willie Lee, I'll See You in the Morning,* we have the simple tale of a colored woman forlorn of love. Deserted by a man she thought she loved, she swears that "I love a man who is not worth / my love," and that the same "love has made me sick." Love, that special sense of warm attachment and sympathetic tenderness has become instead one long, woebegone chapter of lies, deception, and cunning. As a result, she feels a gorgelike emptiness inside, an emptiness she compares to the massive depth of the Arizona Grand Canyon.

> My hand shakes before this killing.
> My stomach sits jumpy in my chest.
> My chest is the Grand Canyon
> sprawled empty
> over the world.

And yet her lovelornness is not hers alone. She shares the same fate with a host of other women, who at one point or another in their chequered lives have had to endure the unsettling disappointments and humiliations of faithless love.

Aside from depicting the ordinary scheme of everyday reality and the people that loom in it, another way in which Walker exemplifies her earthling subjectivity is through the hallowing of the place of nature in the lives of ordinary people. For Walker, the creative mind that perceives nature is an attingent traditional mind that hallows/celebrates the reciprocal dependence of internal and external natural processes. In other words, part of Walker's earthling subjectivity is focused on the sympathetic relationship between her creative intellect and the natural environment. In this relation, the natural environment is not perceived as Other, but instead as an essential part in the expression of one's individuality (in this case the individuality of the poet) as well as one's reciprocal relation to other people, that is, other members of one's community.

The one place where Alice Walker reflects this coordinate and organic perception of nature is in "African Images, Glimpses from a Tiger's Back," one of the longest poems in *Once*. The poem begins:

> Beads around
> my neck
> Mt. Kenya away
> over pineappled hills
> Kikuyuland.

The proximity of Mt. Kenya and the pineappled hills to Kikuyu land is hardly fortuitous. It speaks to, as well as amplifies, the interfusion of nature in the lives of the people of Kenya. The poet is acutely aware of how closely human life here is integrated with physical nature. The pineappled hills, which appear as interlacing arches that weave the lives and destinies of the people, suggest that the people, autochthonous to the Kikuyu land, are farmers whose contact with the earth is fixed, almost like an ineluctable fate or inexorable necessity. The poet says:

> A book of poems
> Mt. Kenya's
> Bluish peaks
> "Wangari!"
> My new name.

She here suggests that from nature the woman artist draws everything, even herself. Consequently, the poetry that she composes is, like nature itself, ultimately concerned with the generative forces of being. For Walker this affinity between benign nature and artistic self situates and defines the matrix of her ecofeminist sensibility. We will return to this point a little later.

Meanwhile, the imposing majesty of Mt. Kenya, strewn across the elongated ridge of "pineappled hills," parallels the graceful charm, the virid brilliance of the "beads around my neck," offering the visiting poet to East Africa a conception of beauty as well as the language in which to express it. Besides, in an esemplastic imagination akin to Wordsworth's in "Tintern

Abbey" and *The Prelude*, the conflation of "a book of poems" and the "bluish peaks" of Mt. Kenya suggests that nature is a creative force to which the human mind (but especially that of the earthling poet) is "exquisitely fitted."[8] It points up the manner in which nature goes about its kind of imaginative creation. According to McNulty, "The process is the 'express resemblance' of the process of imagination in the human mind."[9]

Furthermore, the act of taking on a new name suggests that nature provides the fundamental essence of the process of naming built into the consciousness of the indigenous people. The formal endowment of the praise/heroic epithet "Wangari" upon the visiting poet, apparently by the august assembly of the elders, and the cotangent and correlative processes of naming in the Kikuyu and Leopard clans underscore the unique ontological signification of nature in the thinking of traditional Africans, a thinking that Ernst Cassirer has described as "the myth-making consciousness."[10] This mythmaking consciousness further demonstrates how traditional peoples like the Kikuyus assign names that bear the tutelary influence of primogenitor/ancestor, and how the unique dimensions of clan psychology, which manifest in a variety of formal ritual inductions or initiation rites, all relate to the unique primitivization of nature.

The poet is so delighted, so enthralled by the majestic blossom, almost enchanting comeliness of the East African topography, the distant peaks and virid vistas spread before her very eyes, that she cannot help but catalogue its manifold beauty with a flurry of images. Walker's poetic intelligence is able to transform the grandeur of the manifold objects of sense into an expression of an indissoluble unity of universal poetic thought. This expression reminds us of Plato, for whom "the world of Nature . . . is the expression of an all-dissolving Unity of which the prevailing features are truth and beauty."[11]

With a technique akin to cinematography, the poet-visitor takes the reader on a guided panoramic tour of the East African landforms. First, the poet, from the relative security and comfort of her safari, peers at "a green copse" and "a shy gazelle" and an elephant bulldozing her way through the shifting rents of the morning mists. Next she looks out on "the clear Nile" inside of which "a fat crocodile / scratches his belly and yawns." Then the tropical evergreen woodland of the African rain forest comes clearly into view, lush with red orchids and the spinning cobra. From here, under the overarching blue sky, the poet sails gently on "a placid lake" in "a small boat," then through another "silent lake" along "bone strewn banks / Luminous / In the sun." Earlier the poet had stroked the water buffalo and the two ears of the mammoth hippopotamus with his hand, seen a leopard zap effortlessly through the branches of trees, a giraffe "munching his dinner," while off yonder on a high rise are Uganda mountains with their black soil and white snow, "and in the valley / Zebra."

There is hardly any doubt from the foregoing that our earthling poet on an exhilarating African safari reserves a deep appreciation and a respect for nature, its kaleidoscope of sights and sounds and colors, as well as the intense emotions they stir. The uniqueness of the verdant culture of an East African landscape is a source of incandescent joy for the poet. The safari itself amounts to a kind of initiatory rite. Besides, the topography, especially the verdure of the rain forest, reflects the culture of the indigenous people who occupy it and eke a livelihood out of it. All of that now unfolds before the traveling poet's eye in endless undulations of varying greens, all blending in a delightful, stark harmony of form and texture and color and atmosphere.

In "Torture," the thirty-eighth poem in *Horses Make a Landscape Look More Beautiful*, nature takes on the function of the healer, the regenerative anodyne, serving to assuage the pain and trauma of life, to soothe, to calm and comfort in a moment of grief or seemingly irreparable loss.

> When they torture your mother
> plant a tree
> When they torture your father
> plant a tree
> When they torture your brother
> and your sister
> plant a tree
> When they assassinate
> your leaders
> and lovers
> plant a tree
> When they torture you
> too bad
> to talk
> plant a tree.

The juxtaposition of dissimilar acts of torturing and soothing, of damage and reparation, in the process of self-renewal intensifies the healing and restorative power of nature. The poet ends her injunction with these words:

When they begin to torture
the trees
and cut down the forest
they have made
start another.

Here Walker's ecofeminist convictions ring loud and clear. The speaker is enjoining us to feel the life of the Other, the natural ambience. She is enjoining us to feel a compassion for nature of which the tree and the forest are but synecdoches. According to Judith Plant in *Healing the Wounds: The Promise of Ecofeminism,* "This compassion . . . is the essence of a new paradigm," of the moral necessity of grieving for the loss of our sisters and brothers who are the forests. "Our pain," continues Plant, "for the death of the forests is simply, and most fundamentally, compassion for the senseless destruction of life." [12]

The truth that the poet brings with her injunction is that we are part of this earth, and this fact must predispose us to see "how relations with each other are reflected in our relations with the natural world." Here Walker's message, like that of the ecofeminist spiritualists, becomes "a praxis of hope," the hope "that like the forests we destroy, or the rivers we tame, we are Nature." [13] In her prose work *Living by the Word,* Walker notes how, when she was residing in the northern hills of California, she had witnessed almost with helplessness the daily horror of the loggers' trucks (she calls them "hearses") as they felled the trees and carried, in her words, "the battered bodies of the old sisters and brothers." She also relates another incident at a national park during which she gazed at some gnarled, diseased old trees. "What the trees tell her," writes Winchell, "is that when it comes to human beings, trees do not discriminate; all people must share the guilt for the destruction being done to the planet and all its life forms." Again, Walker writes in *Living by the Word:* "Our thoughts must be on how to restore to the Earth its dignity as a living being; how to stop raping and plundering it as a matter of course. We must begin to develop the consciousness that everything has equal rights because existence itself is equal. In other words, we are all here: trees, people, snakes, alike." [14]

In fact, planting a tree, from the perspective of the poem "Torture," has become for the speaker, in the words of Joanna Macy, "awakening to the ecological self," in which "conventional, customary notions of self and self-interest are being shed like an old skin or confining shell." [15] And the person doing the planting itself has come into a new covenant that transcends separateness and fragmentation. By planting another tree or starting another forest, the planter is no longer just trying to secure it from mindless deforestation; rather, she herself has become a part of the forest protecting herself. She has become that part of nature recently emerged into human thinking.[16] The transition from the grisly scenarios of mindless sadists and assassins to the interdependent plane of regenerative nature is analogous to what Hazel Henderson has described as the shift in consciousness from "phenotype" to "genotype." Henderson writes: "We may be emerging from the 'age of the phenotype,' of separated ego awareness, which has now become amplified into untenable forms of dualism. . . . The emerging view is rebalancing toward concern for the genotype, protection of species and gene pools . . . and the new intergenerational risks being transferred to our progeny, about which economics says little." [17]

A third and final way in which Walker engages her earthling imagination is by a systematic attempt to understand her own personality, a kind of personalist idealism, beyond axiological or moral categories. She does that by asserting her own thoughts, feelings, perceptions, and valuations. The attempt also involves the unique interplay of character, ego, and circumstance vis-à-vis the workings of the artistic intelligence evincible within the processes of imaginative creation. In her essay, "The Black Woman Artist as Wayward," Barbara Christian suggests that what distinguishes Walker's poetry from her prose is that the former is a graph of Alice Walker's self. She writes: "In her poetry, Walker the wayward child challenges us to accept her as she is. Perhaps it is the stripping of bark from herself that enables us to feel that sound of the genuine in her scrutiny of easy positions advocated by progressive blacks and women." [18]

There are many poems in which Walker shows this interest in self and self-analysis. Six of them especially stand out as the most eloquent expression of the trinity of feeling, condition, and character of the poet's self. Each of them, by sheer eloquence of voice and candor, reveals an aspect of the poet's personality predominant at a given time and under certain definable conditions. That personality often is a unique mark of an individual who has grown, fashioned as it were by the processes of self-fertilization/self-pollination beyond easy categories of self-abasement or social adaption.

For Walker the graph of self that Christian speaks about is the ideology of the experience of the self as the essential arbiter of reality. That ideology celebrates autonomy as a fundamental individual right that must not be violated or vitiated by a sentimental or even the most pious appeal to collective experience. It is the ideology of self that Professor Mihaly Csikszentmilhalyi has described as " 'the autotelic self'—a self that has self-contained goals." [19] It is a self that fiercely asserts and guards the validity and integrity of her own experience, a validity and integrity that requires no other validation, morally, socially, or culturally. The epitome of this self is revealed most trenchantly in Walker's "On Stripping Bark from Myself," one of the most significant poems in *Good Night, Willie Lee, I'll See You in the Morning.*

The sheer audacity of voice with which this self announces her presence on this earth is unmistakable. The announcement, which sounds almost bellicose, comes down like a peel of thunder. It is as if out of the nebulous depths of social conformism and conditioned selves a new self emerges to claim her place in the world. The speaker says:

> I find my own
> small person
> a standing self
> against the world
> an equality of wills
> I finally understand.

But the audacity is somewhat weaned within the rhetoric of the underdog, which is intended not so much to elicit sympathy as it is to warn a world that is accustomed to taking advantage of small people that this time there is and must be a new deal. And the new deal, which in metaphorically coextensive terms subserves the agonistic mythos of David and Goliath, is a bold vision of the world as a level playing field where small people and big people, rich people and poor people, the advantaged and disadvantaged, live each in their own space as they see fit without any of them ever assuming for one moment that what is good and right for one is necessarily good and right for another. It is an intensely relativistic world in which one's responses need not be the responses of others dictated by society or political correctness, but instead responses shared with others dictated solely by the individual's defined needs and desires. In this regard, the self becomes the critical medium through which collective responses and sentiments are distilled or crystallized.

Thus, the self swears direly,

> No. I am finished with living
> for what my mother believes
> for what my brother and father defend
> for what my lover elevates
> for what my sister, blushing, denies or rushes
> to embrace.

Here she is warning that often what is passed off as the collective outlook of traditional phallocentric culture from which all reality must receive its legitimating authority is no longer tenable. Back in the days when women were "expected to keep silent about / their close escapes" and felt content living the lie that society's conditioning and customary sanctions had imposed on them, that silence might have appeared perfectly normal. Back in the days when women could not see themselves outside of the assigned roles and normative constructs in society, and others could not see them independently of these roles and constructs, the kind of deviation and subversion of "the common will" contemplated by the Walker self here might have seemed too indefinable, even dangerous. Other poems in which Walker explores the assertive will of the self include, but are not limited to, "So We've Come at Last to Freud" and "Mornings / of an Impossible Love" (*Once*); "Sunday School, Circa 1950," "Will," "Rage," "Beyond What," and "Reassurance" (*Revolutionary Petunias*); and "On Stripping Bark from Myself" and "Early Losses: A Requiem" (*Good Night, Willie Lee, I'll See You in the Morning*). In each of these poems, the capacity and freedom to launch a "ruthless" pursuit of one's inwardness is systematically vocalized. In other words, Walker's intent is to find her own personal turf, and ultimately, this turf is in accord with the thoughts of Hermann Hesse in *Demian:* "Each man had only one genuine vocation—to find the way to himself. He might end up as a poet or madman, as prophet or criminal— that was not his affair, ultimately it was of no concern. His task was to discover his own destiny—not an arbitrary one—and live it out wholly and resolutely within himself. Everything else was only a would-be existence, an attempt at evasion, a flight back to the ideas of the masses, conformity and fear of one's own inwardness." [20]

In closing, I want to return to the remark with which I began this essay, namely, Walker's angry response to the "white Northerner." It is not so much that John Keats was opposed to the earthling subjectivity. As a matter of fact, Keats, through his aesthetic doctrine of negative capability, not only preached about it but in fact practiced it in his poetry. It is not so much that Keats was white, and Alice Walker black. Instead it is that Walker was making a point about the immanent necessities of poetic thought: the contingent particularity of earthly experience that some people like the white northerner would rather ignore or relegate to the back yard. But Walker through her poetry reminds us of the ineluctability of poetic art as the immanent act of the mind and the relation of that mind to experience. What people mistakenly call transcendence with which they identify certain writings and writers is nothing but an epistemic category of a continuum involving a relationship with objects in the actual world and the transcendental universal forms or ideas of which they are embodiments.

Thus the earthling psyche can be appropriately defined as the act of the artistic mind that celebrates immanent reality, a consciousness of the pursuits and interests of earthly life, including the consciousness of essences captured in the objective, as well as those elements such as emotions, sentiments, thoughts, and sensations that constitute a person's unique individuality and identity. It embodies a somewhat primitivist theologic view of reality in which the earth itself is conceived as the primal source of numinous being. Its characteristic elements include, but are not limited to, a concern for the commonplace in the affairs of common people, an impassioned celebration of nature, an exploration of the self, and, sometimes, an engagement in a kind of mild, verbal satirical wit.[21]

Notes

1. Walker identifies this reader as "a white Northerner." As the daughter of indigent sharecropper parents from rural Eatonton, Georgia, Walker is naturally offended by the reader's reckless insensitivity and elitist pose. See Winchell, 15.

2. Walker, *In Search of Our Mothers' Gardens*.

3. For a note on the differences between the two, see McNulty, 104–5, 127. I would like to take the opportunity to acknowledge my indebtedness to McNulty's discussion of the low mimetic era in English and American literature. His discussion alone is the main inspiration for my theory of the earthling imagination.

4. Qtd. in McNulty, 114–15.

5. Ibid., 109.

6. Ibid., 108.

7. Walker, *In Search of Our Mothers' Gardens*, 36.

8. For a fuller discussion of the technique employed by low mimetic poets such as Wordsworth to explain the creative essence of nature, see McNulty, esp. 111–14, 118–25.

9. Ibid., 112.

10. Qtd. in Obiechina, 82.

11. Bryan, 2–3.

12. Plant, 1.

13. Griffin, 10.

14. Qtd. in Winchell, *Alice Walker*, 112.

15. Macy, 201.

16. Macy characterizes the understanding of the significance of this relationship as an "ecological sense of selfhood" (202). She also recalls, in particular, a walk through the jungle of eastern Australia: "One day, under the vine-strung jungle trees of eastern Aus-

tralia, I was walking with my friend John Seed, director of the Rainforest Information Center. I asked him how he managed to overcome despair and sustain the struggle against the mammoth lumber interests. He said, 'I try to remember that it's not me, John Seed, trying to protect the rainforest. Rather I am part of the rainforest protecting myself. I am that part of the rainforest recently emerged into human thinking'" (202).

17. Qtd. in Macy, 210.

18. Christian, 53.

19. Csikszentmilhalyi, 207.

20. Qtd. in Miller, 112.

21. Some of the poems in which Walker displays her satirical wit include: "First, They Said," "Listen," "We Alone," "Killers," "Songless," "A Few Sirens," "SM," "Attentiveness," and "The Diamonds on Liz's Bosom" (*Horses Make a Landscape Look More Beautiful*); "Sunday School, Circa 1950" (*Revolutionary Petunias*); "Janie Crawford" (*Good Night, Willie Lee, I'll See You in the Morning*); and "On Being Asked to Leave a Place of Honor for One of Comfort . . ." (*Once*).

Works Cited

Bloom, Harold, ed. *Alice Walker*. New York: Chelsea House, 1989.

Bryan, J. Ingram. *The Interpretation of Nature in English Poetry*. Tokyo: Folcroft, 1972.

Christian, Barbara. "The Black Woman Artist as Wayward." In Bloom, 39–58.

Csikszentmilhalyi, Mihaly. "The Autotelic Self." In *Reading Critically, Writing Well*. 3d ed. Ed. Rise B. Axelrod and Charles R. Cooper. New York: St. Martin's, 1993. 207–10.

Griffin, Susan. "Split Culture." In Plant, 7–17.

Macy, Joanna. "Awakening to the Ecological Self." In Plant, 201–11.

McNulty, J. Bard. *Modes of Literature*. Boston: Houghton, 1977.

Miller, James E. *Word, Self, Reality: The Rhetoric of Imagination*. New York: Dodd, 1974.

Obiechina, Emmanuel. *Culture, Tradition and Society in the West African Novel*. Cambridge: Cambridge University Press, 1975.

Plant, Judith, ed. *Healing the Wounds: The Promise of Ecofeminism*. Philadelphia: New Society, 1989.

Walker, Alice. *Good Night, Willie Lee, I'll See You in the Morning*. New York: Dial, 1979.

———. *Her Blue Body Everything We Know: Earthling Poems 1965–1990 Complete*. New York: Harcourt, 1983.

———. *In Search of Our Mothers' Gardens*. San Diego: Harcourt, 1983.

———. *Once: Poems*. New York: Harcourt, 1968.

———. *Revolutionary Petunias and Other Poems*. New York: Harcourt, 1973.

Winchell, Donna. *Alice Walker*. New York: Twayne, 1992.

"The Calligraphy of Black Chant": Resiting African American Poetries

A L D O N   L Y N N   N I E L S E N

> *there is a corner just ahead whose turning*
> *is so badly understood that being*
> *upset is included in the tickets.*
> —Ed Roberson (*When, 29*)

ACH YEAR THE NORTON AND HARPER AND HEATH anthologies multiply and grow thicker, yet they seemingly can find no room, even while celebrating the margins and revaluing aesthetic transgression, for a poem like N. H. Pritchard's "junt":

junt

mool oio clish brodge

cence anis oio

mek mek isto plawe (*EECCHHOOEESS*, 28)

Pritchard's poems seem to ask, as did Gertrude Stein's and William Carlos Williams's before him, fundamental questions about the very nature of the poetic. "Words," Pritchard inscribes as the epigraph to his collection *The Matrix Poems*, "are ancillary to content."[1] This statement may not get us very far in our arguments about the form/content controversy, but it no doubt explains a great deal about why so few critics of African American poetry have devoted any time to the works of Pritchard. A more ready-to-hand explanation is that Norman H. Pritchard isn't written about as a predecessor to such important American literary movements as the so-called L=A=N=G=U=A=G=E school: critics of white poetry seldom look at black writers while compiling their genealogies of aesthetic evolution. But Pritchard, who to date has never been mentioned by cultural studies critiques of aesthetic transgression, was not always so marginalized. The book in which "junt" appears was published by New York University Press, and his still more unconventional collection *The Matrix Poems* was published by Doubleday. In June of 1967 Pritchard's photograph filled the cover of the magazine *Liberator,* published in New York by the Afro-American Research Institute, an organization with both Old and New Left affiliations. Inside this issue of *Liberator* was a collection of Pritchard's poetry accompanied by a brief commentary written by W. Francis Lucas. The terminology of Lucas's notes is striking in retrospect. He says of Pritchard's work, "These poems decompose the reader by sight and sound." [2] This in 1967, before English translations of Derrida, Lacan, and Kristeva had become standard fare for graduate literary study, before deconstruction and other forms of poststructuralist critique had had much opportunity to alter the critical vocabularies of book reviewers. More importantly, we see in this instance that Lucas is free of the all too common assumption that experimental approaches to expression and theorized reading are somehow white things. By situating Pritchard "in the balances of language" that include Paul Laurence Dunbar, Geoffrey Chaucer, and Ezra Pound, Lucas manifests, as does William Melvin Kelly in his epigraphs to *Dunfords Travels,* as does Melvin B. Tolson in his later poems, an understanding of English language poetic tradition as having been already implicated in blackness. A poem such as "junt" clearly foregrounds the materiality of the means of signification, but critics have been slow to see black participation in the critical vocabularies of that trend in modern and postmodern verse. Interestingly, even with the emphasis upon the orality of black verse in the work of so many critics, little critical study has been offered of the relationships between the Pritchard poem as scored on the page and, for an excellent example, the chanted versions he recorded for the 1967 Broadside album *New Jazz Poets.* Pritchard's published poems hug to the shifting lines between the composed and the improvised. A poem that appeared in the second issue of the magazine *Umbra,* "From Where the Blues?," shows Pritchard as early as 1963 worrying that line between text and tongue, between writing and intention, singing and speaking, all saturated in the signifiers of black song traditions:

> "The Lady" utters a cantata in "praise"
> of morning heartaches . . . one more chance
> to realize that it's   the unsung
> that makes the song. From where the blues?
> Strange, this combat that selects its soldiers. (51)

The first three words of the second line of this poem exactly follow the rhythm of the Billie Holiday song that is their "real world" referent. Pritchard's poems answer to all the structural criteria outlined by Stephen Henderson in his interpretations of black poetics in *Understanding the New Black Poetry*. They are virtual catalogues of jazzy rhythm effects, virtuoso free rhyming, hyperbolic and metaphysical imagery, understatement, compressed and cryptic imagery, worrying the line, and in both "junt" and "From Where the Blues?," I would argue, black music as poetic reference. Commentary on jazz history makes copious room for the advent and evolution of scat singing on record, but literary criticism, at least mainstream criticism of black writers, seems either to be left speechless by scat's poetic analogue or simply not to have noticed it. The techniques of "junt" have been adopted by other black writers and sometimes adapted to a yet more overt effort to suggest "Africanesque" language thematics, as in the poem titled "Her" by Stephen Chambers that appeared in the *Journal of Black Poetry* in 1969:

                    sue/san
            I - Kemo - San
        Ja - A - Bu
            Ja - A - Bu
                I/kemo/no/san
        San/(frisco???)   (21)

Chambers's poem may also suggest similar passages in works by Amiri Baraka, passages that script the vocal elements of jazz instrumental music and voice American accents in imitation of heard African languages, a speaking in tongues often accompanied by humor. Neither Norman Pritchard nor Stephen Chambers was among the exhibits in the anthology section of Stephen Henderson's *Understanding the New Black Poetry*, but Pritchard was a regular contributor to contemporary anthologies of black poetry, including *The New Black Poetry, You Better Believe It, The Poetry of Black America*, and *Dices or Black Bones*. Later anthologies advertising themselves as records of the period, though, steadfastly ignore Pritchard and most other poets who write in a similar vein.

Norman Pritchard's penchant for concocting sound texts and his interest in concrete poetry should, by now, have attracted much more attention from critics interested in the infinite permutations of orality in black verse and of those historicizing American participation in such international aesthetic movements as concretism. The attention has not come. If W. Francis

Lucas is guilty of anything in his too short note on Pritchard for readers of the *Liberator*, it is overoptimism. Lucas argues that "language and its use in our time is certainly the conveyor of larger and more detailed perceptions about life and art" and predicts that "time inevitably holds a great deal in store" for Pritchard.[3] Pritchard has been, to the contrary, almost wholly forgotten. One of the only critical assessments of Pritchard to appear in the last decade was written by Kevin Young, then a student at Harvard College, in connection with an exhibit at the Harvard College Library on "Material Poetry of the Renaissance / The Renaissance of Material Poetry." Young advances several explanations for the near complete repression of this once well-published poet, perhaps the most convincing being that "Pritchard seems positioned outside whichever definition of 'concrete' is chosen, whether Black reality or reader-oriented physicality."[4]

There lingers an oddness about this explanation; why does the concrete existence of poetry so determinedly given to foregrounding the material of its own workings elude definitions of the concrete? Surely there is something deeply wrong with critical definitions that might have the end result of repressing the reality of a black poet by viewing him and his work as being sited outside black reality. Writing in *Black World* in July 1971, Kalamu ya Salaam declared, "Something is wrong when we mistake everyday Black rapping about our Black condition and experience for strong Black poetry that expresses our realist selves. Something is going wrong with this and we'd better find out now."[5] While the date and the occasion of this declaration will remind us that the "rapping" Kalamu ya Salaam addressed was not quite what the word calls to mind in the 1990s, the essay was a review of recent recordings by Amiri Baraka, The Last Poets, and The Black Voices, the observable fact that essays in cultural studies today are far more likely to look for their valued transgressive readings in the realm of Rap than among publishing black poets should give us pause. In 1968 Stanley Crouch, who was then giving himself to the movement "Toward a Purer Black Poetry Aesthetic," offered a stern binary opposition of his own: "Street speech and street song are two very different things. Many of the younger Black Writers do not really understand this, do not develop their ears so as to tell the difference, a vital difference which, if not understood, most often leads to the flat, ugly sort of thing that Robert Creely, Ginsburg [*sic*], Frank O'Hara and many of the so-called 'avant garde' white writers come up with."[6] Perhaps Crouch hasn't changed *all* that much in the intervening years. In the same issue of the *Journal of Black Poetry*, Crouch, while denouncing new collections by LeRoi Jones, A. B. Spellman, and David Henderson, stated with his accustomed air of certainty, "I am very concerned about Black Literature and do not believe, as do many others, that we are experiencing a renaissance, but, rather, think that we are falling into the same kind of slump Black Music fell into during the soul-funk fad of eight years ago: A whole lot of people are bullshitting under the banner of 'getting down.'"[7] What comes into view in the critical comments of both Kalamu ya Salaam and Stanley Crouch, though I hesitate to yoke them in this fashion, given the quite different routes they have since taken from this shared point, is a growing impatience with some claimed links between black poetics and daily black performance in speech and song, as well as a desire to forge other, perhaps more effective links between those same subjects. While these debates have for the most part not been reexamined by the critical establishment (when I went to check the *Journal of Black Poetry* out of the library at U.C.L.A., I found it had not been requested in twenty years), the residual effects of the debates continue to shape readings and discussions of African American poetry. Mainstream critics today are far more likely to assume they already know what was said during the Black Aesthetic period, and reargue the issues from there, than to revisit the documents themselves. For another take on these issues we might look at Jerry Ward's 1976 study of N. J. Loftis's pioneering volume *Black Anima*. Ward can be seen to share Kalamu ya Salaam's frustrations: "In searching through all the writing devoted to this protean phenomenon, one's attempt to find discussion of the *aesthetics* which inform the Black Aesthetic is a hopeless undertaking. . . . Until such time as we do formulate an aesthetics that will elucidate the concepts involved in critical judgments about black works of art, we will confuse moral and ideological attitudes with aesthetic attitudes."[8] We can say with Jessie Fauset that there is confusion. Ward's article appeared four years after Henderson's attempt to forge a path toward the discussion of the *aesthetics* that might inform the Black Aesthetic. Many of our finest critics, including Hazel Carby, Houston Baker, Hortense Spillers, Henry Louis Gates, Vévé Clark, Deborah McDowell and, as always, Jerry Ward, have done essential work in the critical anatomizing of the aesthetics identifiable in literary works of art by black writers. If we look beyond that important work to the exclusions practiced so regularly against so many black poets in the decades since Ward's article, it appears, at least to this reader, that many of them have been accomplished precisely by masking ideological desire as an aesthetic judgment rooted in concrete particulars. Ward predicted in 1976 that *"Black Anima* will never become a popular book";[9] in *The Dark and the Feeling* Clarence Major offered a stark definition: "To be a black artist is to be unpopular."[10] We need, still, to look carefully at questions about why some are more unpopular, critically unpopular, than others; why, for example, Ward was so right that *Black Anima,* a book he termed "an important and necessary document in the tradition of black writing," has proved to be so consistently unimportant and unnecessary to those critics documenting and theorizing black poetics.[11] We need to ask why it is that, given so much talk of the importance to black poetry of black speech and the avid academic interest in the most popular Rap recordings, so few scholars have been, as Jerry Ward was, "caught by the rhythms of black speech rerapped" in *Black Anima.*[12]

One immense component of the critical operations that have "deaccessioned" (to use a term depressingly current in the language of the library and the gallery) broad swaths of the recent past of black experiment in poetics is a series of nearly hegemonic assumptions about the nature of the relationship between African American oral traditions and writing, with a clear privilege given to the prevailing ideal of the oral. This is not a phenomenon limited to critical discussions of black writing. As Gayatri Spivak has summarized Jacques Derrida's deconstructions of the speech/writing opposition operative in European thought, "Western metaphysics opposed the *general* principle of speech, on the one hand, to writing in the narrowest sense on the other."[13] That categorical error itself remains operative in some of the texts on orality and culture that have assumed the greatest influence among educators and critics in our lifetime. In Walter J. Ong's frequently cited text *Orality and Literacy,* just to take one of the most prominent examples, there is a strange instantiation of this logic. Ong writes that "human beings in primary oral cultures, those untouched by writing in any form, learn a great deal and possess and practice great wisdom, but they do not 'study.' . . . Study in the strict sense of extended sequential analysis becomes possible with the interiorization of writing."[14] Ong takes care to define "study" in such a way that it only becomes possible with the advent of writing, but at the same time he appears less strictly concerned with the largest of epistemological questions. At the most basic level one has to ask how it is that this highly literate writer has come to possess this truth about primary oral cultures, those untouched by writing in *any* form. Has he received this truth in the form of a series of oral reports from previously illiterate informants who have brought the knowledge to him directly upon leaving their primary oral cultures behind, or is this knowledge the result of his reading? Later in this book Ong acknowledges quite openly that "without textualism, orality cannot even be identified," and he does make it clear that his theories of what must have been true for primary oral cultures are derived from his reading of texts. But for all his willingness to engage the debates over textuality, logocentrism, and phonocentrism, Ong never truly comes to grips with the full implications of the transcendent nature of his theories of orality. Similarly questionable assumptions have often been made about the verbal and educational practices of primarily oral cultures, assumptions sometimes mirrored by late twentieth-century theories of education. The relationship of memory and orality is one about which numerous inadequately tested assumptions circulate. Ronald A. T. Judy, in *(Dis)forming the American Canon,* finds a remarkable passage in Theodore Dwight's nineteenth-century ethnological texts. Dwight reports an interview with Lamen Kebe, an African American slave who had been a scholar and teacher in West Africa. Kebe provided Dwight with a description of a West African mode of teaching Qur'anic Arabic that may at first seem to fit with what Westerners generally take to be the case in such African scenes of instruction. But, as Judy observes, "while mnemotechny was emphasized in learning the *Qur'an,* what was practiced in Kebe's school was memorization by graphic reproduction, rather than oral presentation. . . . What is most noteworthy about Kebe's discussion of the . . . pedagogical method is that the written and not the heard word is memorized through recitation. The students are taught to be readers before anything else, and above all readers who can decipher." [15] If we recall the enormous import of such scenes of instruction in African American literature, the regularity with which an atmosphere of nearly religious liberation accompanies the introduction to literacy, we can see that traditions of graphic reproduction and improvisation are part of an iterative continuum with orality, not a secondary or elitist and pale reflection of the spoken, and we can likewise estimate the dangers to our understanding of African American literary history implicit in the construction of an idealized orality in opposition to a devalued writing.

While introducing the poems of Arthur Pfister in a Broadside Press chapbook, Amiri Baraka took a moment to address the devaluing of the written, and we can locate in his remarks a deterritorializing motion against European claims to primacy over supposedly nonliterate societies. Baraka says, "We talk about the oral tradition of African People, sometimes positively, many times defensively (if we are not wised up), and it's always as a substitute for the written. What this is is foolfood, because we were the first writers as well. . . . Thoth is the God of writing, its inventor, and African." [16] It is important to understand that Baraka's statements are made in a historical context of previous attempts to assert the primacy of African inscription. Langston Hughes and Arna Bontemps argued in their introduction to *The Poetry of the Negro* that "articulate slaves belonged to a tradition of writers in bondage that goes back to Aesop and Terence," and we should remember that it was Terence who was memorialized as a predecessor in the poetry of Phillis Wheatley, the first African American to publish a book of poems. In the nineteenth century Martin Delany, writing in *The Origin of Races and Color,* had copied into his text both examples of Egyptian hieroglyphs and the ancient alphabetic script of Ethiopia (and who can forget the

We here introduce the hieroglyphics, the reading of which will be observed, according to our version, or that which we obtained from study among the Africans themselves, by learning the significance or meaning of certain objects or things.

The hieroglyphics are letters forming a literature founded upon the philosophy of nature without an alphabet; but that which we shall now present is of a much higher order, being artificial characters based on metaphysical philosophy of language.

THE OLD ORIGINAL ETHIOPIAN ALPHABET

Alf.	*Zai.*	*Mai.*	*Kof.*
Bet.	*Hbarm.*	*Nabas.*	*Rees.*
Geml.	*Tait.*	*Saat.*	*Saut.*
Dent.	*Jaman.*	*Ain.*	*Tawi.*
Haut.	*Caf.*	*Af.*	
Waw.	*Lawi.*	*Tzadai.*	

—Martin Delany 1879
The Origin of Races and Color

FIGURE 1

importance of ancient Ethiopic script in the mysterious transcriptions of Edgar Allan Poe). Delany's figures are an early instance of black efforts to reassert African inscription as a basis for metaphysical philosophy in language. [17]

In the next century, postmodern poets would again turn to ancient African script for precedence. In a 1967 letter, Stephen Jones expresses his frustration at not being able to locate a copy of Wallis Budge's guide to Egyptian Hieroglyphics at the Boston Public Library and reports that he is ordering a copy of his own from Dover books. Little acknowledgment has thus far been given by white critics to this history of black historical recovery, perhaps in part because, as Frances Smith Foster remarks, "though they have little difficulty acknowledging the complexity of early black music and oral literature, they are reluctant to assume a similar level of sophistication with written language." [18] In positing an African genesis for writing against European attempts to strip the African continent of its history of inscription and its history in writing, Baraka's writing does not offer a simple reversal of the speech/writing opposition. His introduction to Pfister's poetry is, in fact, titled "Pfister Needs to Be Heard!," a title that links together in its inscribed ambiguity the need to hear spoken realizations of Pfister's script and the political need to hear what Pfister has to write.

A criticism that opposes the oral to the written, as opposed to reading their imbrications, may miss a great deal that black poets are doing and have always done. It will miss, as most criticism to date has missed, this passage from Julia Fields's long poem "When That Which Is Perfect Is Come":

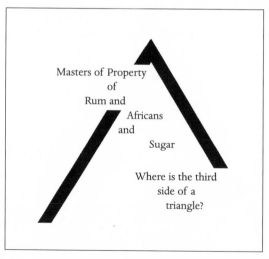

FIGURE 2

Here, Julia Fields writes across the Triangle Trade. It is a writing that disrupts the mastery of the trade it represents, and it is an opening out of the Middle Passage onto contemporary readings. This is a poem that graphically re-masters history, using oral *and* graphic tradition, orature, and historical docu-ment, but using them in a fashion that must be seen to be heard. It is a poem that follows some of the same formal imperatives Nathaniel Mackey has discerned in the poetics of Charles Olson. It is a work that "tends to be tempered by a visual intelligibility ('impenetrable to anything but the eye'), a sense of coherence that resides in shape rather than message or paraphras-able statement, a sense impressed upon the reader by the placement of the words on the page."[19] Likewise, the rest of Fields's poem works with an almost unspeakable, though rebuslike, play between eye, ear, and tongue:

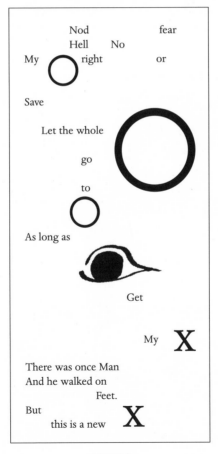

FIGURE 3

In this passage we *can* read "As long as / ✸👁✸ / Get / My X" aloud to one another, but the graphic texture of the poem is essential to its effects; it can be read off the page but cannot be read to another. We must look to this poem to see the wholes becomes eyes (Olson's polis was composed of eyes in heads to be looked out of), to see the X mark itself as absence, burial, and rechristening. The advent of the X in Julia Fields's post-Malcolm poem signifies for us in ways that were unavailable before Malcolm X. As the X emblazoned as both commodity and historic claim on the caps of so many young people in the early 1990s signified so loudly within the silence it marked, the X in Fields's poem is an Xing out and a crossing over. The new X of Julia Fields's "When That Which Is Perfect Is Come," though, continues to be Xed out of critical history, and I doubt that it can be reclaimed by an ethnopoetics that awards primacy to orality.

Notes

1. Pritchard, *The Matrix: Poems 1960–1970.*
2. Lucas, 12–13.
3. Ibid., 13.
4. Young, 36–43.
5. Ya Salaam, 28–33.
6. Crouch, "Toward a Purer Black Poetry Esthetic," 28–29.
7. Crouch, "Books," 90–92.
8. Ward, 195.
9. Ibid., 208.
10. Major, 24.
11. Ward, 208.
12. Ibid., 207.
13. Spivak, 98.
14. Ong, 9.
15. Judy.
16. Baraka, 4.
17. (Including figure) Delany, 47, 53.
18. Foster, 28.
19. Mackey, 134.

Works Cited

Baraka, Amiri. "Introduction: Pfister Needs to Be Heard!" *Beer Cans, Bullets, Things & Pieces.* Detroit: Broadside, 1972. 4–6.

Chambers, Stephen. "HER." *Journal of Black Poetry* 1.11 (1969): 21.

Crouch, Stanley. "Books." *Journal of Black Poetry* 1.10 (1968): 90–92.

———. "Toward a Purer Black Poetry Esthetic." *Journal of Black Poetry* 1.10 (1968): 28–29.

Delany, Martin R. *The Origin of Races and Color.* Philadelphia: Harper, 1879; facs. Baltimore: Black Classic, 1991.

Fields, Julia. *Slow Coins: New Poems (& Some Old Ones).* Washington, D.C.: Three Continents, 1981.

Foster, Frances Smith. *Written by Herself: Literary Production by African American Women, 1746–1892.* Bloomington: Indiana University Press, 1993.

Henderson, Stephen. *Understanding the New Black Poetry: Black Speech and Black Music as Poetic References.* New York: Morrow, 1972.

Hughes, Langston, and Arna Bontemps. *Arna Bontemps-Langston Hughes Letters, 1925–1967.* Ed. Charles H. Nichols. New York: Paragon, 1990.

Jonas, Stephen. *Four Letters.* :that: 23 (1994).

Judy, Ronald A. T. *(Dis)forming the American Canon: African-Arabic Slave Narratives and the Vernacular.* Minneapolis: University of Minnesota Press, 1993.

Kelly, William Melvin. *Dunfords Travels Everywheres.* New York: Doubleday, 1970.

Loftis, Norman J. *Black Anima.* New York: Liveright, 1973.

Lucas, W. Francis. "Norman H. Pritchard, Poet." *Liberator* 7.6 (1967): 12–13.

Mackey, Nathaniel. *Discrepant Engagement: Dissonance, Cross-Culturality, and Experimental Writing.* New York: Cambridge University Press, 1993.

Major, Clarence. *The Dark and the Feeling: Black American Writers and Their Work.* New York: Third Press, 1974.

Ong, Walter J. *Orality and Literacy: The Technologizing of the World.* London: Methuen, 1982.

Pritchard, Norman H. *EECCHHOOEESS.* New York: New York University Press, 1971.

———. "From Where the Blues?" *Umbra* 2 (1963): 51.

———. *The Matrix: Poems 1960–1970.* Garden City, N.Y.: Doubleday, 1970.

Roberson, Ed. *When Thy King Is a Boy.* Pittsburgh: University of Pittsburgh Press, 1970.

Spivak, Gayatri Chakravorty. *Outside in the Teaching Machine.* London: Routledge, 1993.

Ward, Jerry. "N. J. Loftis's *Black Anima:* A Problem in Aesthetics." *Journal of Black Studies* 7.2 (1976): 195–210.

ya Salaam, Kalamu. "On Record." *Black World* 20.9 (1971): 28–33.

Young, Kevin. "Signs of Repression: N. H. Pritchard's *The Matrix.*" *Harvard Library Bulletin* 3.2 (1992): 36–43.

Conversation:

SHERLEY   ANNE   WILLIAMS

and

DEBORAH   MCDOWELL

MCDOWELL: Sherley Anne Williams. *The Peacock Poems, Some One Sweet Angel Chile, Give Birth to Brightness, Dessa Rose,* a score of critical articles: you're a kind of Renaissance woman. This is a conference centered on poetry, but you are by no means writing only poetry. How do you see yourself as a writer, having had a career that combines all of these different modes of writing?

WILLIAMS: Well, I think that the center of my work is really fiction, but I'm not always able to say the things I'd like to say or the things that come to me to be said in fiction, so it's really just a matter of the form the thing kind of takes as it is getting expressed. To a certain extent, I don't see any real distinction. In fact, I just think of myself as a writer, and sometimes that comes out as poetry and at other times it comes out as fiction; occasionally, it comes out as criticism.

MCDOWELL: Interesting. Have you ever tried any drama?

WILLIAMS: Yes, as a matter of fact. I have a play called *Letters from a New England Negro* that's been produced a number of times, most recently at the Chicago International Theatre Festival, where it was the only American entry.

MCDOWELL: Somehow that just passed by me. I like the point that there should be no separation between forms of writing. But as we know—certainly in a publishing market—there is an effort to put writers in a box. I've had experience myself, recently, of just having written something without any generic designs, but being forced to come, after the fact, to put the work in a certain box, when it's neither fish nor fowl. So I like the idea that you are a writer. Whatever form the writing takes is the form it takes.

I also like a couple of comments you have made in past interviews, and I don't want to have you revisit what you've already said, but one was that your topics choose you, which I found fascinating. And the second one was you wait for, and you must wait for, the idea behind the writing, wait for it to come to its own ripeness; it cannot be forced. I'm paraphrasing, but I think that's the essence of what you said and I'd like to hear you say a little more about that.

WILLIAMS: Well, to pick up the second one first, when I am writing poetry, I look upon poetry as more like a kind of gift from God. I mean, you really can't force a poem. It's either going to be there or it's not. And I don't mean you can't work on it after the first burst of inspiration. I can say to myself, "I'd like to write a story about X," and can pretty much go ahead and write a story about X. But to say that I want to write a poem about Y, and to have that poem come, that's not really something that is going to happen. Y is going to be there because it's time to be there, or it wants to be there, or God said, "OK, you can do that," or something on that order. I guess what I'm saying is that I really see poetry as this upwelling of feeling, of thought, of emotion, whereas fiction is much more a kind of calculated act for me, as well as the criticism. That's obviously very calculated and analytical, even though some real interest has to be there first.

MCDOWELL: So, would you say, or would it even be useful to say, that fiction and criticism come more easily to you because they're more calculated?

WILLIAMS: I think in a sense that that is true. I don't have to wait around for them.

MCDOWELL: Not even for characters?

WILLIAMS: One of the things I like about fiction is, once you get into the story, then it really takes on a life of its own, and I become interested in the characters and want to know more and more about them. So, in that sense, everything is like a process of discovery, but with fiction, you're really getting to know a character, whereas with poetry you're trying to get the subject of the poem or all that that subject has to say to you at that moment.

MCDOWELL: And yet you've really done powerful jobs of realizing characters within the context of a poem. I think of the poems in—well, I could think of the poems in either volume—but those in *Some One Sweet Angel Chile* come especially to mind where I have some sense of knowing a Bessie Smith, knowing New England schoolteachers, etc. So it's still a brilliant realization of character within a more compressed form.

WILLIAMS: I started out wanting to write fiction, and I think that that informs everything else that I write, because I always think in terms of story: even in the poems, I'm talking about narrative. Even though there may not be an actual character appearing there, there is always a sense of voice, for example, which is also very much tied to fiction, to the idea of character, and therefore of narrative.

MCDOWELL: I'm going to ask you to talk a little bit, both as a poet and as a critic. I remember your classic essay "The Blues Roots of Contemporary African American Poetry," and obviously music, and particularly the blues, informs your poetry. We can think of other writers, Langston Hughes, for example, who tried self-consciously to incorporate the rhythms and conventions of blues and jazz into his poetry. Do you see this pattern continuing in the work of younger poets, this kind of even self-conscious, theoretical angle on this matter?

WILLIAMS: Yes, I do in fact see African American music as a kind of self-conscious context for many young poets that I read. I think, in particular, of Kate Rushin and Carolyn Beard Whitlow, who've done some very fine lyrical extensions of the blues form. Using the classic form as a kind of starting place for building other kinds of forms: I find that extremely exciting. I think, in a very real sense, that jazz has played a tremendous part in their lives, and the whole rap and hip-hop scene is a kind of poetic force among young writers.

MCDOWELL: Good, good that you said that, because I don't have to tell you how controversial rap music is, focused largely on the lyric content and largely on the reputations of the gangsta rappers.

How would you answer someone who would deny rap a place in the pantheon of contemporary black American poetry?

WILLIAMS: To a certain extent I don't think that you really can, because even though I am appalled at some of the lyrics, I can still see rap as a continuation and see how, in fact, rappers build upon previous generations of music. What they've added is a kind of rhythmical, lilting, chanting of the words. But the kinds of things that many of them talk about, for example, are very much related to what Gil Scott-Heron was doing in the seventies, so it's not as though they have created a completely new form, and it's not as though they have really cut themselves out of the continuity of Afro-American culture. Whether or not critics want to deal with it in that way, the continuity is still there.

MCDOWELL: I agree with you, but certainly the level of the lyrics poses an obstacle to any kind of open-minded view of the form. Have you seen Trisha Rose's latest book *Black Noise*?

WILLIAMS: No, I haven't got a copy of that yet, but we have some very different views about what—I don't know how to say this. I think that, in terms of gangsta rap, there has to be some kind of self-policing going on there. It's not just a matter of self-expression, and it's not just an economic matter of making more money; young people need to realize that words do, in fact, have meaning, and that they have consequence. I know, my own son says, "I don't really listen to the words, I'm just into the rhythm." But words can affect people, and whether or not you're listening to them consciously, those values are in fact being incorporated, and people have to be made aware of that.

MCDOWELL: I agree with you, and that is my resistance to part of her thesis, because what she wants to do is say that rap has been demonized, particularly in the dominant press, and so her mission is to recuperate or rehabilitate it, and I think in the process, there's a lot of sanitation and idealization going on along precisely the lines you mention. This brings me to another question that's related to rap: the concept of "culture" as an explanation for, or as a rationale for, what's happening in rap music. Trisha Rose will say, "Well, yeah, there's a lot of misogyny; yeah, there is a lot of woman-bashing, but if you put this in the tradition of the toast, in the tradition of rapping and capping, then it's cultural"; so we've come to a critical pass where whatever we can designate as "cultural" is untouchable.

WILLIAMS: If you want to take that everything is in fact cultural, everything is. And just because it's cultural does not mean it's not open for analysis or criticism. Or that people don't have to take responsibility, in some sense, for its effect and consequence. To do that, it seems to me, is just about the height of irresponsibility. I think what disturbs me about the criticism—I'm just now talking about the commentary on it—what disturbs me about rap music having the same kind of stature as the poetry of Amiri Baraka or serious poetry in general is that rappers are not held to account in the same way that we hold Amiri to account when he comes out with some of that stuff he says: we're up in arms, saying you shouldn't say things like that; this is anti-any kind of constructive purpose, and you need to do something about that. And if we can say that to Amiri Baraka, surely we can say that to 2 Live Crew.

And what happens is, because we're talking about 2 Live Crew in the academy, that seems to give our stamp of approval to what they're saying. And I think that to comment on rap without talking about its very negative aspects is to agree with the children that, yes, this is reality and a reality that we cannot change.

MCDOWELL: That's right, absolutely, and that's one of my tics, that is the rappers' notion that "We're simply reflecting what we see." And I think all artists understand, especially those who take their craft seriously, that an artist isn't ever simply reflecting reality; an artist is creating reality and recreating reality, not in the sense that this is just out here and I'm recording in some documentary way. It's pernicious, and I'm glad to have someone else go on record to say that, because I don't think we can abandon our responsibility to offer critique. The kind of unqualified approval of rappers just because they try to express themselves artistically doesn't do them any good. It might make them feel good for the moment, but it doesn't give them any opportunities to stretch, to grow, to realize some still more latent possibilities in the form.

WILLIAMS: I think there is a potential in rap to get these young people to really examine their circumstances and to see how, in fact, they can be changed in a positive, constructive manner, and that too often we're missing that opportunity.

MCDOWELL: Completely missing it and completely missing the oppor-
                    tunity to hold the recording industry to account. Some-
how the industry gets exempted from all of this, and nobody really talks
about that. To move to another arena altogether, I'm really interested in
the kind of twinning of film and rap by young black men; the ways in
which a lot of the music underwrites and reinforces the films. I think that,
collaboratively, they are working to project a really disturbing position in
which women and particularly mothers, black mothers, are criminalized,
and I think when we get to that point, we have come to a very dangerous
pass. Somebody needs to say stop, pause, enough.

WILLIAMS: We have been reluctant to do so because I think the
                    larger society, white people in particular, have been so
ready to jump on rap music and black rappers, and we don't want to seem
to be vilifying them that way. Too often, even now, as people have begun
to speak out about these things, we are not listened to, but rather are
classed in the same way that a Tipper Gore or that kind of coalition was
cast. I always make it plain that this is not some kind of academic question
for me. I am in fact a mother and a grandmother, and this is affecting the
lives of my children and of my grandchildren.

And it is affecting *my* life because I live in a predominantly black neigh-
borhood; these children who are listening to this stuff are my neighbors. I'm
talking about my world and this is the world that I want to change. I have
some responsibility in helping to make the changes I want to see are made.
I've decided that I can't allow the fact that, in many quarters, it's not consid-
ered politically correct to point out the ways in which these things are de-
structive and the pernicious effects that they have to me, because it really
does have an effect upon me personally. Rap comes out of a kind of male
venting or something like that, and I think that's fine, male venting, but
when you bring that out into the larger culture and begin to set that up as
the standard of that culture, then you are in some real trouble.

MCDOWELL: Could you say a bit more about the importance of under-
                    standing, if you want to look at rap in a historical/cul-
tural context: the rapping, capping, boasting, toasting.

WILLIAMS: It comes out, mostly, of an exclusively male world. As
                    children, you may have a male/female thing going on
there, but the older you get, the more the male/female worlds diverge.

I think by the time you are into your late teens and early twenties, it becomes exclusively a kind of male preserve. I think of male venting in that kind of way, and as long as that's what it's used for, in that subculture, OK; but now it's being purveyed as a kind of standard of the whole culture, and this is just simply not the case. What has gone on and what ought to go on between grown men and women is very different from that adolescent world of boast and toast, from that kind of exclusively male thing.

MCDOWELL: That needs to be said, and the comment speaks to the understanding of culture itself as a historical phenomenon that grows and changes. You don't just simply say this took place here; we're going to transplant it. You're trying to transplant it without the context that surrounded it and, as you say, without understanding its role in matters of socialization.

WILLIAMS: Exactly. I'm glad to see that Trisha Rose's book is out there, because there's a lot of things that can now be said in reaction to it, and it serves as another starting point, I hope, for real discussion and debate about these two different positions. And hopefully, we get something that will in fact move us beyond this point.

MCDOWELL: I hope we do. The consumers of that music are largely white kids in suburbia. What is their voyeuristic reaction to this so-called abnormal subculture they're listening about?

WILLIAMS: If the majority of the listeners of this are white people, then in fact their whole view of Afro-Americans is being based upon this one tiny bit of our culture, and so everything else is really distorted. It's so dangerous, and for the artists themselves not to see that danger, it is almost criminal.

MCDOWELL: It *is* almost criminal. But a large part of the problem is that so many of these people are very young, and they're having tossed at them possibilities for making money that are more astronomical than they could ever have imagined. It blows them out of the water. For the recording industry, this money is a drop in the bucket, it's nothing. It's equivalent to, say, Columbia Studios investing 2.6 million dollars in a film by a twenty-year-old filmmaker, and then reaping 26 million dollars from that investment. It gives you some sense of the disparity here.

But 2.6 million to somebody whose prospect is making minimum wage at McDonalds or staking out a place in the drug economy, this seems like an astronomical sum of money. So it's youth, it's inexperience, and it's a loss of faith in what the elders are teaching; it's a loss of faith in the wisdom of the elders, in a fashion that I don't know that I've ever encountered before in the same form.

WILLIAMS: I think that the elders—not to seem conceited or ego-
                 istic, but I would include myself in that because I did
come of age in the sixties—I think a lot of it is our responsibility. This is an abandoned generation. My generation spent a lot of time on tearing down some institutions and trying to build up other institutions. We learned how difficult it is to build new institutions. Many of us abandoned the attempt, but we had already torn down or damaged institutions like the black church that had held us up in the past, so that our children were left with very little: certainly with less to lean on than we had. And, as you said, I think this is the first time in our history that our music is controlled by children. Most grown people cannot listen to or participate in rap. Although blues singers, jazz singers traditionally start out very young, they always grow up; their audience aged with them and at the same time older people were listening to them, too. But now you have this terrible schism where grown black people can't even understand what these young rappers are saying.

MCDOWELL: Absolutely. I have gone on record to say, "Deliver me
                 from Snoop Doggy Dogg!" I hate to interrupt this be-
cause it's been such a good flow about the rap music, but I want to ask you about a related matter in *Dessa Rose*, which I think is one of the most significant novels of the past decade. And I think it's precisely on this allegorical dimension of Dessa's scars, because I don't want to overread your work or ask you to go back and interpret it for the reader, but I see you doing something very powerful and very necessary there that has implications for this question of rap music and the responsibilities of the artist to the word and the power of the word. This business with Rufel wanting to see the scars before she could believe the story of Dessa's pain, Dessa's oppression; and those scars are writ about her privates. And I thought that image was so powerful and a metaphor for the dangers of parading the extent of our scars as black people for the amusement of those who have dominated and controlled us.

WILLIAMS: Rufel, who is in fact a slave owner, has not allowed her-
                   self to know that these things take place, and before
Dessa comes along she could have gone out to her slaves and said, "Is this
happening?" or could have watched what her husband was doing with
them. But she did not choose to do that, but now she has this young
woman under her control, and now she's going to say, "Let me see before
I believe."

MCDOWELL: And Dessa's reluctance to let her see, unaware of what
                   she's going to do then.

WILLIAMS: And why should we keep baring this pain for our fellow
                   citizens who have lived through the time, who ought to
know the history? Why should we have to keep baring this pain in order
for them to believe that it took place? I read an interview with one of
those black neoconservatives, whose name I can't remember, and one of
those questions that was asked him, it was couched in such a way that the
"perceived" deprivations—as though slavery and segregation were only
our perception. It didn't happen; it was just our perception. The black neo-
conservative did not say, "Wait just a minute. We're not talking about per-
ception here. This stuff really happened; you can go back and read."
    So it's always as if we're trying to parade that out, to put that on the
table. To put that out because if we don't, it will be slipped right under the
rug. People think you can hold people in subjugation for three or four
hundred years and then pass the laws that abolish that subjugation and
then they're going to be just like the people that subjugated them. Just like
that. That those three or four hundred years have no consequences.

MCDOWELL: I really thought that to be one of the most striking
                   achievements in a generally well-wrought and wonderful
novel; when I teach it, I make sure we go there, to talk about this history
writ about our privates. For whom must we continue to bare this pain?
What is the cost to us?

WILLIAMS: One of the things about Rufel as a character that I liked
                   was her ability to change; that, seeing Dessa's scars, she
was in fact changed by the scars; so it was not just amusement or enter-
tainment, Rufel's look at Dessa's scars: it was a real education and she had
to face what she had previously refused to face: her own complicity, not

only in what was going on on her plantation, but the whole system and setup of slavery.

MCDOWELL: The way you capture that: in her words, "It was a shame
                    to beat a body so." The language of the text captures
that moment when she does enter emotionally into that knowledge, into that experience, and makes way for change. I know writers are famous, and I think this is a good thing, for not talking about work in progress, but you're working on a novel, right?

WILLIAMS: That's right, I am. It's called, at this point, *Meanwhile
                    in Another Part of the City,* and it's going to go back and
forth over the last thirty years. The central character is a professor of history named Amah Dean Graham. She came of age during the sixties. I really want to write about our generation of intellectual women. I think that this is something important to be said: that we have had a greater effect and that our experiences are more important than we have allowed ourselves to know, and that having it out there for our children, for ourselves, is something that might in fact serve as some forum of debate, a point of change, a point of departure.

MCDOWELL: Very interesting. That's a subject I can't think of anybody
                    tackling. I'm trying to go back; I have a pretty compre-
hensive knowledge of contemporary fiction by black Americans.

WILLIAMS: I can only think of one novel that deals with college
                    women, and this was young women, students, as op-
posed to professionals in the field. I'm very interested in it and very excited about it. It's moving along by fits and starts.

MCDOWELL: I like the idea, and the other thing that appeals to me
                    about it is what I know about your work. I can expect
you not to do this, but we as black people are oftentimes quite ambivalent about intellectual activity. We want it, and then we don't want it somehow. And that "don't want it" expresses itself, in fictional representation, in a tendency to demonize women who are educated, women who are making a living as intellectuals. We have certainly seen women who have educations get demonized in books.

WILLIAMS: The core of this is the relationship between Amah and a
                   woman who has been—I hate the word "role model," I
hate the word "mentor." As you said, "our tendency to demonize women."
Her relationship with this woman who is somewhat older than she is,
who, just by being there—she too is a professional woman—just by being
there gives her an example, tells her it is possible to be an intellectual and
be black. All that she has seen by way of professors are the ones with the
heavy tweed, the brogans, people trying to be English or British, and she
comes across this woman who is as fly as she wants to be, do you hear
me? and who knows the literary tradition, knows everything she needs
to know to be a top-notch professional. This says to her, "Yes, I can do
it too."

So it's that kind of thing that is going on there, because this is also
something that confronts many of our children. I know it was one of
those things that was oppressive; even my son, while growing up, wanted
to know how you can be really smart and still be black. How is it that you
can use Standard English and still keep in touch with the black vernacular?

MCDOWELL: And not just, can you keep in touch with the black ver-
                   nacular, but can you still be accepted, by the "folk" if
you're an intellectual?

WILLIAMS: It really does. I've seen reporters talking to black children
                   on TV where I see children who say that to read, to get
good grades, is to be white.

MCDOWELL: This is a recent phenomenon, and I want somebody to
                   historicize it, because this was not a part of my formative
years. In fact, it was just the opposite.

WILLIAMS: Integration. When I say integration, I'm not talking
                   about the concept of integration and the way we fought
for it in the fifties and early sixties; I'm talking about the actuality of inte-
gration as it was lived from the sixties on, which was that you were always
taking black children out of their environment and putting them into a
white environment. Saying to them that you cannot have a quality educa-
tion in a black environment, and you have to be over here if you're going
to be smart or get on in the world. This was absolutely the wrong mes-
sage to send out. You were saying to them that the only way to get on in

this world is to go into this hostile environment where people literally wanted to kill you, where we cannot protect you, where the people who are in charge do not have to follow the rules. I think that really has a lot to do with it.

In my own neighborhood, living in a predominantly black, working-class neighborhood, there are two kinds of children, two sets of children, two classes of children: those who are bused out of the neighborhood and those who go to schools in the neighborhood. And those children who are bused out of the neighborhood, when they come back during the week and are there for the weekends, they have to prove they are still black, they are still part of the neighborhood. I think that has a lot to do with the rise of gangs, and these are the kinds of things we don't talk about and nobody investigates. But I'm telling you this is my life. I have lived it.

MCDOWELL: And it is important to put it on record, it's important to say it, because this is a critical point, and it's just so obscenely obvious. We are in a crisis insofar as finding a way to talk about the casualties of integration is concerned. As you say it is important to distinguish between integration as fought for by black people, grassroots people, and the thing that came to be realized, the form that integration has taken. You're not saying integration as a concept was misguided, but that the realization of this ideal has had some very devastating consequences on black communities, particularly on black children who have come to fear education, who have come to fear knowledge.

I grew up knowing if you do not get anything else, what you get in your head is yours and it cannot be taken from you, knowing that education was to be prized above all else. I feel so lucky I have never lost the love of learning, and sometimes, like a child, I feel utterly frustrated when I realize this is the middle-age point. I want to know how much time I have left to learn all I want to know.

PART 3

Writing a Literary History of African American Poetry

African American Epic Poetry: The Long Foreshadowing

R A Y M O N D   R .   P A T T E R S O N

LITERARY HISTORY OF AFRICAN AMERICAN POETRY would be incomplete without an examination of the African American epic poem. Called "The Tale of the Tribe" by Michael Bernstein in his 1980 study of the modern verse epic, the epic poem—the long narrative of actions and ideas involving characters of heroic dimension—offers a valuable lens through which to view major themes and periods in African American literature and life.

"The function of the epic," Northrop Frye reminds us in *Fearful Symmetry,* "is to teach the nation, or whatever we call the social unit which the poet is addressing, its own traditions."[1] Epics, "in any case," Nigerian scholar Isidore Okpewho would add, "reflect some significant stage in the political or cultural histories of the communities that tell them."[2] This connection between poet, community, and cultural traditions, at the center of epic poetry, has deep historical resonance in African American life.

Sterling Stuckey's *Slave Culture: Nationalist Theory and the Foundations of Black America* offers the following observation regarding the African American slave's sense of community: "The final gift of African 'tribalism' in the nineteenth century was its life as a lingering memory in the minds of American slaves. That memory enabled them to go back to the sense of community in the traditional African setting and to include all Africans in their common experience of oppression in North America."[3]

E. Franklin Frazier in *The Negro Church in America* called this sense of community among slaves "social cohesion." He attributed it to the influence of the Christian religion and not to any African cultural or religious survival.[4] Recent scholars, however, have more convincingly traced the origins of social cohesion among American slaves to African survivals. Using postbellum accounts and contemporary evidence, Lawrence W. Levine in *Black Culture and Black Consciousness* cites a rich West African musical tradition as a source for "the presence of a compelling communal ethos at slave religious meetings."[5] John W. Blassingame, examining plantation culture, documents the social cohesion among slaves in *The Slave Community: Plantation Life in the Antebellum South*. He cites, for example, frequent references in the spirituals to relatives and friends by name, as evidence of the strong sense of family and community solidarity that existed on plantations.[6] Regarding its origin, he concludes: "A communalism born of oppression led to an emphasis on mutual cooperation, joyful camaraderie, humor, respect for elders, and an undisguised zest for life. The slave's culture bolstered his self-esteem, courage, and confidence and served as his defense against personal degradation."[7] This communal sense, Blassingame points out, was noticed by contemporary observers: "Masters frequently noted the sense of community in the quarters; they reported that slaves usually shared their few goods, rarely stole from each other, and the strong helped the weak. Whitemarsh Seabrook asserted in 1834 that 'between slaves on the same plantation there is a deep sympathy of feeling which binds them so closely together that a crime committed by one of their number is seldom discovered through their instrumentality.'"[8]

The *Narrative of the Life of Frederick Douglass* gives an intimate account of this sense of community typical of slave society. Douglass recalls his life after his experience with the notorious slave-breaker Edward Covey, and prior to his first attempt to escape with four other slaves:

> For the ease with which I passed the year, I was, however, somewhat indebted to the society of my fellow-slaves. They were noble souls; they not only possessed loving hearts, but brave ones. We were linked and inter-linked with each other. I loved them with a love stronger than any thing I have experienced since. It is sometimes said that we slaves do not love and confide in each other. In answer to this assertion, I can say, I never loved any or confided in any people more than my fellow slaves, and especially those with whom I lived at Mr. Freeland's. I believe we would have died for each other. We never undertook to do any thing, of any importance, without a mutual consultation. We never moved separately. We were one; and as much so by our tempers and dispositions, as by the mutual hardships to which we were necessarily subjected by our conditions as slaves.[9]

It is interesting to note that Douglass attributed the slaves' sense of community to a common temper and disposition as much as to a common experience of oppression.

The relatively few, though sensational, betrayals of slave revolts notwithstanding, substantial evidence indicates that a sense of community and an emphasis on cooperation, solidarity, and mutual support were the rule among slaves.

Alain Locke observed this sense of community among African Americans at the beginning of the twentieth century. He saw in the New Negro "the belief in the efficacy of collective effort, in race co-operation. This deep feeling of race," Locke felt, "is at present the mainspring of Negro life." [10]

In *The Souls of Black Folk,* W. E. B. Du Bois movingly describes the struggle of African Americans to sustain a sense of community at the beginning of the century. Du Bois lays bare the complexity of this struggle and its ironic legacy of "double consciousness, this sense of always looking at one's self through the eyes of others." "One ever feels his twoness," Du Bois explains, "—an American, a Negro; two souls, two thoughts, two unreconciled strivings; two warring ideals in one dark body, whose dogged strength alone keeps it from being torn asunder." [11]

The African American pursuit of community, in Du Bois's analysis, is a striving for "the ideal of human brotherhood, gained through the unifying ideal of race." [12] The goal of this striving is for the African American "to be a co-worker in the kingdom of culture," and thereby "to escape both death and isolation." Frustrated by racism, the pursuit of this goal becomes the striving for "two warring ideals." [13]

This African American striving for community is not surprising when seen as a need for kinship and transcendence through participation in a larger human enterprise ("the kingdom of culture"). In traditional African societies such participation assures physical and spiritual survival and is the foundation of a viable social, economic, and political life. Its alternative is isolation and death. [14] Ironically, attempts to achieve a sense of community by African Americans in a racialized America have historically, more often than not, resulted in figurative and literal forms of isolation and death.

Full of paradox and ambiguity, the theme of the pursuit of community touches all other themes in African American life and literature. Unlike the theme of freedom, which has engaged African American poets from Phillis Wheatley to the present, community has roots in African American experience predating American slavery. Freedom implies independence, self-assertion, and self-reliance. Community implies cooperation, solidarity, and mutual support. How the pursuit of community is addressed in African American epic poetry offers a revealing history.

Few examples of African American epic poetry appear before the Civil War. The marginal relationships slave poets like Phillis Wheatley, Jupiter Hammon, and George Moses Horton had with both American society and their slave communities (whose traditions they might have drawn upon) no doubt presented obstacles to the creation of an African American epic. John C. Shields in his essay "Phillis Wheatley's Use of Classicism" asserts, however, that Wheatley did write two short epics, "Goliath of Gath" (based on the biblical account of David and Goliath), and "Niobe in Distress for Her Children Slain by Apollo" (a retelling of the Greek myth). Both poems, he points out, use epic devices including an invocation to the muse, and both poems use elevated language and references to pagan and Christian deities.[15]

Among free African American poets who attempted the epic during the nineteenth century was George Boyer Vashon. His contribution was "Vincent Ogé," published in 1854. Vashon, the son of a prominent abolitionist, was born in 1824 in Carlisle, Pennsylvania. He attended Oberlin College and was its first African American graduate. Later he studied law but was refused examination by the Pennsylvania bar because of his race. In disgust, he left the United States for Haiti, where he taught school, returning after thirty months to begin a law practice in New York State, whose bar he had passed before leaving the country.

"Vincent Ogé" no doubt gained inspiration from Vashon's self-imposed exile. It is a poem in 391 lines about a hero of the 1790–91 Haitian insurrection. It opens on an Eden-like setting and follows Ogé, a mulatto, as he prepares to fight the French tyrants. Its conclusion depicts the horrors of the prison where Ogé dies, a martyr to freedom. Although its ending is tragic, notes Joan R. Sherman in her analysis of the poem in *Invisible Poets,* "Vincent Ogé" "burns with race pride and bittersweet yearnings for retributive justice."[16] In *African-American Poetry of the Nineteenth Century,* Sherman states that "Vashon's epic of the Haitian insurrection is surely the most imaginative poem by an African American of his century."[17]

Before the Civil War, under the influence of the abolitionist movement, the majority of African American writers turned to prose as the effective weapon against slavery. Abolitionist poets like Frances Ellen Harper and the slave poet George Moses Horton to the contrary, it was the writers of the slave narratives and the developing African American novel who most powerfully sustained the epic vision of African American life. The profound dislocations caused by the Civil War and, in its aftermath, the failure of Reconstruction, left the African American community largely confused, but determined, as far as possible, to leave every vestige of slavery in the past and enter the larger American society as full citizens.

"The struggle for freedom had bonded black writers of North and South, free blacks and slaves, to each other and to like-minded white Americans," writes Joan R. Sherman in *African-American Poetry of the Nineteenth Century*. Once achieved, "freedom imposed uncertainties about racial identity and the role of blacks in America's future. Reconstruction brought an urgent need for racial solidarity, as newly won civil rights were undermined by trickery, intimidation, and the South's black codes; the race's social, economic, and political security seemed fearfully precarious." [18] Responding to the times, African American poets acted in either of two ways: they avoided racial issues as a subject, or they wrote poems designed to elevate the image of the African American in order to demonstrate the absurdity of racism. [19] Both strategies, each designed to hasten the integration of African Americans into American society, can be seen in African American epic poetry of the nineteenth century.

One of the earliest poems of truly epic length by an African American is *Columbiana, or the North Star*, published in Chicago in 1870. Its author, Francis A. Boyd, an evangelist and ardent abolitionist, was born of free parents in Lexington, Kentucky, in 1844. He was twenty-six years old when *Columbiana* appeared, a volume of sixty-nine pages, dedicated to the clergyman and abolitionist Henry Ward Beecher.

Columbiana's five cantos range widely in language and style. They narrate the journey of Freedom, personified by a maiden driving a winged chariot from ancient Egypt through Israel and Greece to America, toward the North Star. In the course of her journey, Freedom meets various antagonists. Among those in America is Sesessia, an allegorical figure representing the Confederacy. Blyden Jackson's *A History of Afro-American Literature* describes *Columbiana*, with its mythological allusions and grandiose language, as an attempt to place the abolitionist era in the perspective of all human history. [20] Rather than address the particular aspirations of the African American community, the poem focuses on the universal struggle for freedom. Eugene B. Redmond in *Drumvoices: The Mission of Afro-American Poetry* calls *Columbiana* a "notable step in the development of African American poetry" and suggests that Boyd in some way anticipates Melvin B. Tolson's twentieth-century epic ambition. [21]

Frances Ellen Watkins Harper, abolitionist, orator, author, and the most popular African American poet of the nineteenth century, published in 1869, the year before Boyd's *Columbiana,* a forty-nine-page poem entitled *Moses: A Story of the Nile.* Choosing a familiar epic figure, Harper narrates the biblical life and death of the eponymous lawgiver and leader. The poem draws no parallel between the African American experience of slavery and the ordeal of Moses and the Israelites. However, Joan Sherman in *Invisible Poets* suggests that its composition was probably inspired by the Emancipation Proclamation and the death of Abraham Lincoln.[22] The poem ends with the death of Moses as he gazes across the Jordan River into the Promised Land, a place reserved for future generations.

In Harper's vision of the Promised Land, community is achieved through a recognition of "the unity of God"—which, as the narrator of *Moses* says:

> Should bind us closer to our God and link us
> With our fellow man, the brothers and co-heirs
> With Christ.[23]

Undoubtedly, the finest African American poet of the abolitionist era was Albery A. Whitman.[24] Praised alike by Frederick Douglass, Longfellow, Whittier, and William Cullen Bryant, Albery Whitman was considered the premier African American epic poet of the nineteenth century. Born a slave in Kentucky in 1851, Whitman was orphaned at the age of twelve. After emancipation, with little more than a year of formal education, he taught school, attended Wilberforce University for six months under the guidance of Bishop Daniel A. Payne and published, as a young minister, his first collection of verse. The epic, *Not a Man, and Yet a Man,* his third book, appeared in 1877.

Dedicated to "The Abolition Fathers," *Not a Man, and Yet a Man* shows the influence of Longfellow, Whitman's idol. It narrates, in over 5,000 lines, the larger-than-life adventures and loves of Rodney, a slave who is "eighty-five percent Anglo-Saxon" and the only slave of the evil Sir Maxey in a frontier settlement in Illinois. Rodney possesses an indomitable love of freedom coupled with a spirit of self-reliance. These qualities gain him, after many trials, his freedom in Canada.

Highly melodramatic, the plot moves the hero across a vast and crowded stage representative of nineteenth-century American life. Rodney single-handedly rescues Sir Maxey's beautiful daughter from the Indians following their retaliation for Sir Maxey's unprovoked attack upon their peaceful village. Rodney is betrayed by Sir Maxey, who sells him south to avoid keeping his pledge of rewarding his daughter's hand in marriage to whoever rescues her. Imprisoned on a Florida plantation by his new owner when both he and Rodney become attracted to the same beautiful and innocent octoroon slave, Leeona, Rodney succeeds in escaping with Leeona after she is made pregnant by the degenerate plantation owner, and they begin a perilous journey north to eventual safety in Canada, where the baby dies, but Rodney and Leeona live happily ever after. In Canada they have two sons who grow up and return south with Rodney to fight as Union soldiers in the Civil War. Whitman ends his epic with a plea to the nation to become a true community: "A common country and a common cause" without which "Freedom is an empty name, / And war-worn glory is a glaring shame." He hopes for a time when

> Our country's hosts shall round one interest meet,
> And her free heart with one proud impulse beat,
> One common blood thro' her life's channels flow,
> While one great speech her loyal tongue shall know.
> And soon, whoever to our bourne shall come,
> Jew, Greek or Goth, he here shall be at home.
> Then Ign'rance shall forsake her crooked ways,
> And poor old Caste there end her feeble days.[25]

The Rape of Florida, another Whitman epic, appeared in 1884. It narrates in Spenserian stanza several events of the Seminole War, 1816–42, fought in Florida between the U.S. Army and the Seminole Indians supported by their black Maroon allies and slaves. The narrative, notes Joan Sherman, "is often interrupted by Whitman's musings on honor, freedom, race pride, love, death, and nostalgia for an Edenic pastoral world. The treacherous rape of Florida is a parable of the American experience: a land once paradisical is corrupted by greed, hatred, and hypocrisy, and its native peoples, red and black, are doomed by race prejudice" (AAP, 258).

A third and shorter epic by Whitman, The Octoroon, was published in 1901. Written in ottava rima, it records the unhappy fate of the handsome, noble, and aristocratic Sheldon Maury and his beautiful octoroon slave Lena, whom he attempts to marry. Both epics, The Rape of Florida and The Octoroon, end in tragedy, but Whitman imbues each with an element of hope. In The Rape of Florida, the noble Indian warrior Atlassa and his "sweet-eyed Southern maid," although exiled to Mexico, begin a new life in freedom. In *The Octoroon,* the hero, his beloved, dead, is granted a vision of "a home for love and beauty in the skies," where her spirit resides, free, among "all the spirits of the just" (*AAP,* 263–64).

The Rape of Florida and *The Octoroon* can be read as Whitman's comment on the state of African American hope for community at the beginning of the twentieth century. Progress toward the "ideal of human brotherhood, gained through the unifying ideal of race," later articulated by Du Bois, meant little more than exile (isolation) and death. In the introduction to another edition of *The Rape of Florida* (*Twasinta's Seminoles,* 1885) Whitman states that he had dedicated his genius to the task of producing creations "of real merit," which would "correct the world's judgement and force its respect." [26] He died in 1901 at the age of fifty, the world's judgment, for the most part, unaltered.

With similar ambitions, more than a generation later, poet Robert Hayden would "set out to correct the misconceptions and destroy some stereotypes and clichés which surround Negro history," by writing his poem "Middle Passage." [27] Hayden's "Middle Passage" is clearly not an epic. However, he credits the poem's genesis to a challenge to write the "black-skinned epic, epic with the black spear" predicted by poet Stephen Vincent Benét in lines 933–44 of *John Brown's Body.* Originally, Hayden's work was to be "a poem on slavery and the Civil War, but this time from the black man's point of view." [28]

"Middle Passage," first published in 1943 in *Phylon* magazine, where W. E. B. Du Bois was editor, is an orchestration of voices and documents that relate the circumstances of the 1839 *Amistad* rebellion in which slaves, en route to America aboard the ship *Amistad,* overpowered their captors and attempted to sail back to Africa. The ship was subsequently captured off the Long Island coast by an American man-of-war. A celebrated court trial followed, and eventually the Africans were set free to return home.

The poem projects the rebel African leader Cinquez as a heroic figure, symbolic of "the deep immortal human wish, / the timeless will." [29] In her essay "Changing Permanence: Historical and Literary Revisionism in Robert Hayden's 'Middle Passage,'" Vera Kutzinski observes that "Cinquez is an epic hero who survives the 'Voyage through death' and returns from it a wiser man. But Hayden did not, in the final analysis, write an epic poem. In fact his revisions of the poem on the whole show that he carefully excised all vestiges of the epic mode" from later versions of "Middle Passage." [30] Not until Melvin Tolson's *Harlem Gallery,* more than a half century after

Albery Whitman's work, do we encounter another African American poem that can be called an epic.

Harlem Gallery: Book I, The Curator, published in 1965, was the last of Tolson's four collections of poetry. It was intended to be the first of five books in a single epic that would present the history of African America, from its African origins to contemporary times. Tolson's plan was to parallel the history of African Americans with that of the Old Testament history of the Hebrews, in a way quite different from Frances Harper's earlier use of Old Testament history in *Moses: A Story of the Nile.* In Tolson's epic, book 2, Egyptland, would deal with the slave trade and southern bondage. Book 3, the Red Sea, would cover the Civil War. Book 4, the wilderness, would treat Reconstruction. Book 5, the Promised Land, would focus on present conditions of African America and its class divisions.[31] Of the five books, only the first was completed.

Harlem Gallery, Book I is divided into twenty-four sections, each named for a letter of the Greek alphabet. In a complex, modernist style, it presents a variety of characters who inhabit a community—Harlem, a symbol for African America's creative potential as well as its problems. The main character of the poem, The Curator, is of "Afroirishjewish" ancestry.[32] As the artist-hero of the epic, he shares the weaknesses and virtues of Harlem and, by extension, the entire African American urban community. It is through his genius and vision that positive change can be effected. Tolson writes, "The *Gallery* is an attempt to picture the Negro in America before he becomes the great auk of the melting-pot in the dawn of the twenty-second century."[33] Isolated in urban ghettos, the genius of Tolson's African American community is, paradoxically, threatened by extinction in the American melting-pot. The larger community—America—is equally fated. Says the narrator of *Harlem Gallery:*

> The moving finger in the Harlem Gallery
> paints dramatis personae in the dusk of dawn,
> between America's epigraph and epitaph.[34]

With the publication of Gwendolyn Brooks's *In the Mecca* in 1968, African American epic poetry received a vivid and disturbing portrait of urban African American life at mid-twentieth century. An early proposal for the work describes it as "a book-length poem, two thousand lines or more, based on life in Chicago's old Mecca Building."[35] The completed poem consists of 807 lines in fifty-six stanzas.

Haki Madhubuti, who makes a brief appearance in *In the Mecca* as Don Lee, refers to Gwendolyn Brooks's poem as "her epic of black humanity." [36] Its setting is a decaying, once luxurious, ghetto apartment building on Chicago's Southside. Mrs. Sallie Smith, a domestic, comes home at evening to discover that Pepita, the youngest of her nine children, is missing. As the family undertakes a search, a variety of Mecca inhabitants are introduced. We witness their individual isolation, confusion, anger, and despair, and realize the ethical values of an entire community have been inverted. What is more, we apprehend, by implication, the wider tragedy that is contemporary American life. As D. H. Melhem observes in *Gwendolyn Brooks: Poetry and the Heroic Voice,* "Brooks's black world mirrors the psychic isolation of its white environment." [37]

The Mecca represents the poet's assessment of urban African America's progress toward community a century after emancipation. The Mecca's inhabitants are isolated not only from the larger society but also from each other. The search for the missing Pepita makes this clear by causing doors to open, ultimately revealing the body of the murdered child hidden beneath the bed of one of the inhabitants.

Du Bois's description of frustrated African American need and desire for community is epitomized in the Mecca, a place of both isolation and death. However, as a symbol, the Mecca is not without hope. Despite its tragic conclusion, the poem enacts a search for a lost child—a pilgrimage by a family, door to door, toward reclamation and possible redemption. Like its narrative, many of the poem's devices, including the use of irony and ambiguity of character and incident, convey this possibility of redemption:

> I hate it.
> Yet, murmurs Alfred—
> who is lean at the balcony, leaning—
> something, something in Mecca
> continues to call! Substanceless; yet like mountains,
> like rivers and oceans too; and like trees
> with wind whistling through them. And steadily
> an essential sanity, black and electric,
> builds to a reportage and redemption.
>   A hot estrangement.
>   A material collapse
> that is Construction. [38]

There is hope even in isolation and death. This African knowledge African American epic poets have perennially asserted. "One who is self-alienated must see, must think, must define, must act," writes poet Jay Wright, author of *The Double Invention of Komo*, published in 1980. "To be self-divided," Wright goes on to say, "is not necessarily to be defeated but to be more radically alert to the claims of human experience, human history and creativity." [39] Ritual isolation and death as a preparation for rebirth and integration is an essential element of Wright's vision of community as represented in his epic poem.

Drawing upon African myths and rituals from the Dogon and Bambara of Mali, West Africa, *The Double Invention* presents a quest for self-knowledge by means of initiation through Komo clan ritual. Such a process, if completed successfully, allows the initiate knowledge of self and entry into the larger community as a fully participating member. Wright's poem, an epic of the soul's progress toward "true self-consciousness," seems to address that absence which Du Bois laments in *The Souls of Black Folk*. [40] The hero must ritually pass through sectors of painful history and personal experience, and undergo numerous journeys, in order to evolve a multicultural—American—personality.

In an essay on Jay Wright, Isidore Okpewho points out that *The Double Invention* takes its hero on a journey toward a personality that has a traditional African sensitivity. It is a personality that has gained, by means of ceremonial initiation, knowledge of the principle of duality, or doubling, that underlies all creation in Dogon cosmology. The individual is therefore able, according to Okpewho, to "accommodate a cultural Other," Du Bois's "double-consciousness." [41] The narrator-hero of *The Double Invention of Komo* calls this knowledge "the trinity of races [African, European, Native American] in my blood." [42]

The initiated personality, the epic's poet-hero, awakes in the end from his ritual death, firm in his African identity and more capable of reconciling his personality's multiracial dimensions.

Wright, in an essay on black poetry's ritual and historical voice, suggests that Okpewho's assessment of the role of the African artist in society agrees with his own view, that the artist is "'the truly guiding sensibility of his community' who 'leads the way in recreating the progressive forms of communal myth.'" [43] By "progressive" we assume that Wright refers to forms of myth that, like the epic poem, "teach the nation, or whatever we call the social unit which the poet is addressing, its own traditions"; or which "reflect some significant stage in the political or cultural histories of the communities that tell them."

A glance at the achievements of Wheatley, Vashon, Boyd, Harper, Whitman, Tolson, Hayden, Brooks, and Wright scarcely suggests the riches to be discovered by a close examination of the African American epic poem. The lives of early African American epic poets are themselves epics. Twentieth-century forms of epic poetry, specifically the long poem and the poetic sequence, enlarge the area of investigation. Questions of gender, class, and the changing field of heroic action call for study. A list of contemporary works would certainly include N. J. Loftis's *Black Anima* and Yvonne Chism-Pease's three-volume epic *Iwilla,* with its heroic female figures. Seeing how African American epic poetry approaches the need and desire for community, and resolves the double goals of racial solidarity and human brotherhood in a racist society, offers challenges to both poets and scholars.

Notes

1. Frye, 316.
2. Okpewho, *African Oral Literature,* 202.
3. Stuckey, 3.
4. Frazier, 6.
5. Levine, 27.
6. Blassingame, 145.
7. Ibid., 148.
8. Ibid., 315–16.
9. Douglass, 304–5.
10. Locke, 11.
11. Du Bois, 16–17.
12. Ibid., 22.
13. Ibid., 17.
14. Mbiti, 135–41.
15. Shields, 104–05.
16. Sherman, *Invisible Poets,* 56.
17. Sherman, *African-American Poetry of the Nineteenth Century,* 153.
18. Ibid., 7.
19. Ibid., 8.
20. Jackson, 256.
21. Redmond, 98.
22. Sherman, *Invisible Poets,* n. 71.
23. Harper, 161.
24. Jackson, 272.

25. Sherman, *African-American Poetry,* 247; hereafter cited in text, with page numbers, as *AAP.*

26. Sherman, *Invisible Poets,* 115.

27. Hayden, *Collected Prose,* 162.

28. Ibid., 163.

29. Hayden, "Middle Passage," 859.

30. Kutzinsky, 179–80.

31. Russell, 12.

32. Tolson, *Harlem Gallery,* 24.

33. Tolson, *Gallery of Harlem Portraits,* 259.

34. Tolson, *Harlem Gallery,* 153.

35. Brooks, *Report from Part One,* 189.

36. Ibid., 22.

37. Melhem, 158.

38. Brooks, *Blacks,* 433.

39. Wright, "Desire's Design," 20.

40. Du Bois, 16.

41. Okpewho, "From a Goat Path in Africa," 720.

42. Wright, *Double Invention of Komo,* 105.

43. Wright, "Desire's Design," 27.

Works Cited

Benét, Stephen Vincent. *John Brown's Body.* New York: Holt, 1968.

Bernstein, Michael. *The Tale of the Tribe: Ezra Pound and the Modern Verse Epic.* Princeton: Princeton University Press, 1980.

Blassingame, John W. *The Slave Community: Plantation Life in the Antebellum South.* New York: Oxford University Press, 1979.

Boyd, Francis A. *Columbiana; or, The North Star, Complete in One Volume.* Chicago: Steam Job & Book Printing House of B. Hand, 1870.

Brooks, Gwendolyn. *Blacks.* Chicago: Third World, 1987.

———. *Report from Part One.* Detroit: Broadside, 1972.

Douglass, Frederick. *Narrative of the Life of Frederick Douglass, An American Slave.* In *The Classic Slave Narratives,* ed. Henry Louis Gates Jr. New York: New American Library, 1987. 243–331.

Du Bois, W. E. B. *The Souls of Black Folk.* New York: Fawcett, 1961.

Frazier, E. Franklin. *The Negro Church in America.* New York: Schocken, 1964.

Frye, Northrop. *Fearful Symmetry: A Study of William Blake.* Princeton: Princeton University Press, 1947.

Harper, Frances Ellen Watkins. *Moses: A Story of the Nile.* In *A Brighter Coming Day: A Frances Ellen Watkins Harper Reader,* ed. Frances Smith Foster. New York: Feminist, 1990.

Hayden, Robert. *Collected Prose.* Ed. Frederick Glaysher. Ann Arbor: University of Michigan Press, 1984.

———. "Middle Passage." In *The Norton Anthology of Modern Poetry*, ed. Ellmann and O'Clair. New York: Norton, 1973. 854–59.

Jackson, Blyden. *A History of Afro-American Literature, Vol. I, The Long Beginning, 1746–1895*. Baton Rouge: Louisiana State University Press, 1989.

Kutzinsky, Vera M. "Changing Permanences: Historical and Literary Revisionism in Robert Hayden's 'Middle Passage.'" *Callaloo* 9.1 (1986): 171–83.

Levine, Lawrence W. *Black Culture and Black Consciousness: Afro-American Folk Thought from Slavery to Freedom*. New York: Oxford University Press, 1977.

Locke, Alain. *The New Negro*. New York: Antheneum, 1983.

Loftis, N. J. *Black Anima*. New York: Liveright, 1973.

Mbiti, John S. *African Religions and Philosophies*. New York: Anchor, 1970.

Melhem, D. H. *Gwendolyn Brooks: Poetry and the Heroic Voice*. Lexington: University Press of Kentucky, 1987.

Okpewho, Isidore. *African Oral Literature*. Bloomington: Indiana University Press, 1992.

———. "From a Goat Path in Africa: An Approach to the Poetry of Jay Wright." *Callaloo* 14.3 (1991): 692–726.

Redmond, Eugene B. *Drumvoices: The Mission of Afro-American Poetry*. New York: Anchor, 1976.

Russell, Mariann B. "Evolution of Style in the Poetry of Melvin B. Tolson." In *Black American Poets between Worlds, 1940–1960*, ed. R. Baxter Miller. Knoxville: University of Tennessee Press, 1992.

Sherman, Joan R., ed. *African-American Poetry of the Nineteenth Century: An Anthology*. Urbana: University of Illinois Press, 1992.

———. *Invisible Poets: Afro-Americans of the Nineteenth Century*. Urbana: University of Illinois Press, 1992.

Shields, John C. "Phillis Wheatley's Use of Classicism." *American Literature* 52 (1980): 97–111.

Stuckey, Sterling. *Slave Culture: Nationalist Theory and Foundations of Black America*. New York: Oxford University Press, 1987.

Tolson, Melvin B. *Gallery of Harlem Portraits*. Ed. Robert M. Farnsworth. Columbia: University of Missouri Press, 1979.

———. *Harlem Gallery, Book I, The Curator*. New York: Twayne, 1965.

Vashon, George Boyer. "Vincent Ogé." In *Autographs for Freedom*, ed. Julia Griffiths. Auburn: Alden, 1854. 44–60.

Wheatley, Phillis. *The Collected Works of Phillis Wheatley*. Ed. John Shields. New York: Oxford University Press, 1988.

Whitman, Albery Allson. *Not a Man, and Yet a Man*. Springfield, Ohio: Republic, 1877.

———. "The Octoroon." In *An Idyl of the South: An Epic Poem in Two Parts*. New York: Metaphysical, 1901.

———. *The Rape of Florida*. St. Louis: Nixon-Jones, 1884. Reissued as *Twasinta's Seminoles; Or, Rape of Florida*, 1885, 1890.

Wright, Jay. "Desire's Design, Vision's Resonance." *Callaloo* 10.1 (1987): 13–28.

———. *The Double Invention of Komo*. Austin: University of Texas Press, 1980.

Yvonne (Chism-Peace). *I Willa, Book I, Soil*. New York: Chameleon, 1985.

———. *I Willa, Book II, Scourge*. New York: Chameleon, 1986.

Personal and Public: Three First-Person Voices in African American Poetry

ERIC A. WEIL

LACK POETS, BECAUSE SO MANY IN THEIR AUDIENCE are white, must constantly be aware that they speak not only as individuals but as representatives of their race. This fact of persona is at the root of racism, but it is also at the heart of any ethnic minority's self-identity. How do poets deal with both personal and public personae in their work? One way, with which we are familiar, is the first-person-plural narrator, which is used when the poet wishes to speak directly as a voice for his or her race. Paul Laurence Dunbar's "We Wear the Mask" is a well-known example. Of course, the first-person-singular narrator, to communicate an intensely personal experience to a wider audience, is as available to black poets as to any, and Countee Cullen's "Incident" may be the most anthologized poem in this voice. Influenced perhaps in part by such poets as Edgar Lee Masters (*Spoon River Anthology*) and T. S. Eliot ("Prufrock"), black poets such as Gwendolyn Brooks also used the first-person-singular narrator as a voice for individual characters created to speak the poems. There is another first-person-singular narrator, one that makes a poem sound either personal or character-driven, but on a second reading, it is clear that readers should assume that the "I" of the poem is a racially identified "We." An early example is Frances E. W. Harper's "Bury Me in a Free Land," in which the speaker enunciates, following a catalog of injustices, the desires not only of self but of race:

> I ask no monument, proud and high,
> To arrest the gaze of the passer-by;
> All that my yearning spirit craves,
> Is bury me not in a land of slaves. (*BWA,* 225)[1]

Poets of the Harlem Renaissance and the post–Harlem Renaissance periods have used these voices, particularly the last, in their work. Since racism still exists, the need remains for both personal ("I") and public ("We") voices for black poets. And there is no reason to believe that the need for a special personal/public voice (the "I" that means "We," or a particular kind of dramatic monologue), with which black readers can identify and through which white readers can appreciate black pain, would have faded with either increased African American publications or the successes of the civil rights movement.

In a revolution, some of the past is cast off as useless or irrelevant, and some is kept for its continuing usefulness. The use of a variety of first-person voices, including the "I" that means "We," is not universal among African American poets, but enough examples can be found in the Harlem Renaissance poetry of Hughes, Cullen, and McKay, and in the post-Renaissance poetry of Sterling Brown, Gwendolyn Brooks, Nikki Giovanni, Amiri Baraka, and Haki Madhubuti to demonstrate a continued need for this variety of racial self-expression. Despite the differences among these poets in their attitudes about race or social conditions or other poetic techniques, a continuity of various first-person narrative stances has been valuable to succeeding generations of black poets. I am not writing about any poet's oeuvre but points of intersection among disparate black poets. Also, it is not my intent to suggest that only race matters to black poets, but it is to explore the range of expression that occurs in poems when race does matter. J. Saunders Redding, in the groundbreaking work *To Make a Poet Black,* refuses to acknowledge that race is all that matters to a black poet, yet in many cases he has no praise for the poems that do not deal with race.[2] This paradox also is borne out in anthologies of black poetry, whose editors make selections almost exclusively on the basis of the poems' messages about race. In sum, what we end up with is a kind of "meta-autobiography," personal writing in which the poet creates a place for himself or herself within the larger framework of a racial heritage. This writing might also be called "activist autobiography," particularly in the poetry of the 1960s and later, as poets strive for an overt political positioning in the American capitalist culture.

"MY POETRY is whatever I think I am," writes Amiri Baraka in his early essay "How You Sound?"[3] This concise "ars poetica" raises questions relevant to most poets: When am I myself? When am I a character created for a poem? And it raises another question for black (or any minority) poets: When am I my people? Later, in the 1960s essay, "State/meant," Baraka creates a clearer picture of his poetics: "The Black Artist must draw out of his soul the correct image of the world. He must use this image to band his brothers and sisters together in common understanding of the nature of the world (and the nature of America) and the nature of the human soul." [4] A goal this broad must use all the techniques available to connect the individual with the masses. Indeed, by the eighties, in "The Revolutionary Tradition in Afro-American Literature," Baraka theorizes another version of this connectivity by calling for a constantly evolving Black Arts ideology that is willing to focus not simply on antiwhite sentiment but on "the real enemies of black people," imperialism and capitalism. [5] Donald B. Gibson rejects the notion that any black writer "considers his blackness to define his *essential* self," [6] despite what seems to be a growing willingness to move in that direction on the part of Baraka and others. I agree that no one's color should be his or her "essential self," yet many black poets have accepted this stance in some of their poems, because speaking for more than the self has been an important strategy for them. In his introductions to two anthologies published in the late 1960s, *Anger and Beyond* and *Soon, One Morning,* Herbert Hill writes of the necessity for black writers to combine social protest with serious artistic technique. He feels that they share "a determination to break through the limits of racial parochialism into the whole range of the modern writer's preoccupations." [7] Implicit in Hill's argument is the idea that black writers must somehow get "beyond" race. Others, such as Henry Louis Gates, Houston A. Baker, and Kimberly W. Benston, are not so hopeful. [8] The bitter truth, of course, is that although black poets might avoid the issue of race in a few poems, race inevitably preoccupies their art as it preoccupies their lives. Fortunately, a variety of narrative points of view can be used to keep poetic presentations of race issues fresh. Changes of point of view are evidence of another kind of double consciousness—first there is the double consciousness created by being a free black in racist America; then there is the double consciousness created by speaking both for oneself and for one's race.

Point of view is a choice writers make as they form their work. For black writers, this choice involves creating an indication of just how "black" they want the work to sound. Houston Baker, in *Afro-American Poetics: Revisions of Harlem and the Black Aesthetic,* notes the frequency with which black poets choose the role of "spokesperson" for their race. [9] In *Loose Canons: Notes on the Culture Wars,* Henry Louis Gates notes that when earlier black scholars explicated poems by black writers, they asserted that "if the 'blackness' of a text was to be found anywhere . . . it would be in the practical uses of language."[10] One of these scholars is Stephen Henderson. In his Introduction to *Understanding the New Black Poetry,* Henderson hypothesizes a tripartite evaluation of black poetry: theme (discussed as "subject"), structure (discussed in terms of black music), and "saturation" (defined as a "descriptive category" in which the reader feels that the character described must be black).[11] Henderson does not discuss point of view in any of these areas, but I feel that point of view cuts across all three. The narrator is part of the subject, an integral part of the structure, and in black poetry, a great deal of "saturation," especially when the poet chooses the role of "spokesperson."

Langston Hughes probably is still the best-known African American poet, one who made use of a wealth of narrative points of view, one who makes a good beginning to this study. In "The Negro Artist and the Racial Mountain," Hughes writes of the necessity to avoid imitating white writers, acting as if white culture were superior to black. He acknowledges the role of race: "Most of my poems are racial in theme and treatment, derived from the life I know."[12] The sum is that the issue of race is unavoidable for minority writers in America, and few of these writers have tried to avoid it. In some poems Hughes creates a first-person black character, as in "Daybreak in Alabama," where the speaker imagines composing great music. The first-person speaker of the italicized lines in many of the poems of *Montage of a Dream Deferred* also seems to be made for the occasion. In other poems, such as "Dinner Guest: Me" and "Theme for English B," Hughes is writing directly from personal experience and clearly the "I" is intended to be taken with considerable autobiographical emphasis with, perhaps, the kind of mask, or persona, that Gibson sees in all of Hughes's poetry. "Theme" is a catalog of Hughes's physical, mental, and racial situation as he attends a college class (*TBE,* 535–56). "Dinner Guest: Me" is interesting for its portrayal of self as aware of the (white) audience's tendency to see him as a representative of his race, one who can either "explain" blacks to whites or one to whom liberal whites can express their guilt for the way blacks have been treated in America. It is, of course, not unusual for blacks to be put in this position of "representative" or to be uncomfortable in the role.

At other times, however, Hughes was, like most black poets, willing to accept the role of spokesperson for the black race. The difference is made through choosing the circumstances of race representation. In "Peace," Hughes uses the first-person-plural narrator instead of the singular in order to foster group identification in his readers: "We passed their graves; / The dead men there" (*TBP,* 82). In this ironic "Peace," "We" are the heirs of the lynched or the slaves or others who gave their lives to improve civil rights.

More interesting, in terms of the use of various narrative voices, are poems in which Hughes uses "I" to mean "We"—"We blacks." Here, Hughes creates another spokesperson voice, one that is both personal and public, speaking through an individual's pain to reach that of a race. The most anthologized of these poems is "The Negro Speaks of Rivers." This brief outline of African American heritage is spoken in the first person— "I've known rivers ancient as the world" (*BWA*, 517)—but every black reader is to identify with the poem's "I." Hughes frequently employed the "I" that means "We" voice in poems depicting the savagery and injustices of whites during the long struggle for civil rights. See, for example, such poems as "Third Degree" ("Hit me! Jab me! / Make me say I did it"); "Ku Klux" ("They took me out / To some lonesome place"); "The Backlash Blues" ("Mister Backlash, Mister Backlash, / Just who do you think I am?") (*TBP*, 80, 81, 90). Whereas in the first two of these poems the speaker represents that segment of the black population that directly faced the violence and paid the price, the third poem seeks to literally put a first-person voice on the entire race. Hughes could also employ the I (We) voice in a more positive poem, "I, Too": "I, too, sing America. / I am the darker brother" (*BWA*, 519). The poem ends hoping (perhaps a bit naïvely) to unify the disparate racial and social forces that constantly tear at the American social fabric. With even this small cross-section of poems, we can see that Hughes created a variety of poetic voices, all of which could be used to sing frustrations as well as joys: his own and those of his race.

Other Harlem Renaissance poets also utilized various first-person points of view; Countee Cullen and Claude McKay are the best known. "Incident" is Cullen's most anthologized personal cry against the remembered racist slight, and he wrote many other poems that, in their first-person-singular voices, speak Cullen's own pain. But Cullen could also choose the more public, spokesman's plural voice of "We." "The Litany of the Dark People" is a comparison of black suffering with Christ's suffering (53). "From the Dark Tower" is a sonnet that follows in the footsteps of Dunbar's "We Wear the Mask" and McKay's "If We Must Die." It ends "So in the dark we hide the heart that bleeds, / And wait, and tend our agonizing seeds" (47). This poem, with that most hated word, "wait," need not be censured, for it also counsels action, the tending of the seeds that will, in time, produce for the speaker and not for others.

Cullen also found the "I" that means "We" voice useful. "Hunger" is another Dunbar-like poem of the black mask, only with a singular voice:

"Inevitable is the way I go, / False-faced" (66). In "The Shroud of Color," a poem of some one-hundred heroic couplets, Cullen makes his first-person-singular narrator symbolize the black condition of the early twentieth century: "I strangle in this yoke drawn tighter than / The worth of bearing it, just to be man" (16). Primarily a psalmic questioning of God's ways that allow so many to suffer so much, and partly a dream-vision saying that blacks' natural affinity for music gives them the courage to endure, this poem ends with the speaker (and, by extension, the black race) joyous in his cathartic knowledge that he has the spiritual fortitude to continue. The ambiguities of Christianity as the religion of the oppressor and at the same time a source of comfort for the oppressed are treated again in "Heritage," a poem whose fame demands brevity. At the beginning, Cullen seems to be at his most personal, his speaker obviously a descendant of Keats. In comparing Western and African cultures, differences in worship are at the fore, and as the speaker tries to resolve his dual-culture heritage, he becomes a racial spokesman: "Lord, forgive me if my need / Sometimes shapes a human creed" (28). It takes community to shape a creed, but this speaker is uncertain in his dualism: *"Not yet has my heart or head / In the least way realized / They and I are civilized"* (italics Cullen's) (28). Certainly the intent of the poem is to match, in the reader's mind, the third-person-plural "they" with an assumed first-person plural "We," with the individual narrator of the poem standing in for the race.

Like Cullen's "Incident," Claude McKay's "The Tropics in New York" is a short poem of intense personal suffering, here, a longing for "the old, familiar ways" (*BWA*, 493) of Jamaica. "The Harlem Dancer," with its male first-person observation of the woman, is another example of the singular narrator, watching and withholding judgment. McKay's most anthologized poem, "If We Must Die," corresponds exactly to the mode of the plural narrator-as-spokesperson and needs no further discussion here. But McKay, like Hughes, wrote a number of poems in the "I" that means "We" voice, usually again like Hughes, to express disgust with the treatment accorded blacks in America, and in many cases to call for a brand of separatism within American society. McKay's early poetry is "dialect verse" in which he creates characters who speak in first person. Wayne Cooper points out that after 1912, when McKay stopped writing in dialect, he "would henceforth project in all his verse the image of the romantic revolutionary, defiant of all injustices." [13] And I would add that McKay often projected this image through the "I (We)" point of view. In "The White City" ("I will not toy with it nor bend an inch"); "Tiger" ("The white man is a tiger at my throat"); "America" ("I stand within her walls with not a shred / Of terror, malice, not a word of jeer"); and "The White House" ("Your door is shut against my tightened face, / And I am sharp as steel with discontent" (*TBP*, 61; *BWA*, 494, 496, 497);[14] McKay takes upon himself the voice of his people, yet is one step removed, from "We" to the "I" that means "We." As the Harlem Renaissance was a period of deep and continuing exploration into both the situation of blacks in America and into their African roots and heritage, the major poets of the time found it necessary to produce in a variety of voices suited to different expressions of their personal and their racial identities.

In the post–Harlem Renaissance decades, Sterling Brown and Gwendolyn Brooks are two poets who value the melange of narrative possibilities so richly maintained by Hughes, Cullen, and McKay. In Sterling Brown's poetry an array of first-person narrative strategies can be found. Following the lead of some of Cullen's and McKay's sonnets, "Salutamus" uses the first-person-plural speaker. The octave expresses the familiar complaint of injustice: "The bitterness of days like these we know; / Much, much we know, yet cannot understand / What was our crime"; but the sestet reveals the certainty of proper resolution through effort: "And yet we know relief will come some day / For these seared breasts; . . . / *We must plunge onward; onward, gentlemen*" (italics Brown's) (106). A similar poem in the same voice is "Crossing," which catalogs the American rivers black history has passed over: "We know only / That there lies not Canaan / That this is no River Jordan" (195). The "one wide river" left to cross, as the spiritual puts it, is that of justice and equality.

Much more commonly, Brown depicts individual characters and allows them to speak their own stories. There are a number of poems written in the third person—he, she—describing the travail of a working-class man or woman. And there is probably an equal number written in the first-person singular. Usually, the speaker's name or occupation is given in the title, for example, "Scotty Has His Say," in which the conjuring and the joyful song and dance of his black culture are contrasted with the spiritless work of white culture, and "Tin Roof Blues," the lament of a railroad worker. Most of these poems are spoken in a southern rural-black dialect, such as "Slim in Atlanta," a poem about the danger blacks face by laughing in public, and "Ruminations of Luke Johnson," in which the speaker meditates on the legacy of slavery. I think it is safe to say that all of these poems presenting the lives of many different individual black characters add up to a presentation of the lives of "We," the black race in America. In Brown's

Collected Poems there is one poem employing the "I" that means "We" voice, "Bitter Fruit of the Tree." Not about lynching, the poem depicts the economic injustices of the slavery and Reconstruction periods. The first stanza recalls "my grandmother" and how her first child was sold away from her and how her husband escaped, was recaptured, and beaten. The second stanza recalls "my father" and the spirit-killing system of tenant farming. In both stanzas the voice of white people ("they") is heard, telling blacks they should not feel bitterness. The speaker is intended to be any African American, thinking about his or her heritage.

Like Sterling Brown, Gwendolyn Brooks creates many individual characters to speak her poems, representing in their sum the situation and struggles of blacks in America. She, too, as Richard K. Barksdale has pointed out, finds some occasions when either she or a narrator takes on the role of spokesperson.[15] In the group-written book *A Capsule Course in Black Poetry Writing,* Brooks is emphatic about the relationship between author and audience: "The prevailing understanding: black literature is literature BY blacks, ABOUT blacks, directed TO blacks."[16] Brooks is most clearly a spokeswoman in her tribute poem, "Malcolm X": "He had the hawk-man's eyes. / We gasped. We saw the maleness" (441).[17] She plays the same role in "The Second Sermon on the Warpland." Here, the implied singular narrator through the first three sections takes up the cause of the race in the fourth section with a plural speaker enjoining "you"—all black folk—to be positive: "It is lonesome, yes. For we are the last of the loud. / Nevertheless, live" (456).

These poems are from later in her career, *In the Mecca,* 1968. Early in her career, as in *A Street in Bronzeville,* 1945, Brooks's technique echoed Sterling Brown's, creating individual characters to speak the poems. Sometimes in first person, sometimes in third, these portraits delineate a picture of a Chicago neighborhood, and through that picture the black situation in America. D. H. Melhem, in *Gwendolyn Brooks: Poetry and the Heroic Voice,* discusses this portraiture in relation to form and content. In aggregate, the "I" portraits speak the "We" of black circumstances in America. The much anthologized poem "The Mother" serves as one example, with its character both bemoaning and rationalizing her choice of abortion: "I have heard in the voices of the wind the voices of my dim killed children / . . . / Believe me, I loved you all" (21–22). This theme is picked up again in *Annie Allen,* in part 2 of "The Children of the Poor": "What shall I give my children? who are poor, / Who are adjudged the leastwise of the land" (116). The children are given their voice by the girl who sings "A Song in the Front Yard," who wants "a peek at the back / Where it's rough and untended and hungry weed grows" (25). But women and children are not the only representative characters Brooks creates; men get their voices in poems such as "Negro Hero" and "The Chicago *Defender* Sends a Man to Little Rock," in both of which a first-person-singular narrator documents attitudes necessary to the civil rights movement. The poems from *Riot* and after are primarily in the third person. Characters, often apparently based on real people, are the focus, as with "The Life of Lincoln West." Twice Brooks takes on the "We" spokeswoman voice, in "Young Afrikans" and in "To John Killens." The former is a call to action, and the latter is a tribute to one who died for the cause of equality. A later long poem that uses a more autobiographical-sounding first person voice to speak for the pain of all African Americans (and many others) is "In Montgomery," an exploration of reactions to the assassinations of the 1960s. Brooks is at her most personal and public in expressing a rage that was both personal and public for all who experienced it. Neither Gwendolyn Brooks nor Sterling Brown seems to have chosen to write in an obviously personal mode, in the way of Cullen's "Incident" or Hughes's "Dinner Guest: Me," choosing instead to keep their own personalities behind the scenes and allowing the assortment of personae they created to speak both for themselves and for all—or at least most—African Americans.

Of black poets who came to prominence in the 1960s and 1970s, who created, in Donald B. Gibson's words, "a significantly definable black poetry,"[18] Amiri Baraka, Nikki Giovanni, and Haki Madhubuti display a variety of first-person voices. In large part, I believe their variety is the result of passing through more distinguishable phases of their careers than some of the earlier poets. In writing about the dialect verse of the Reconstruction period, J. Saunders Redding notes that the poet "discovered that in order to be heard at all he must speak in the voice and accents that his hearers recognized."[19] To an extent, this statement can be applied to black poetry of the 1960s, not for the same kind of dialect use, but for the increased use of urban street slang and experiments in form. Larry Neal, with Baraka a spokesman in both poetry and prose for the Black Arts Movement, wrote, "The Black Arts Movement is radically opposed to any concept of the artist that alienates him from his community."[20] Houston Baker, writing of Baraka and Neal's anthology *Black Fire,* notes that "the words strive to recreate a primordial black logos, or word, through sheer lyricism and assertiveness."[21] This assertiveness takes part of its form in the narrative stances the poets chose. These poets either started out writing more lyrical, personal poetry and later grew more politically militant as the civil rights movement increased its prominence, or their writing began in a militant mode and later resolved, at least in part, toward more personal expression. In either case, they maintained the tradition of the use of a variety of first-person points of view.

If his poetry is whatever Amiri Baraka thinks he is at the moment, it is no surprise that he has thought of himself in a variety of ways throughout his career. In any form, he has "nonetheless pointed the way for younger poets," to borrow Gibson's words.[22] Yet from the Beat period through his Pan-Afrikan Marxist period, Baraka has wielded a variety of first-person points of view, in general moving from purely personal expression to a mode that incorporates elements that exemplify the role of racial spokesman he has increasingly taken upon himself. Clyde Taylor calls Baraka "the most personal so far of the Afro-American poets."[23] Baraka's strong personality lends itself to speaking for the race, allowing his own antiwhite rhetoric to be stamped onto his people. "Preface to a Twenty Volume Suicide Note," with its marking of modern uncertainties followed by observation of his small daughter, and poems from *The Dead Lecturer,* such as "The Liar," in which Baraka refers specifically to himself, and "Short Speech to my Friends" are examples of the early, more personal first-person-singular mode of address.

Also in *The Dead Lecturer* is the beginning of Baraka-as-spokesman. "The Politics of Rich Painters" demands of those who once were poor the compassion and political insight to help those who remain poor. "You know the pity / of democracy, that we must sit here / and listen to how he made his money" (60–61).[24] "An Agony. As Now." is an early example of the "I" narrator who stands in for the race. The first stanza of the poem relates the well-documented feeling that the oppressed always knows his oppressor better than the oppressor knows himself: "I am inside someone / who hates me" (52). And the remainder of the poem details the difficulty of understanding your feelings, or understanding whether you have feelings, in a society that tries to minimize your selfhood.

Not surprisingly, the poems of Baraka's Black Nationalist period provide the most examples of the "We" spokesman narrator, as Baraka became more of a literary (and political) force in America. At the end of the essay "State/meant" he incorporates a challenge: "The day will not save them / and we own / the night" (170). In *Black Magic,* "Return of the Native" moves from personal impressions on a visit to Harlem to an identification with the struggles of and the search for joy in the lives of all black people. And juxtaposed against the intensely personal "leroy" is "Ka 'Ba," with its social consciousness and its encouragement. Primarily, however, as Baraka's Black Nationalist poems grew longer, they grew more exhortatory—"It's Nation Time," "Afrikan Revolution," and "When We'll Worship Jesus," for example. In these poems the "I" is assumed; the poems are in the voice of a leader, calling "you," his people. Only in the later poems of *Why's/Wise* is there a return to the "I" speaker who directly represents "We," the black people. "Wise 2" is a heritage poem, recalling that "I still hear those songs, and cries" of an enslaved people. It ends: "I am among those / to be avenged!" (482). Surely a call to political arms. "Wise 4" is a similar evocation of the general through the individual, as the speaker says, "I have never got nothing but hard times and punishment / Any joy I had I made myself" (484). It appears that late in his career, Baraka has experimented with dialect and point of view in a fashion resembling that of Sterling Brown.

Another major poet of the 1960s, Nikki Giovanni, also adapted several points of view to her poetic purposes. Called by R. Roderick Palmer "the poet most impatient for change," Giovanni is in many poems just as personal as Baraka and just as willing to step from the personal role to the role of spokesperson.[25] Some of her earlier and more frequently anthologized poems are the most personal, such as "My Poem" ("I am 25 years old / black female poet") and "For Saundra" ("I wanted to write / a poem / that rhymes / but revolution doesn't lend / itself to be-bopping") (*TBP*, 319, 321). Giovanni slips on the mantle of spokeswoman by using the first-personplural narrator. Sometimes she is speaking for all African Americans; sometimes she is speaking on behalf of women. In "The Funeral of Martin Luther King Jr." she speaks the pain of the race; in "Always There Are the Children" she speaks of the hope of the race:

> we feed the children with our culture
> that they might understand our travail
>
> we nourish the children on our gods
> that they might understand respect
>
> we urge the children on the tracks
> that our race will not fall short (n.p.)

In other poems, "We" are women. "The Women" is the first section of the volume *The Women and the Men,* and the first poem is "The Women Gather." This poem of the early 1970s still resonates in the nineties, as it speaks of women's pain upon the deaths of young men and of their ability to cope with this pain: "we judge a man by his dreams / not alone his

deeds / we judge a man by his intent / not alone his shortcomings" (n.p.).
In most of the remaining poems of "The Women" Giovanni employs the
dramatic monologue, creating individual women characters who, when
considered together, speak for the whole. Other poems speak even more
directly and widely to and for the black race. An example is "Ego Tripping":
"i was born in the congo / i walked to the fertile crescent and built the
sphinx / i designed a pyramid" (n.p.). Another monologue exploring the
black heritage is "Africa," with its refrain, "i am a teller of tales / a dreamer
of dreams" (n.p.). The later poems are marked by a return to the personal,
for example, in the volumes *Cotton Candy on a Rainy Day* and *Those Who
Ride with the Wind*. These poems are addressed primarily to friends and
acquaintances, more personally reflective observations of her own life, her
son's, her husband's, and those of the people around her. The revolution
has been left behind.[26]

A contemporary of Giovanni is Don L. Lee/Haki Madhubuti, another
"revolutionary" writer of "protest Literature."[27] "If you are Black, you will
always be Black first and a writer second," Madhubuti asserts.[28] Despite his
experiments with vocabulary, spelling, punctuation, and line breaks even
more severe than Giovanni's, Madhubuti has chosen to set his poems in a
variety of first-person narrative stances, just as his predecessors have done.
Some brief examples from his most anthologized poems will suffice to dem-
onstrate his continuation of this technique. "The Self-Hatred of Don L. Lee"
reveals the poet in his most confessional mode, protesting against white
society's desire to include only token blacks and relating his self-education
and the difficulty he had in accepting the role of color in America. Certainly
it is a poem with which many African Americans can identify, as it ends:

```
I               is all
began           black—
to love         &
only a          developed a
part of         vehement
me—             hatred of
my inner        my light
self which      brown
                outer. (TBP, 298)
```

As with other black poets, when treating the heritage, singular gives way to
plural. In "The Primitive," Lee restates the injustices of slavery:

> taken from the
> shores of Mother Africa.
> the savages they thought
> we were—
> they being the real savages

and the shallowness of contemporary American culture: "raped our minds with: / T.V. & straight hair, / Reader's Digest & bleaching creams" (*TBP*, 297). The "I" and the "We" come together in "a poem to complement other poems." The one celebrates the many in this poem that celebrates "change," particularly the slow end of Jim Crow laws and the development of more racially positive attitudes within black people: "change. I say change into a realblack righteous aim. like I don't play / saxophone but that doesn't mean I don't dig 'trane.' change" (*TBP*, 301). Haki Madhubuti bases a large part of his revolution on tactics retained from earlier black poets working toward the same ends.

When they write about race, all black poets have the same ends in sight: equality, identity, solidarity. In this respect, they have a kinship with the autobiographies stretching back through the slave narratives. As a whole, the poems, particularly those that seem to have the "I" that means "We" voice, form a "collective autobiography" in a loosely Jungian sense; it is not unconscious, but it does make a connection with an entire race of people. In this way, African American poets contribute to a racial history as autobiographers have. That said, I would like to avoid the charge of "essentializing" by reiterating a point made earlier: that his "I" that means "We" voice is not universal among African American poets; for example, I believe that Michael S. Harper and Alice Walker are two poets who do not use this voice. Further study will reveal the extent of this special-use voice. Of course, once in print, even the most personal poem becomes public and available for varieties of interpretations and responses. One reaction may be the tactic of literary critics who theorize only a "function" in the place of an author, but I believe that for many black poets there is a very real sense of both self and belonging that is revealed in their poetry.

Notes

1. Most of the poems quoted can be found in a number of anthologies of American or African American literature. I will abbreviate within the text as follows: *BWA: Black*

Writers of America, ed. Barksdale and Kinnamon; *TBP: The Black Poets,* ed. Randall; *TBE: The Black Experience,* ed. Kearns. Page references for quotations without title abbreviations refer to a volume listed under the author's name unless some confusion may result.

2. Redding, 109.

3. Baraka, 16.

4. Ibid., 169.

5. Ibid., 321.

6. Gibson, xi.

7. Hill, *Soon, One Morning,* 3.

8. Gates connects twentieth-century black poetry with the slave narratives, as both "represent the attempt of blacks to *write themselves into being*" (75–76, 57; his emphasis). Baker writes that "the necessity [of black writing] was to continue speaking in a manner that both counteracted the repressions of the white world and clarified the black situation for those who shared it" (*The Journey Back,* 132). Bentson generalizes most broadly about African American literature: "For the Afro-American, then, self-creation and reformation of a fragmented familial past are endlessly interwoven: naming is inevitably genealogical revisionism. All of Afro-American literature may be seen as one vast genealogical poem that attempts to restore continuity to the ruptures or discontinuities imposed by the history of black presence in America" (152).

9. Baker, *Afro-American Poetics,* 4.

10. Gates, 94.

11. Henderson.

12. Hughes, 228.

13. Cooper, 108.

14. Additional poems in this mode that are seldom anthologized are "Invocation" (Cooper, 117), "Outcast" (121), and "Mulatto" (126). "Passive Resistance" (115) employs the "We" spokesman narrator as in "We Wear the Mask."

15. Barksdale, "Humanistic Protest in Recent Black Poetry," 160.

16. Brooks et al., 3.

17. Unless otherwise indicated, all quotations from Gwendolyn Brooks's poems are from *Blacks.*

18. Gibson, *Modern Black Poets,* 1–17, 9.

19. Redding, 51.

20. Neal, 187.

21. Baker, *Afro-American Poetics,* 134.

22. Gibson, *Modern Black Poets,* 16.

23. Taylor, 127–34.

24. All quotations from Amiri Baraka's poems are from *The LeRoi Jones/Amiri Baraka Reader.*

25. Palmer, 135–46.

26. There is one exception. The first poem in *Those Who Ride the Night Wind,* "Lorraine Hansberry: An Emotional View," contains a section on the black heritage in America (14).

27. Palmer, 135–46, 136.

28. Brooks et al., 33.

Works Cited

Baker, Houston A., Jr. *Afro-American Poetics: Revisions of Harlem and the Black Aesthetic.* Madison: University of Wisconsin Press, 1988.

———. *The Journey Back: Issues in Black Literature and Criticism.* Chicago: University of Chicago Press, 1980.

Baraka, Amiri. *The LeRoi Jones/Amiri Baraka Reader.* Ed. William J. Harris. New York: Thunder's Mouth, 1991.

Barksdale, Richard K. "Humanistic Protest in Recent Black Poetry." In *Modern Black Poets,* ed. Donald B. Gibson. Englewood Cliffs, N.J.: Prentice-Hall, 1973. 157–64.

Barksdale, Richard, and Keneth Kinnamon. *Black Writers of America.* New York: Macmillan, 1972.

Bentson, Kimberly W. "I Yam What I Am: The Topos of Un(naming) in Afro-American Literature." In *Black Literature and Literary Theory.* New York: Methuen, 1984. 151–72.

Brooks, Gwendolyn. *Blacks.* Chicago: Third World, 1991.

———. *To Disembark.* Chicago: Third World, 1981.

———, et al. *A Capsule Course in Black Poetry Writing.* Detroit: Broadside, 1975.

Brown, Sterling A. *The Collected Poems of Sterling A. Brown.* Sel. Michael S. Harper. New York: Harper, 1980.

———. *Negro Poetry and Drama.* New York: Atheneum, 1969.

Cooper, Wayne, ed. *The Passion of Claude McKay: Selected Prose and Poetry 1912–1948.* New York: Schocken, 1973.

Cullen, Countee. *On These I Stand.* New York: Harper, 1947.

Gates, Henry Louis, Jr. *Loose Canons: Notes on the Culture Wars.* New York: Oxford University Press, 1992.

Gibson, Donald B. Introduction. *Five Black Writers,* ed. Gibson. New York: New York University Press, 1970. xi–xxviii.

———. Introduction. *Modern Black Poets,* ed. Gibson. Englewood Cliffs, N.J.: Prentice-Hall, 1973. 1–17.

Giovanni, Nikki. *Cotton Candy on a Rainy Day.* New York: Quill, 1978.

———. *Those Who Ride with the Night Winds.* New York: William Morrow, 1983.

———. *The Women and the Men.* New York: William Morrow, 1975.

Henderson, Stephen. *Understanding the New Black Poetry.* New York: William Morrow, 1973.

Hill, Herbert. Introduction. *Anger and Beyond: The Negro Writer in the United States,* ed. Hill. New York: Harper, 1968. ix–xxii.

———. Introduction. *Soon, One Morning: New Writing by American Negroes 1940–1962,* ed. Hill. New York: Knopf, 1969. 3–18.

Hughes, Langston. "The Negro Artist and the Racial Mountain." In Gibson, *Five Black Writers.* 225–29.

Kearns, Francis E., ed. *The Black Experience.* New York: Viking, 1970.

Melhem, D. H. *Gwendolyn Brooks: Poetry and the Heroic Voice.* Lexington: University Press of Kentucky, 1987.

Neal, Larry. "The Black Arts Movement." In *The Black American Writer, Vol. 2: Poetry and Drama,* ed. C. W. E. Bigsby. Deland: Everett, 1969. 187–202.

Palmer, R. Roderick. "The Poetry of Three Revolutionaries: Don L. Lee, Sonia Sanchez, and Nikki Giovanni." In Gibson, *Modern Black Poets.* 135–46.

Randall, Dudley, ed. *The Black Poets.* New York: Bantam, 1971.

Redding, J. Saunders. *To Make a Poet Black.* 1939. Repr. Great Neck: Core Collection, 1978.

Taylor, Clyde. "Baraka as Poet." In Gibson, *Modern Black Poets.* 127–34.

Conversation:

M A R G A R E T   W A L K E R   A L E X A N D E R
and
J O A N N E   V .   G A B B I N

GABBIN: Fifty-four years ago, you won the Yale Series of Younger
Poets Award for your first volume of poetry, *For My
People,* making it the first collection by an African American writer to
win a national award. Now you are the dean of African American writers
and respected and revered for your work. When did you begin writing
and who were the people who most influenced your burgeoning literary
interests?

WALKER: I started writing poetry when I was eleven years old. My
father told my mother, "Pay her no attention, don't get
excited; it's just a puberty urge," which made me very angry. By the time
I had filled the date book that he gave me I was at Northwestern; I think
I'd written in those three hundred and sixty five pages by the time I was
eighteen. I told him, "Do you still think this is a puberty urge?" He said,
"I guess you're going to write as long as you live." When someone asked
me the other day, "When are you going to retire?" I said, "Retire from
what? Retire from life?" I'd retired from teaching, and I said, "I will retire
from writing when I'm dead. I won't write anymore after I die, but until I
do I'll keep trying."

I think my mother's music and my father's books were my first inspi-
ration, but I had wonderful teachers—mostly women—throughout the
grade school years, and then in high school a few men. My teachers were
always encouraging me. I had little composition books that I wrote in and
I wrote poetry in class, but I managed to answer the questions when they
asked me: I just looked up and said "so-and-so" and started writing again.

I think the earliest I can remember reading the Harlem Renaissance writers was when I was eleven. The Harlem Renaissance took place when I was a child. I saw a little booklet, *Four Lincoln Poets*—including Langston Hughes and Waring Cuney and Edward Silvera, when I was eleven. By the time I was sixteen I saw my very first living writer. I told my father and mother that when the white president said he didn't think people would pay a dollar to listen to a Negro read poetry, not even a few people, that he had to have Langston come to New Orleans. So we wrote eight hundred letters and we filled the auditorium of that campus. He must have sold hundreds of dollars of books that night. All the books that he had stacked up went away. I will never forget it, because it was the first time I had ever seen a living black writer. It was important for me, and it meant the beginning of my whole career.

Langston was a friend until 1967 when he died. I had seen him just the October before, when I went to New York just after *Jubilee* was published. Langston was the kind of person who would write you a letter of congratulations. He wrote when *For My People* was published, he wrote when *Jubilee* was published, and I still have those letters. I got a letter from Countee Cullen saying, "I understand you are one of these unusual poets who can read the poetry as well as write it."

He said, "The next time you come to New York, my wife and I would like you to come to dinner." I have that letter. I went to dinner and there I saw Claude McKay for the first time. Langston of course was there, and there were others. That was really the beginning of my professional career, with the publication of *For My People*. I had another wonderful experience at Northwestern when I met the great Dr. W. E. B. Du Bois. He came to speak at Northwestern, and afterward I had the courage and the nerve to go up and tell him, "I write poetry, too." He said, "Send me some." I said, "Where shall I send it?" He said, "To the *Crisis*." I did, and the next year in May, while I was still a teenager, the poem came out. Some of my friends who are very kind critics say that that is the poem I have fulfilled with my whole career.

I Want to Write
I want to write
I want to write to write the songs of my people.
I want to hear them singing melodies in the dark.
I want to catch the last floating strains from their sob-torn throats.
I want to frame their dreams into words; their souls into notes.
I want to catch their sunshine laughter in a bowl;

fling dark hands to a darker sky
and fill them full of stars
then crush and mix such lights 'till they become
a mirrored pool of brilliance in the dawn.

GABBIN: That's wonderful—"a mirrored pool of brilliance in the
dawn." "I Want to Write," also called "Daydream."

WALKER: It's had three or four different titles. Every time it's pub-
lished, there's another title. I got tired of "Daydream"—
I thought, "Oh, I don't want to use 'Daydream'"—and then I saw a book
Songs of My People, and I said, "Oh, there's my poem: 'I want to Write the
Songs of My People.'"

GABBIN: You mentioned Langston Hughes, and you also men-
tioned Du Bois, but there's one other person you met
when you were young.

WALKER: Well, I saw Langston when I was sixteen, I saw Du Bois
when I was seventeen, and I met Richard Wright when
I was twenty. Those three men have had tremendous influence on my
thinking and on my writing. They were not members of my family and
they were not my classroom teachers, but I read them. I read Langston,
I read Du Bois, I read Richard Wright. They were men that I always
thought of in terms of a great protest movement of black people. People
who were constantly writing for the sake of our people—not for art's
sake, but for the *people's.* I think they influenced me more than any others.
I had wonderful teachers, yes; and my parents encouraged me. I was for-
tunate to that extent. But those three men represented for me everything
that we try to do when we write. They represent the *humanity* of black
people; the fact that every individual is a human being. Nobody can be
more than a human being, and nobody can be less. That is what I taught
my students all those years.

GABBIN: A major theme in your poetry, in your fiction, your es-
says is freedom. Stephen Henderson says in his seminal
work *Understanding the New Black Poetry* that the overarching theme of our
literature is liberation, and you consistently use that theme in your writ-
ing. Why have you stayed with it?

WALKER: When I was about eleven years old—I guess eleven and
                   a half—I went to high school, and one of the first things
I studied then was the French Revolution. I had already read about the
American Revolution, but for some reason Patrick Henry and George
Washington didn't excite me.

But when I read about the French Revolution—Robespierre, Danton,
Marat—I was excited. I heard them saying *freedom*—"égalité, fraternité,
liberté." It became a motto for my life, and it began when I was only
eleven. I was much older when I read about the Russian Revolution. In
school they talked about "the barbaric Russians"—"the Communists,"
they called them. They had pictures in the book that showed you these
people with shining whiskers and they were devils; they told you these
people were no-good people.

One of the first books I read after meeting Wright was *Ten Days That
Shook the World*. If you ever read that book and you are not moved to think
in terms of freedom for people who were living under the terror of the
czars, even going beyond the Kerensky government—something is wrong
if you aren't affected by it. I was tremendously impressed, and when I read
the short stories that Wright wrote in *Uncle Tom's Children,* you've got
the essence of what we were in the thirties, the writers of social protest.
That's what he was saying in everything. Baldwin and the postmodernists
look down on those writers of social protest. They're not popular any-
more, and our black men are not writing social protest; they're doing . . .
what is it, "deconstruction"?

GABBIN: "Deconstruction of the language," "tropes," "analysis of
                   texts" . . .

WALKER: I've been reading some of the postmodernists. One man
                   is a marvel with language, and he doesn't ever have a
plot. He doesn't *believe* in a plot. He says, "Language is everything." The
writer knows that the word is powerful, that it has more than emotional
and intellectual meaning. But I am still a student of the old school of fic-
tion; I believe you have to tell a story. Postmodernists are very wonderful
writers, but they'd be better if they had a plot.

GABBIN: You know, I've been trying—and I know my story's
                   probably like a lot of other people's—for many years to
write down a story that's really important in my life. In fact, it's the story
of how I met my husband . . . I've been trying to write this story, about

our meeting, and every time I put down the facts, they don't come alive. They're just there; it's not a story. How do you do that? I know other people want to know.

WALKER: That was my problem with *Jubilee* for years and years
                and years. I wrote those first 300 pages when I was nine-
teen at Northwestern. Then I looked at that stuff and I said, "Oh, this is not right." I didn't know what was wrong with it, but nobody there could tell me what to do. In the fifties I went up to Yale, and I worked with Norman Holmes Pearson, who had coedited the *Oxford Book of Verse* with Auden. When I left in May I was still not understanding what to do, and Professor Pearson said, "You're telling the story but it doesn't come alive. You're telling it but you're not showing it." I left Yale deciding I would not stay there and try to get a Ph.D., that I'd go back where I learned to put the poetry together and had written the ballads for the first time. I'd throw my hat in and see if Paul Engle would let me come in, because we fussed all the time.

Anyway, when I went back, I spent a summer working under a man who taught me how to do it. His name was Verlin Cassill and he had a little book on writing fiction. I think he's done more potboilers than prize winners, but he absolutely is the most marvelous teacher of fiction I ever encountered. He told me, "You've got to read Chekhov. Not the plays"— I had read *The Cherry Orchard* and *Three Sisters*—"but read the short stories and see how he puts incidents together." What you're talking about is what was one of Wright's greatest assets. That was the ability to drama-tize the material. What do we mean? Well, what is a plot? A plot is a series of related incidents that tell a story. Through the actual dramatization of material, taking the facts and making fiction by showing the action, by actually getting the person reading it to see the action. What is going on? What are they saying, and what does it mean? If they're walking, if they're thinking, if they're acting—actually dramatizing that material means showing the story rather than telling the story.

I thought that I would never learn. I spent eight weeks before I could turn in to him the first chapter, the revised first chapter, of *Jubilee* as you know it. He said, "You got it." I thought about: Here I was now in my late forties, and I'd been fooling around trying to learn that ever since I was nineteen years old. That's why it took so long. I did all the research, I read all the books, but until I learned how to create a scene I could not write fiction. Everybody's got a story. Everybody knows a story. Can you write the story without telling it by showing? It's not easy, and I recommend exactly who he recommended to me: Chekhov. Chekhov's stories show you line for line, page for page, what you have to do.

GABBIN: You know that I've worked with Sterling Brown's work
                 for a long time, and I'm a devotee of the folk tradition.
You remember Sterling Brown, don't you, out there? Sterling Brown of "Old Lem," Sterling Brown of "Odyssey of Big Boy" and "Sister Lou." Sterling Brown's work taught me a love for the folk tradition. I know that you are in that tradition as well, and I want you to tell us how you show your debt to that tradition in *Jubilee* and the other writing that you have done.

WALKER: I think one of the first conversations I ever had with
                 Richard Wright was on that folk tradition. Both of us
were tremendously interested in what we thought at the time was limited to the South, but it isn't limited to the South. It's a part of black life all over this country. It's the way we live, it's the religion we believe, it's our spirit, our art, it's our music . . . it's our daily living, that folk life.
     I know you have read Zora Hurston and have read Richard Wright. I don't think Wright ever wanted to admit that Zora had affected him, because he was so chauvinistic that he wouldn't want to say that a woman did that. But she did. You open Richard Wright and read, "Your mama don't wear no drawers." Where did he get it? He got it from Zora. Sterling writes about the working man, the roustabout, the stevedore. Langston writes about the culture of the cities, particularly Harlem; the menials, the maids, the cooks and washerwomen. But all of us know that when we speak in the vernacular of black people we have gone to the root of black life. We are dealing with everyday living, and everyday believing, and the everyday actions of black people. "I talked to old Lem, and old Lem said: They do the so-and-so, and we carry the cross . . . and they get the money."

GABBIN: "And they don't come by ones . . ."

WALKER (AND OTHERS):   "And they don't come by twos; they come
                       by tens."

GABBIN: In your essay "The Humanistic Tradition of Afro-
                 American Literature," you developed a line of thinking
that I think is essential to appreciate the continuity and the connections

in our literature. I'm going to read this: you say that "this tradition began in the ancient Oriental world, in black Africa, in Egypt, some 3,500 years ago with *The Book of the Dead*. The literature of black people, like that of all people, grew out of the cosmogony and the cosmology that developed around the Nile River, and not from Greece or Rome at the end of the ancient world, nor in the Middle Ages with the European Renaissance, nor with the modern expansion of the European man. But black America is tied to her ancient African heritage in all her physical and cultural manifestations." I want you to talk about that heritage.

WALKER: I think that very few English teachers in the Western world have a tendency to tell their students that the descent into the underworld did not begin with Homer.

GABBIN: She's signifying, isn't she, Baraka?

WALKER: They failed to say that this is an epic convention that began with *The Book of the Dead;* the pyramids and the coffin texts in Egypt were far earlier than anything Greece or Rome produced. You know, white professors in the white universities—when you talk about pre-Homeric epics, they say "Was there any such thing?" They don't believe that, because they never read *The Book of the Dead,* and it's very hard for them to bring themselves to realize that these so-called savages understood how to go from this world to the next world without the white man telling them how.

GABBIN: Back in 1975 you did an interview with Charles Rowell. In that interview he asked you about writing a biography of Richard Wright and he said he thought there was no person in this country more suited, more prepared to write that biography than you. Of course, we all know you wrote that biography: *Richard Wright: Daemonic Genius.* However, because of the sensitive and controversial material, it cost you dearly writing that book. I want you to share with us some of the problems, some of the issues, that you dealt with.

WALKER: Well, I tell, in the book, of the six areas that he wished to deal with, and the problems were all growing out of that. The first problem was that this man was a card-carrying Communist for twelve years, and if I proceeded to talk about this man's Communism, how was I going to know anything about it when I was never a Communist? That was the first problem.

The second problem was dealing with interracial marriage. In the friendship that Wright and I had together—that was a very close friendship—there was never a romance, never anything like a romance between us. Early in the friendship, he told me that if he ever married, he'd marry a white woman. Since I didn't look white, I knew he wasn't going to marry me.

Then there was the question of money. Richard Wright had two Book-of-the-Month Club selections. Well, did he have a lot of money? Did he make a lot of money? He lived in Europe in a very bourgeois fashion, in a nice apartment; he traveled around the world. But did he ever have a lot of money? That was another question. How did he get along with those agents and publishers and people who helped him to reach a great pinnacle of fame in this country, and in Europe, too?

Then there was the question of the Jewish-Arab conflict. If you started talking about, "This man is a pan-Africanist . . ." Pan-Africanism is really a black thing: most Jewish people are opposed to it, and he was married to two Jewish women. Now how are you going to deal with that?

And finally . . . I have to tell this little bit and then I'll be through with it. Wright's family—his second wife, Ellen—was bitterly opposed to my publishing the book. She spent close to a hundred thousand dollars and wrote letters to publishers like Harper's telling them, "Don't give her any permission to use any of his material," and threatened three publishers with a suit: first Howard [University Press], and then Dodd Mead, and finally Warner, and told them that as sure as I published the book she was going to sue.

Howard was scared to death; they said they'd had enough suits, and they didn't need any more. Dodd Mead was perfectly willing, but they didn't have any money. So finally Warner said, "Oh, we don't mind taking her on." They knew when they took the manuscript that Ellen Wright was going to sue, which meant that I didn't have the authority from the family to write the biography, as Michel Fabre had. Six months after the book appeared—it appeared in November of '88, and in May of '89 she sued. One of our very dear friends who's a critic, and who's been teaching in some of our white universities, said he felt sorry for me, because that was that woman's husband, and I couldn't do anything if she didn't want it done. I got word of what he said, and I had nerve enough to do what I had to do.

I wonder . . . we live through lots of things, and I thought in 1977 and '78 . . . well, Alex Haley published a book in 1976 called *Roots,* and

I thought that thing was going to kill me. I thought I was going to die under *Roots*. Everybody talked about that jealous woman wanting this man's money, an agitated old woman; how she ought to go somewhere and sit down, and how "that dumb woman thinks she's going to do thus-and-so," and I said to my husband and my sons, "I don't know what I've done to anybody to deserve this. Anybody can pick up a book of *Roots*, and pick up a book of *Jubilee*, and they can see what's happening there. All you got to do is read it: it's there." You know, we have a saying in the black community: "We'll understand it better by and by." Well, when I wrote the Richard Wright book, and Ellen Wright sued Warner *and* Margaret Walker, I "understood it better by and by."

I had read every book I could find on fair use and copyright infringement. I told Charlie Harris, "That book is clean, there's nothing wrong there, there's nothing in there that anybody can say I've used without saying that I have a right to do this." That's what the lawyers said, and when it went to court that's what the court said. Then despite the fact that her lawyers and her children told her not to push it, she went to the appellate court and the lawyers in the appellate agreed with the lower court. One of them wrote an additional statement about it, which if you read the paperback copy of *Daemonic Genius* you'll see that the appellate court and this extra statement would all be there to explain, and I "understood it better by and by." I couldn't understand why I had to live through the horrible ordeal of *Roots*. I know now. Without *Roots*, I never would have known what "fair use" meant.

GABBIN: In a 1993 interview with Maryemma Graham, you talk about the responsibility of the writer. You say, "The writer's responsibility is like God's. He's supposed to, or she's supposed to, show the way."

WALKER: Well, I meant by that not that we are divine to the extent that all human personality is not potentially divine. But I'm thinking in terms of the prophetic nature of the writer. The writer is like the prophet: he has to see the future by looking at the present. He has to understand that what's happened in the past is happening now, and will happen in the future. That is the role of the writer: to write about that future that you do not see, but that is evident in everything you do and hear. You know what's going to happen tomorrow because the seeds of it are happening today.

GABBIN: Talk about what's happening tomorrow. I know you love
to write, and you're going to continue to write. What
are your projects?

WALKER: I saw a young lady here just before we began—Junette
Pinckney. She was the person at CBS that had Charlie
Rose have an interview with me when the Richard Wright book came
out. He asked me, he said, "My, you've done all these things. What are
your dreams? What do you dream about for the future?" I answered very
flippantly, "All my dreams have already come true." But I will add that
some of the dreams are still in the making. I would like to return to the
fiction, and I have three short novels—one about education, one about
sociology of religion, and one a sequel to *Jubilee*. If I could live long
enough I'd like to write those books.

GABBIN: We've been talking about your life as a writer, but we
know there are so many other dimensions to your life;
I think we'd be remiss if we didn't talk about your work as an activist. You
say in *I Dream a World* and elsewhere that the three enemies of black
women are racism, sexism, and fascism. How have you personally done
battle with these three *isms*?

WALKER: There are three examples of actions I took in civil rights
and the community that did just that. In 1964, with the
sponsorship of the NAACP, we sued to get the Jackson television station
WLBT to operate with a staff that is 51 percent black. I was instrumental
in changing the "confederate" history book to *Challenge and Change* by
Sallis and Loewen. I am gratified to see my grandchildren using this book.
I was also one of the first witnesses in the Ayers court trial to desegregate
higher education in Mississippi. We consider ourselves loyal, good Ameri-
cans, and to say that we live under a fascistic system is talking about going
to the devil and living in Hell. But fascism is what we have. We live with it
every day. It's in every part of our lives. It's not just the judicial system; it's
not just that awful Supreme Court; it's not just Congress and that man—
what's his name?—Newt Gingrich. It's all of it, and what we have to un-
derstand is, that's what we live with. It's racism, it's sexism, it's fascism;
and it's the role—and the right—of the black writer to put it on paper,
and tell the truth.

GABBIN: In 1988 our literary diva, the brilliant Eleanor Traylor, did an article, "Measures Crashing Through: Margaret Walker, Poem of the Century." In this article she equates you with Ogun, or the first artist or forger. And she talks about . . .

WALKER: I didn't know what Ogun was. I had to go and look it up.

GABBIN: Margaret, I did, too. You know, Eleanor coins these words—"Ogunic." She calls your voice Ogunic, and she says in *Prophets for a New Day* you equate biblical heroes with modern heroes.

WALKER: Eighth-century prophets.

GABBIN: Yes. Who are those heroes, those modern heroes, for you?

WALKER: Well, you know, we went through two revolutions: I don't know whether we got all we needed from either one. Dr. Martin Luther King caused us to see the end of legal segregation—whether you admit it or not, the civil rights movement really ended legal segregation. Then Malcolm X came along and he told us, "Make something of yourself—your manhood and your womanhood are the things out there that matter." We changed our way of dress and our hair: we did everything to deny ourselves as purely Americans and show that we are African Americans. We learned a lot from both King and Malcolm X.

We lost three men through assassination. My neighbor Medgar Evers, killed the same year that the president of the United States was assassinated. Then we lost King by assassination, and we lost Malcolm X by assassination. What greater price can you pay for heroism? Who can you think of that deserves to be a hero who has not given his life for what he believes? They are our heroes. We have had women heroes too. My mother said something one day during the civil rights movement. She said, "You know, we had great women like Harriet Tubman and Sojourner Truth and Mary McLeod Bethune—all these women, but we could not get a revolution going until we had intelligent, intellectual men. The world didn't listen until they heard those men."

Now, I *know* you're not going to say that I'm a woman-basher. I'm not a basher of men or a basher of women. I was married thirty-seven years to a wonderful man; I have two wonderful sons; my father was a wonderful man. I admire men as much as women. I think God intended us to be partners and to get along with each other.

All of us have our weaknesses and our strengths, and we have to strive to be better, to live out our humanity as we reach toward divinity. That is the spiritual destiny of us all.

I don't think we have as many heroes or she-roes as we should have. I think about all the black men in prison who are not in the classrooms, and how many of us work for nothing when we ought to be making dollars. We have a tendency to rise above ourselves and transcend our realities. We have a tendency to think if you scrub a floor, you're the floor. Scrubbing the floor doesn't mean you're the floor. I taught my students that it's as important to know how to make a good lemon meringue pie as it is to write a poem because there is *dignity* in all labor.

We cry out for heroes. You walk along the street and you see them every day, and you don't credit them with being heroes. If you live in the Deep South as I do, and you go to church or you go to school, you don't know whose money keeps it going, do you? It's that washerwoman's money. She's the one that does anything that she can do honestly to send her child to school. That's what we do every day; that's part of our life, that's our living. And the day we understand that is the day we'll step a little higher up the ladder.

GABBIN: After all of your years, and all that you've been through—wars and the civil rights movement; attacks on our community in terms of drugs and guns and AIDS; attacks on affirmative action; and the latest assault on our churches, the very heart of our community—somehow through it all, you seem to maintain a kind of faith in humanism; a faith in humanity. I want to know: what is it that keeps you hopeful?

WALKER: I think that any day you believe that every human being has a spark of divinity within him, you will not destroy yourself by trying to destroy somebody else.

You will have to believe in the goodness of the future if you believe that we are constantly striving toward a real divinity. We are black people of spirit. That spirit is the basis of animism and ancestor worship in Africa. The African believed for a while in animism, and he said, "Spirit is in everything. It's in the water; it's in the grass and the trees; it's in the wind; and it's in us." We have the greatest amount of spirit in us, and if we don't think positively, how can that spirit live?

GABBIN: Dr. Margaret Walker Alexander, thank you for your poetry, your writing, your essays; for the pool of brilliance that you've mirrored in this part of the world.

Note

This conversation took place on July 2, 1996, at the Black Arts Festival in Atlanta. It was taped in front of an audience of more than two hundred people whose response to Margaret Walker's call was electric.

Blooming in the Whirlwind:
The Early Poetry of Gwendolyn Brooks

J O A N N E   V .   G A B B I N

INCE THE EARLY 1940S GWENDOLYN BROOKS HAS exhibited in her poetry a deep and cogent sense of living black and female in America. Her portraits of women—vibrant in color, diverse in the degree of their heroic response to their circumstances, and complex in the social and psychological dimensions of their lives—refute the libels of monolithic and stereotypical treatment of women in American literature and reveal a creative consciousness rawly aware of the major racial and social traumas of her time. Whether exposing the tenuous ego of chocolate Mabbie, who too readily accepts her inferiority to "a lemon-hued lynx"; or the diminished, desiccated life of Mrs. Small, tyrannized by domestic cares; or the death-defying spirit of Cousin Vit, "too vital" to be forgotten, Brooks anticipates black writers like Sonia Sanchez, Alice Walker, and Audre Lorde who have also successfully explored the triple consciousness of women confronting race, gender, and caste.[1]

For Gwendolyn Brooks, being a black woman poet is synonymous with being a revolutionary. Even in her earlier poems, when she cultivated her themes in the modernist aesthetic tradition of T. S. Eliot, Ezra Pound, and Wallace Stevens and the popular regionalism of Langston Hughes, Carl Sandburg, Vachel Lindsay, and Edgar Lee Masters, she conducted her "blooming in the noise and whip of the whirlwind."[2] Her poetry carried with it the questioning and disapprobation of a society winking at social injustice. The opening lines taken from "The Second Sermon on the Warpland" in *In the Mecca* (1968) suggest a time of awakening, outrage, and militant poise. As such, they also describe the development of Brooks's poetry. "The time / cracks into furious flower." Like the oxymoronic "furious flower," her poetry represents both beauty and fury, lyricism and shriek, peace and turmoil in elegant upheaval. The icons of the mammies, whores, tragic mulattos and bitches so prevalent in American literature give way in Brooks's poetry to complex multifaceted images. The poet's delicate acceptance of her blackness and racial strength grows into affirmation. "Lifts its face / all unashamed. And sways in wicked grace" (456). It is with this dual focus of Brooks's deep-rooted womanhood and her armed social vision that her poetry will be examined. Though selected poems from *A Street in Bronzeville* (1945), *Annie Allen* (1949), *The Bean Eaters* (1960), *In the Mecca* (1968), and *To Disembark* (1981) will be discussed, "The Anniad" and "In the Mecca" have been chosen for closer analysis because of their sustained, thematic treatment of male-female relations, motherhood and children, women's self-concept, and their commitment to survival and positive social change.

From the earliest publication of *A Street in Bronzeville,* Brooks's poetry has had strength of conviction. The themes of mothering, nurture without neglect; loving, the tentative encounters of first love or the comfortable meanderings of mature love; the pain of betrayal and loss; the heroism of simply "being" are uncompromised in her writing. Brooks is unsentimental in her portrayal of Jessie Mitchell's mother, who confronts her illness and impending death by finding solace in the notion that her "shabby" dark-skinned daughter's youth will never compare to her "exquisite yellow" one. In "A Bronzeville Mother Loiters in Mississippi, Meanwhile a Mississippi Mother Burns Bacon," Brooks is clear-eyed as she looks at the Emmett Till murder through the eyes of the white woman on whose account the boy of fourteen was slain. Brooks avoids the hysteria of protest and special pleading by skillfully registering the encroaching revulsion the woman feels as she becomes convinced of her husband's guilt. The "Ballad of Pearl May Lee" also reveals a poet whose tone ranges from mild irony to derisive sarcasm as she exposes the outrage of a black woman who has been spurned by her black lover who preferred "a taste of pink and white honey."

This poem is her treatment of the black woman—black man—white woman triad of revenge, pain, and death that is played out in a scenario made illicit by the ethics of a racist and chauvinistic society. The speaker is not the black man who is torn between forbidden desire and fear of violence. The speaker is not a chorus of Sirens warning of the dangerous lust for white flesh. On the contrary, the speaker is a forlorn, enraged black woman whose voice had rarely been heard in American literature. "Though never was a poor gal lorner," she has urged her despair and personal rejection into a private vengeance. As he had cut her passion cold, she coldly views his fate.

> You paid for your dinner, Sammy boy,
> And you didn't pay with money.
> You paid with your hide and my heart, Sammy boy,
> For your taste of pink and white honey,
>   Honey,
>   Honey,
> For your taste of pink and white honey. (63)

Admitting that this woman's rage was not foreign to her sensibility, Brooks says in an interview with Claudia Tate in *Black Women Writers at Work*, "I hope you sense some real rage in the 'Ballad of Pearl May Lee' [*A Street in Bronzeville*]. The speaker is a very enraged person. I know because I consulted myself on how I have felt." [3]

Because Gwendolyn Brooks, like Zora Neale Hurston, Margaret Walker, Ntozake Shange, Toni Morrison, and others, has consulted herself, she has been compelled even in the midst of travail and faltering self-esteem to reveal women in the fullness of their struggle for self-definition. Joyce Ann Joyce writes in "Gwendolyn Brooks: Jean Toomer's November Cotton Flower" of the strength of the poet to nurture her creative spirit in a literary world whose very nature sought its destruction. "Having bloomed under the light of Robert Hillyer's *First Principles of Verse*, Brooks brought to modern American poetry her own peculiar sensibility which manifests at once the embodiments of both Wallace Stevens's blue guitar and the African griot's drum. Even though they have the visual and stylistic attributes of a Euro-American poetic tradition, her earlier ballads, free verse poems, and the sonnets reveal the same feelings of racial integrity and record the same malaises of racism as those poems published after 1967 when Brooks's blackness confronted her 'with a shrill spelling of itself.'" [4]

Joyce's comments also speak to the continuity of Brooks's developing sensibility. Brooks often points to 1967 as a significant juncture in her understanding of her own developing consciousness and her awareness of a new spirit of radical black activism. In the spring of 1967 at a writers' conference at Fisk University, she became aware of "a general energy, an electricity, in look, walk, speech, gesture of the young blackness" that she encountered there. [5] The urgent voices of spokesmen like Imamu Amiri Baraka (LeRoi Jones), John Killens, David Llorens, Hoyt Fuller, Ron Milner, John Henrik Clarke, Lerone Bennett punctuated the air with the rhetoric of racial pride and fierce contempt for the oppressive status quo. Back at home in Chicago, Brooks met Don L. Lee (Haki Madhubuti), Walter Bradford, Carolyn

Rodgers, Etheridge Knight, Jewel Latimore (Johari Amini) and other young poets; they were committed to carrying out the ideals of black solidarity and empowerment that she heard about at Fisk. These young poets, especially Don L. Lee and Walter Bradford, had a profound effect on her, for they had a youthful enthusiasm that urged a vision of change that seemed real, relevant, and within reach. What Brooks absorbed from them was their tempered optimism and political savvy, their cogent awareness of the importance of cultivating and speaking directly to a black audience, and their reliance upon new poetic forms that reflected the rhythms, texture, and richness of folk music and speech. The blooming of her poetry would now turn toward a stronger, more insistent sun and be watered by a greater understanding of the reality of living black in America.

Some critics, however, have attempted to assert that Brooks's poetry made a radical departure in 1967 from what she had created previously. With too great simplicity, they have declined to see the political assertiveness and protest in her earlier poems. In the above-mentioned interview in *Black Women Writers at Work*, Claudia Tate says, "Your earlier works, *A Street in Bronzeville* and *Annie Allen*, don't seem to focus directly on heightened political awareness. Do your more recent works tend to deal directly with this concern?" After proffering the examples "of DeWitt Williams on his way to Lincoln Cemetery" and "The Sundays of Satin-Legs Smith," Brooks says,

> Many of the poems, in my new and old books, are "politically aware"; I suggest you reread them. You know, when you say "political," you really have to be exhaustive. You aren't always to think of Andy Young and his comments on Africa, for example. I try to picture in "The Sundays of Satin-Legs Smith" a young man who didn't even know he was a tool of the establishment, who didn't know his life was being run for him from birth straight to death, and even before birth. As I say in that poem: "Here are hats / Like bright umbrellas; and hysterical ties / Like narrow banners for some gathering war." Now this book was published in '45 and even then I could sense, although not brilliantly, not in great detail, that what was happening to us was going to make us erupt at some later time.[6]

Not unlike Richard Wright's Bigger Thomas, whose act of killing acknowledges his life, Satin-Legs, in perverse oblivion of his oppression, is merely the walking dead. Brooks understood the forces that could make people give up. From the window of her kitchenette at 623 East 63rd Street in Chicago, she had seen the faces of those who had stopped warming their dreams, those who manipulated the remnants of existence and called that living, those who simply went through the motions. She was aware that the forces in society that would diminish people in that way would ultimately cause them to rise up in desperate refusal.

When Tate followed up in the interview with the question of whether any of her early work assumed "the blatant, assertive, militant posture we find in the 'new black poetry' of the early seventies," Brooks shot back, "Yes, ma'am. I'm fighting for myself a little bit here, but not overly so, because I certainly wrote no poem that sounds like Haki's 'Don't Cry, Scream' or anything like Nikki's 'The True Import of Present Dialogue, Black v. Negro,' which begins: 'Nigger / Can you kill / Can you kill?' But I'm fighting for myself a little bit here because I believe it takes a little patience to sit down and find out that in 1945 I was saying what many of the young folks said in the sixties."[7] In poems such as "The Sundays of Satin-Legs Smith," "Negro Hero," "The Lovers of the Poor," and "The Children of the Poor," Brooks's tone of militancy and rage is "crowded back into the language." For example, the same intense awareness of the need for struggle that was endemic to the poetry of the late sixties and seventies is present in the magnificent "The Children of the Poor" sonnets, especially sonnet 4 of the quintet. The poet, speaking through Annie, commands, "First fight. Then fiddle. Play the slipping string / With feathery sorcery." She admonishes her children that there would be time enough for making beautiful music when circumstances no longer necessitated "malice" and "murdering." Though Gwendolyn Brooks readily admits that her poems were not generally those that would be taken into the taverns (a goal she now has for her poetry), in those days she soon realized her importance to the younger poets. The respect that they accorded her was based on her inimitable genius at expressing human yearning whether it be for resignation or revolution. Surveying her status as a developing writer/activist, she says with nuances that appear to be too deprecating,

> I—who have "gone the gamut" from an almost angry rejection of my dark skin by some of my brainwashed brothers and sisters to a surprised queenhood in the new black sun—am qualified to enter at least the kindergarten of new consciousness now. New consciousness and trudge—toward—progress.
>
> I have hopes for myself.[8]

The essence of Gwendolyn Brooks's genius is her ability to distill experience and create artful magic that doubles for life. Nowhere is this ability more apparent than in her forty-three-stanza poem "The Anniad," which appeared in *Annie Allen* (1949). Organically connected with the volume as a whole, "The Anniad" represents the portion of Annie's life in which she is seen flowering into womanhood. Yet, as the title suggests, the poet has in mind something larger, more elevated for a plebeian Annie than an ordinary story of a girl growing into womanhood. Brooks, in relating her intent behind the title during an interview with George Stavros in *Contemporary Literature*, says, "Well, the girl's name was Annie, and it was my little pompous pleasure to raise her to a height that she probably did not have, and I thought of the *Iliad* and said, I'll call this "The Anniad."" [9]

Obviously, such a title is not the result of a random and unrelated selection but is the product of a complex network of feelings and ideas, illusions and images, ghosts of the past and flesh and bone of the present that come together to conjure up in the poet's mind Annie as fit material for epic-making. Brooks, in raising Annie "to a height that she probably did not have," brings the young woman, simply by poetic declaration, into the illustrious company of epic figures. No Amazon woman of extraordinary strength or beauty, she does not conquer lands, found sprawling nations, fight glorious battles, or make voyages. Instead, her story is one of the futile strivings of a young black woman to experience and sustain, despite the damaging forces of war and rejection, an eagerly awaited and cherished love. Annie's trials, though, are not unique; hers are the longings and sorrows of many women who enter starry-eyed into communion with a man only to come out of it irrevocably sadder for their experience.

In the opening stanza of the poem, Brooks commands that we consider a girl "of sweet and chocolate."

> Think of sweet and chocolate,
> Left to folly or to fate,
> Whom the higher gods forgot,
> Whom the lower gods berate;
> Physical and underfed
> Fancying on the featherbed
> What was never and is not. (99)

Brooks wastes no time getting us imaginatively, if not intimately, involved with the fate of this lonely brown woman. She posits Annie in a universe bereft of celestial concern. "Left to folly or to fate," she has no higher gods to watch her tenuous progress and direct her faltering step. Even the lower gods who preside over her circumstances have spurned her. Annie offends their standard of beauty, sense of propriety, and notion of cultural superiority. "Fancying on her featherbed," she has only the sovereignty of her dreams for protection.

Paradoxically, the reality of Annie's life ("What is ever and what is not") is fantasy. "Pretty tatters blue and red, / Buxom berries beyond rot, / Western clouds and quarter-stars, / Fairy-sweet of old guitars" converge with fantasies about her dream man. Her "paladin" comes trailing grand epithets, "Prosperous and ocean-eyed," "Paradisiacal and sad / With a dimple in his chin / And the mountains in the mind." He will be entrusted with the ripe harvest of her womanhood; he "shall rub her secrets out / And behold the hinted bride" (99–100). The image "hinted bride" is suggestive and recalls Zora Neale Hurston's Janie, another innocent girl who senses acutely her forages into womanhood and anticipates fulfillment.

However, creating this magical world and positing her hero in it is far less difficult than transforming the plainness that stares back at her from her mirror.

> Think of thaumaturgic lass
> Looking in her looking-glass
> At the unembroidered brown;
> Printing bastard roses there;
> Then emotionally aware
> Of the black and boisterous hair,
> Taming all that anger down. (100)

The reality of the image wins out; she is confronted with the plain brown face scarcely relieved by rouge and "the black and boisterous hair." George Kent writes, "There is no single verse or poem which as brilliantly sums up the conflict which a Black woman could feel before the natural hair movement made some moderation of the necessity to keep one eye focused upon white standards of beauty." [10]

Throughout Brooks's poetry and fiction, she has revealed the inner tensions and emotional turmoil created when black girls and women become aware of these extrinsic standards and face self-denigration. These feelings are often complicated by the anxiety they are made to associate with a black man's ultimate choice of beauty. In the above-mentioned "the ballad of chocolate Mabbie," Brooks portrays a young girl who early becomes painfully aware that sweet and chocolate were not enough. Mabbie, who is "all of seven," imagines Willie Boone and herself in a heaven of her making. Yet her imaginings are as fragile as "the bubble of song" that bursts when Willie appears in the schoolyard with a little yellow girl who has "sand-waves loving her brow." In ballad quatrains that barely mute the pain, the poet intimates that Mabbie will not outgrow this intense disappointment but will relive it when she is grown. Brooks also explores in the deeply moving and delicately written novel *Maud Martha* the problems that result from intraracial color prejudice, a further complication of an already serious racial malady. As Arthur P. Davis suggests in *From the Dark Tower*, the black-and-tan motif figures prominently in the difficulties that arise in "The Anniad" and "plays a crucial role in the lives of the two lovers."[11]

When Brooks introduces the "man of tan" into Annie's life, she does so in an array of nature images to suggest the diligence of his pursuit and the eagerness with which she awaited it. As Annie would surround her long-sought-after lover with the language of courtly love, "celestial function" and "bejewelled diadem," these gilt images are immediately undercut by the insurgence of reality. The succeeding stanzas show Annie insisting upon creating out of her relationship something it can never be. The poet, playing on the sacredness and sanctity in which Annie has swaddled her marital relationship, reveals in a masterful use of religious images her passion as "hot theopathy," her advances like those of "a nun of crimson ruses," the lowly room as a chapel "Where she genuflects to love / All the prayerbooks in her eyes / Open soft as sacrifice / Or the dolour of a dove." Brooks exposes Annie's fanatical obsession with her "man of tan" that obscures and diminishes her sense of self and predicts the decimated personality Annie becomes at the end of the poem.

As Brooks sets in motion the inevitability of Annie's downfall, war mercilessly intrudes upon the couple's lives. "Names him. Tame him. Takes him off / Throws to columns row on row." To fight off a paralyzing melancholy, Annie reminds herself, "Skirmishes can do / Then he will come back to you." The soldier/husband does come back; but, his return is no occasion for joy. Diseased and troubled, he cannot shake himself free of the "eerie stutter" of the war. Nor can he reconcile himself to the utter boredom or feeling of inconsequence that he experiences upon his return. With his illusions to hero status vanquished by civilian life and unable to restore the "candy crowns" of glory, he turns to another woman as recompense and rejects his wife. Annie's rejection is complete. Her husband gone; her marriage ruined; her dreams wrecked, "all things suave and bright" spent. Not only is her physical appearance spurned for one "gorgeous and gold" but the magic that surrounded the marriage is dispelled.

Skillfully juxtaposing the stages of Annie's emotional breakdown with the passing of the seasons, Brooks shows Annie seeking solace in nature. "Crusted wintertime" brings on "fluting spring"; spring merges with "summer gourmet fare." Yet summer turns again to autumn, and Annie finds no consolation there. Time has spent time but not her grief.

> Runs to parks. November leaves
> All gone papery and brown
> Poise upon the queasy stalks
> And perturb the respectable walks.
> Glances grayly and perceives
> This November her true town;
> All's a falling falling down. (105)

The beauty of Brooks's highly original tetrameter seven-line stanza is nowhere more startling than in these lines on nature. In every stanza Brooks carefully and exquisitely chisels the images. In the stanza beginning "Seeks for solaces in snow," the poet creates the icy, jeweled glow of snow, "half blue and silver," and the alliterative wonder, the "crunching in the crust / Chills her nicely, as it must." In the stanza that begins "Seeks for solaces in green," the rich, fecund smell of spring bombards the senses. "Bubbles apple-green, shrill wine, / Hyacinthine devils sing" (105). As Brooks admits, every stanza in the poem "was worked on, revised, tenderly cared for." She describes the poem as one "that's very interested in the mysteries and magic of technique." [12] Years later, recalling the technique of "The Anniad," Brooks exclaims, "What a pleasure it was to write that poem." In response to the question of whether she was "trying something totally new," she says, "No, not something new. I was just very conscious of every word; I wanted every phrase to be beautiful, and yet to contribute sanely to the whole, to the whole effect." [13] Though Brooks admits that it is a labored poem and others including Haki Madhubuti have been disturbed by its tendencies toward obscurantism and excessive delight in dazzling its readers, who were presumed to be white, [14] it is a striking example of the originality of her poetic technique. As Gloria Hull suggests, part of the pleasure and the difficulty of experiencing Brooks's poetry is recognizing the elements of her compressed, elliptical style: a quaint and unusual diction, imperative tone, personification, economical language, alliteration, and slyly satiric humor—which, in combination, make Miss Brooks unique and define her to the poetic ear." [15]

However, "The Anniad," conspicuous for its highly developed and stylized form, is treasured because of the poignant truth it reveals about this male-female relationship. Brooks becomes the thaumaturgic seer divining more than beautiful lines that hold in stark relief the ironies and tragedy of small groping lives; she plumbs their very souls with compassion and truth. The "Anniad" is invaluable in any analysis of the poetry of Gwendolyn Brooks because it is one of the earliest examples of the mature, courageous, innovative poetic voice that she dared claim as her own. What Brooks did in this poem was uncommon. Among the established literary circles, it was rare to consider the interior lives of black women as important. Not only had white male writers virtually ignored them but few men of her own race had given more than surface treatment to black women characters who could have been treated with depth and complexity. Brooks dared in mid-1940s America, where its black citizens were politically and socially invisible, to bring into stark view a woman whose deep humanity could not be denied. Well aware of the pressure that publishers and critics exerted to influence her style, she continued to experiment and was adamant about her right to do so despite the criticisms of obscurity and excessive preoccupation with form that were leveled at *Annie Allen* and especially "The Anniad." She chose experimentation when it would have been safer to devise a poetic formula based on the successful poems in *A Street in Bronzeville* and stay with it. Yet by taking literary risks, she brings to creation Annie, whom Nikki Giovanni, recognizing her spiritual kinship, called "my mother." [16] Even in 1949 Brooks was writing/building with the kind of love that the speaker in "The Sermon on the Warpland" urges.

> Build with lithe love. With love like lion-eyes.
> With love like morningrise.
> With love like black, our black—
> luminously indiscreet;
> complete; continuous." (452)

It took a "luminously indiscreet" love to expose Annie with all of her self-doubting and feelings of inferiority that were rooted in sexism and racism.

It took a "complete" and "continuous" love to portray her empathetically in a time when consciousness-raising had scarcely become more than exercises in dualism.

Brooks, in relating the dimensions of male-female relations, brought to them what she knew of love. In "when you have forgotten Sunday: the love story," Brooks clothes her remembrances of the early days of her own marriage in bright bedclothes and a deliciously sensuous gush of details. According to critic D. H. Melhem, this poem refers to Gwendolyn Brooks and Henry Blakely, her husband of more than forty years, when they lived at "623 East 63rd Street, our most exciting kitchenette." [17] In "A Lovely Love" (*The Bean Eaters*), Brooks captures the tension and titillation that accompanied premarital love encounters before the freedom of the sixties released the strictures. Though this love appears expansive and cavernous, it is restrictive, even as the poet's expressiveness is confined to the strict sonnet form.

> That is the birthright of our lovely love
> In swaddling clothes. Not like that Other one.
> Not lit by any fondling star above.
> Not found by any wise men, either. Run.
> People are coming. They must not catch us here
> Definitionless in this strict atmosphere. (363)

In alluding to the Nativity, the poet effectively suggests the lowly beginnings of this love that, unlike the "Other one," must be concealed.

However, "A Sunset of the City" reveals the end of love mourned by a woman who faces the sunset of her years. Brooks writes of this woman: "She knows it is fall, and that winter is on the way. She feels done and dusty as she stands among the echoes of her past—echoes from which all the vitality and richness, even the richness of life's debris, have been cruelly scrubbed away. Her lines belie her own intimacy with the disappointing loss of love in her fragile, waning years of middle age." [18]

> It is summer-gone that I see, it is summer-gone.
> The sweet flowers indrying and dying down,
> The grasses forgetting their blaze and consenting to
>   brown. (353)

Brooks's powerful signature metaphor of flowers appears here to represent this once-vital woman whose very soul is drying up. Prayers avail nothing;

only a "dual dilemma" remains. "Whether to dry / In humming pallor or to leap and die" (354). In all of these poems Brooks consults herself and reveals her willingness to explore the depth of her emotional life and that of women she understands intimately.

It is with this same depth of understanding that she explores mother-hood and children. No other major American poet has given such consistent treatment to these themes. In her often-quoted poem "The Mother," appearing in *A Street in Bronzeville*, Brooks introduces a mother whose decision to abort her children seems to defy the boundaries that are predestined for their lives. Writing about the poem in her autobiography, Brooks says, "Hardly your crowned and praised and 'customary' Mother; but a Mother not unfamiliar, who decides that *she*, rather than her World, will kill her children. The decision is not nice, not simple, and the emotional consequences are neither nice nor simple." [19] Interestingly, Brooks's description of this mother could well fit the woman that Toni Morrison immortalizes in her novel *Beloved*. Determined to kill her children before she will see them dragged back into slavery, Morrison's Sethe succeeds in cutting her daughter's throat before the slave catchers stop her. Though the circumstances appear dramatically different, the urgency and the anguish associated with the choices are similar.

However, Brooks insists that this poem is not so much about abortions as it is about mothering and refuses to allow any group whether pro-choice or pro-life to use it to promote its cause. In the opening ten lines of the poem, the speaker achieves a relative distance from the subject of abortions. Addressing an indefinite "you," the mother attempts to shield herself from the remorse and guilt she feels.

> Abortions will not let you forget.
> You remember the children you got that you did not
>   get,
> The damp small pulps with a little or with no hair,
> The singers and workers that never handled the air.
> You will never neglect or beat
> Them, or silence or buy with a sweet.
> You will never wind up the sucking-thumb
> Or scuttle off ghosts that come.
> You will never leave them, controlling your luscious
>   sign,
> Return for a snack of them, with gobbling mother-eye. (21)

In evoking the unfinished lives of the unborn, Brooks registers significant poignancy; however, the corresponding loss of the mother, forever tied emotionally to her "dim killed children," is overwhelming. The artificial distance erected in the opening lines must be abandoned and we find the mother confessing and accepting her portion of responsibility. Brooks powerfully suggests the tyranny choices exercise in the life of this woman. Written in irregularly metered couplets, her monologue is faltering and strained, and the tone is wistful and deeply remorseful.

When the choice is made to bear children and seek to ensure their survival within the context of life's inexorable limitations, great courage is needed. In poem 2 of "the children of the poor," the narrator, who has now become a mother, asks,

> What shall I give my children? who are poor,
> Who are adjudged the leastwise of the land,
> Who are my sweetest lepers, who demand
> No velvet and no velvety velour. (116)

When one of these limitations is racism that defines and separates, that makes them feel "quasi," "contraband," the mother is helpless "to ratify [her] little halves."

In Brooks's long narrative poem, "In the Mecca," in the book of the same title, she takes a sustained look at the dimensions of mothering and the fierce grip on reality that is required if a mother is to nurture her children and prevail against a society that plots their destruction. In the poem Brooks's central character is on a desperate search for her child through the chaotic maze of halls in a blighted Chicago apartment building. When Mrs. Sallie Smith comes home to the Mecca weary with the spoils from her domestic job and starts a meager dinner for her nine children, she discovers that her baby girl Pepita is missing. As Mrs. Sallie enlists the aid of her children and neighbors to join her in the search, the hysteria and pathos of her search grow, even as the reader is drawn into a dangerous world, overcrowded and teeming with possibilities for both growth and decay.

> In twos!
> In threes! Knock-knocking down the martyred halls
> at doors behind whose yelling oak or pine
>   many flowers start, choke, reach up,
>   want help, get it, do not get it,
>   rally, bloom, or die on the wasting vine. (416–17)

Unlike Brooks's development of character in "The Anniad," in which she peels back the layers of Annie's consciousness, layer after painful layer, to reveal her essence, in "In the Mecca," Brooks creates the character of Mrs. Sallie by making her a synthesis of all that touches her. Not only is Mrs. Sallie's search used as a device to introduce the various inhabitants of the Mecca, she is also paradoxically a symbiont living apart from ("a fragmentary attar") and living immersed in ("armed coma") (407) this pulsing urban organism.

As Mattie Michael is the thread that runs through the emotional warp of Gloria Naylor's *Women of Brewster Place* and stands as a symbol of resilience to its residents, Mrs. Sallie is a fitting symbol for the poet's vision of the "destruction and nurturing aspects of the black urban environment" that Brooks proposed for the work.[20]

> I wish to present a large variety of personalities against a mosaic of daily affairs, recognizing that the *grimmest* of these is likely to have a streak or two streaks of sun.
> In the Mecca were murders, loves, lonelinesses, hates, jealousies. Hope occurred, and charity, sainthood, glory, shame, despair, fear, altruism. . . .
> To touch every note in the life of this block-long, block-wide building would be to capsulize the gist of black humanity in general.[21]

Brooks introduces Mrs. Sallie, "low-brown butterball," as she "ascends the sick and influential star" of the Mecca, once a luxurious architectural wonder for the wealthy, now a decrepit tenement crumbling under the weight of thousands of poor, dispossessed blacks.

> The eye unrinsed, the mouth absurd
> with the last sourings of the master's Feast.
> She plans
> to set severity apart,
> to unclench the heavy folly of the fist. (407)

Brooks in a clever use of synecdoche suggests the bone-tiredness and soul-weariness of this woman dragging herself home from a job she resents not only because of the severe demands that her employers exact but also because of her awareness that time exacts its own spoils. Her slow steady movement up the stairs gives Brooks a vehicle to bring in other characters who serve to amplify Mrs. Sallie's character.

Mrs. Sallie, unlike old St. Julia Jones, is "all innocent of saints and sig-
natures" (408); she is content to pay her respects abstractly through the
communion sacrament. However, she is fervent in her righteous indigna-
tion against the depraved nature of Prophet Williams, "who reeks with lust
for his disciple," and who so impoverished the spirit of his own wife that
she "died in self-defense." As Mrs. Sallie approaches another landing she
sees Alfred, the resident writer/teacher. Mrs. Sallie, herself a frustrated art-
ist without a means to express her creativity beyond the art of procreation,
"wants to decorate." She is a secret sharer with Alfred with a clear prefer-
ence for his God.

> Sallie sees Alfred, Ah, his God!—
> To create! To create! To bend with the right intentness
> over the neat detail, come to
> a terrified standstill of the heart, then shiver
> then rush—successfully—
> at the rebuking thing, that obstinate and
> recalcitrant little beast, the phrase! (408–9)

By delineating the creative process, Brooks gives credence to her own and
appears to empathize with the seeker/artist.

At the fourth and final landing, Mrs. Sallie daily confronts the paradox
of her existence: the abject poverty of her surroundings alongside the aban-
doned wealth that her children represent. This paradox intensifies when she
becomes aware of the glaring disparity between the condition of her own
children and the child she cares for at work. Her children, appendages of
herself, have been left to their private worlds of fantasy, hate, violence, pain,
and deprivation. The eldest daughter, Yvonne, waits for her errant lover
and rationalizes his unfaithfulness.

> It is not necessary, says Yvonne,
> to have every day him whom
> to the end thereof you will love. (411)

The awkward, tortured syntax adequately reflects the contortions her mind
must go through to believe that he will "touch" her again. For others of
Mrs. Sallie's children, love or the romantic illusion of it is not enough,
for their seeds have been sprinkled on hard sod and hatred is the harvest.

And, like other inhabitants of the Mecca, their machinations are toward
escape. Briggs who "is adult as stone / (who if he cries cries alone)" epito-

mizes the gang psychology that is quicksand that swallows up love, hope, individuality, even the conscience that would not accept "the unacceptable evil." Thomas Earl loves Johnny Appleseed. He, like the mythic American hero, wants to touch growth and cultivate life and see it propagate. In his love is the anlage for growth, but in the Mecca "the ground shudders" and "hits you with gnarls and rust / derangement and fever, or blare and clerical treasons." Emmett, Cap, and Casey "are skin wiped over bones," a trinity of deprivation. Perhaps when Alfred says, "The faithless world! / betraying yet again / trinities!" (414), he grasps the irony of the secular order that cannot promise abundance or salvation. However, despite their disparate pain, their defensive alienation, they all come together to search for Pepita. For she is "their joining thing."

Much of the magic of the poem results from Brooks's ability to reveal the emotional anguish of a mother who almost immediately intuits tragedy.

> SUDDENLY COUNTING NOSES, MRS. SALLIE SEES NO
> PEPITA. "WHERE PEPITA BE?"
> . . . where may our Pepita be?—
> our Woman with her terrible eye,
> with iron and feathers in her feet,
> with all her songs so lemon-sweet,
> with lightning and candle too
> and junk and jewels too?
> My heart begins to race.
> I fear the end of Peace. (415–16)

This vivid description of Pepita owes greatly to Mrs. Sallie's growing dementia. With the clairvoyance of Cassandra her mind races to capture her child's essence as though to freeze it in secure permanence. When premature memorials are done, however, the tortuous fears and denials return, everyone is suspect. Mrs. Sallie's brave rationalizations cannot conceal her encroaching sense of loss.

The Mecca is not a place for innocence, and Mrs. Sallie knows that few care about Pepita; few are concerned whether she will live out the meaning of her name: seed of fruit. As Brooks uses the search as a way of introducing the inhabitants of the Mecca, their introductions are crowded with almost unbearable intensity and hysteria. Brooks ingeniously recreates the chaotic, despairing, hope-tinged atmosphere she experienced firsthand as the secretary to a patent-medicine salesman who, resembling the parasitic prophet Williams, purveyed the nostrums necessary for escape and disengagement.

The diverse residents of the Mecca peer from behind their oak and pine doors. Great-great Gram, an ancient resident whose age mocks the premature decay of the once-splendid building, lives more comfortably in the past with her vivid memories of slavery and sleeping "curled in corners" of dirt floors. The "striking debutante" Hyena, a female counterpart of Satin-Legs, loses herself in "special oils and fumes" and sun-gold hair. She cares nothing for the child she thinks of as "puny" and "putrid." Insane Sophie cannot reach out to Pepita, for she was withdrawn to a place "in which to scream" a constant, silent scream that conceals her deepest regrets: "What have I done, and to the world, / and to the love I promised Mother?" (428). Some can only be oblivious to the fate of this little girl, for they tend their own agonizing seeds, anticipating greener days. Loam Norton, who "considers Belsen and Dachau" and "regrets all old unkindnesses and harms," feels the sufferings of victims whether Jewish or black. Regretting the remoteness of their God and the inability of organized religion to affect survival, he acknowledges: "I am not remote / nor unconcerned" (418). Way-out Morgan, a tour de force of character development, has not considered Pepita. He has grown lean nurturing the coming blood-harvest.

Alfred, who has been the voice of skepticism throughout the poem, in one final moment of revelation is redeemed by a spirit of caritas and witnesses God, "Substanceless; / yet like mountains, / like rivers and oceans too; and like trees / with wind whistling through them" (433). It is at this time that the poet in a dramatic reversal reveals the murder of innocent Pepita, having destruction and redemption contiguous in a mother's pain.

> Hateful things sometimes befall the hateful
> but the hateful are not rendered lovable thereby.
> The murderer of Pepita
> looks at the Law unlovably. Jamaican
> Edward denies and thrice denies a dealing
> of any dimension with Mrs. Sallie's daughter.
>   Beneath his cot
> a little woman lies in dust with roaches.
> She never went to kindergarten.
> She never learned that black is not beloved.
> Was royalty when poised,
> sly, at the A and P's fly-open door.
> Will be royalty no more.
> "I touch"—she said once—"petals of a rose.

A silky feeling through me goes!"
Her mother will try for roses. (433)

Mrs. Sallie will try for roses. Violence and death in the form of Jamaican Edward have choked another flower, yet all the forces of destruction have not prevailed in killing Mrs. Sallie's determination to build, to create a new community, like the one envisioned by Don Lee, who "wants / new art and anthem; will / want a new music screaming in the sun" (423–24). For Brooks the message is clear, the grimmest circumstances, whether abject poverty of matter or spirit, whether hellish confusion precipitated by loss of identity, whether paroxysms of fear and revenge, all are relieved by "a streak or two streaks of sun." Articulating a mother's abiding faith in the emergence of life even amid destruction, Brooks addresses in "In the Mecca" her own belief in the reemergence of a black nation transplanted in America.

In *In the Mecca* (1968), called by some her pivotal work, her poetry "lifts its face all unashamed. / And sways in wicked grace." Significantly, the tropism in her poetry is a consequence of her audience. Brooks did not start saying things so differently; her use of ellipsis, ironic and humorous nuances, unusual syntax and wordplay remains characteristic. Nor were the pressing social and political concerns that appeared in *A Street in Bronzeville* (1945), *Annie Allen* (1949), or *The Bean Eaters* (1960) put aside.

From the time her mother, Keziah Wims Brooks, announced that she was going to be "the lady Paul Laurence Dunbar," Brooks was aware of racism, so virulent that it demanded death of its victims, so subtle that it made victims wish to imitate their victimizers. Early, she observed the double standards of caste and class and the amazing paradoxes prevalent in a society where black boys were killed for acting like men and black men were made to act like boys. As she developed as a poet, she distilled in her poetry the complex nature of women often maligned in a society that accepted only the cosmetic parts of their womanhood.

What truly changed after 1967, however, was her awareness of her audience and her sense of connectedness with it. With the publication of *In the Mecca*, she became clearly aware that black people, her people, were listening and that what she said could and did make a difference. For Brooks, the audience transformed the art. In an article published in 1975, she said that in the late sixties there was the recognition of the fact "that shrieking into the steady and organized deafness of the white ear was frivolous." "There were things to be said to black brothers and sisters, and these things, annunciatory, curative, inspiriting, were to be said forthwith, without frill and, without fear of the white presence. There was impatience with idle embroidery, with what was considered avoidance—avoidance of the gut issue, the blood fact. Literary rhythms altered. Sometimes the literature seemed to issue from pens dipped in, *stabbed* in writhing blood."[22]

Gwendolyn Brooks has spent the last thirty years of her literary career as a mother/mentor to younger black writers. She has taken this role seriously, always cognizant of their revolutionary turnings and ever critical of her own timid beginnings. She has cautioned them against falling into the timidity that she experienced in the 1940s and 1950s when her shrieking against racial and social injustices was muted and camouflaged in language more tenable to the ears of her audience. In 1975 she wrote, "The Forties and Fifties were years of high poet-incense; the language-flowers were thickly sweet. Those flowers whined and begged white folks to pick them, to find them lovable. Then—the Sixties: independent fire."[23] Because she was there, she understands the temptation of younger writers, frustrated at the slowness of change and confounded by future dictions, to settle for "the pretty little thing."[24] When she sees them moving away from the fire of the late sixties, moving away from poetry that singed the enemies of equality and hurled word-weapons at the thwarters of justice, she admonishes them not "to creep back to the weaker flowers" and "not to forget the Fire."[25]

With the pervasive metaphor of the flower, Brooks ingeniously charts the race's emotional journey. From the delicate shrinking violet of Annie, to the children-flowers who "rally, bloom or die on the wasting vine" of the Mecca, she arrives at "rowdy" flowers that "must come out to the road." In "Young Afrikans," first published in *Family Pictures* (1970), the poet says,

> If there are flowers flowers
> must come out to the road. Rowdy!—
> knowing where wheels and people are,
> knowing where whips and screams are,
> knowing where deaths are, where the kind kills are. (494)

This important metaphor reappears in "The Second Sermon on the Warpland," a poem in which Brooks unself-consciously embraces the imperatives for life and growth, blooming, "the greening of the universe," as Sonia Sanchez calls it, even in the midst of turmoil and struggle. Written for Walter Bradford, to whom Brooks gave the affection of a son, the poem has an urgency issuing from a deep maternal insistence on the value of life and the dignity of struggle. The poet in sections 1 and 2 challenges the youth to produce, create, salvage the outcasts, and give new expression to worn-out forms. Hers is an ecclesiastical fervor. There will be no reassuring calm for self-discovery; the whirlwind of struggle tosses about the initiates even as they grow in strength.

In section 3, which is descriptive and profoundly prophetic, she paints a city colder and uglier than any Gotham because it is real.

> All about are the cold places,
> all about are the pushmen and jeopardy, theft—
> all about are the stormers and scramblers but
> what must our Season be, which starts from Fear?
> Live and go out.
> Define and
> medicate the whirlwind. (455)

This place and time will require great courage and heroism of those who seek to ride out the storm. In the final section of "The Second Sermon on the Warpland," the poet suggests that the youth are not alone and that they must look for comrades among common folk who have always managed their share of heroism. Witness Big Bessie, who "stands—bigly— under the unruly scrutiny . . . in the wild weed." The poet ends the sermon as she began it, with an imperative and a prayer.

> It is lonesome, yes. For we are the last of the loud.
> Nevertheless, live.
> Conduct your blooming in the noise and whip of the whirlwind. (456)

"Annunciatory, curative, and inspiriting," Brooks's poetry is the furious flower that younger poets came to treasure and countless others have returned to again and again to glimpse its magic and its ferocious beauty.

Notes

1. Brooks, "the ballad of chocolate Mabbie," "Mrs. Small," and "the rites of Cousin Vit," *Blacks*, 30, 341–43, 125. Hereinafter *Blacks* will be cited in the text with page numbers only.

2. Mootry, 3–4.

3. Brooks, "Gwendolyn Brooks," 43–44.

4. Joyce, 82.

5. Brooks, *Report*, 42.

6. Brooks, "Gwendolyn Brooks," 42.

7. Ibid.

8. Brooks, *Report*, 86.

9. Stavros, 12.

10. Kent, 45–46.

11. Davis, 186.

12. Stavros, 12.

13. Ibid., 13.

14. Lee, 17.

15. Hull, 281.

16. Giovanni, 26.

17. Melhem, 30.

18. Brooks, *Report*, 184.

19. Ibid.

20. Guy-Sheftall, 154.

21. Brooks, *Report*, 189–90.

22. Brooks, "Of Flowers and Fire and Flowers," 16.

23. Ibid., 18.

24. Ibid.

25. Ibid.

Works Cited

Brooks, Gwendolyn. *Blacks*. Chicago: Third World, 1992.

———. "Gwendolyn Brooks." In *Black Women Writers at Work*, ed. Claudia Tate. New York: Continuum, 1985.

———. "Of Flowers and Fire and Flowers." *Black Books Bulletin* 3 (fall 1975).

———. *Report from Part One*. Detroit: Broadside, 1972.

Davis, Arthur P. *From the Dark Tower*. Washington, D.C.: Howard University Press, 1974.

Giovanni, Nikki. "To Gwen Brooks from Nikki Giovanni." *Essence* (Apr. 1971).

Guy-Sheftall, Beverly. "The Women of Bronzeville." In Moorty.

Hull, Gloria. "A Note on the Poetic Technique of Gwendolyn Brooks." *CLA Journal* 19 (Dec. 1975).

Joyce, Joyce Ann. "Gwendolyn Brooks: Jean Toomer's November Cotton Flower." In *Say That the River Turns: The Impact of Gwendolyn Brooks*, ed. Haki R. Madhubuti. Chicago: Third World, 1987.

Kent, George. "The Poetry of Gwendolyn Brooks." *Black World* 20 (Oct. 1971).

Lee, Don L. "Gwendolyn Brooks: Beyond the Wordmaker—the Making of an African Poet." In Brooks, *Report*.

Melhem, D. H. *Gwendolyn Brooks: Poetry and the Heroic Voice.* Lexington: University Press of Kentucky, 1987.

Mootry, Maria K. "'Down the Whirlwind of Good Rage'—an Introduction to Gwendolyn Brooks." In *A Life Distilled: Gwendolyn Brooks, Her Poetry and Fiction,* ed. Maria K. Mootry and Gary Smith. Urbana: University of Illinois Press, 1987.

Stavros, George. "An Interview with Gwendolyn Brooks." *Contemporary Literature* 11 (winter 1970).

Conversation:

G W E N D O L Y N   B R O O K S
and
B .   D E N I S E   H A W K I N S

HAWKINS: Some literary critics have charged that when Black poets don't confine themselves to writing about the "Black experience" then they are not "legitimate" Black poets.

BROOKS: A Black poet writes only from the Black experience. What else can he write from?

HAWKINS: What is the Black experience?

BROOKS: The Black experience is any experience that a Black person has.

HAWKINS: You receive hundreds of solicited and unsolicited manuscripts and poems to be reviewed. How do you determine what is good writing? How do you evaluate?

BROOKS: The first thing I do is look for clichés. Then I want to be sure that the poet is speaking honestly and saying what he or she really means.

HAWKINS: How should African American poetry be critiqued, evaluated, and chronicled?

BROOKS: Anybody writing about the literary history of Black poetry should be interested in really trying to understand what the poets were trying to do. The first thing that any critic writing about the history of Black poetry should do is read the poetry. There are many people writing about my poetry who have read "A Song in the Front Yard," "We Real Cool," and "The Bean Eaters." Then they're through. They know nothing about my book *Winnie,* which marks a very significant change in my writing. They know nothing about *In the Mecca.* They know nothing about *Children Coming Home.*

They need to know that I am interested in Winnie Mandela, not just in Harriet Tubman and Sojourner Truth. They need to know that I am interested in what goes on in the streets, that my *own* home on 74th and Evans was invaded, that I started a workshop for some of the hardest youngsters—parts of a group called the Blackstone Rangers, and got to know some of the things that motivated them, and wrote on this subject in a poem that I think is very well written.

The poem is called "The Blackstone Rangers." Critics need to read that. Many critics are not going to read that. They are satisfied with trying to give the public the impression that I'm an "old-fashioned" writer, simplistic and outmoded. They want to use "A Song in the Front Yard" to represent my entire output and intent. I have been changing all along. None of my books is exactly like the other.

HAWKINS: Since your childhood you have lived and worked in Chicago. How has that city and its people influenced your writing?

BROOKS: Of course, living in the city, I wrote differently than I would have if I had been raised in Topeka, Kansas, where I was born and lived for six weeks. I'm so glad my parents decided to move to Chicago. I am "an organic" Chicagoan.

HAWKINS: When you sit down to write, what is your thought process?

BROOKS: I write and rewrite and ask myself the sterling question—Is this really what *I* want to say? With an emphasis on *really* and *I.* I started using a ballpoint pen, which is still what I use to this day. At some point, of course, you have to see how what you are writing looks like in print. (At that stage I use an ordinary old-fashioned typewriter.)

HAWKINS: A few years ago, when the works of both Toni Morrison and Terri McMillan flourished for weeks on the best-seller list, critics attempted to force a wedge between them and force readers to choose—"scholarship" as in Morrison's *Beloved*—or "pop culture," as in McMillan's *Waiting to Exhale*. Are you concerned about fitting in either literary camp? Should readers, especially Black readers, be forced to choose?

BROOKS: I'm not interested in fitting in. To what? Into T. S. Eliot's mode of writing? What I find very fascinating is that young Black women are reading both of those authors. They seem just as excited about one as the other, and they want to have both on their bookshelves. In the white race there was some of that same kind of dissension involving Katherine Mansfield and Virginia Woolf. Katherine Mansfield . . . well nobody could say that she wasn't literary. Virginia Woolf's style was a more studied "literariness." There will always be those kinds of comparisons. *All* these books are available to us. All we have to do is put down our money.

I am not a "scholar." I'm a writer who loves to write and will always write. I want to report; I want to record. I go inside myself, bring out what I feel, put it on paper, look at it, pull out all of the clichés. I will work hard in *that* way.

HAWKINS: You continue to attract throngs of students and young writers who admire and study your work.

BROOKS: They like poetry that means something to them. Most of the young people that you saw me with today have already heard me on this campus or that campus. I travel a lot. I visit about fifty campuses a year. For some of them, it's like saying hello to Mommy or Sister or Friend.

HAWKINS: The language in many of your poems is very familiar, especially to African Americans. One such poem that comes to mind is "To Black Women." Did you intend to send a special message to African American women through this particular work?

BROOKS: I never say to myself that I am going to "send a message." In the poem "To Black Women" I thought about the horrors that many Black women endure. They *oblige* themselves to prevail.

I put so much into that poem. I hope that a good many people have taken much from it. Each line there is loaded. An essay could be written on each line.

HAWKINS: Discuss your formal education in literature.

BROOKS: I've had very little formal education in anything. I graduated from a junior college in Chicago that was once called Woodrow Wilson Junior College. It is now Kennedy-King College. That is the limit of my "formal" education. I did not consider pursuing a four-year degree. I knew that I was going to be a writer. I knew that I would read read read.

HAWKINS: What has your experience been like in higher education as a professor?

BROOKS: Most of my "job-work" was as a typist for lawyers. I had to make a living. Frank London Brown, the novelist who wrote *Trumbull Park,* was teaching at the University of Chicago and invited me to teach a course in American literature. That was my first teaching experience. When I was teaching at the University of Chicago, it did not matter if I had a degree or not. Later Frank London Brown tried to get a job for me at Roosevelt University. I was not allowed to teach because I had only an Associate Degree. That was in 1961. Several years later, Roosevelt University did invite me to come and teach. (At *that* time I did not want to teach.)

Maybe they came to their senses and realized that if you are going to teach a class in poetry writing, it's better to have a practicing poet than someone who has a string of degrees and has not written anything. In 1990, Roosevelt gave me an Honorary Degree.

I'm working now—in various ways—at Chicago State University. Haki [Madhubutil] fought for years to get me on that campus and to create the center that is named for me. I try to do what I can to excite the students about writing—and about literature itself.

HAWKINS: When did you discover Black literature and poets? What books did you read growing up?

BROOKS: When I was fifteen, I discovered a little book called
                Caroling Dusk. It featured the writings of poets like Lang-
ston Hughes and Sterling Brown. And the two Cotters—Joseph Cotter Sr.
and Jr. Before that (*and* after) I read from the Harvard classics, which my
wonderful father had given to my wonderful mother as a wedding pres-
ent. And my mother would take my brother and me downtown to buy
books for us (poor though we were). Rest well, Mama. You certainly did
your job.

   It was exciting to see all those writers. Of course I knew about Paul
Laurence Dunbar. We had many of his books in the house, and my father
used to recite his works to my brother and me. One day I told myself that
if these people could write poetry and become well known, maybe I
would also become well known one day. I knew that I was going to write,
even if I were never published. I knew that I wanted to write poetry. I
never wanted to write novels. I did write a few short stories when I was
young. (Finally, my one novel, *Maud Martha* was published in 1953. It was
beautifully received.)

HAWKINS: In your Pulitzer Prize–winning book, *Annie Allen,* was it
                the social climate, the message, the character, or a com-
bination of those things that appealed to the selection committee?

BROOKS: I never thought about whether it was right for the time. I
                just wanted to write about a little Black girl growing into
womanhood. I start her at her birth, a birth in a narrow room. I wanted to
consider what would happen in the life of such an individual. I will tell
you one thing about that poem that not many people know. I thought
about the kind of impression that book would have. I was trying in that
long poem, "The Anniad" to be arty and to be ever so "poetic." I would
never write such a poem again. I wouldn't have the patience and I don't
see the point. There are some good things about many expressions I used,
however.

HAWKINS: In 1950 you became the first African American to win a
                Pulitzer Prize in any category. How differently would
your literary career have been shaped if you had won the prize in 1994
instead of in 1950?

BROOKS: It would be different because I would be just one more
                Black woman winning the prize. Until May 1950, no

Blacks had won *any* of the significant awards of our time, and that is why people keep talking about me in terms of "grandeur"; just because I happen to have been "the first." Isn't that ridiculous? Before me there was W. E. B. Du Bois and Langston Hughes. . . . There was Claude McKay. There was Countee Cullen, wonderful writers who certainly deserved whatever prizes were available for writers. But they were denied.

HAWKINS: How did your contemporaries respond when you won the Pulitzer?

BROOKS: *I* was very happy of course! I was thirty-two and it was my second book. Things were quite different in those days. When one of us got recognition, the others seemed happy about it. Langston Hughes, who often wrote to me, discussed my work in his column. Langston certainly should have won a Pulitzer a long time ago for all his work. When I won, he was like a father beaming over a daughter, who was getting this wonderful prize.

HAWKINS: You are as particular about what you are called as the words that you choose for your poems. Discuss your preference for the term *Black* over *African American.*

BROOKS: I don't like the term *African American.* It is very excluding. I like to think of Blacks as *Family.* Parts of that family living in Brazil or Haiti or France or England are not going to allow you to call them African American because they are not. I would like to read to you my poem that speaks to this.
[Gwendolyn Brooks excerpting from "I Am A Black"]:

> According to my Teachers,
> I am now an African-American.
> They call me out of my name.
> BLACK is an open umbrella.
> I am Black and *a* Black forever.

I've talked to little boys, big boys, little girls, and big girls, and they say that my writing gives them the strength to express their preference. I don't expect to change the world! As a people, we are not of one accord on what we should be called. Some people say it doesn't matter, "call me anything." I think *that* is a pitiful decision.

HAWKINS: In your 1991 book of poetry, *Children Coming Home,* you chronicle contemporary issues such as incest in "Uncle Seagram," interracial families in "Our White Mother Says We Are Black But Not Very," drug dealing in "Song: White Powder." Do you plan to capture other significant issues of our day—AIDS, crime, the L.A. uprising—in future poems?

BROOKS: I have a long poem called *Riot,* that came out in book form in three parts. I think it is a very good impression of the riots of '68. When the [1992] riot broke out in Los Angeles, I said "I've got to write about this" and started taking notes as I watched it on TV. But then I quit because I said, "my poem *Riot* says as much about the Los Angeles riot as any newer poem I would write."

HAWKINS: What does that realization say about our time and about racism?

BROOKS: That we are not making as much progress as we should be making. It's sad, very sad.

HAWKINS: What entered into your decision to leave Harper and Row [now HarperCollins]?

BROOKS: I was with Harper, my first publisher, from 1945 to 1969. That's quite a while to stay with one publishing house. Dudley Randall [then publisher of Broadside Press] at that time was giving a platform to young Black poets, people that Macmillan and Harper wouldn't accept. I thought joining Broadside Press was the right thing for me to do. Instead of staying in the "Harper harbor" I decided to go with a Black publisher and give some assistance to them. It has been thirty years since I published with Harper. My publisher is now Third World Press of Chicago.

HAWKINS: Thank you for sharing this time with me.

Song of Herself: Lucille Clifton's Poems about Womanhood

HILARY HOLLADAY

T
O READ ONE OF LUCILLE CLIFTON'S POEMS IS TO EX-
perience an epiphany, a swift flowering of personal observation into
social insight. To read all of them is to apprehend a far-reaching,
essentially hopeful vision of humanity. Clifton has dedicated her
work and her life to "the celebration of the spirit and flesh of what is a
whole human."[1] Starting with *Good Times* (1969), her free-verse lyrics con-
sistently speak to the spirit and the flesh, not only because she writes mainly
about human connections and relationships, but also because a Clifton
poem has the effervescence of unbidden thought. If "the purpose of lyric,
as a genre, is to represent an inner life in such a manner that it is assumable
by others," then that purpose is repeatedly fulfilled in Clifton's verse.[2]

Her mastery of the lyric recalls the stylistic pleasures of imagism and
the visceral emotion of confessional poetry. Like William Carlos Williams,
Ezra Pound, H.D., and Wallace Stevens, Clifton is capable of the stunning
miniature. She shares Williams's interest in vernacular speech and Stevens's
penchant for wordplay. But whereas the imagists went on to longer, more
complicated forms to accommodate their increasingly meditative verse,
Clifton has rather stubbornly remained brief and to the point: "I have never
believed that for anything to be valid or true or intellectual or 'deep' it had
to first be complex. . . . I am interested in trying to render big ideas in a
simple way," she maintains.[3] Both the clarity and breadth of her poetry
stem in large part from her persona's varying moods and aspects. By turns
joyfully resilient and perilously vulnerable, Clifton's persona brings to mind
the strong female voices of confessional poetry. Like her contemporaries
Anne Sexton and Sylvia Plath, Clifton constructs an autobiographical iden-
tity for herself in her poems; she writes passionately about the strengths

and frailties of the female body; she bravely chronicles every hill and shadow in the landscape of her spirit.

But growing up black and working-class in Depew, New York, and later in Buffalo, Thelma Lucille Sayles came of age in a very different milieu from the white middle-class Boston suburbs that produced Plath and Sexton. The first in her family to go to college, she attended Howard University and Fredonia State Teachers College and then married Fred Clifton, an educational consultant. The couple moved to Baltimore, where they reared six children, four daughters and two sons. Though her popular books (for children as well as adults) and a series of university teaching positions—most recently as distinguished professor of humanities at St. Mary's College in Maryland—have brought her mainstream status, Clifton still speaks from the racial and social margins of American society. The fact that she has outlived Plath by three decades and Sexton by two also distinguishes Clifton's poetry from theirs: Her later life is marked by the multiple sorrows of loss and the singular triumph of her own endurance, and her poetic "confessions" naturally reflect these developments. Clifton's ever-evolving persona is a survivor, deeply anxious about mortality yet still delighted by her living, vibrant, female self.

Throughout her career as a poet, the nature of womanhood has been Clifton's consuming subject. Many of her poems challenge pervasive societal attitudes casting women, especially black women, in the role of victim, adversary, or nonentity. For Clifton, being female is a fine starting point rather than a sorry end. She recognizes the shining facets of womanhood that many people, including many women, choose to ignore. A look at one of her frequently anthologized poems is instructive here. Published in *Two-Headed Woman* (1980), "there is a girl inside" focuses on an older woman's abundant vitality: "she is a green tree / in a forest of kindling." [4] If we take the poem autobiographically, then Clifton's third-person description of herself as "a green girl / in a used poet" is a witty play on racial identity as well as a proclamation of her own youthful spirit. But even if "there is a girl inside" Clifton, the poem is not solely about her, as the expansive imagery makes clear. This woman's body may look old, but like "a nun," she is waiting for the sexually suggestive "second coming, / when she can break through gray hairs / into blossom." Effectively combining images of nature, sex, and spiritual renewal, the poem concludes with an orgy of all the senses: "and her lovers will harvest / honey and thyme / and the woods will be wild / with the damn wonder of it." More than one lover is anticipated for this energetic woman, and the word *damn* suggests a gleeful abandonment of her chaste, nunlike existence. The harvest is also significant: Sweet, sensual honey is a compound of amazing staying power. It never grows stale. There is a parallel, then, with the sweet, sensuous woman, who only needs time (or "thyme") to share herself with others. Given the opportunity, she will inspire delight and gratification in those around her and, indeed, in her whole environment. The poem thus proposes that women, no matter what their age, are a wondrous resource waiting to be tapped both creatively and sexually.

Her poems consistently arguing for the special properties of the female spirit and body, Clifton belongs to the long tradition of poets mythologizing womanhood. But hers is a uniquely female vision, which sometimes does not even allow men or male perceptions of women into her poems. By keeping men out of the metaphorical picture, she is better able to isolate the aspects of womanhood that interest her. Like "there is a girl inside," for instance, "female" and "nude photograph" put womanhood front and center. The seven-line "female" in *Next* (1987) begins, "there is an amazon in us. / she is the secret we do not / have to learn,"[5] thereby implying that women possess an internal fortitude of mythic proportions. Rather than suggesting a pathologically divided female self (as Anne Sexton does in "Her Kind"), Clifton creates the illusion of objectivity in order to develop her notion of a multilayered, inherently female identity. If "The Child is the father of the man,"[6] then Clifton would have it that the "girl inside" every woman is not only sexy but amazingly strong. Wordsworth may have yearned for the innocent, seemingly pure vision of youth, but Clifton implies that real insight comes from a mature recognition of one's role at the vanguard of history.

If "female" mythologizes the spirit, then "nude photograph" does the same to the female body. Here, Clifton relishes "the woman's / soft and vulnerable body, / every where on her turning / round into another / where."[7] Like Wallace Stevens's "Study of Two Pears," this poem seems to be both a representation of and an alternative to the physical object being described. It is hard to say whether Stevens's "Study" depicts a painting of pears, an idea about pears, or the pears themselves; nor can we be sure whether Clifton's "nude photograph" describes a photographic image, an imagined rendering of the female body, or a real woman's body, perhaps the speaker's own. But whereas Stevens, bemused by his own paradox, pulls back from his material and states, "The pears are not seen / As the observer wills,"[8] Clifton moves closer, finally identifying with the body she describes:

who could rest one hand here or here
and not feel, whatever the shape
of the great hump longed for
in the night, a certain joy, a certain,
yes, satisfaction, yes.

Her rhetorical question swiftly becomes a rhythmic, even orgasmic, affir-
mation of female beauty and potency. This climax effectively collapses the
distance between observer and object that Stevens takes such pains to pre-
serve. Clifton's imagery is much less specific than Stevens's, yet "nude
photograph" definitely has an erotic momentum. That momentum comes
partly from the suggestive-sounding off-rhymes ("where" and "here")
and partly from the absence of detail, an absence requiring one to imagine
the woman's body as one wants it—or, as Stevens would say, as one wills
it—to be.

The evocative "nude photograph" is one of an impressive concentra-
tion of poems concerning the female body in Clifton's sixth book, *Quilting*
(1991). Elsewhere in the volume, "poem in praise of menstruation," "poem
to my uterus," "to my last period," and "wishes for sons" all take on the
still-delicate topic of menstruation in ways that are by turns joyous, poi-
gnant, and funny. A celebration of women's fertility, "poem in praise of
menstruation" compares the menstrual flow to a river "bright as the
blood / red edge of the moon" (36). Its central metaphor and its tone bring
to mind Langston Hughes's "The Negro Speaks of Rivers," the famously
dignified poem and benchmark work of the Harlem Renaissance.[9] While
Hughes focuses on the role of blacks, especially black men, in the shaping
of civilization, Clifton looks at the female experience through the ages. By
fusing images of nature, female sexuality, and matriarchal mythology, the
poem transcends the familiar taboos surrounding the fertile woman, and
menstruation becomes an awe-inspiring life force. Should a stronger force
exist, it would only be another version of "this wild / water," and one could
only "pray that it flows also / through animals / beautiful and faithful and
ancient / and female and brave." In one conditional sentence, which five
times repeats the phrase "if there is a river," the poem represents the cycli-
cal and periodic aspects of menstruation.

Later in *Quilting*, however, her approach to menstruation is much
less lofty. Her "poem to my uterus" and "to my last period" are com-
panion pieces, appearing on facing pages and addressing related events.
They resemble "there is a girl inside" and "female" in their use of per-
sonification. In the woeful "poem to my uterus" the poet addresses her

soon-to-be-removed uterus as an "old girl"—a term that is both wry and affectionate. She goes on to compare her uterus to a "stocking i will not need / where i am going, / where am i going" (58), lines implying both uncertainty about the future and a heightened awareness of mortality. The woman and her reproductive organs are in a mutually dependent relationship:

> my black bag of desire
> where can i go
> barefoot
> without you
> where can you go
> without me

With her essential "black bag," the woman is a well-prepared traveler. Without it, she anticipates a loss of direction and a lack of purpose. The word *barefoot* brings to mind an undressed woman, alone with her body. If a woman's mind and body create and continually define each other, then the loss of a body part represents a partial death. In the case of a sex organ, the loss is all the more profound since it means the woman can no longer conceive or bear children. The woman in this poem mourns the loss of creative potential as well as the seeming erasure of her sexual history. Caught in limbo, she asks questions that neither her mind nor her body can answer.

Perhaps because the dreaded change is now fully upon her, the speaker in "to my last period" is less anxious and more resilient than the one in "poem to my uterus." From the start, it is clear that the poet's imagination and humor have already rescued her from the dangers of self-pity:

> well girl, goodbye,
> after thirty-eight years.
> thirty-eight years and you
> never arrived
> splendid in your red dress
> without trouble for me
> somewhere, somehow. (59)

The stanza's syntactically delayed meaning brings to mind the anxieties preceding and then attending menstruation, whereas the unexpected image of the "red dress" celebrates the vividness, the privately riveting beauty, of the blood itself. The rest of the poem develops the female conceit. The uterus may have been a reliable "old girl," but the menstrual flow was a willful, brazen spirit:

> now it is done,
> and i feel just like
> the grandmothers who,
> after the hussy has gone,
> sit holding her photograph
> and sighing, *wasn't she*
> *beautiful? wasn't she beautiful?*

In contrast to "poem to my uterus," this poem blends nostalgia and humor rather than fear and sorrow. Here the poet's component parts are imagined as female: The "hussy" and the grandmothers represent her youthful and postmenopausal selves, respectively. Fortified by the vivid memory of menstruation, a process that both enriched and complicated her life, the woman turns away from her body ("now it is done") and addresses an unspecified audience. This is a subtle indication that she is willing to accept her altered body. The mournful tone of "poem to my uterus" has given way to a gently self-mocking, yet more accepting, outlook. Even in the face of a major crisis of identity, it seems, the fertile mind will see the mortal body through.

In "wishes for sons," the poem immediately following "to my last period" in *Quilting*, Clifton is still ruminating on the subject of menstruation, but now her concern is cultural rather than mythic or personal. Her comically spiteful "wishes"—or curses—would inflict both the small and large burdens on the menstrual cycle on men. Although the poem sounds vindictive ("later I wish them hot flashes / and clots like you / wouldn't believe"), it is an accurate record of the annoyances women deal with every month (60). The poem could have dissolved into a joke, but instead Clifton ends it on a scathing note:

> let them think they have accepted
> arrogance in the universe,
> then bring them to gynecologists
> not unlike themselves.

This indictment of men, especially male doctors, is social commentary, but it is also a gloss on women's lives. By transposing female experience onto men, the poem asks us to think about that experience anew. The poem is outlandish, not just because it imagines men menstruating, but because it imagines them in a culture fundamentally hostile to their most basic needs. Therein lies the poem's wit and its final cold blast of rage.

Elsewhere in *Quilting*, we find "water sign woman" and "moonchild," seemingly personal poems (alluding to Clifton's birth sign, Cancer) that nevertheless speak to the experience of many women. In "water sign woman," "the woman who feels everything" is set against an amorphous group that dismisses her yearnings: "they say to the feel things woman / that little she dreams is possible, that there is only so much / joy to go around, only so much / water" (50). But the woman rejects these imposed limits, preferring instead to believe that "water will come again / if you can wait for it." In the context of the poem, the title takes on new meaning: The "water sign woman" is waiting for a sign of water—that is, of renewed possibility in her life. The long-suffering woman in "moonchild" is likewise hopeful about the future. For her, the moon is a "small light" assuring her that she will "rise again and rise again to dance" (68).

The first poem in *The Book of Light* (1993), "climbing," seems to take up where "water sign woman" and "moonchild" leave off. No longer waiting for a sign or promising herself that things will get better, the woman now seems much more actively engaged in her own life. Perhaps alluding to Langston Hughes's "Mother to Son," in which the speaker compares her life to climbing a staircase, the single-stanza poem begins,

> a woman precedes me up the long rope,
> her dangling braids the color of rain.
> maybe i should have had braids.
> maybe i should have kept the body I started,
> slim and possible as a boy's bone.
> maybe i should have wanted less.[10]

We don't know the identity of the woman on the rope; she could be a friend or fellow traveler, an ancestor or an emblem of a life that the poet chose not to lead. Calvin Bedient has called this figure a "mysterious, barely specified *other* Clifton, the elementally ageless one (part child, part cyclically renewable rain) who nonetheless precedes the poet up the rope of her life."[11] More important than the other woman's identity is the narrator's anxious, self-referential response to her. The poet's doubts concentrate on her body and the life she might have led if she hadn't had sex or children.

But thoughts of what might have been only remind her of the life that was and is her own:

> maybe i should have ignored the bowl in me
> burning to be filled.
> maybe i should have wanted less.
> the woman passes the notch in the rope
> marked Sixty. i rise toward it, struggling,
> hand over hungry hand.

A questing soul, the poet knows she cannot dwell in limbo forever. Although she is not rising to dance as she had imagined she would in "moon-child," at least she is rising and climbing. In her climb, furthermore, there is the same burning desire for fulfillment that motivated her earlier decisions in life. The figure ahead of her on the rope is an archetypal role model, a woman growing old but not giving up. If the woman with braids can climb bravely and stubbornly into old age and the unknown, so can the poet; so can all women who share her profound hunger for life.

When her race enters into her poems about womanhood, Clifton's emphasis on survival and self-affirmation grows adamant. This is evident in *Good Times* and each successive volume. As Clifton herself put it in a free-wheeling 1993 interview, in response to a question about the role of black women in the women's movement: "I've always enjoyed being female and not felt myself put upon because of it. If I were put upon, I always believed it was for race. I believe in the women's movement. I know there are things that need to be addressed but I think black women have to address our own agendas, not address an agenda that is decided for us." [12] Some of her poems about black women inevitably define themselves in opposition to white people, especially white men. In *"if I stand in my window,"* a black woman refuses to yield to the expectations of a white male establishment. Published in *Good Times*, the poem begins with the woman literally and figuratively taking a stand:

> if i stand in my window
> naked in my own house
> and press my breasts
> against my windowpane
> like black birds pushing against glass
> because i am somebody
> in a New Thing (*GW*, 25)

In its subject matter and conditional syntax, this poem resembles William Carlos Williams's "Danse Russe" (1916), in which a man delights in his nude body while his family sleeps. But unlike Williams's insouciant persona, who asks rhetorically, "Who shall say I am not / the happy genius of my household?," [13] Clifton's seems braced for a real battle. The unnerving image of the "black birds," combined with the woman's nudity, ironically plays off the stereotype of the black woman as a sexual primitive who simultaneously threatens and titillates. In this poem, the woman is chafing against social and cultural confines even as she holds her ground.

The poem is characteristic of the Black Arts Movement of the 1960s and early seventies, when authors such as Amiri Baraka, Sonia Sanchez, and Clifton challenged mainstream white society through their writings. In the second stanza, the poet imagines "the man" who would object to her, "saying I have offended him / I have offended his / Gods." Any talk of "Gods"—which Clifton pointedly capitalizes and pluralizes—will not frighten off the "New Thing" whose singular (also capitalized) presence hovers over the poem. It is the white man who is in for a shock:

> let him watch my black body
> push against my own glass
> let him discover self
> let him run naked through the streets
> crying
> praying in tongues

The poem rails against the disenfranchisement of black women and effectively turns the tables on the white men whose self-image seems to depend on oppression and segregation. Here the black woman is an emblem of self-determinacy and self-possession, and, in imagining her enemy, the white man, undergoing an identity crisis of biblical proportions, she transforms herself into an apocalyptic vision. During the socially turbulent 1960s, a vision of a distinctly black, female self really was a whole New Thing, not just in a colloquial sense but also in a political one. The black woman angrily demanding her rights represented a tangible new social force that had to be accepted because its members would no longer be locked out, beaten down, or ignored.

Just as it infuses angry tension into *"if I stand in my window,"* race complicates many of Clifton's other poems about womanhood. This is true of "the lost baby poem," from *Good News about the Earth* (1972), which addresses a baby lost through abortion. Here, the narrator implies that even if she'd had the baby, she would have given the child up for adoption: "we would have made the thin / walk over genesee hill into the canada wind / to watch you slip like ice into strangers' hands" (*GW*, 60). If there is regret in this poem, it is regret tinged by a weary recognition that the child, had it survived, would have had a difficult life: "you would have been born into winter / in the year of the disconnected gas / and no car," the mother says, adding that "you would have fallen naked as snow into winter." In the conclusion, she vows that

> if i am ever less than a mountain
> for your definite brothers and sisters
> let the rivers pour over my head
> let the sea take me for a spiller
> of seas   let black men call me stranger
> always   for your never named sake

Memorialized by the gap, the visible silence, in the last two lines, the "never named" child contributes to the narrator's identity just as her fully realized children have. As an intractable mountain of maternal strength, moreover, the mother feels a special obligation to black men, the poem's only indication of her own race. To fail her children in any way, the poem implies, would be to fail as a black woman, a partner in the shaping of the race. In her fervent desire to fulfill her maternal and racial duties, she threatens herself with Old Testament–style punishments worthy of a terrible sinner. For those who fail in their moral and social duties to others, Clifton insists, apocalypse is just around the corner.

When Clifton considers the black female body, she is considerably more upbeat than she is in "the lost baby poem." For her, a vibrant body represents emotional as well as physical strength. We see this in the exuberant "homage to my hair" and "homage to my hips," both published in *Two-Headed Woman*. Although "homage to my hips" does not refer to race directly, the hips in question evidently belong to a black woman: "these hips have never been enslaved, / they go where they want to go / they do what they want to do" (*GW*, 168). The poem recognizes not only the black woman's joie de vivre but also her sexual allure: "these hips are magic hips. / I have known them / to put a spell on a man and / spin him like a top!" In "homage to my hair," she once again bestows gender on a part of the woman's identity: "when I feel her jump up and dance / i hear the music! my God / i'm talking about my nappy hair!" (*GW*, 167). As the rest of the poem reveals, the black woman's hair is feisty, sexy, and inspirational—presumably like the black woman herself. As Joyce Johnson points out, the poem's verbs "capture the character and vitality of nappy hair; together with the word 'music,' they present images we readily associate with celebration, and thus, operate on two levels, as description and exultation." [14] The ending underscores the black woman's identification with her hair: "she can touch your mind / with her electric fingers and / the grayer she do get, good God, / the blacker she do be!" As in "there is a girl inside," this poem applauds the aging woman, but here the focus is on black women as proud representatives of both their race and gender. Using a colloquial, exclamatory style that still manages to be reminiscent of the biblical psalms, Clifton infuses wit into a poem of fervent, even reverent, self-affirmation.

Nowhere is this more clear than in "what the mirror said," which immediately follows the two "homage" poems and precedes "there is a girl inside" in *Two-Headed Woman*. The poem comically alludes to the talking mirror in "Cinderella," a fairy tale notably preoccupied with female beauty and skin color. Clifton's mirror, speaking in the black vernacular, affirms the black woman's pride in her body: "listen, / you a wonder. / you a city / of a woman" (*GW*, 169). The poem goes on to detail the woman's complexity ("somebody need a map / to understand you") and to reassure her of her value ("you not a noplace / anonymous / girl"). Like the poems about hips and hair, this one marvels over the black woman's sexual power:

> mister with his hands on you
> he got his hands on
> some
> damn
> body!

The word *damn* adds zesty emphasis and turns a worthy "somebody" into a sexy body. The repeated references to black men in these lively poems suggest that she is asking them to join in all the fun.

The black woman's resilience is the theme of *"won't you celebrate with me,"* which appears in *The Book of Light*, thirteen years after the poems of praise in *Two-Headed Woman*. But this one finds Clifton in a much more serious state of mind. Her speaker asserts that she "had no model" for her life (25): "born in babylon / both nonwhite and woman / what did I see

to be except myself?" The woman seems to represent many generations;
convinced that her survival is a profound achievement, the narrator views
herself as not so much a self-made woman as a woman-made self:

> i made it up
> here on this bridge between
> starshine and clay,
> my one hand holding tight
> my other hand; come celebrate
> with me that everyday
> something has tried to kill me
> and has failed.

Even as it recognizes the value of the hard-fought life, the poem strikes a
plaintive note. The woman who must hold her own hand is surely lonely,
in need of companionship. In Clifton's poems, total self-reliance never
sounds like much fun. Just as the narrator of "climbing" clings to the image
of the woman with braids preceding her up the rope, the would-be hostess
in "won't you celebrate with me" clings to the possibility of a party—a glad
gathering of like-minded souls.

While the poems discussed thus far may reflect Clifton's own experi-
ences, they do not contain enough details to be considered truly auto-
biographical. Beginning with An Ordinary Woman, however, Clifton has
periodically published poems that contain obvious autobiographical refer-
ences. These poems are about womanhood and more particularly about
black womanhood, but they are also about being a black woman, born in
1936, known variously as Lucy, Lucille, Thelma Lucille, and Lucille Clifton.
The name "Lucille" derives from the same root as "light," a derivation
Clifton refers to frequently—as in "the light that came to lucille clifton"
(both a poem and a section title in Two-Headed Woman) and the biblical-
sounding The Book of Light, which contains a preface titled "LIGHT."
Clifton makes frequent use of her own name and includes unmistakable
autobiographical references in numerous other poems. Sometimes she even
invokes her appearance: her large size, her one good eye, and her two extra
fingers, a deformity once considered proof that a woman was a witch.
Though her extra fingers were removed when she was an infant, Clifton has
not let go of their metaphorical significance. In fact, the defining character-
istics of her weight and her eye, and the legacy of seemingly supernatural fin-

gers, have been decidedly welcome gifts to her self-exploratory verse.

We see this perspective in the humorous *"lucy one-eye,"* where Clifton describes herself as a "big round roller" who sees "the world sideways" (*GW*, 145). The poem ends with her assuring us, and herself, that "she'll keep on trying / with her crooked look / and her wrinkled ways, / the darling girl." No matter how old she is, Clifton always remembers the "girl inside," the essence of an ebullient, distinctly female self. Similarly, in *"I was born with twelve fingers,"* she draws strength from the feature linking her with her mother and daughter: "each of us / born wearing strange black gloves / extra baby fingers hanging over the sides of our cribs and / dipping into the milk" (*GW*, 166). Alluding to the supernatural power once attributed to twelve-fingered women, she mourns the loss of "our wonders" but declares that the magic remains intact:

> and we connect
> my dead mother   my live daughter   and me
> through our terrible shadowy hands.

The fingers, or at least the memory of them, link Clifton with other women in her family and suggest that this important bond is in itself magical.

Any time the familial bond feels tenuous, Clifton grows uneasy, as in "speaking of loss." In this poem, she says, "I began with everything; / parents, two extra fingers / a brother to ruin" (*GW*, 174). But now, bereft of those family members and "wearing a name I never heard / until I was a woman," she feels uncertain of her identity: "my extra fingers are cut away. / I am left with plain hands and / nothing to give you but poems." As in "poem to my uterus," this poem defines the spirit in terms of the body. The poems Clifton writes are a consolation of vast importance, because they record her identity and are themselves a "body" of work, enduring evidence of who she was and is.

Collected in *An Ordinary Woman* (1974), which was published the year Clifton turned thirty-eight, *"the thirty eighth year"* is an autobiographical poem exploring the poet's identity as she heads into middle age. One of her strongest, most moving works, this sixty-line meditation is twice the length of most of her other poems. Partly due to this expansiveness, *"the thirty eighth year"* illustrates the overlap among the three categories discussed here; it is a definitive poem of womanhood, black female identity, and Clifton's own experience:

the thirty eighth year
of my life,
plain as bread
round as a cake
an ordinary woman.

an ordinary woman.

i had expected to be
smaller than this,
more beautiful,
wiser in afrikan ways,
more confident,
i had expected
more than this. (GW, 158–59)

In the opening stanza, Clifton asserts her gender but not her race. The fragments seem like private, even random thoughts, but the imagery deftly sketches a woman in her kitchen, the "ordinary" woman's home base. The opening imagery is homely but pleasant, since bread is life-sustaining and cakes are sweet. In the second stanza, the surprise, and humor, of the admission, "i had expected to be / smaller than this," comes from the improbable syntax, but the rest of the carefully constructed litany implies that this black woman *is* beautiful and does have some confidence, some knowledge of Africa.

The rest of *"the thirty eighth year"* continues to weigh hope against disappointment, strength against vulnerability. Clifton admits to loneliness, despite being "surrounded by life, / a perfect picture of / blackness blessed." Remembering her "very wise / and beautiful / and sad" mother, who died young, she feels the winds of mortality swirling around her as she approaches forty. Midway through the poem, Clifton directly addresses her deceased mother, an indelible presence in her poetry, and then invokes the family's new generation of women: "I have taken the bones you hardened / and built daughters / and they blossom and promise fruit / like afrikan trees." Having opted for motherhood, Clifton has taken the usual path in life. But that path is filled with the wonderment of blossoming daughters, the fruits of a new generation and a reminder of the past ones.

The penultimate stanza is a kind of prayer in which Clifton yearns for a distinct, comfortable identity of her own as she approaches "the final turn" of her life:

> let me come to it whole
> and holy
> not afraid
> not lonely
> out of my mother's life
> into my own.
> into my own.

Her daughters are not the only ones blossoming: Clifton herself is still growing, preparing for the future, whatever it may hold. The poem finally emerges as a meditation on inner strength rather than on shortcomings. And by the time we read the words "an ordinary woman" for the fourth time in the poem's conclusion, even this seemingly bland expression has taken on a luminous resolve. "The strong sense of general disappointment coupled with the sinking suspicion that one's life has missed the mark strikes responsive chords in many readers," Wallace R. Peppers has commented. "And worse still, from the speaker's point of view, is the growing realization that this enormously unsatisfying condition is probably permanent." [15] And yet the persistent repetition of "an ordinary woman" calls to mind its opposite as well as its literal meaning. The "ordinary" woman is on a profound journey, after all. Aware of her compounded identity as daughter and mother, as a black woman, and as an autonomous, ambitious self, the "ordinary" woman can truly come into her own, as the last lines suggest. The poem is not so much one of hopes dashed or dreams deferred as it is one of hopes tempered and dreams revised.

For Clifton, womanhood is a powerful, even awe-inspiring, foundation for the individual self. Her images of the female body are infused with tenderness and affection; her images of the female spirit radiate strength and humor. Although her poems admit to feelings of sorrow, vulnerability, and self-doubt, these emotions do not hold sway. As one critic notes, "Clifton speaks from the freedom of an individual who acknowledges her full female self, including the losses suffered by heart and body." [16] Even "poem to my uterus" is a loving poem, reminding us that true self-love involves an enormous generosity of spirit: The woman who accepts the terms of her own body sets an admirable example for others to follow.

Clifton's own life provides the impetus for most of her poems, but, like Whitman, whom she quotes in the epigraphs to her family memoir, *Generations: A Memoir* (1976), she creates a wide-ranging, multitudinous self. As in "Song of Myself," a composite identity gradually emerges from Clifton's poetry, one that both absorbs and reflects the surrounding world. The more of Clifton one reads, the more distinct yet universal that self becomes.[17] Her poems invite widespread identification across race and gender lines, though they are determinedly about women, especially black women, often Clifton herself. No matter what their mood, her poems all manage to affirm the essential dignity of womanhood. When considering this subject without reference to race, her poems often concern the strengths and vulnerabilities of the female body. In "there is a girl inside" she finds youthful enthusiasm and sexual energy within an old, seemingly depleted woman. In her poems about menstruation, she does not flinch from the awkward realities of the process, nor does she ignore the beauty of it. In "homage to my hair," "homage to my hips," and "what the mirror said," she honors the black woman's body, while in the somber "climbing," "speaking of loss," and "*won't you celebrate with me*" she chronicles the challenges of survival. In "an ordinary woman" the woman who emerges from the poem is at once usual and unique. Many of Clifton's poems themselves play out a similar paradox: They are small yet vast, clear but complex. Reading them closely, we find that they, too, "blossom and promise fruit like Afrikan trees."

Notes

1. Clifton, quoted in Baraka and Baraka, 403.
2. Vendler, xi.
3. Clifton, "A Simple Language," 137–38.
4. Clifton, *Good Woman*, 170. Clifton's first four volumes—*Good Times, Good News about the Earth, An Ordinary Woman,* and *Two-Headed Woman*—are collected in *Good Woman*. Hereafter, all page citations from the first four volumes will refer to *Good Woman,* abbreviated in text as *GW.*

Note also that italicized titles indicate poems that are, in fact, untitled; the italicized words are the poem's first line.

5. Clifton, *Next,* 33; hereafter cited in text.
6. Wordsworth, 279.
7. Clifton, *Quilting,* 31; hereafter cited in text.
8. Stevens, 197.
9. I am indebted to Professor Wilfred Samuels of the University of Utah for this insight.

10. Clifton, *The Book of Light*, 11.

11. Bedient, 348.

12. Clifton, "Lucille Clifton," 48.

13. Williams, 86.

14. Johnson, 74.

15. Peppers, 58.

16. Ullman, 180.

17. Anaporte-Easton, 120.

Works Cited

Anaporte-Easton, Jean. "'She Has Made Herself Again': The Maternal Impulse as Poetry." *13th Moon* 9 (1991): 116–35.

Baraka, Amiri, and Amina Baraka. *Confirmation: An Anthology of African American Women.* New York: Quill, 1983.

Bedient, Calvin. "Short Reviews," *Poetry* 163.6 (March 1994): 336–53.

Clifton, Lucille. *The Book of Light.* Port Townsend: Copper Canyon Press, 1993.

————. *Good Woman: Poems and a Memoir 1969–1980.* Brockport, N.Y.: BOA Editions, 1987.

————. "Lucille Clifton." Interview with Shirley M. Jordan. *Broken Silences: Interviews with Black and White Women Writers.* New Brunswick, N.J.: Rutgers University Press, 1993. 38–49.

————. *Next.* Brockport, N.Y.: BOA Editions, 1987.

————. *Quilting: Poems 1987–1990.* Brockport, N.Y.: BOA Editions, 1991.

————. "A Simple Language." *Black Women Writers (1950–1980): A Critical Evaluation.* Ed. Mari Evans. Garden City, N.Y.: Anchor, 1984. 137–38.

————. *The Terrible Stories.* Brockport, N.Y.: BOA Editions, 1996.

Johnson, Joyce. "The Theme of Celebration in Lucille Clifton's Poetry." *Pacific Coast Philology* 18 (Nov. 1983): 70–76.

Ostriker, Alicia. "Kin and Kin: The Poetry of Lucille Clifton." *The American Poetry Review* 22 (Nov.–Dec. 1993): 41–48.

Peppers, Wallace R. "Lucille Clifton." *Afro-American Poets since 1955. Dictionary of Literary Biography.* Vol. 41. Ed. Trudier Harris and Thadious M. Davis. Detroit: Gale, 1985.

Stevens, Wallace. "Study of Two Pears." *The Collected Poems of Wallace Stevens.* New York: Vintage, 1982, 196–97.

Ullman, Leslie. Book reviews. *The Kenyon Review,* n.s. 14.3 (1992): 174–88.

Vendler, Helen. *The Given and the Made.* Cambridge: Harvard University Press, 1995.

Williams, William Carlos. "Danse Russe." *The Collected Poems of William Carlos Williams.* Vol. I, 1909–1939, 86. Ed. Walton Litz and Christopher MacGowan. New York: New Directions, 1986.

Wordsworth, William. "My Heart Leaps Up When I Behold." *English Romantic Writers.* New York: Harcourt, 1967. 279.

"Flashbacks through the Heart": Yusef Komunyakaa and the Poetry of Self-Assertion

ANGELA M. SALAS

YUSEF KOMUNYAKAA'S LIFE AND CAREER FIT ALMOST perfectly into the American ideal of the self-made man, arising from the ashes of harsh childhood and youth to attain success and power by dint of hard work, good luck, and fierce intelligence. The prototypical American ideal is most often a lad who finds himself a mentor and rises through the ranks of the business world, attaining money and power, yet remembers his humble beginnings. He is a practical man, doing practical things, and he never challenges the social or economic status quo; he fits in, gets to work, and by his good fortune reassures others that anyone can succeed—with Horatio Alger luck and pluck.

Komunyakaa both embodies and redefines this American dream. From his birth in Bogalusa, Louisiana, where he admits he never really learned to play his part in the tragicomedy that was the Jim Crow South, through youthful service as a military correspondent during the Vietnam War, Yusef Komunyakaa survived and thrived. Now having reached middle age, Komunyakaa is respected, well known, and increasingly influential. Like Alger's heroes, he is hard-working, courteous, generous, intelligent, and observant. Unlike Alger's exemplars of the American dream, Komunyakaa is an African American man, a poet who argues that poetry is and must be political.[1] In his career, Komunyakaa has successfully questioned both the world's ills and the conventions of poetry as he has found them. He critiques and pushes limits, adding to the treasurehouse of American poetry while leaving a rich legacy for other, younger, poets. Indeed, while it is unlikely that Komunyakaa ever conceived of his life and career in terms of the American myth of the self-made man, one can imagine him taking delight in both embodying and rewriting this pale ideal, leaving it enriched for generations to come.

Any reader who engages with Yusef Komunyakaa's lush and frequently disturbing work realizes that he is an ambitious poet who, as Alvin Aubert has written, "approaches the intensity of no less a figure than prototypical canon quester Ralph Ellison in his bid for mainstream American literary status."[2] Michel Fabre, introducing Komunyakaa at a French conference on southern literature in 1994, asserted that the poet "calls our souls to bright daylight . . . make[s] them stumble forth from their hiding place into the open . . . become[s] the midwife of our more profound humanity."[3] In a review of the 1998 volume *Thieves of Paradise*, Donna Seaman suggests that Komunyakaa "gets inside language, achieving a complexity and a naturalness of form, and reflecting a knowingness born of scholarship and imagination, experience and empathy."[4] For his part, Garrett Hongo has written that Yusef Komunyakaa "is perhaps the most original poet of his generation, and one of the most brave both in stylistic innovation and commitment to handling difficult subjects and dark emotions."[5] Yusef Komunyakaa, a shy young man mentored through the Vietnam War by what he found in poetry anthologies, has come into his own. He is now *in* the anthologies.

An omnivorous reader of poetry, drama, and prose, Komunyakaa is influenced by Walt Whitman, by Margaret Walker, by the literature of the Harlem Renaissance, by French and Russian literatures, by Shakespeare, by Borges, by Marquez and—quite unmistakably—the Bible. A former double major in English and sociology, Komunyakaa understands the ways the human soul can be either nourished or starved. His own work is powerfully surrealistic, steeped in the work of the Language poets, masterful at intertextual riffs and resonant with his passion for music.

These are only some of the reasons Yusef Komunyakaa won the Pulitzer Prize in 1994 for *Neon Vernacular: New and Selected Poems,* after having become widely recognized for *Dien Cai Dau,* his collection of Vietnam War poetry. His first book, *Dedications and Other Darkhorses,* was published in 1977; yet it was *Dien Cai Dau,* an uncompromising volume addressing the collective, as well as individual, horror and guilt of the African American soldier in Vietnam, that brought Komunyakaa wide acclaim and the attention of a large reading audience. *Neon Vernacular* and the Pulitzer Prize have earned Komunyakaa a permanent position at Princeton University, as well as the peripatetic life of that rarity in belle lettres: the poet whose presence lends cachet to any serious literary gathering.

I suggest that Komunyakaa actually hit his literary stride in *I Apologize for the Eyes in My Head* (1986), which announced his presence as a poet to be reckoned with and which, while critically successful at the time of its release, has been overlooked after *Dien Cai Dau*. In *I Apologize* and every volume thereafter, readers get an articulation of Komunyakaa's presence as a poet and as a man. From "Unnatural State of the Unicorn," the opening poem of *I Apologize*, through "Anodyne," the closing piece in *Thieves of Paradise*, readers follow Komunyakaa's continuing preoccupation with his place, as an African American man who wears the scars of racism and war, in the world of letters. To a world that would have denied the young black child he was any place in the world, Komunyakaa firmly replies with a reminder that he still lives—that poverty, violence, racism, booby traps, snipers, guilt, and pain have neither silenced nor destroyed him. Indeed, as Toi Derricotte asserts, "for Komunyakaa, poetry is the expression of an embattled ego determined by whatever means necessary to survive."[6]

While Komunyakaa's work has evolved in the twelve years since *I Apologize* was published, his voice is much the same as it was in "Unnatural State of the Unicorn":

> Introduce me first as a man.
> Don't mention superficial laurels
> the dead heap up on the living.
> I am a man. Cut me & I bleed.
> Before embossed limited editions,
> before fat artichoke hearts marinated
> in rich sauce & served with imported wines,
> before antics & Agnus Dei,
> before the stars in your eyes
> mean birth sign or Impression,
> I am a man. I've scuffled
> in mudholes, broken teeth in a grinning skull
> like the moon behind bars. I've done it all
> to be known as myself. No titles.
> I have principles. I won't speak
> on the natural state of the unicorn
> in literature or self-analysis.
> I have no birthright to prove,
> no insignia, no secret
> password, no fleur-de-lis.
> My initials aren't on a branding iron.

I'm standing here in unpolished
shoes & faded jeans, sweating
my manly sweat. Inside my skin,
loving you, I am this space
my body believes in.[7]

From the opening, where the speaker demands to be introduced as a man, rather than as a list of static accomplishments, to the final lines, in which he claims the space his "body believes in," the poem is physical. The speaker asserts ownership of the space he inhabits, insisting that his words, read or spoken, will not be about "the natural state of the unicorn / in literature or self-analysis," but will instead be about those things *he* deems important, such as fighting for survival in mudholes and the nauseating feeling of breaking teeth "in a grinning skull / like the moon behind bars"—subjects that might be deemed unpoetic and ungenteel by the sort of prattling dilettante only impressed by "embossed limited editions," ethereal discussions, and catered delicacies. The space Komunyakaa claims is not simply corporeal; it is emotional and poetic as well. He will write about things readers might prefer not to address: life and murder—fear and sweat.

Perhaps as interesting as the tone of the poem and the way Komunyakaa weaves his way through the demands of high and low seriousness ("antics & Agnus Dei") is the poem's structure. The poem begins and ends with assertions of what the speaker of the poem *is*; however, these assertions bracket a long list of negations—a list of things the speaker either *is* not or *will not* do. He will not speak on anything as specious as the natural state of the unicorn in literature; he will not fight for or claim titles; nor will he assert a personal or a professional pedigree. Instead, he will be a man, claiming the space he inhabits and the past that, paradoxically, both imprisons him and makes him the man he is proud to be.

It is profitable to read "Unnatural State of the Unicorn" as the manifesto that signals the beginning of Yusef Komunyakaa's career as one of the most influential poets of this generation. Having established his terms of engagement in the poem, Komunyakaa continues through *I Apologize for the Eyes in My Head,* giving readers various gritty insights into life as an African American man—and Vietnam War veteran—in the United States. Indeed, the speaker of "Touch-up Man" leans "over the enlarger, / in the light table's chromatic glare / where [he's] king, doctoring photographs, / airbrushing away the corpses"—an apt comment upon the capacity of technology to disguise harsh reality—and of the responsibility of the poet to reclaim that truth.

"How I See Things," another manifesto-cum-poem in *I Apologize for the Eyes in My Head,* consists of seven stanzas of five lines each. The poem is constructed with Komunyakaa's characteristic enjambment of lines, as the poet remembers and evokes the eventful 1960s, with its freedom marchers, nightriders, lynchings, conflict in Vietnam and daily, dull realities. This interwining of personal and collective history, of guilt implicating the very soil of Louisiana, is classic Komunyakaa: personal and standoffish; visual and aural; ironic and pained:

> I hear you were
> sprawled on the cover of *Newsweek*
> with freedom marchers, those years
> when blood tinted the photographs,
> when fire leaped into the trees.
>
> Negatives of nightriders
> develop in the brain.
> The Strawberry Festival Queen
> waves her silk handkerchief,
> executing a fancy high kick
>
> flashback through the heart.
> Pickups with plastic Jesuses
> on dashboards head for hoedowns.
> Men run twelve miles into wet cypress
> swinging bellropes. Ignis fatuus can't be blamed
>
> for the charred Johnson grass.
> Have we earned the right
> to forget, forgive
> ropes for holding
> to moonstruck branches?
>
> Every last stolen whisper
> the hoot owl echoes
> turns leaves scarlet.
> Hush shakes the monkeypod
> till pink petal-tongues fall.

You're home in New York.
I'm back here in Bogalusa
with one foot in pinewoods.
The mockingbird's blue note
sounds to me like *please,*

please. A beaten song
threaded through the skull
by cross hairs.
Black hands still turn blood red
working the strawberry fields.[8]

The poem, itself a series of "flashbacks through the heart," seems at first to be addressed to some hero of the civil rights movement—perhaps to writer Galway Kinnell. Kinnell was a field director for CORE near where Komunyakaa grew up; his bloodied face appeared on the cover of a national news magazine, calling attention to the violence directed at anyone working to end Jim Crow.[9] Komunyakaa soon moves into a meditation of a time "when blood tinted the photographs, / when fire leaped into the trees," as he muscles incongruous images together to show the perverse reality of those years, when "negatives of nightriders / develop[ed] in the brain" and were seared into memory.

With this image Komunyakaa draws attention to the associations of the images of white and black. His readers live in a culture in which white is associated with purity, and black with evil or madness, as in Conrad's *Heart of Darkness;* yet these nightriders dressed themselves in white, camouflaging their identities and hoping to disguise the "blackness" of their hearts. In a photographic negative, of course, white hooded men would appear black, while their black victims would be transformed into white images. Komunyakaa thus employs and comments ironically upon the tropes of white and black and gives a visual representation of the reversal of those associations, since the "white" men are devils, while the black targets of their hostility are sacrifices to madness.

Meanwhile, an image no photographer could capture is that of a "beaten song / threaded through the skull / by cross hairs." The bird's song, usually so hopeful, is transformed by its association with the cross hairs of a weapon's scope—an image certainly the legacy of the Vietnam War. And that final image, "Black hands still turn blood red / working the strawberry fields" reminds readers that, while some things, such as field labor, did not change during the Vietnam War and the civil rights era, strawberry juice on the hands is no longer a simple occupational hazard—it is a reminder of Vietnam and hands that have literally been bloodied by war.

Twelve years and four volumes after the publication of *I Apologize for the Eyes in My Head*, Yusef Komunyakaa still meditates upon complexities, rendering them back in word portraits that, like *Newsweek* covers, arrest the reader. In "The Wall," his second poem about the Vietnam Veterans Memorial in Washington, D.C. ("Facing It," the past poem in *Dien Cai Dau* is the first), Komunyakaa characteristically comments upon the multiple legacies of violence and war. "The Wall" is prefaced by these lines from William Shakespeare's Sonnet 55: "But you shall shine more bright in these contents / Than unswept stone, besmeared with sluttish time." The diction of the poem is of a lower order than Shakespeare's, but is just as serious:

> Lovenotes, a bra, lipstick
> kisses on a postcard, locks
> of hair, a cerulean bouquet,
> baseball gloves broken in
> with sweat & red dirt,
> a fifth of Beefeaters,
> everything's carted away.
> Before it's tagged & crated,
> a finger crawls like a fat slug
> down the list, keeping record
> for the unborn. All the gunshots
> across America coalesce here
> where a mother sends letters
> to her son. As time flowers
> & denudes in its whorish work,
> raindrops tap a drumroll
> & names fade till the sun
> draws them again out of granite nighttime.[10]

From the epigraph, lending Shakespeare's gravity to the Vietnam Veterans Memorial and to the war itself, to the lines "a finger crawls like a fat slug / down the list," which acknowledge John Balaban's masterful poem "After Our War," Komunyakaa's "The Wall" is highly compressed, aural and visual, allusive and elusive, horrible and ordinary. One might say that this poem is vintage Komunyakaa, aligning incongruous images (the sun drawing names "out of granite nighttime"), juxtaposing the peculiar ("cerulean" bouquets) with the clichéd ("baseball gloves broken in / with sweat & red dirt").

One would be wrong, however, in making such an assumption. In fact, "The Wall," like most of *Thieves of Paradise*, is more fraught with significance than Komunyakaa's earlier work. While much of Komunyakaa's work before *Thieves of Paradise* has been an articulation of the perspective of a man who comes to his work from his racial experiences, from his war experiences, from his former status as correspondent, not participant, in grim events, the poems of *Thieves of Paradise* are more universal in scope and intent. Thus, while the renowned poem "Facing It" renders a particular set of moments at the Vietnam Veterans Memorial, "The Wall" comments upon the memorial as site of cultural commentary—the place where "All the gunshots / across America coalesce," and where the groundskeepers who inventory and store each day's offerings at the Wall are "keeping record / for the unborn." This is not Komunyakaa's America—it is *America*—and Komunyakaa is accepting the challenge of universality and insisting that he be read by that standard. The question now is whether all his readers will have the heart to follow him as he ventures away from the particular experience of an African American Vietnam War veteran (an experience he's rendered to stunning effect) and begins to write about many of the troubling legacies America will leave its unborn. And how will these readers follow him as he reminds us that the Vietnam War, while always with us, is now more history than current events? The Wall is, itself, a site of history, where the once-spontaneous gesture of gift-leaving has become the highly ritualized subject of coffee-table books and museum exhibits that display the pain of the living, rather than the legacy of the dead. Additionally, Komunyakaa places the dead of the Vietnam War in the long line of history's fallen warriors. After all, the sonnet to which "The Wall" alludes concludes with this couplet: "So, till the judgement that yourself arise, / You live in this, and dwell in lovers' eyes." Like Shakespeare, Komunyakaa immortalizes the lost warrior through poetry, while commenting ironically upon the transience of marble and of "gilded monuments." "The Wall" is Sonnet 55 for the twenty-first century, and Komunyakaa is suggesting that *he* might be our new Bard.

There can be no doubt that Yusef Komunyakaa, with volumes of work and much success behind him, is spreading his wings and demanding to be read as an American poet. This demand may be discomfiting for some readers, since it has been possible thus far to maintain slight distance from the immediacy of Komunyakaa's vision, mediated, as it has been, by history. Good readers have been stunned into silence by Komunyakaa's subject matter and methods of engagement, but they have also been able to reassure themselves that the issues Komunyakaa raises are blessedly past. After all, while lynchings and napalm are horrible, the Vietnam War is over, and the upheaval for civil rights was largely successful. And if, as Komunyakaa has always suggested, the effects of past violence and horror linger and leave their marks in the present, those horrors have always lingered in limboed *individuals,* not in the country at large.

It is somehow easier to sympathize with an abstract victim, someone "out there," who suffers at the Vietnam Veterans Memorial, than it is to accept that we *all* suffer, that the Vietnam Veterans Memorial is a national wailing wall, the manifestation of all of our nation's unresolved grief and humiliation. Yet in "The Wall," and in most of *Thieves of Paradise,* Komunyakaa makes readers face the continuing implications of slavery, of racism, of the Vietnam War, of Manifest Destiny and of "the dark history of Western culture."[11] These implications are not outside us—they are inside, and they *are* us. We can no more escape our history than we can our DNA. From the child who reads his father's resentment of Vietnamese tourists in "Frontispiece" to the resurrection of Charlie Parker, in "Testimony," Komunyakaa forces readers to come to terms with our personal and collective ghosts. And, playing "point and counterpoint" with our literary heritage, Komunyakaa both revivifies that heritage and asserts his intention to be counted among the greats.

Indeed, many of the selections in *Thieves of Paradise* do not resemble poetry as much as they do paragraphs, essays, and stories. It is as though, in "Nude Interrogation," "Phantasmagoria," "A Reed Boat" and other such pieces, Komunyakaa is suggesting that the very *idea* of poetry be reconsidered. T. S. Eliot, in pondering the course of Western civilization, offered to show us fear in a handful of dust; Komunyakaa offers electric, almost postapocalyptic, moments of clarity in various moments, packaged in sundry ways. And yet he returns, circles back, to his primary concerns: endurance, celebration, and posterity.

The closing poem of *Thieves of Paradise,* "Anodyne" might be an inheritor of Whitman's tradition of poetic and physical self-assertion, but, like "Unnatural State of the Unicorn," it veers into unexpected places:

> I love how it swells
> into a temple where it is

held prisoner, where the god
of blame resides. I love
slopes & peaks, the secret
paths that make me selfish.
I love my crooked feet
shaped by vanity & work
shoes made to outlast
belief. The hardness
coupling milk it can't
fashion. I love the lips,
salt & honeycomb on the tongue.
The hair holding off rain
& snow. The white moons
on my fingernails. I love
how everything begs
blood into song & prayer
inside an egg. A ghost
hums through my bones
like Pan's midnight flute
shaping internal laws
beside a troubled river.
I love this body
made to weather the storm
in the brain, raised
out of the deep smell
of fish & water hyacinth,
out of rapture & the first
regret. I love my big hands.
I love it clear down to the soft
quick motor of each breath,
the liver's ten kinds of desire
& the kidney's lust for sugar.
This skin, this sac of dung
& joy, this spleen floating
like a compass needle inside
nighttime, always divining
West Africa's dusty horizon.
I love the birthmark
posed like a fighting cock

on my right shoulder blade.
I love this body, this
solo & ragtime jubilee
behind the left nipple,
because I know I was born
to wear out at least
one hundred angels.

It is fitting that the last selection in this "break-out" collection meets Whitman's song of celebration on its own terms and surpasses them. Both corporeal and ethereal, it is a dizzying piece of writing. With eight assertions of self-love, it rises into abstraction ("rapture & the first / regret") and swoops into startling corporeality ("This skin, this sac of dung / & joy"), and reminds readers of the assertions Komunyakaa made in "Unnatural State of the Unicorn." The poet is still a man. He no longer simply announces his presence in the world of poetry; he celebrates his own endurance and his strength and poet and man. After all, one must listen to a man "born / to wear out at least / one hundred angels," particularly when he speaks so persuasively.

In *I Apologize for the Eyes in My Head* Yusef Komunyakaa refused to apologize for anything. He offered complicated and allusive poems, self-consciously asserting the validity of his vision. In *Dien Cai Dau, Magic City,* and *Neon Vernacular,* Komunyakaa established himself as a poet of enormous range and depth, writing about blues, jazz, childhood, racism, war, and even the legacy of the Vietnam War for the Vietnamese. In *Thieves of Paradise,* bolstered by a decade of critical acclaim and success, Komunyakaa takes the challenge of universality. He quests for the canon, not as an African American writer, as a southern writer, or as a Vietnam War veteran. He is, and he celebrates, all those things, but he writes, too, as a poet with such extraordinary range and imagination that he renders the foreign familiar, capturing the thoughts of women, Vietnamese, the dead and the maimed so well that we think we are hearing from them without the poet's mediation. Komunyakaa places himself beside Shakespeare, out-Whitmans Whitman and out-Komunyakaas Komunyakaa.

Like T. S. Eliot, Yusef Komunyakaa shores up fragments against the ruins; unlike Eliot, he does so with energy and with hope for the future. Komunyakaa may exhaust his reader, but it's a good, cleansing, sort of exhaustion. One is grateful for a poet willing to endure "flashbacks through the heart" for his readers and for the sake of the future.

Notes

1. Gotera, "'Lines of Tempered Steel': An Interview with Yusef Komunyakaa," 215–29.
2. Aubert, 671–77.
3. Fabre, 5–8.
4. Seaman, 970.
5. Garret Hongo, book jacket blurb for *Thieves of Paradise* (Hanover: University Press of New England, 1998).
6. Derricotte, 217–22.
7. Yusef Komunyakaa, *I Apologize for the Eyes in My Head.*
8. Ibid.
9. Gotera, 218.
10. Yusef Komunyakaa, *Thieves of Paradise.*
11. *Publishers Weekly*, 70.

Works Cited

Aubert, Alvin. Review of *Neon Vernacular*. *African American Review* 28 (1994): 671–72.
Derricotte, Toi. "The Tension between Memory and Forgetting in the Poetry of Yusef Komunyakaa." *Kenyon Review* 13 (1993): 217–22.
Fabre, Michel. "On Yusef Komunyakaa." *Southern Quarterly* 34 (winter 1996): 5–8.
Gotera, Vince. "'Lines of Tempered Steel': An Interview with Yusef Komunyakaa." *Callaloo* 13 (1990): 215–29.
———. *Radical Visions: Poetry by Vietnam War Veterans*. Athens: University of Georgia Press, 1994.
Komunyakaa, Yusef. *Dien Cai Dau*. Hanover: University Press of New England, 1988.
———. *I Apologize for the Eyes in My Head*. Hanover: University Press of New England, 1986.
———. *Thieves of Paradise*. Hanover: University Press of New England, 1998.
Publishers Weekly. "Review of *Thieves of Paradise*." February 23, 1998. 70.
Seaman, Donna. Review of *Thieves of Paradise*. *Booklist*. February 15, 1998. 970.

What Is This New Thing?

JABARI ASIM

T THE OUTSET, I'M COMPELLED TO OFFER A DIS-claimer: I am merely a visitor here in the academic arena; I am not a permanent resident. I make my living as a book review editor sure enough, but as a journalist, not as a scholar. Journalistic criticism, I believe, is easily distinguished from that which appears in literary and academic journals. The former must conform to extremely tight limitations regarding length and depth of discourse. Explorations of the literature must be summary, decisive, and tailored to meet the educational level of the greatest possible cross-section of the newspaper's readership. Reviewers must enter the text quickly and exit almost immediately afterward; opportunities to plumb the true depths of a work, its various levels of allusion and meaning, are rare.

Scholars, on the other hand, dive deeper, touch bottom, and sift the contents of the ocean floor, as it were. They get dirt under their nails. They lift the evidence to their nostrils and sniff for authenticity. They, if need be, sleep with the material, digest it, and sweat it through their pores in a quest for deeper understanding, eternal truths. Fellow scholars may want to know if the material in question honors the tradition to which it belongs, whether it speaks to humanity's eons-long confrontation with questions about life, love, justice, death, immortality. My readers simply want to know: Should I buy this book or not?

In the best of circumstances I am able to touch the skin of a work. I rarely make contact with its muscle, its bone, its marrow. So I speak as one who views his role as that of an advocate, a defender of a pursuit challenged—if not besieged—by the electronic onslaught and brief attention spans of the late twentieth century. I also speak as a writer identified by age with a group of literary artists designated as emerging writers. In some cases, this designation is probably accurate; in others it is more than charitable.

How best to characterize this new generation of poets? I hesitate to use terms such as *movement* because I don't see much evidence of the kind of cohesion such terms imply. It's probably safer to say that here are writers coming of age in a time and place where the idea of poetry is reemerging and evolving.

Coffeehouses and open mikes are once again in vogue, and poetry slams and spoken-word performances are taking place nightly in many major cities. Rap, some of which is poetry, is an explosive and magnetic force in the popular consciousness. Of course, some of these developments have happened before. They don't herald a brave new world unless they result in the creation and maintenance of significant institutions and bodies of work. In *Eyeball*, a literary arts journal that I cofounded with Ira Jones, and elsewhere, I have used the phrase, "new thing." Not new movement, new renaissance, or new poetry, because the only thing truly new about it is us, newly born into poetic awareness.

I also have written about some of the places where the new poets are working: The Nuyorican Poet's Cafe in New York; the Dark Room in Boston; Cafe Afrika in Cleveland; The Good Life in L.A.; the Vaughn Cultural Center in St. Louis; the Eugene B. Redmond Writer's Club in East St. Louis; a multitude of college campuses and many other sites. There's no question that something is happening, but just what that something is, is subject for debate. I will say, though, that coverage of this new thing has been profoundly uneven. MTV, network television, and even some mass-market publications aimed at black readers have focused almost exclusively on the East Coast and, to a lesser extent, the West Coast. As if a great cultural vacuum engulfs the rest of the country. Further, much of this coverage has focused on the mike-happy and the photogenic. *Interview, Elle, Harper's Bazaar, The Source*, the *Village Voice*, and *American Visions* all have recently hyped marginally talented performance artists at the expense of young writers who are proving their mastery on the printed page, such as Alison Joseph, Elizabeth Alexander, Rohan B. Preston, Darryl Holmes, and Paul Beatty.

This discrepancy forces the following mission: as we attempt to study and understand this new thing, we must also examine the changing and challenged role of the printed page. So far, books have not held their own against compact discs and music videos, the popularity of which encourages sound-bite poetry and devalues complex literary explorations.

Witness the birth of *In the Tradition: An Anthology of Young Black Writers*, published in 1992 by Harlem River Press and ably edited by Kevin Powell and Ras Baraka. Its presence has caused hardly a ripple outside the generation for which it aspires to speak, and has thus far escaped scrutiny in many of the popular media organs. One can't help but wonder how it would have been received if it had been a CD instead. Or maybe a new jack movie? Picture this: two young brothers from the ravaged streets of New Jersey aspire to be gangsta poets. Along the way they shoot up a housing project, have sex with dozens of half-naked, underage girls, and take over the East Coast cocaine trade. They live to publish their hardcore anthology, only to collapse in a bloody clash of brother against brother, poet versus poet. "You stole my metaphor," one pissed-off poet hisses to the other as he strangles him to death with a cheap gold chain.

For all its significance, *In the Tradition* is heavily weighted toward East Coast writers, perhaps because that's where the editors live and operate. There's also the inevitable comparisons with other seminal anthologies, such as *The New Negro* and the immortal *Black Fire*. The histories surrounding those collections suggest that in those cases the use of terms such as *movement* is not so far-fetched.

But, without pausing to devote much attention to questions of ideology, let's focus for a moment on technique, on the actual applications of language. Here, I think, is where a generation gap looms, and to the detriment of the younger ranks. While *In the Tradition* is filled with earnest expressions of sentiments typically found in African American poetry, many of its poems lack the devices commonly used to convey those same sentiments. It is possible to read through many pages and many poems without encountering a metaphor. Is this a redefining of what poetry is or a failure to understand what it is? Is it harsh to say that prose broken into fragments does not equal poetry? Is it oversimplification to suggest that poetry, to be effective, needs to sing a little?

For example, when Claude McKay felt sad he didn't write, "I am sad." He wrote, "My spirit is a pestilential city, / With misery triumphant everywhere." Similarly, Gaston Neal wrote in his poem "Personal Jihad": "The seed of my day begins / as the tortuous night ends / the common birds gray shrill / interrupts the flushing of a morning pee." When Langston Hughes wanted to say the black man gets no respect he wrote, "They send me to eat in the kitchen / When company comes." When he wanted to say that blackness is timeless, he wrote, "I bathed in the Euphrates when dawns were young." When Baraka writes of enslavement in "Ka 'Ba" he says, "we sprawl in grey chains in a place / full of winters, when what we want is sun." Rage, misery, resistance—they are all there, but at the same time, metaphors and illustrative language are in abundance.

I'm reminded of the time when I boldly, and with a total absence of humility, decided to call myself a poet. I gathered a bunch of my scribblings and went to my campus advisor, the novelist Leon Forrest. I remember one poem was written from the perspective of a man who was about to be lynched. Its climax read something like, "Go ahead, hang me if you dare. I'm black and a spirit and can do whatever I want." Broken up into about two dozen lines.

Professor Forrest looked at the poem a long time, rubbing his chin. He'd look at me a while, then he'd return to the poem, sigh and rub his chin some more. I'd arrived expecting his immediate approval. Well, he was taking too long. As each minute passed, my previously puffed-out chest deflated a little more. Finally, he thumbed through his many books and handed me one containing the poem called "Between the World and Me" by Richard Wright. I shuddered after reading the last lines: "Now I am dry bones and my face a stony skull staring in yellow surprise at the sun."

"Now, son," Professor Forrest said, "do you see?" Not only did I see, but I also felt, smelled, and tasted everything the poem described. The lesson for me was clear: I had quite a bit of reading and absorbing to do before tackling the task of actually writing. And that's the single significant flaw of *In the Tradition:* the least successful of its contributors apparently have little or no knowledge of black poetry's rich history, its glorious past. The shameful flatness of their work betrays them. Typographical tricks perpetrated for no apparent reason, arbitrary punctuation, spelling, and capitalization, and artless repetition mar most of these efforts. Grocery-list recitations of names and whimsical italics don't help the cause much either, resulting in rhythmless prose fragments that tell but don't show. It's impossible to advance or honor the tradition without first acknowledging its power and its precedence. Racism is bad, black is beautiful, and unity is strength. These are all unassailable truths best conveyed via metaphor, simile, allusion, and other poetic devices.

The most accomplished poets in *In the Tradition* are on intimate terms with technique. Thus in Elizabeth Alexander's "The Venus Hottentot," the title character can say, "In this newspaper lithograph / my buttocks are shown swollen / and luminous as a planet." Elsewhere in the same poem, "A drop of water swirls like marble."

In Michelle T. Clinton's "I Wanna Be Black," irony and distance blend with personal history to create a percussive exhortation that seems both rhythmic and natural. But first let's look at a passage from Amiri Baraka's "Black Art":

> Let Black People understand
> that they are the lovers and the sons
> of lovers and warriors and sons
> of warriors Are poems & poets &
> all the loveliness here in the world.

Now see how Clinton echoes Baraka's comprehensive urgency, ampersands and all:

> Nigguhs need to pick themselves up out of the drug scum,
> the numb come, up out the sphere of the white man's
> life plan & history & logic & systematic self hate
> for black & funk & nap & snap & pop & fuck & fun
> & just 'bout most the best thangs folks love to do.[1]

Paul Beatty proves the possibility of stretching the limits of language, of persuading it to match rhythms with the music in one's mind. More than any other emerging poet, Beatty has an arsenal that is fully armed to capture the imaginations of the hip-hop, post-Nintendo, megabyte generation. His poem "Gription" offers the funkadelic fundamentals of a street encounter:

> whuddup
> whaz hat-nen
> you man
>
>   two nigguh
>   hands swing
>
> in mid arc
> fingers hesitate
> wait is he bringin
> that ol school soulshake
> or he gonna skip step 2
> do a quick slide n glide
>   hope he don't trip
>   and go into

all that post grip
flip wilson
royal order of the
water buffalo shit

finger snappin
hand clappin
elbow taps
twists

then i'll improvise
my handshake guise
and just bang fists[2]

Despite the uneven quality of its contents, In the Tradition deserves recognition as a seminal event on the timeline of this still-evolving new thing. First, it should be lauded for its audaciousness. Second, Powell and Baraka have erred on the side of inclusiveness, which perhaps is the best message to transmit to a generation striving to make itself heard. Third, their prescience is impressive. They have managed to include several poets who are destined to be among the best of their generation: Elizabeth Alexander, Darryl Holmes, Paul Beatty, Sharan Strange. Other landmarks include our own Eyeball literary arts journal and Muleteeth, a Dark Room publication that is multigenerational in scope but features many promising younger writers. Other writers to watch include Chicagoan Rohan B. Preston, author of Dreams in Soy Sauce from Tia Chucha Press, and Alison Joseph, author of What Keeps Us Here, from Ampersand Press.

I also think some of the deficiencies evident in the new thing result from pressure exerted by hip-hop's pervasive influence. Its emphasis on the visceral tends to submerge the intellectual impulse (the rare exceptions include Arrested Development and most notable, Digable Planets). Also, rap's ability to provide instant stimulation may encourage poets laboring under its huge shadow to take shortcuts and expose their work before it's ready. This premature willingness to share is readily visible at slams and coffee houses. Long-term damage can result when audiences begin to get the idea that the half-baked verse they're hearing is good poetry. When that happens the problem that Alexander, Beatty, and others face will become multi-faceted. When the young listeners chance upon a book of well-written poetry, will they recognize it? Will they understand it? Will they care?

Notes

1. Clinton, in Kevin Powell and Ras Baraka, 136.
2. Beatty, 92.

Work Cited

Powell, Kevin, and Ras Baraka, eds. *In the Tradition: An Anthology of Young Black Writers.* New York: Harlem River, 1992.

CONTRIBUTORS

MARGARET WALKER ALEXANDER, poet, novelist, teacher, activist, was one of the most important literary voices of the century. Her first book of poetry, *For My People* (1942), contains her signature poem that is a metaphor for the cultural connections she continued to make throughout her career. Her other books include *Jubilee* (1966), *Prophets for a New Day* (1970), *October Journey* (1973), and *This Is My Century* (1989). She won numerous awards and recognitions such as a Rosenward Fellowship (1944), a Fulbright Fellowship to Norway (1971), a Senior Fellowship from the National Endowment for the Humanities (1972), and the Furious Flower Lifetime Achievement Award (1994). In 1979 Margaret Walker retired after thirty years as a teacher at Jackson State University. She died in November 1998.

JABARI ASIM is an assistant editor of *Washington Post Book World*. He is a published poet, playwright, and fiction writer whose work has appeared in a number of collections, including *Brotherman: The Odyssey of Black Men in America* and *Soulfires: Young Black Men on Love and Violence*. His reviews have appeared in the *Los Angeles Times Book Review*, *Hungry Mind Review*, *Emerge*, and *Salon*. He lives in Silver Spring, Maryland, with his wife and four children.

AMIRI BARAKA, poet, activist, and playwright, is one of the most exciting and prolific authors in America. Considered an architect of the Black Arts Movement, he has published fifteen books of poetry including *Preface to a Twenty Volume Suicide Note*, *The Dead Lecturer*, *It's Nation Time*, *Spirit Reach*, and *Reggae or Not*, a novel, five books of essays, twenty-four plays, and four anthologies. Baraka, born LeRoi Jones, was educated at Rutgers University and Howard University. Since 1962 he has combined his artistic and literary activities with teaching, and has taught poetry and drama at the New School for Social Research, Columbia University, University of Buffalo, Yale University, and George Washington University. He is currently teaching at the State University of New York at Stony Brook as a professor of African Studies. Amiri Baraka has also been a prime and dynamic force in the Black Arts Repertory Theater School in Harlem and Spirit House in Newark. From 1968 until 1975, he was one of the founders and chairmen of the Congress of African People, a nationalistic Pan-African organization and one of the chief organizers of the National Black Political Convention in 1972. He also edited *Cricket*, a magazine of African American music, and directed the publication of new literature through Jihad Press and People War Publications. He is currently editor of *The Black Nation*. His latest volume of poetry is *Transbluesency: The Selected Poems of Amiri Baraka/LeRoi Jones* (1961–1995).

GWENDOLYN BROOKS, the inspiration for the Furious Flower Conference, describes writing poetry as "delicious agony," a process that has produced some of the most outstanding poetry written in the twentieth century. Her career has garnered a magnificent array of achievements. In 1950 Brooks won the Pulitzer Prize for *Annie Allen*, becoming the first black writer to win this award. In 1968 she was named Poet Laureate of Illinois, succeeding the late Carl Sandburg, and holds that post to this date. Brooks was named Consultant-in-Poetry to the Library of Congress, 1985–1986 and was the first black woman to be so honored. She is the recipient of over seventy honorary doctorates, and in 1980 she was nominated to the Presidential Commission on the National Agenda for The Eighties.

She has written more than twenty books including *A Street in Bronzeville*, *Annie Allen*, *The Bean Eaters*, *In the Mecca*, *Blacks*, *Maud Martha* (a novel), *Report from Part One* (an autobiography), *Report from Part Two* (1996), and *Children Coming Home* (1991).

In 1988 she was selected for an award by *Essence Magazine*—one of seven internationally renowned black women to be so honored. The next year the Poetry Society of America bestowed on her the Frost Medal, its highest honor; and that same summer she was the focus of an entire issue of the *Colorado Review* which was devoted to her in conjunction with a conference celebrating her life and work. In 1986, *Gwendolyn Brooks, Poetry and the Heroic Voice*, a comprehensive biocritical study, was written by D. H. Melhem. In 1990, the long-awaited book by the late George Kent, *A Life of Gwendolyn Brooks*, was published and is a full-scale biography of this major poet. She was also named the 1994 Jefferson Lecturer by the National Endowment for the Humanities.

A chair has been named in her honor at Chicago State University: The Gwendolyn Brooks Distinguished Chair in Black Culture and Literature, and she serves as writer-in-residence at that university.

EUGENIA COLLIER, a native of Baltimore, is a writer and a critic. She taught English at colleges and universities in the Baltimore-Washington area until her retirement in 1996. She has published scholarly and critical articles as well as stories, personal essays, and poems in numerous periodicals. With Richard A. Long, she coedited an anthology, *Afro-American Writing*. Her stories are collected in *Breeder and Other Stories*. Her work is motivated by her love for African American literature, drama, and culture.

IKENNA DIEKE is Associate Professor of African American Studies at the University of Arizona. He is the author of *The Primordial Image: African, Afro-American, and Caribbean Mythopoetic Text*. A literary comparatist by force of habit, Dieke is currently putting together *Critical Essays on Alice Walker* (forthcoming from Greenwood Press). He has published widely in journals and has just completed a monograph, *Self and Subjectivity in Alice Walker's Writing*.

JOANNE V. GABBIN is a professor of English at James Madison University, where she directs the university's Honors Program. She is author of *Sterling A. Brown: Building the Black Aesthetic Tradition*, which was published in a new edition by the University Press of Virginia in 1994. Gabbin has published essays in *Wild Women in the Whirlwind*, edited by Joanne M. Braxton and Andrea Nicola McLaughlin, and *Southern Women Writers: The New Generation*, edited by Tonette Bond Inge. Her articles have also appeared in *The Dictionary* of *Literary Biography, The Zora Neale Hurston Forum, The Oxford Companion to Women's Writing,* the *Langston Hughes Journal, Callaloo,* and *Black Books Bulletin.* She has received numerous awards for excellence in teaching and scholarship. Among them are the College Language Association Creative Scholarship Award for her book *Sterling A. Brown* (1986) and the Outstanding Faculty Award, Virginia State Council of Higher Education (1993). She is also the founder and organizer of the Wintergreen Women Writers Collective, and organized and directed the historic Furious Flower Conference: A Revolution in African American Poetry in 1994.

MICHAEL S. HARPER, the poet laureate of Rhode Island, is one of the country's most prolific writers. Author of eight books of poetry, he began his distinguished career with *Dear John, Dear Coltrane* (1977). His other books include *History Is Your Own Heartbeat* (1971), *Nightmare Begins Responsibility* (1975), *Images of Kin: New and Selected Poems* (1977), and *Healing Songs for the Inner Ear Poems* (1984). Harper has also made a significant contribution as the editor of *Chant of Saints: A Gathering of Afro-American Literature of Art and Scholarship,* which he edited with Robert B. Stepto and *Every Shut Eye Ain't Asleep: An Anthology of Poetry by African Americans since 1945,* edited with Anthony Walton. Nominated twice for the National Book Award, he has been honored by the National Institute of Arts and Letters, the National Endowment for the Arts, and the Guggenheim Foundation. He is University Professor of English at Brown University, where he directs the writing program.

B. DENISE HAWKINS, a print journalist, has worked as a senior writer and news editor at *Black Issues in Higher Education Magazine,* where she covered the nation's historically black colleges and universities. During her tenure at the magazine, she was the reporter of note on the landmark, higher education desegregation case, *United States v. Fordice.* She coedited and wrote a chapter in the upcoming book *Reforming Teacher Education through Accreditation: Telling Our Story* (1998). She earned her B.A. degree from the Howard University School of Communications and her M.A. from the Pennsylvania State University.

HILARY HOLLADAY is an associate professor of American literature at the University of Massachusetts, Lowell. She is the author of *Ann Petry* (Twayne, 1996). Her critical essays on African American literature have appeared in *Studies in Short Fiction* and the *South Carolina Review,* among other journals. She is also a poet and the founding director of Beat Literature Symposium.

JOYCE A. JOYCE was a recipient of the American Book Award for Literary Criticism for her collection of essays *Warriors, Conjurers, and Priests: Defining African-centered Literary Criticism.* She is also the author of *Richard Wright's Art of Tragedy, Ijala: Sonia Sanchez and the African Poetic Tradition,* and the coeditor of *The New Cavalcade: African American Writing from 1760 to the Present.* Joyce is currently chairperson and professor of the African American Studies Department at Temple University. Receiving her Ph.D. from the University of Georgia in 1979, Professor Joyce taught for ten years at the University of Maryland, College Park, three years at the University of Nebraska, Lincoln, and five years at Chicago State University, where she was professor of English, associate director of the Gwendolyn Brooks Center, the chairperson of the Black Studies Department, and coordinator of the Honors Program. Joyce has published articles on the works of a number of writers and novelists, such as James Baldwin, Richard Wright, Toni Morrison, Nella Larsen, Zora Neale Hurston, Sonia Sanchez, E. Ethelbert Miller, Gil Scott-Heron, and Gwendolyn Brooks. Among Joyce's many other credentials, she edited the first two volumes of the Gwendolyn Brooks Center's annual publication *Warpland: A Journal of Black Literature and Ideas.*

DEBORAH MCDOWELL is Professor of English at the University of Virginia. She is the author of *"The Change Same": Studies in Fiction by Black American Women, Leaving Pipe Shop,* and *Memories of Kin;* period editor of *The Norton Anthology of African American Literature;* and coeditor, with Arnold Rampersad, of *Slavery and the Literary Imagination.*

ALDON LYNN NIELSEN, Professor of English at Loyola Marymount University, is the author of *Reading Race: White American Poets and the Racial Discourse in the Twentieth Century* (1988) and *Writing between the Lines: Race and Intertextuality* (1994). Nielsen's two collections of poetry are *Evacuation Routes* and *Heat Strings.* In 1997 Nielsen published *Black Chant: Languages of African-American Postmodernism,* which "traces the embrace and transformation of black modernism and postmodernism by African-American poets in the decades after World War II."

RAYMOND R. PATTERSON is the author of *26 Ways of Looking at a Black Man and Other Poems* (Award Books) and *Elemental Blues* (Cross-Cultural Communications), as well as an unpublished book-length poem on the life of Phillis Wheatley and an opera libretto, *David Walker.* His poetry has appeared in *The Transatlantic Review, The Ohio Review, The West Hills Review, The Crisis,* the *Beloit Poetry Journal,* and elsewhere. Many of his poems have been anthologized and can be found in *The Poetry of the Negro, New Black Voices, Soulscript,* the *Norton Introduction to Literature,* and *A Geography of Poets,* and have been translated into a number of languages. In addition, they have been performed over PBS. In 1985 the Hale Smith composition "Three Patterson Lyrics" received its world premiere at Alice Tully Hall. For his poetry, Raymond Patterson has received a National Endowment for the Arts award and a Creative Artists Public Service fellowship. He has served on the executive boards of the Poetry Society of America and PEN American Center, and is a trustee of the Walt Whitman Birthplace Association. He was born in New York City and educated at Lincoln University, Pennsylvania, and New York University. He is a professor emeritus of the City College of the City University of New York, where he taught for many years in the English Department and directed its annual Langston Hughes Festival.

EUGENE REDMOND, the first and only official poet laureate of his native East St. Louis, Illinois, since 1976, teaches at Southern Illinois University, Edwardsville, his alma mater. He has written several books, including *Songs from an Afro/Phone: New Poems* and *Drumvoices: The Mission of Afro-American Poetry, a Critical History* (1976). He, along with Henry Dumas and Sherman Fowler, founded the Black River Writers Publishing Company, which has published most of his poetry. His boundless energy has propelled him into countless creative projects including his work with Katherine Dunham at Southern Illinois University's Performing Arts Training Center and his biographical study of the late poet and fiction writer Henry Dumas. Redmond has been poet-in-residence at Southern Illinois

University, Oberlin College, California State University, Southern University in Baton Rouge, and the University of Wisconsin at Madison. Redmond is the founding editor of *Drumvoices Review*, a multicultural literary magazine. The recipient of the 1993 American Book Award for his collection of poems *The Eye in the Ceiling*, he received the 1993 Pyramid Award from the Pan-African Movement USA for his writing achievements and his lifetime dedication to multiculturalism. He is presently at work on a poetic biography of former prima ballerina Katherine Dunham.

MARIANN RUSSELL, retired Professor of English, studied on a John Hay Whitney Fellowship and earned her Ph.D. at Columbia University. She has written *Melvin B. Tolson's Harlem Gallery: A Literary Analysis* (1980), published by University of Missouri Press. The work was completed during her tenure on a fellowship from the National Endowment for the Humanities and later won the College Language Association Award for Creative Scholarship.

KALAMU YA SALAAM, a native of New Orleans, Louisiana, is a professional editor/ writer and arts administrator. He served as the editor of *The Black Collegian* magazine for thirteen years. Salaam is the author of seven books of poetry: *The Blues Merchant* (1969), *Hofu Ni Kwenu/My Fear Is For You* (1973), *Pamoja Tutashinda/Together We Will Win* (1974), *Ibura* (1976), *Revolutionary Love* (1978), *Iron Flowers* (1979), and *A Nation of Poets* (1989). He has also written two books of essays: *Our Women Keep Our Skies From Falling* (1980) and *Our Music Is No Accident* (1987). His most recent edited volume, *360° A Revolution of Black Poets* (1998), was coedited by Kwame Alexander.

ANGELA M. SALAS earned her Ph.D. in English from the University of Nebraska–Lincoln in 1995. She is currently Assistant Professor of English and Honors Chair at Adrian College, Adrian, Michigan. Salas has published articles about Willa Cather and Edith Wharton. She is currently working on a full-length study of Yusef Komunyakaa's poetry.

MARK A. SANDERS, currently Assistant Professor of English at Emory University, earned his graduate degree from Brown University. Under the direction of Michael S. Harper and Thadious M. Davis, he wrote his dissertation, "Distilled Metaphysics: The Dynamics of Voice and Vision in the Poetry of Sterling A. Brown," focusing upon Brown's formulation of African American aesthetics and its response to American and English modernism. His work on Brown and the Harlem Renaissance has deepened his interest in American and African American poetics, folklore, autobiography, and narrative form. Focusing on the implications of narrative form, he published "Theorizing the Collaborative Self: The Dynamics of Contour and Content in the Dictated Autobiography," in *New Literary History*, spring 1994. He also recently published in *Callaloo*, "Responding to Contemporary Crisis, a Review of Cornel West's *Race Matters*." His latest book is *A Son's Return: Collected Essays of Sterling A. Brown.*

EDWARD A. SCOTT is Associate Professor of Philosophy at Mary Baldwin College in Staunton, Virginia. He received his Ph.D. in philosophy from Duquesne University. He has taught philosophy at the University of Calabar, Nigeria, Payne Theological Seminary in Wilberforce, Ohio, and Monmouth College in Monmouth, Illinois. He is also an ordained

A.M.E. minister and is pastor at Allen Chapel A.M.E. Church in Staunton. His scholarly interests emphasize the relation between philosophical discourse and the narrative imagination.

THERESE STEFFEN was born and raised in Switzerland. She studied English, art history, and literary criticism at the San Francisco State University, at the University of California at Berkeley, and at the University of Zurich where she completed her doctorate on Shakespeare in 1992 (*Twelfth Night or, What you will/Zwölfte Nacht oder, Was ihr wollt/Sonderband im Rahmen der Englisch-deutschen Studienausgabe der Dramen Shakespeares.* Tübingen: Francke). She was assistant and lecturer/Lehrbeauftragte in the English Department of the University of Zurich and published articles on Eudora Welty, "The New Yorker" cartoon captions, Shakespeare, and Rita Dove. She recently completed the first monograph of the U.S. poet laureate (1993–1995), forthcoming as *Crossing Color: Rita Dove's Poetry, Drama, Fiction.* From 1995 until 1996 she was a fellow of the W. E. B. Du Bois Institute for African American Studies at Harvard University, where she remains an associate. Since 1996 Therese Steffen has been Professor of "Gender Studies" at the University of Basel and concentrates on the intersections of gender, ethnicity, and ethics.

ASKIA TOURÉ, one of the architects of the Black Arts/Black Aesthetic Movement, has responded on many levels to the culture of black liberation. His poems and essays, widely published in *Black Scholar, Soulbook, Black Theatre, Black World, Freedomways,* embody the ideology of a people seeking to reclaim their images and history. Touré has also been a member of the legendary Umbra Group. Touré's books include *Earth* (1968), *JuJu: Magic Songs for the Black Nation* (with Ben Caldwell) (1970), *Songhai!* (1972), and *From the Pyramids to the Projects* (1990), which won an American Book Award.

JERRY W. WARD JR., Lawrence Durgin Professor of Literature at Tougaloo College, was born in Washington, D.C., in 1943 and has lived in Mississippi since 1949. He received a B.S. from Tougaloo College (1964) and a Ph.D. from the University of Virginia (1978). His poetry and essays have appeared in anthologies and such magazines as *The Georgia Review, African American Review, Callaloo, Southern Exposure,* and the *Mississippi Quarterly.* He is coeditor with John Oliver Killens of *Black Southern Voices* (1992) and editor of *Trouble the Water: 250 Years of African American Poetry* (1997). His work-in-progress includes *Hollis Watkins: An Oral Autobiography* and *Reading Race, Reading America: Social and Literary Essays.*

ERIC A. WEIL is an assistant professor of English at Shaw University in Raleigh, North Carolina, where he teaches American Literature, World Literature, and composition. His poems have appeared in *Poetry, The American Scholar, The Greensboro Review,* and other journals; articles on Chaucer and on Hawthorne were published in *Medieval Perspectives* and *Postscript.* His interview with the African American novelist Linda Beatrice Brown appeared in the premier issue of *North Carolina Literary Review.*

SHERLEY ANNE WILLIAMS, poet, critic, and novelist, began writing seriously after she received a bachelor's degree in history from California State University at Fresno in 1966. Her first story, "Tell Martha Not to Moan," was published in 1967 while Williams continued graduate study at Howard University. She earned her master's degree in 1972 from Brown University, where she taught in the Black Studies Program. Her volume of literary criticism, *Give Birth to Brightness*, was published the same year. Williams is the author of two volumes of poetry, *The Peacock Poems* and *Some One Sweet Angel Chile*. Describing *Some One Sweet Angel Chile*, she sees it as a "series of self-affirmations, each rooted in a sense of the sisterhood of black women and dealing with some aspect of self-image. Each arises out of a deeper and wider sense of the group experience." Williams often renders that sense of group experience with the poignance and transcendence of the blues. Author of the novel *Dessa Rose*, she has published several books, as well as stories, criticism, and a play. Williams currently teaches at the University of California at San Diego.

JON WOODSON is Associate Professor of English at Howard University. He is the author of *To Make a New Race: Toomer, Gurdjieff, and the Harlem Renaissance*. For his Ph.D. from Brown University, he wrote a dissertation on Melvin B. Tolson. He has published articles in *African American Review*, *The Western Journal of Black Studies*, *Black American Poets between Worlds, 1940–1960*, *Poetry Criticism*, and *The Oxford Companion to Women's Writing*. He has published poetry in numerous journals and in two chapbooks, *Solos* and *I Dreamed I Slept like Liquid Paper*.

INDEX